Adobe® Premiere® For Dummies®

Cheat Sheet

W9-BYF-853

Playback Controls

Macintosh	Action	Windows
Spacebar *or* L	Play (press L again to increase speed)	Spacebar *or* L
J	Play backwards (press J again to increase speed)	J
Spacebar *or* K	Pause	Spacebar *or* K
Right arrow	Frame forward	Right arrow
Shift+right arrow	5 frames forward	Shift+right arrow
Left arrow	Frame back	Left arrow
Shift+left arrow	5 frames back	Shift+left arrow
Up arrow *or* Home	Beginning of Timeline	Up arrow *or* Home
Down arrow *or* End	End of Timeline	Down arrow *or* End
Page Up	Previous edit point	Page Up
Page Down	Next edit point	Page Down

Marker Controls

Macintosh	Action	Windows
D	Clear in point	D
F	Clear out point	F
I	Mark in point	I
O	Mark out point	O
Command+Option+(0-9)	Set numbered marker at edit line	Shift+Alt+(0-9)
Command+Option+=	Set unnumbered marker at edit line	Shift+Alt+=
Command+(0-9)	Go to numbered marker	Shift+(0-9)
Command+right arrow	Go to next marker	Shift+W
Command+left arrow	Go to previous marker	Shift+Q

Adobe® Premiere® For Dummies®

Cheat Sheet

View Controls

Macintosh	Action	Windows
+ (plus sign)	Zoom in on Timeline	+ (plus sign)
- (minus sign)	Zoom out on Timeline	- (minus sign)
\	Zoom out to show entire Timeline	\
Command++ (plus sign)	Move up one video track in Timeline	Ctrl++ (plus sign)
Command+- (minus sign)	Move down one video track in Timeline	Ctrl+- (minus sign)
Command+Shift++ (plus sign)	Move up one audio track in Timeline	Ctrl+Shift++ (plus sign)
Command+Shift+- (minus sign)	Move down one audio track in Timeline	Ctrl+Shift+- (minus sign)
Command+Tab	Toggle between Timeline and Monitor	Ctrl+Tab
Esc	Toggle between Source and Program in Monitor	Esc

Editing Controls

Macintosh	Action	Windows
C	Toggle razor tools	C
H	Hand tool	H
M	Toggle range select tools	M
N	Toggle in/out point tool	N
P	Toggle edit tools	P
T	Match Timeline edit line with original source clip frame	T
U	Toggle cross-fade tools	U
V	Selection tool	V
Z	Zoom tool	Z
,	Insert edit	,
.	Overlay edit	.
Command+M	Export Movie	Ctrl+M
Command+Z	Undo	Ctrl+Z
Command+Shift+Z	Redo	Ctrl+Shift+Z
Option+right arrow	Slide edit one frame right	Alt+right arrow
Option+left arrow	Slide edit one frame left	Alt+left arrow
Option+[	Begin work area at edit line	Alt+[
Option+]	End work area at edit line	Alt+]
Option+Delete	Ripple delete selected clip	Alt+Backspace

Copyright © 2002 Wiley Publishing, Inc.
All rights reserved.

Item 1644-2.

For more information about Wiley Publishing,
call 1-800-762-2974.

For Dummies: Bestselling Book Series for Beginners

by Keith Underdahl

Wiley Publishing, Inc.

Adobe® Premiere® For Dummies®

Published by
Wiley Publishing, Inc.
909 Third Avenue
New York, NY 10022

www.wiley.com

Copyright © 2002 by Wiley Publishing, Inc., Indianapolis, Indiana

Published by Wiley Publishing, Inc., Indianapolis, Indiana

Published simultaneously in Canada

For general information on our other products and services or to obtain technical support, please contact our Customer Care Department within the U.S. at 800-762-2974, outside the U.S. at 317-572-3993, or fax 317-572-4002.

Wiley also publishes its books in a variety of electronic formats. Some content that appears in print may not be available in electronic books.

Library of Congress Cataloging-in-Publication Data:

Library of Congress Control Number: 2002106047

ISBN: 0-7645-1644-2

Manufactured in the United States of America

10 9 8 7 6 5 4 3 2 1

1B/SZ/QY/QS/IN

Ⓦ**Wiley Publishing, Inc.** is a trademark of Wiley Publishing, Inc.

About the Author

Keith Underdahl is an amateur movie maker residing in Albany, Oregon. Professionally, Keith is an electronic publishing specialist for Ages Software, where he serves as program manager, interface designer, multimedia specialist, graphic artist, programmer, customer support manager, resident Portable Document Format (PDF) guru, and when the day is over he even sweeps out the place. Mr. Underdahl has written numerous books, including *Teach Yourself Microsoft Word 2000*, *Microsoft Windows Movie Maker For Dummies*, and *Macworld Final Cut Pro 2 Bible* (co-author).

Dedication

My beloved brethren, let every man be swift to hear, slow to speak, slow to anger.

— *James 1:19*

Author's Acknowledgments

So many people helped me complete this project that I hardly know where to begin. First and foremost I wish to thank my family for allowing me to work two full time jobs as I completed *Adobe Premiere For Dummies*. My wife Christa has been my entire support staff, head cheerleader, and inspiration throughout my entire writing career. She was the one who urged me to start writing for a small motorcycle magazine in 1995, and that endeavor has led to so many great adventures and challenges in the years since. I owe everything to Christa.

My undying gratitude also goes out to my two very favorite movie subjects, Soren and Cole Underdahl. Not only do my boys take direction well, but they are also incredibly intelligent and look great on camera!

I worked on several movie projects during the course of writing this book, and a lot of friends and associates provided assistance. For help with my movies I'd like to thank Cassandra and Scott Turner, Luke Difalco, havoc23, the FSR riders, and The Common.

I wish I could take full credit for the quality and content of *Adobe Premiere For Dummies,* but many other kind folks contributed to this work to make it what it is. I'd like to thank Steve Hayes for hiring me to write this book, my Project Editor Paul Levesque, my Technical Editor Dennis Short, my Copy Editor Barry Childs-Helton, and the many other folks at Wiley who toiled to make this one of the best references on Adobe Premiere to be found. I'd like to thank John Matson for his assistance, as well as Kim Adams at ContourDesign. Finally, thanks to Marcus Chang and all the folks at Adobe for inviting me to help develop this excellent video-editing tool; I've been on the user side of Adobe software for so long that it was great to finally get a chance to contribute and be useful!

Publisher's Acknowledgments

We're proud of this book; please send us your comments through our online registration form located at www.dummies.com/register/.

Some of the people who helped bring this book to market include the following:

Acquisitions, Editorial, and Media Development

Project Editor: Paul Levesque

Acquisitions Editor: Steve Hayes

Copy Editor: Barry Childs-Helton

Technical Editor: Dennis Short

Editorial Manager: Leah Cameron

Permissions Editor: Carmen Krikorian

Media Development Manager: Laura VanWinkle

Media Development Supervisor: Richard Graves

Editorial Assistant: Amanda Foxworth

Production

Project Coordinator: Erin Smith

Layout and Graphics: Gabriele McCann, Jackie Nicholas, Laurie Petrone, Jeremey Unger, Erin Zeltner

Proofreaders: Laura Albert, John Bitter, Andy Hollandbeck, Angel Perez, Carl Pierce, Dwight Ramsey, TECHBOOKS Production Services

Indexer: TECHBOOKS Production Services

Publishing and Editorial for Technology Dummies

Richard Swadley, Vice President and Executive Group Publisher

Mary C. Corder, Editorial Director

Andy Cummings, Acquisitions Director

Publishing for Consumer Dummies

Diane Graves Steele, Vice President and Publisher

Joyce Pepple, Acquisitions Director

Composition Services

Gerry Fahey, Executive Director of Production Services

Debbie Stailey, Director of Composition Services

Contents at a Glance

Introduction 1

Part I: Introducing Digital Video and Adobe Premiere 7
Chapter 1: Introducing Adobe Premiere 9
Chapter 2: Setting Up Your Production Studio 23
Chapter 3: Preparing Adobe Premiere 35

Part II: Beginning a Video Production 57
Chapter 4: A Crash Course in Video Production 59
Chapter 5: Starting and Managing Your Movie Projects 79
Chapter 6: Capturing, Importing, and Managing Media 91

Part III: Editing in Premiere 117
Chapter 7: Editing Clips 119
Chapter 8: Working with the Timeline 133
Chapter 9: The Fine Art of Transitioning and Compositing 157
Chapter 10: Affecting Effects in Your Movies 175
Chapter 11: Working with Audio 193

Part IV: Wrapping Up Your Project 205
Chapter 12: Giving Credit with Titles 207
Chapter 13: Finalizing the Project 225
Chapter 14: Sending Your Project to the World 237

Part V: The Part of Tens 273
Chapter 15: Ten Online Resources 275
Chapter 16: Ten Plug-ins for Adobe Premiere 283
Chapter 17: Ten Tools (And Toys) for Your Production Studio 293

Part VI: Appendixes 307
Appendix A: Glossary 309
Appendix B: Finding Help! 313

Index 317

Cartoons at a Glance

By Rich Tennant

page 117

page 273

page 57

page 307

page 7

page 205

Cartoon Information:
Fax: 978-546-7747
E-Mail: richtennant@the5thwave.com
World Wide Web: www.the5thwave.com

Table of Contents

Introduction 1

Why This Book? 2
Foolish Assumptions 2
Conventions Used in This Book 3
How This Book Is Organized 3
Part I: Introducing Digital Video and Adobe Premiere 3
Part II: Beginning a Video Production 4
Part III: Editing in Premiere 4
Part IV: Wrapping Up Your Project 4
Part V: The Part of Tens 4
Part VI: Appendixes 5
Icons Used in This Book 5
Where to Go from Here 6

Part 1: Introducing Digital Video and Adobe Premiere 7

Chapter 1: Introducing Adobe Premiere 9

What's Adobe Premiere? 9
Taking the Grand Tour 10
Project window 13
Monitor 15
Timeline 16
Palettes 17
Commanding the interface 18

Chapter 2: Setting Up Your Production Studio 23

Selecting a Computer 23
Identifying your needs 24
Choosing a Macintosh 26
Choosing a Windows PC 28
Choosing Video Gear 30
Cameras 30
Video decks 31
Audio recorders 32
Capture hardware 32

Chapter 3: Preparing Adobe Premiere **35**

Setting Up Your Workspace 35
    The A/B Editing workspace 36
    The Single-Track Editing workspace 37
    The Effects workspace 38
    The Audio workspace 39
Adjusting Program Settings 40
    Setting up your scratch disks 40
    Customizing other options 42
    Setting online preferences 44
Customizing Premiere's Windows 45
    Changing the Project window 45
    Modifying the Timeline 47
    Adjusting the Monitor 49
    Mixing up the Audio Mixer 50
    Using keyboard commands 51
Installing Premiere Plug-Ins 53

Part II: Beginning a Video Production **57**

Chapter 4: A Crash Course in Video Production **59**

What Is DV? 60
    Comparing analog and digital video 61
    Understanding video fundamentals 62
Analyzing DV Tape Formats 67
    MiniDV 67
    Other consumer-grade formats 67
    Professional-grade formats 68
    Analog formats 69
Understanding Codecs 70
Comparing Editing Methods 71
    Linear versus nonlinear editing 71
    Online versus offline editing 72
Shooting Great Video 73
    Plan the shot 73
    Compose the shot 73
    Light the shot 75
    Shoot the shot 76

Chapter 5: Starting and Managing Your Movie Projects **79**

Starting Your Project 79
    Saving a project 81
    Opening an existing project 82
Adjusting Project Settings 83
    Modifying settings for your project 83
    Creating your own presets 89
Documenting a Project 89

Chapter 6: Capturing, Importing, and Managing Media **91**

Capturing Media 91
    Setting up your hardware 92
    Capturing with the Movie Capture window 99
    Doing batch captures 108
Importing Media 111
    Preparing stills for your movie 112
    Importing stills and other fun stuff .113
Organizing Your Media 114
    Managing source clips 114
    Using the Project window 115

Part III: Editing in Premiere *117*

Chapter 7: Editing Clips **119**

Getting to Know Your Clips 119
    Analyzing clip details 120
    Playing clips 121
The Ins and Outs of In and Out Points 123
    Setting in and out points 124
    Using other markers 125
    Deleting markers 126
Modifying Clips 126
    Copying clips 127
    Controlling a clip's duration 128
    Speeding up (or slowing down) your clips 128
"Oops!" Undoing Mistakes 130
    Adjusting Undo levels 131
    Using the History palette 132

Chapter 8: Working with the Timeline **133**

Editing Clips into the Timeline 133
    Inserting clips 134
    Controlling Timeline options 136
    Overlaying clips 137
    Moving clips 138
    Replacing frames with three- and four-point edits 144
    Selecting clips 145
    Using virtual clips 147
    Freezing frames 148
    Changing the speed of clips 148
    Working with tracks in the Timeline .150
Using Markers in the Timeline 152
    Adding markers to the Timeline 153
    Moving around with markers 154
Creating a Storyboard 154

Chapter 9: The Fine Art of Transitioning and Compositing **157**

Using Transitions in the Timeline 157
    Using the Transitions palette 158
    Adding a transition to your project 159
    Using a default transition 164
    Previewing transitions 166
Using Transparency 166
    Adjusting the opacity of a clip 167
    Using keys 168
    Creating a matte 171
    Creating a split-screen effect 172

Chapter 10: Affecting Effects in Your Movies **175**

Understanding Effects 175
    Applying effects 177
    Using keyframes 177
    Removing effects 180
Fixing Imperfect Video 182
Animating Clips 183
Using Other Video Effects 186
    Distorting video 186
    Disorienting your audience 188
    Working in the Golden Age of Cinema 188
    Flipping video 190
    Adding Web links to movies 191

Chapter 11: Working with Audio **193**

Understanding Audio 193
    Understanding sampling rates................................194
    Delving into bit depth 194
    Making sound audio recordings 194
    Acquiring music and stock audio 195
Playing Audio Clips 196
Working with Audio in the Timeline 196
    Adjusting volume 197
    Adjusting audio balance 198
    Adjusting audio gain 199
    Cross-fading audio 200
    Linking audio and video 201
Using Audio Effects 202

Part IV: Wrapping Up Your Project *205*

Chapter 12: Giving Credit with Titles **207**

Creating Titles in Premiere 207
    Setting up the Adobe Title Designer view 208

Creating text 209
Adding graphics to titles 219
Adding Titles to Your Project 221
Adding titles to the Timeline 221
Importing titles from other programs 222
Previewing titles 223

Chapter 13: Finalizing the Project **225**

Previewing the Timeline 225
Previewing your project in real time 226
Casting a critical eye upon your project 227
Speeding up your renders 227
Previewing on an external monitor 229
Adding Final Video Elements 230
Creating a leader 230
Adding bars and tone to the project 234
Generating black video 235

Chapter 14: Sending Your Project to the World **237**

Exporting for Digital Playback 237
Selecting a player 238
CD-ROM 244
World Wide Web 247
DVD 260
Exporting for Analog Playback 264
Videotape 265
Exporting for Further Editing 269
Creating edit decision lists 269
Exporting for Adobe After Effects 270
Exporting Audio 270
Exporting Still Images 271

Part V: The Part of Tens *273*

Chapter 15: Ten Online Resources **275**

Adobe User-to-User Forums 275
AppleErrorCodes 276
C|NET 277
Digital Producer 278
DV.com 278
eBay 279
Tiffen 279
VCDHelp.com 280
VersionTracker.com 281
videoguys.com 282

Chapter 16: Ten Plug-ins for Adobe Premiere **283**

AccessFX 284
Adobe After Effects 284
Adobe Photoshop 285
BorisFX 287
Media Players 288
PanHandler 288
Panopticum Effects 289
Pixelan Effects 289
SmartSounds QuickTracks 290
Ultimatte Compositing Plug-ins 291

Chapter 17: Ten Tools (And Toys) for Your Production Studio **293**

Audio Recorders 294
Dream Camcorders 295
DVD Burners 297
Filters 297
Microphones 298
Monitors 300
Multimedia Controllers 300
Tripods and Other Stabilization Devices 302
    Monopods 303
    Mobile stabilizers 303
Video Converters 304
Video Decks 305

Part VI: Appendixes *307*

Appendix A: Glossary **309**

Appendix B: Finding Help! **313**

Using Premiere's Built-in Help 313
Using Online Resources 314
    Adobe's online support 314
    Getting third-party help 315

Index *317*

Introduction

● ●

Some of you young folks may not remember all the way back to the twentieth century, but the waning years of that century were a heady time indeed. Hyped up on $4.00 coffee drinks and biscotti, overdosed on cathode rays, we'd spend hours sitting around and making wild predictions about the future. Through a fog of whipped soymilk we foresaw that humans (or possibly mutants) of the year 2002 would buy all their groceries online, check e-mail on their refrigerators, and edit high-quality movies on devices that fit inside most overhead storage bins. Of course, all these predictions were contingent upon whether or not the apocalypse came at the turn of the millennium.

Thankfully, many of our predictions proved untrue. We don't have to trust Joe DotCom to pick out firm tomatoes, we don't wonder if the light stays on when we close the door on our eIceBoxes, and doomsday appears to be delayed at least until February 2012 (the end of the Mayan calendar) if not longer. We can, however, easily edit movies on devices that fit into most over-head storage bins. Those devices are called *laptop computers,* and they're even affordable. Hey, we got one prediction right. I think I'll take the rest of the day off.

Okay, I'm back.

As you've probably heard, movie editing is one of the hottest topics in the com-puter business today. High-quality digital camcorders are now widespread, and computers that are capable of editing the video shot by those camcorders are now affordable if not downright cheap. Software vendors are rushing to provide programs that can take advantage of all this new hardware, and Adobe Premiere is among the best.

If you recently purchased a computer that has a FireWire (IEEE-1394) inter-face, it probably also came with some free movie editing software. Apple Macintoshes come with a program called iMovie, and Windows Me and Windows XP include Windows Movie Maker. Countless other low-cost pro-grams are available from companies like MGI, Pinnacle, and Ulead. You might have gotten one of these programs with a video capture card or FireWire card that you recently bought. Are those programs any good? Sure, but Adobe Premiere 6.5 is better. Premiere is widely recognized as the best midpriced video-editing program available for both Windows and Macintosh platforms. If you want professional-grade video editing capabilities but don't want to spend thousands of dollars, Premiere is your best choice.

Why This Book?

Adobe Premiere is an advanced program, so you need an advanced reference. But you do not need a gargantuan textbook that causes your bookshelf to sag. You need easy-to-follow step-by-step instructions for the most important tasks, and you need tips and tricks to make your work more successful. You need *Adobe Premiere For Dummies*.

Needless to say, you're no "dummy" or else you wouldn't be reading this book and trying to figure out how to use Adobe Premiere correctly. Video editing is fun, and it is my hope that you'll find this book fun to use as well. I have included instructions on performing the most important video editing tasks, including lots of graphics so that you can better visualize what it is that I'm talking about. You'll also find tips and other ideas in this book that you wouldn't otherwise find in Adobe's own documentation.

Adobe Premiere For Dummies doesn't just help you use the Adobe Premiere program. I have also designed this book to serve as a primer to movie making in general. Sections of this book will help you choose a good camcorder, shoot better video, publish movies online, and speak the industry technobabble like a Hollywood pro.

Foolish Assumptions

I've made a few basic assumptions about you while writing this book. First, I assume that you have an intermediate knowledge of computer use. Movie editing is one of the more technically advanced things you can do with a computer, so I assume that if you're ready to edit video, you already know how to locate and move files around on hard drives, open and close programs, and perform other such tasks. I don't assume that you're using a Macintosh (or, for that matter, a Windows PC); I used both Mac and Windows versions of Premiere 6.5 while writing this book, so it can be of use to you no matter which platform you use.

Another basic assumption I made is that you are not an experienced, professional video editor. I explain the fundamentals of video editing in ways that help you immediately get to work on your movie projects. Most of the coverage in this book assumes that you're producing movies as a hobby or working in a semiprofessional ("prosumer") environment. Prosumer projects could include wedding videos, company training videos, school projects, or other nonbroadcast situations.

Conventions Used in This Book

Adobe Premiere For Dummies helps you get started with Adobe Premiere quickly and efficiently. The book serves as a reference to this program, and because Premiere is a computer program, you will find that this book is a bit different from other kinds of texts you have read. The following are some unusual conventions that you will encounter in this book:

- ✔ Filenames or lines of computer code will look like THIS or this. This style of print usually indicates something you should type in exactly as you see it in the book.

- ✔ Internet addresses will look something like this: www.dummies.com. Notice that I've left the http:// part off the address because you almost never have to actually type it into your Web browser anymore.

- ✔ You will often be instructed to access commands from the menu bar in Premiere and other programs. The menu bar is that strip that lives along the top of the Premiere program window and usually includes menus called File, Edit, Project, Clip, Timeline, Window, and Help. If I'm telling you to access the Save command in the File menu, it will look like this: File➪Save.

- ✔ You'll be using your mouse a lot. Sometimes you have to click something to select it. This means you should click *once* after you've put the mouse pointer over whatever it is you're supposed to click — and use the *left* mouse button if you use Microsoft Windows. I'll specify when you have to double-click — in which case, use the *left* mouse button if you are using Windows.

How This Book Is Organized

Believe it or not, I did put some forethought into the organization of this book. I hope that you will find it logically arranged and easy to use. The chapters of *Adobe Premiere For Dummies* are divided into five major parts, plus appendices. The parts are described below.

Part 1: Introducing Digital Video and Adobe Premiere

Adobe Premiere is a highly advanced program, and if you're new to video editing, many of its parts may seen unfamiliar. Part I helps you get started with your movie-making adventure by introducing you to Adobe Premiere. You'll begin by touring the Premiere program and getting familiar with its tools and basic features. Since Premiere is just one of many tools that you will use to produce movies, I will spend some time helping you prepare your production studio. I'll also show you how to prepare Premiere for use with a variety of media formats.

Part II: Beginning a Video Production

Once you are comfortable with Adobe Premiere, you should familiarize yourself with the basics of video production. The first chapter in Part II introduces you to the fundamentals of movie making, a thorough understanding of which is crucial if you want to produce great movies. Next, you'll start new projects in Premiere and manage the media and content that Premiere uses. I will also show you how to import and manage material in Premiere so that you have something to work with when you start editing.

Part III: Editing in Premiere

Adobe Premiere is first and foremost a video-editing program, so this part could be considered the heart of *Adobe Premiere For Dummies*. In this part you will edit clips, create movies using the Timeline, and give your project a high-quality soundtrack. You also utilize Premiere's more advanced editing features. You create and manipulate transitions between scenes in the movie, you will create and use special effects, and you learn how to combine (or *composite*) multiple video scenes into one, in much the same way the special-effects pros do in Hollywood.

Part IV: Wrapping Up Your Project

Just as pancakes are not truly finished until the syrup is poured, your movie project requires some finishing touches as well. Title screens tell viewers the name of the movie and who is responsible for it. Bars and tone help others calibrate video equipment to your movie. The final movie format that you choose will vary depending upon how you plan to distribute it. Part IV guides you through the finishing process for your movie projects.

Part V: The Part of Tens

I wouldn't be able to call this a *For Dummies* book without a "Part of Tens" (really, it's in my contract). Actually, the Part of Tens always serves an important purpose. In *Adobe Premiere For Dummies* it gives me a chance to show you ten great online resources for Adobe Premiere and movie making, ten Adobe Premiere plug-ins and accessory programs that you may find useful, and ten toys, er, tools to help you make better movies.

Part VI: Appendixes

The appendixes provide quick handy references on several important subjects. First up is a glossary to help you decrypt the alphabet soup of video editing terms and acronyms. Next, you will find help on finding, er, help for Adobe Premiere. Finally, a list of keyboard shortcuts for common Premiere actions is provided.

Icons Used in This Book

Occasionally you'll find some icons in the margins of this book. The text next to these icons includes information and tips that deserve special interest, and some warn you of potential hazards and pitfalls you may encounter. Icons you'll find in this book are easy to spot:

Although every word of *Adobe Premiere For Dummies* is important, I sometimes feel the need to emphasize certain points. I use Remember to occasionally provide this emphasis.

Tips are usually brief instructions or ideas that aren't always documented but that can greatly improve your movies and make your life easier. Tips are among the most valuable tidbits in this book.

Heed warnings carefully. Some warn of situations that can merely inconvenience you; others tell you when a wrong move could cause expensive and painful damage to your equipment and/or person.

Computer books are often stuffed with yards of technobabble, and if it's sprinkled everywhere, it can make the whole book a drag and just plain difficult to read. As much as possible I have tried to pull some of the deeply technical stuff out into these icons. This way, the information is easy to find if you need it, and just as easy to skip if you already have a headache.

I wish I could cover everything in one book, but I can't. In some cases, you'll see a cross-reference, where I have suggested another book that can help you out if you want more information on a subject. Some cross-references show you where to look in this book to get more information right away.

Where to Go from Here

You are about to enter the mad world of video production. Exciting, isn't it? Video editing is *the* hot topic in computer technology today, and you're at the forefront of this multimedia revolution. If you still need to set up your movie studio or need some equipment, I suggest that you start off with Chapter 2, *Setting Up Your Production Studio*. If you aren't quite ready to start editing yet, you may want to spend some time in Chapter 4, *A Crash Course in Video Production*. Otherwise, you should go ahead and familiarize yourself with Adobe Premiere, beginning with Chapter 1.

Part I

Introducing Digital Video and Adobe Premiere

The 5th Wave   By Rich Tennant

"I found these two in the multimedia lab morphing faculty members into farm animals."

In this part . . .

It wasn't so long ago that moviemaking was "magic" that came from the shining temples of Hollywood. But thanks to the home-video revolution that got started in the mid-1990s, anyone with a reasonably modern personal computer, an affordable digital camcorder, and a video-editing program like Adobe Premiere can now produce a high-tech motion picture.

This part of *Adobe Premiere For Dummies* begins the moviemaking adventure by exploring Adobe Premiere and finding out just what this program can do. It also looks at what's needed for your personal video production studio and walks you through configuring Premiere to make movie magic.

Chapter 1

Introducing Adobe Premiere

· ·

In This Chapter

▶ Getting a look at Adobe Premiere

▶ Taking the Grand Tour

· ·

The field of video editing software is getting pretty crowded these days. If you want to spend money like the pros (that is, by the bucketful), you can use a program like Avid Xpress DV ($1,699). Or you can save $700 and use Apple Final Cut Pro ($999, for Macintosh only). At the other end of the price spectrum, you can use some simple video-editing tools that come with your operating system, such as Apple iMovie and Microsoft Windows Movie Maker. Plenty of other programs fill the middle ground, pricewise — and of those, Adobe Premiere is generally regarded as the best.

This chapter introduces you to Adobe Premiere by showing you what this program is designed to do and what it has to offer. You'll also take a tour of Premiere to help you find your way around this feature-packed program.

What's Adobe Premiere?

Adobe Premiere is a video editing program — although that term is almost too modest, given the versatility of Premiere. Editing movies on affordable PCs has been a dream since multimedia-ready computers became common in the mid-1990s. For years, the *reality* of affordable video editing lagged well behind the dream. But today, video can be easily edited on computers that cost less than $1,000, and powerful programs like Premiere give you editing tools that were previously available only to video and film professionals, working on systems that cost hundreds of thousands — if not millions — of dollars. With Adobe Premiere, you can skip the glitz and get right to the gist:

✔ Capturing audio and video from your camcorder or video deck (if your computer has the right hardware).

✔ Picking and choosing scenes to include in a movie. You can move frame by frame through video to precisely place your edits.

✔ Making use of up to 99 separate video tracks that can be composited and combined to make a single image.

✔ Adding and editing audio soundtracks to your program. Up to 99 separate audio tracks can be added to the program.

✔ Creating titles and adding still graphics to your movie projects. Titles and graphics can be animated in a variety of ways.

✔ Applying one of 75 different transitions to video.

✔ Modifying your movie with 79 video and 24 audio effects.

✔ Outputting movies to videotape at full broadcast quality or outputting tightly compressed movies for the World Wide Web.

Even these hefty capabilities are only a smattering of what you can do with Adobe Premiere. It's one of the most versatile programs you'll ever use. And unlike many other video editing programs, Adobe offers versions of Premiere for both Macintosh- and Windows-based computers. You can use this program on almost *any* modern computer. (What a concept!)

Taking the Grand Tour

As you might expect from a program that can do so many things, the Adobe Premiere program interface may seem complex and intimidating the first time you look at it. The first time you launch Premiere, you see the dialog box shown in Figure 1-1; it's where you select your initial *workspace*. The workspace is the basic layout of the Premiere features and is where you perform your movie editing magic. The dialog box suggests that if you're new to video editing, you should click the Select A/B Editing button. Ignore this advice. "Start out right," I always say — and if you really want to get off on the right foot in Premiere, I recommend you click the Select Single-Track Editing button. There's nothing wrong with the A/B Editing workspace, I just think that doing *real* editing is easier when you use the Single-Track Editing workspace.

To find out more about workspaces, see "Setting Up Your Workspace" in Chapter 3.

The next dialog box you see — the Load Project Settings dialog box (which looks something like Figure 1-2) — is a bit more complicated. From now on, this is probably the first dialog box you'll see when you launch Premiere. This dialog box is more complicated because you have to actually make a decision about what kind of project you want to create. This is where you choose a *preset* — a standard collection of settings that apply to a certain kind of video or media.

Adobe Premiere 6.*What?*

This version of *Adobe Premiere For Dummies* was written primarily with Premiere version 6.5 in mind. However, I'm guessing that more than a few of you have version 6.0 of Premiere instead. Don't worry. Premiere 6.0 and 6.5 are very closely related, and the information in this book will still be very useful for you. In most cases, the programs look and work exactly the same. Perhaps the greatest difference between 6.0 and 6.5 is the titling tool, which has been totally revised for Premiere 6.5.

Most other differences between Premiere 6.0 and 6.5 are minor. Admittedly, there are a few new audio and video effects in Premiere 6.5, the Online Settings dialog box is new, real-time previews have been improved, and the DV Device Control Options have been simplified. The Windows version of Premiere 6.5 now can output directly in MPEG-2 format, which is the video format used for DVD movies, and both versions offer better support for DVD creation right in Premiere.

Which preset you choose depends on the video you're working with; preset settings are specific to frame size, frame rate, audio quality, and the video broadcast standard for your area. For example, if you live in North America and will be editing video you recorded with your digital camcorder, you'll probably choose DV-NTSC⇨Standard 48kHz. If you aren't sure what to choose, click Standard 48kHz (under either DV-NTSC or DV-PAL), and then click OK.

Figure 1-1: You see this dialog box the first time you launch Premiere. Despite the recommendations in the dialog box, I suggest you click the option on the right.

Initial Workspace

Please select an initial workspace:

A/B Editing

This workspace provides editors with a visual view of the timeline, where clips and transitions are displayed on separate tracks. Select this workspace if you are new to video editing.

Select A/B Editing

Single-Track Editing

This workspace provides editors with a traditional timeline, where clips and transitions are displayed on the same track, but can be viewed as two tracks. Select this workspace if you have experience in video editing.

Select Single-Track Editing

Many factors affect your choice of a preset when you first open Premiere. For more on picking the preset that is right for you (including explanations of terms such as DV-NTSC and DV-PAL), see "Starting Your Project" in Chapter 5.

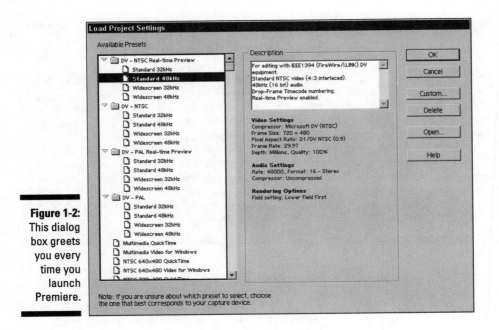

Figure 1-2:
This dialog
box greets
you every
time you
launch
Premiere.

When you have chosen a project preset, Adobe Premiere opens (at last) to the editing workspace. The exact appearance of your workspace depends upon several things:

> ✔ Are you working on a Macintosh or a Windows PC?
>
> ✔ Did you choose A/B Editing or Single-Track Editing for your initial workspace?
>
> ✔ What's the current screen resolution setting on your computer?

Although the *exact* appearance varies, you still see at least the three fundamental windows that make up the Premiere interface — the Project window, Monitor, and Timeline, as shown in Figure 1-3. These three windows are explained in greater detail in the following sections.

If you chose to start with the A/B Editing workspace rather than Single-Track Editing, your Monitor window has only one pane instead of the two shown in Figure 1-3.

Project window

Monitor

Timeline

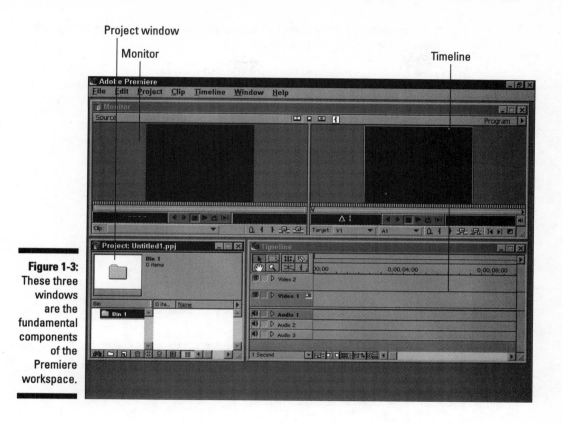

Figure 1-3:
These three
windows
are the
fundamental
components
of the
Premiere
workspace.

Project window

Think of the Project window as a sort of filing cabinet that helps you organize
the various files and clips you use in your project. Whenever you capture
video from your camcorder or video deck, import still graphics, or capture
audio from an audio CD, the files show up in the Project window. If you're
working on a big project, you'll end up with many different files in this
window; a full project window looks similar to Figure 1-4. You can create new
bins in the Project window to help organize your files. Bins work like folders
in your operating system. To create a new bin, follow these steps:

1. **Click in the Project window to select it and make it active.**

2. **From the menu bar at the top of the Premiere screen, choose
   File⇨New⇨Bin.**

   The Create Bin dialog box appears.

3. Type a name for your new bin in the Bin Name field of the Create Bin dialog box and then click OK.

Your new bin now appears in the Bin list on the left side of the Project window. Click the bin to view its contents. To add items to a bin, simply click-and-drag them into the bin from the File list on the right side of the Project window. Figure 1-4 shows a Project window for a project I'm working on; as you can see, I've imported and captured a lot of files into it.

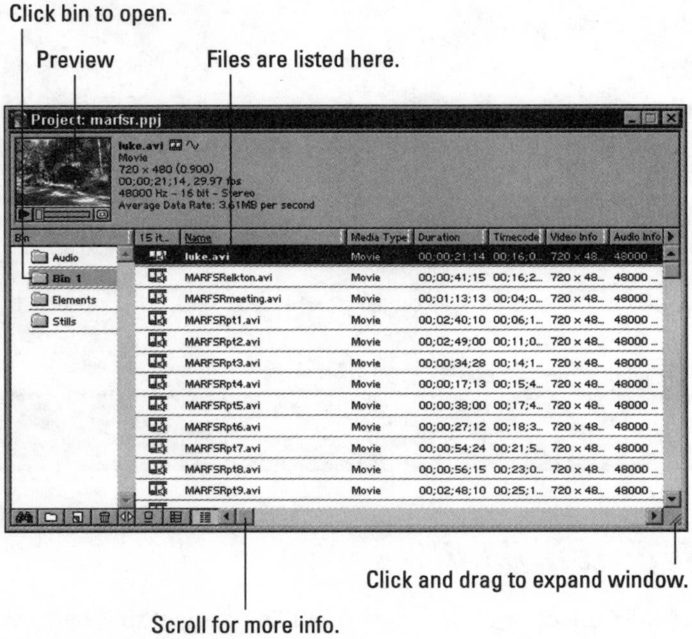

Click bin to open.

Preview   Files are listed here.

Figure 1-4:
The Project window serves as your storage cabinet for the files you use in your movie projects.

Click and drag to expand window.

Scroll for more info.

Although the Project window is primarily a storage place, you can also

- ✔ **Review data about a file.** What's the frame size of the image? Is the file an audio clip, video, or a still graphic? How long is the clip? Columns in the Project window provide many different kinds of information about your files.

- ✔ **Preview the file.** If you click a file in the Project window, a preview of it appears in the upper-left corner of the Project window as shown in Figure 1-4. If you click the little Play button under the preview, you can play audio and video clips to get a better idea of what's in them.

Monitor

Try to imagine editing video without being able to look at it. Your task would be daunting. Thankfully, Premiere makes sure you can always see exactly what your movie looks like as you work on it. The Monitor window is where you view your work. The Monitor window has controls for playing video and audio clips and for performing other editing tasks. In the Monitor, you

✔ Play through clips you plan to add to a movie project. As you play each clip, you decide which portions to add to the movie by setting *in points* and *out points*. When you set in and out points, only the portions of the clip between those two points will be added to your movie program.

✔ Play through the edits you have already made in your project.

The Monitor shown in Figure 1-5 has two panes. The left pane is called the Source view, and this is where you review clips before you edit them into the movie. To load a video file into the Source view, simply drag the file from the Project window and drop it on the Source view side of the Monitor.

The right pane of the Monitor is the Program view, which shows what's in the actual movie project you're assembling in the Timeline (a feature described in the next section).

Change view mode.

Source view   Program view

Figure 1-5:
The Monitor
window —
shown here
in dual-pane
view —
allows you
to preview
and edit
clips before
and after
you edit
them into
the movie.

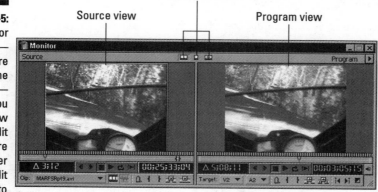

If you're working with the A/B Editing workspace, your Monitor probably only has one pane rather than the two shown in Figure 1-5. The single-pane view of the Monitor only has the Program view. Instead of dragging clips from the

Project window to the Monitor, you simply double-click a clip in the Project window to open the clip in a window that (coincidentally) looks exactly like the Source view of a dual-pane Monitor. Confused? Me too. That's why I prefer to work in the Single-Track Editing workspace with its dual-pane Monitor. If you want, you can switch between single-pane and dual-pane view in the Monitor using buttons at the top of the Monitor window (see Figure 1-5).

The Monitor window also has a Trim Mode view, which is described in greater detail in Chapter 8. Use the Trim Mode when you're trimming clips you've already added to the Timeline and you want to see the exact in- and out-point frames of a particular clip and both adjacent clips. For more on setting in and out points in the Monitor, see Chapter 7.

Timeline

The Timeline could be considered the heart and soul of Adobe Premiere. As with virtually every other video-editing program, Premiere's Timeline is the place where you craft your movie by putting its pieces in the desired order. You assemble clips, add effects, composite multiple clips on top of each other, and add sound. As you can see in Figure 1-6, the Timeline shows audio tracks on the bottom and video tracks on top. You can have up to 99 video tracks and 99 audio tracks in the Premiere Timeline.

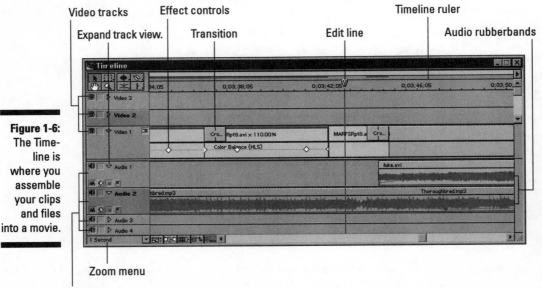

Figure 1-6: The Timeline is where you assemble your clips and files into a movie.

Video tracks   Effect controls   Timeline ruler

Expand track view.   Transition   Edit line   Audio rubberbands

Zoom menu

Audio tracks

I can't completely explain the Timeline here. That would fill a chapter all by itself. (In fact, it does — see Chapter 8.) However, I do want you to know that by using the Timeline you can

- Expand the view of a track by clicking the right-facing arrow on the left side of the Timeline.
- Figure out where you are in the project by using the Timeline ruler.
- Use the Edit line (see Figure 1-6) to set the current playback location in the Timeline.
- Control aspects of a clip directly in the Timeline. You can set keyframes for effects or adjust audio levels using audio rubberbands (Figure 1-6).
- Use the Zoom menu to adjust the zoom level from 1 Frame up to 8 Minutes.
- Move items by simply dragging-and-dropping them to new locations in the Timeline. If your clip calls for some effects and transitions, you can add them by simply dragging them to the Timeline as well.

Palettes

Admittedly, the Project window, the Monitor, and the Timeline are the three primary components of Adobe Premiere. An introduction to Adobe Premiere can't stop there though. You should also know about palettes. Premiere stores many of its advanced features and effects in small floating windows called *palettes*. If you're familiar with other Adobe programs such as Photoshop and Illustrator, you're probably already familiar with palettes. To view a couple of palettes, do this:

- Choose Window⇨Show Transitions.
- Choose Window⇨Show Commands.
- Choose Window⇨Show Video Effects.

You should now have three floating palettes on your screen that look something like the ones in Figure 1-7. You can move these palettes around by dragging the title bar, close them by clicking the little *x* in the upper-right corner, or minimize them by clicking the Minimize button. (The Minimize button is right next to the Close button. Minimizing a palette means the palette takes up less space on-screen without completely disappearing.) Many items in palettes are organized into folders. Click an arrow on the left to open a folder, as shown in Figure 1-7. Each floating palette also has tabs at the top, which you can click to view other items.

Expand folder

Click tab to view.

Click here to move palette.

Close

Minimize

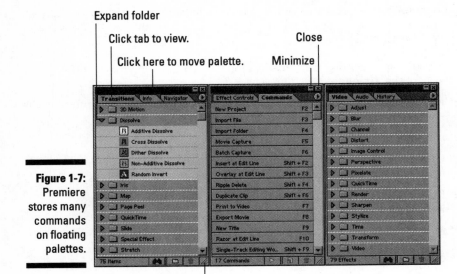

Figure 1-7:
Premiere
stores many
commands
on floating
palettes.

Resize palette

Many of Premiere's most powerful features can be found in the palettes. All the palettes can be accessed through the Window menu, and you may want to spend some time exploring them to see what features and tools are available.

Commanding the interface

As I mention in the "Foolish Assumptions" section of the Introduction, one of the assumptions I make about you is that you already know how to open and close programs on your computer. You probably also know how to open menus, click buttons, and even resize or minimize windows.

That said, Adobe Premiere is so advanced (and video editing is so demanding of a computer's resources) that I suspect you've recently bought a new computer — and have recently "switched camps" from Macintosh to your first Windows PC (or vice versa). Therefore the following two sections provide a brief overview of the basic interface controls in both Macintosh and Windows versions of Adobe Premiere.

If you're new to your operating system, I suggest you purchase a book with more detailed information on using and managing the system. Depending on which operating system you're using, I recommend *Mac OS 9 For Dummies*, *Mac OS X For Dummies*, *Macs For Dummies*, *Microsoft Windows Me For Dummies*, or *Windows XP For Dummies*.

Using the Macintosh GUI

The Apple Macintosh *graphical user interface* (GUI) has been gradually refined over the years, but the basic elements have remained unchanged from the ancient days of OS 7.5 to today's OS X. Whether you have Mac OS 9 or OS X, you can launch Premiere by double-clicking its desktop icon.

How you control the Premiere window varies, depending upon which OS version you have. Figure 1-8 shows how Premiere looks and works in the typical OS 9 interface. To switch between open programs in OS 9, use the Application menu in the upper-right corner. The basic window controls are

- **Apple menu:** Use this menu to access basic system controls or recently opened items. In OS X, this menu also provides controls for shutting down and restarting the computer (in OS 9 and earlier, the shutdown and restart controls are in the Special menu). The Apple menu is similar in purpose and function to the Start menu in Windows.

- **Close:** Use this button to close the window or program.

- **Zoom:** Use this to change the size of the window. The Zoom button works much like the Restore/Maximize button in Windows.

- **Collapse (OS9) or Minimize (OS X):** Use this button to minimize the window to just its title bar. Use the Collapse or Minimize button like you would the Minimize button in Windows.

Mac OS X looks a bit different, but the basic operation is similar. Figure 1-9 shows interface controls in OS X. In OS X, you can use the Dock at the bottom of the screen to switch between open programs on your computer.

Using the Windows GUI

The fundamental look and feel of the Microsoft Windows interface has not changed significantly since Windows 95 was released in (ahem) 1995; Figure 1-10 shows a typical Windows version of a Premiere screen. To launch Premiere, click the Start button to open the Start menu and choose Programs⇨Adobe⇨Premiere 6.5⇨Adobe Premiere 6.5. You can switch between open programs using the Windows Taskbar at the bottom of the screen. Basic controls include

- **Start menu** — Use this menu to access programs on your computer, as well as shut down and restart controls. The Start menu is similar in concept to the Apple menu on a Macintosh.

- **Minimize** — Click this to minimize a window. When a program is minimized, it becomes a button on the Taskbar. Use this button like you would the Collapse or Minimize buttons on a Mac.

- **Restore/Maximize** — Use this button to change the window size. Restore/Maximize works like the Zoom button in the Mac OS.

- **Close** — Click this to close a program or window.

If you don't like digging through the Start menu every time you want to launch Premiere, right-click the Adobe Premiere 6.5 link in the Start menu and choose Send To⇨Desktop (create shortcut) from the menu that appears. Doing so creates a desktop icon that you can double-click to launch Premiere.

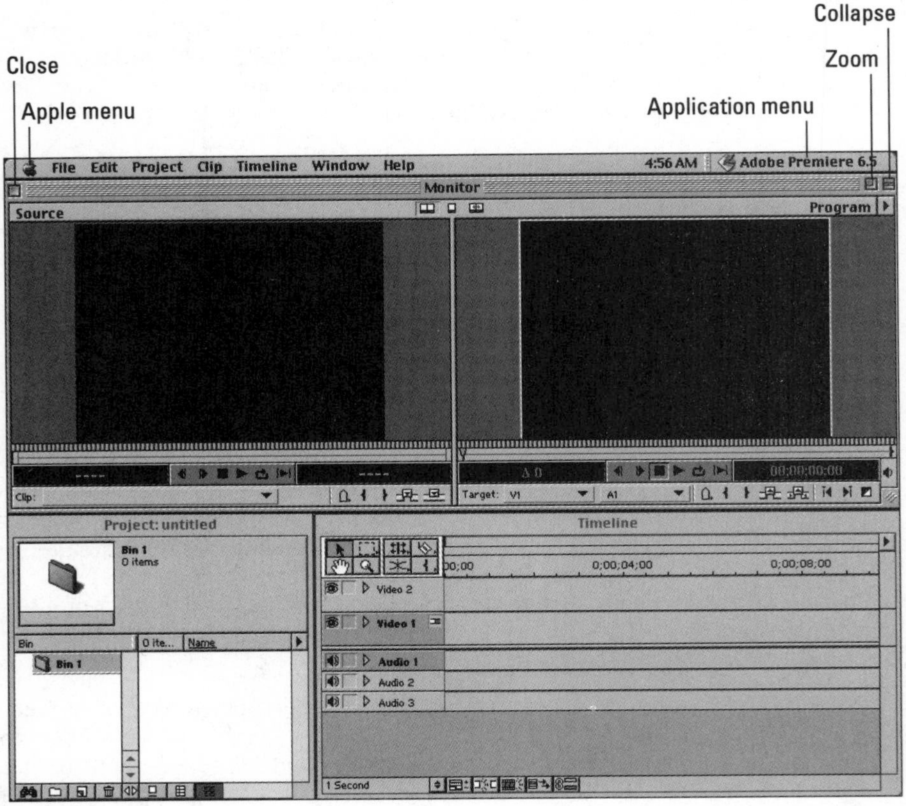

Collapse

Close

Zoom

Apple menu

Application menu

Figure 1-8:
Premiere
presents
a familiar
face in the
Mac OS 9
interface.

Close

Apple Menu

Minimize

Zoom

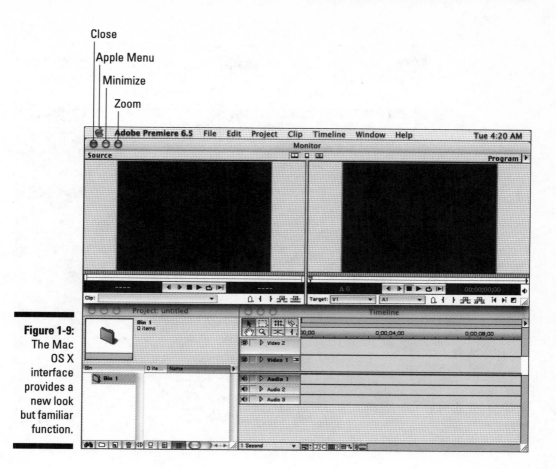

Figure 1-9:
The Mac
OS X
interface
provides a
new look
but familiar
function.

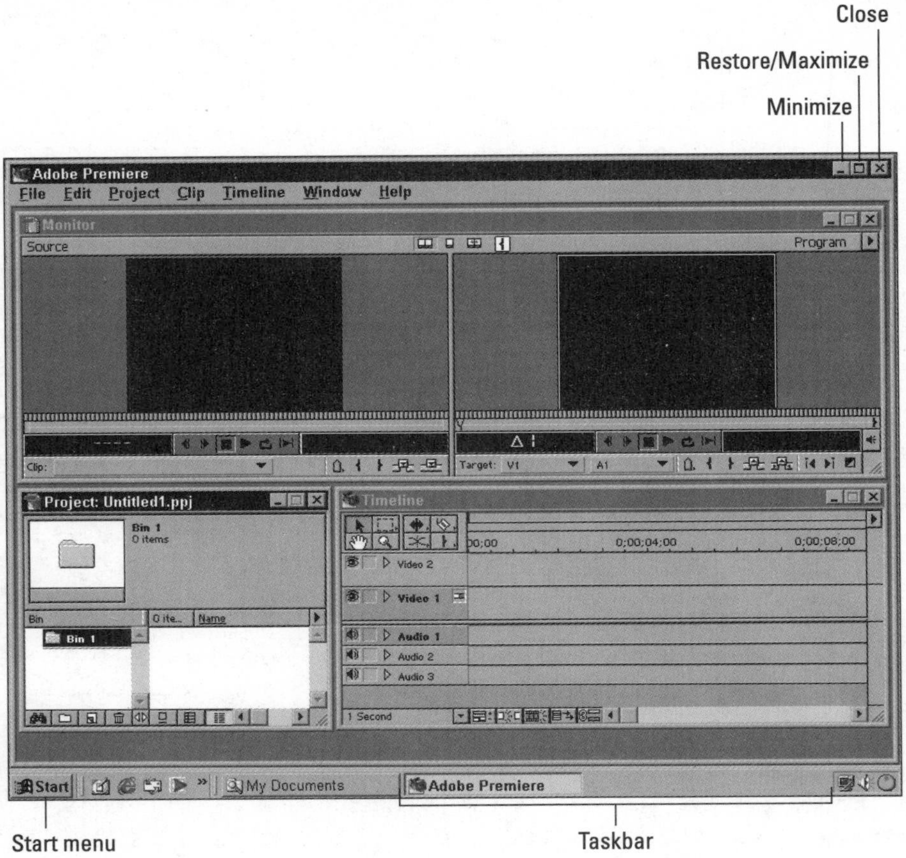

Close

Restore/Maximize

Minimize

Adobe Premiere

File   Edit   Project   Clip   Timeline   Window   Help

Monitor

Source

Program

Clip:

Target: V1   A1

Figure 1-10:
The
Windows
interface is
similar
across all
modern
versions of
Microsoft
Windows.

Project: Untitled1.ppj

Bin 1
0 items

Bin   0 ite...   Name

Bin 1

Timeline

00;00   0;00;04;00   0;00;08;00

Video 2

Video 1

Audio 1
Audio 2
Audio 3

1 Second

Start   My Documents   Adobe Premiere

Start menu   Taskbar

Chapter 2

Setting Up Your Production Studio

● ●

In This Chapter

▶ Choosing the right computer

▶ Comparing video cameras

▶ Selecting capture cards and other hardware

● ●

*N*ot so long ago, the price of a good video-editing system could have bought you a pretty nice home in the suburbs. But thanks to programs like Adobe Premiere, many of those suburban homes now *have* good video-editing systems — and the owners of said homes didn't have to take out second mortgages to purchase the equipment. Premiere revolutionized video by providing professional-grade editing capabilities in a software package that runs on affordable computers.

Another revolution has been the newfound affordability of digital video (DV) hardware. Amateur videographers can now shoot near-broadcast-quality video on cameras that cost less than $1,000. Then Apple created the FireWire interface a few years ago — and suddenly digital video can be edited on personal computers — both Macintoshes *and* Windows PCs — because the interface is fast enough to handle large video files at full playback speed. These three things — video-editing software, digital camcorders, and FireWire — have come together and created a synergy that is changing the way we think about and use moving pictures.

When you have the software (Adobe Premiere), you need the hardware to go with it. This chapter guides you through the process of finding a computer to serve as a video-editing platform. You also get a look at digital cameras and other hardware that you may need or want as you get serious about video.

Selecting a Computer

Although video-editing systems have certainly become affordable, you should be aware that you can't expect to edit video on just any old computer. That PC your parents bought you for college ten years ago, for example, won't cut it. In fact, almost any computer that is not new or has not been significantly upgraded in the last year or so is probably barely adequate when using Adobe Premiere. The following sections help you identify what kind of computer you need, including specific requirements for both Macintosh- and Windows-based systems.

One thing you will not find here is a recommendation on whether a Mac or Windows PC is better. That debate has raged tirelessly for years and often reaches an almost religious fervor. The truth is, Adobe Premiere works pretty well on either platform. I suggest you stick with whichever platform you are already comfortable with, fits best in your budget, or best matches the décor in your office.

Identifying your needs

First, you need a computer that will run Adobe Premiere without crashing. Beyond that, your computer should run Premiere efficiently without making you wait for hours on end while simple actions take place. You need lots of storage space for your video files. And you need special hardware tailored to video editing. The next two sections describe the computer that you need.

Minimum system requirements

Like virtually all software programs, Adobe Premiere has some minimum system requirements that your computer must meet. You'll find them emblazoned on the side of Premiere's retail box, as well as in the "INSTALL READ ME" file located on the Premiere CD-ROM. The minimum requirements are surprisingly low. For the Macintosh version of Premiere 6.5, you need

- ✔ PowerPC processor or higher
- ✔ Mac OS 9.2 or later
- ✔ 64MB of RAM available to Premiere
- ✔ 50MB of free hard drive space
- ✔ Apple QuickTime 5.0 or higher

The minimum requirements for the Windows version are

- ✔ Pentium-class processor, 500MHz or higher
- ✔ Windows 98 or higher; Windows NT4 with Service Pack 4 or higher
- ✔ 64MB of RAM
- ✔ 85MB of free hard drive space
- ✔ 256-color video display

Yes, Adobe Premiere 6.5 is compatible with Windows XP! You must be logged in as an administrator to install the software. Although Premiere 6.0 is *not* compatible with Mac OS X, Premiere 6.5 will run in OS X classic and native modes.

The real system requirements

You've seen the *minimum* system requirements. I dare you to try to edit video on a system that exactly meets those minimum specs. It would be an exercise in futility. The lowliest computer on which I have ever run Premiere was a Windows PC with an AMD K6-2-400 processor and 128MB of RAM. Premiere would run, but my work was tediously s-l-o-w and video frames were frequently dropped.

Video editing puts unusually high demands on a computer. Video files require massive amounts of disk space, as well as special hardware to capture video and lay it back to tape — and the computer's memory and processor are utilized to their maximum capabilities when you render video for playback. Whether you are buying a new computer or upgrading, you really need some relatively souped-up capabilities:

- ✔ **A seriously powerful processor:** The *central processing unit* (CPU) can be thought of as the brain of the computer, and a faster processor affects how well everything else runs. The faster the processor, the less time you'll spend twiddling your thumbs as your video renders. On a Macintosh, I recommend at least a G3-500 or G4 processor. For a Windows PC, I recommend any Intel Pentium III or higher that is at least 800MHz, or an AMD Athlon or Duron of at least 800MHz.

- ✔ **Lots of memory:** Your CPU uses *random-access memory* (RAM) as its working space. More RAM means you can run more programs, and processes like video rendering happen much more efficiently. I recommend 512MB of RAM as a bare minimum; if your computer uses DDR (double data rate) RAM, you can safely get away with as little as 256MB. Check the computer's documentation if you're not sure.

- ✔ **Big, fast hard drives:** Video requires lots of storage space. You can get a good start with 80GB (gigabytes) of disk space but more is always better. If your computer uses IDE hard drives (check the spec sheet), always choose 7200-rpm drives over 5400-rpm drives.

- ✔ **A large monitor:** Premiere takes up a lot of screen real estate. Unless you want to spend half your life scrolling back and forth in the Timeline and moving windows and palettes this way and that, you need a monitor that can display a screen resolution of *at least* 1024 x 768 pixels. If you try to work at 800 x 600 pixels on a small 15-inch monitor, your workspace will be cramped and confusing like the one shown in Figure 2-1. Thankfully, big CRT (cathode ray tube) monitors are pretty cheap these days. I recommend at least a 19" monitor.

✔ **FireWire interface:** FireWire ports are essential for working with digital video. Even if you don't currently have a DV camcorder, you will probably need a FireWire port before long. All new Macintosh computers from Apple include FireWire (IEEE-1394) ports. Many new PCs do as well, but double-check before you buy. FireWire ports can be added to most PCs for less than $100.

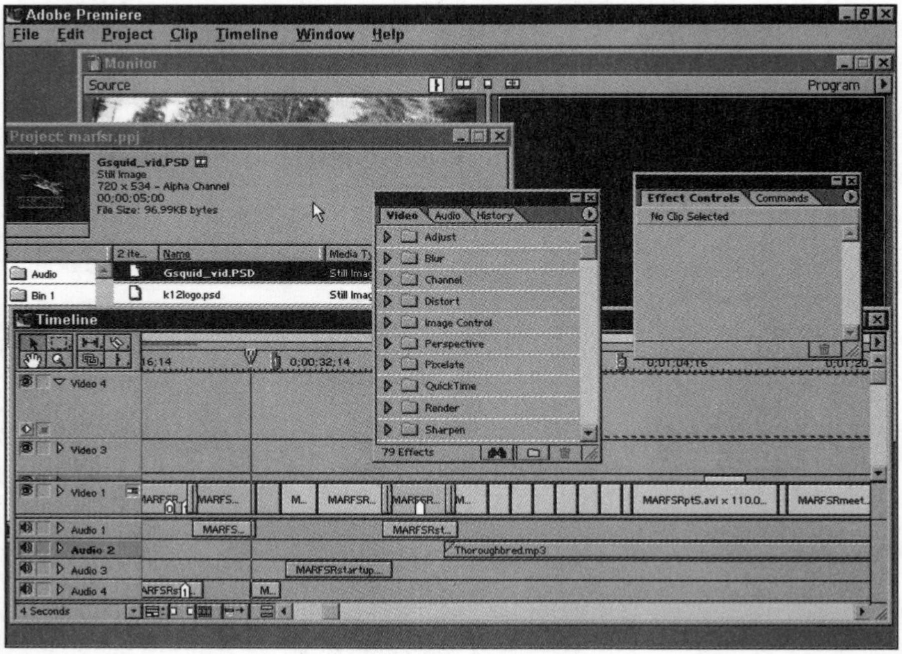

Figure 2-1:
This is what Adobe Premiere looks like with a screen resolution of 800 by 600. Good luck trying to get any work done in this cramped workspace.

A lot of interesting hard-drive alternatives have appeared in recent years. These include external hard drives that plug into FireWire or USB ports. I recommend against using such drives for video storage when you're editing in Premiere. External drives are seldom fast enough to keep up with video's demands, meaning you may experience dropped frames and other problems when you try to output your video.

Choosing a Macintosh

I told you that I wasn't going to get into the Mac-versus-Windows debate, and I won't. However, it must be said that Apple makes some really good video-editing systems right out of the box. As I mention earlier, all new Macs — even lowly iMacs that retail for as little as $1,000 — come with at least one FireWire port built in. Macs also tend to use high-quality CPUs, RAM, video cards, and other hardware — meaning fewer problems when you edit video. However, there are some things to check for when purchasing a new Mac:

- ✔ **Does it have enough hard drive space?** Lower-priced iMacs tend to have hard drives that are not big enough for serious video work. Some iBooks, for example, have as little as 15 or 20GB of disk space, which is unacceptably small for your purposes. (You really need at least 80GB for serious video work.)

- ✔ **How fast is the processor?** Actually, any new Mac has an adequate processor. If you're buying a used Mac or a closeout model, make sure you get at least a 500MHz G3 or any G4 processor.

- ✔ **Is the display adequate?** Apple is known for offering high-quality displays with its computers, due largely to the fact that a lot of graphic-arts professionals prefer the Macintosh. However, some iMacs have really small monitors, and you may find that using Premiere with these systems is difficult. "Oh, I can live with it," you might say. But if your budget allows, I strongly recommend at least a 17-inch display.

- ✔ **Is the FireWire adapter QuickTime-compatible?** This isn't a problem with newer Macs, but if you have an older unit with a FireWire adapter you should double-check for QuickTime compatibility.

- ✔ **Is a SuperDrive included?** Apple has been a real trailblazer in the world of DVD authoring. The SuperDrive, which is available with many new Macs, allows you to record your own DVDs. SuperDrive-equipped systems start at under $2,000, and the drives are also available as add-ons for other Macs.

What about flat-panel monitors?

I haven't mentioned flat-panel monitors yet, which may seem hard to believe because these advanced displays are all the rage today. Most flat-panel monitors use LCD (liquid crystal display) technology to generate the display, and they offer several advantages over CRT monitors, including these:

- ✔ LCD monitors use less electricity.

- ✔ LCD monitors generate less heat.

- ✔ LCD monitors usually cause less eyestrain.

- ✔ Flat-panel monitors take up less space on your desktop.

Sounds great, right? Personally, I am not very impressed by most of the flat-panel monitors I've seen so far. Most of them tend to be darker than CRT monitors, and the screen resolution is not as fine. This does not mean that flat-panel monitors cannot be superior. Apple has a sharp, brilliant example in its 21-inch Widescreen Studio Display.

Clearly, flat-panel monitors are the wave of the future. But I recommend that you observe any monitor in action before you make a purchasing decision. You'll want bright, clear images when you fine-tune your video — and that means a high-quality monitor is crucial.

Choosing a Windows PC

Don't let anyone tell you that Macs are always better for video editing than Windows PCs. Yes, most new Macs are great video-editing machines right out of the box. But a properly equipped PC running Windows can be just as effective. You just need to take a bit more time (and spend a bit more money) to make sure you're getting the right kind of system, if only because when you are shopping for a Windows machine there are so many more choices.

When shopping for a Windows-based video-editing system, follow the system recommendations I made earlier, and also look for the following:

- ✔ **A fast processor.** I can't think of a reason to buy any new PC these days with less than a 1GHz CPU. Adobe recommends a Pentium III or Pentium IV processor for use with Premiere, though I have had success with an AMD Duron processor as well.

- ✔ **A big hard drive.** As with Macs, cheaper PCs usually have smaller hard drives. If you are ordering a more affordable PC, ask about upgrading to at least an 80GB hard drive. (And make sure you get a 7200-rpm drive!)

- ✔ **A good video card.** Many new PCs have the display adapter built into the motherboard. When you're reading the spec sheet, you may see something like "16MB on-board AGP video." I usually don't like on-board video because it almost always uses up some system RAM, and many on-board display adapters perform quite slowly. The better solution is to buy a system with a separate video card in an expansion slot, like PCs have had for over a decade. I recommend a video adapter card with at least 32MB of video RAM.

  Speaking of video cards, many good cards (such as the ATI All-In-Wonder cards) include composite or component video inputs/outputs. This means that the video card can also be used to capture analog video. This feature is worth paying a little extra for.

- ✔ **A FireWire card.** Many PCs still don't come with built-in FireWire adapters, so double-check to ensure that the PC you buy has FireWire.

  If you get a computer without a FireWire adapter, you can usually add one for less than $100. FireWire adapters should be Microsoft-certified and OHCI-compliant. This information should be noted in the documentation that comes with the computer or adapter card.

- ✔ **A DVD recorder.** Some Windows PCs now include DVD-Recorder drives. It's an expensive option (expect to pay $400 or more), but you can have a lot of fun creating your own DVDs.

Buy a PC or Build Your Own?

If you are considering an Apple Macintosh, your only reasonable option is to buy a complete computer. This is not necessarily a bad thing, because most new Macs make great video-editing machines right out of the box. But if you are considering a Windows PC, you can either buy a complete system, or build your own from parts. Building PCs from scratch (or upgrading an older PC) has been a vaunted geek tradition for years, and many people — myself included — still practice it. Components are available from mail-order companies, Web sites, and some retail electronics stores.

For most PC users, building a computer from scratch doesn't make a whole lot of sense anymore. You must purchase a case, motherboard, processor, RAM, sound card, video card, modem, network card, FireWire card, hard drive, CD-RW drive, DVD-ROM drive, floppy drive, keyboard, mouse, monitor, some cooling fans, speakers, Windows software, and various cables. Expect to go back to the computer shop at least three times to get the things you forgot to list. Now you have a pile of parts that you must put together, and that pile probably cost hundreds of dollars *more* than a preassembled unit from a PC maker like Dell or Hewlett-Packard. And unlike your homebuilt computer, that affordable premade PC from Dell or H-P comes with a pretty good warranty and technical support.

But for some maniacs — like me — building your own PC can be a lot of fun. Besides, if you need a video-editing system, building your own can help you ensure that you're getting the best possible components. A preassembled unit is bound to include some cost-cutting measures to give it more mass-market appeal. Furthermore, because mass-produced computers usually use proprietary case and motherboard designs, gutting them for an extensive upgrade in the future may not be practical.

If you have never built a computer from scratch, this probably isn't a good time to start. I couldn't possibly tell you how to do it in this sidebar, because PC building and upgrading is a subject that fills many books. (May I recommend *Building a PC For Dummies* by Mark L. Chambers?) But if you are comfortable with PC upgrades and construction — and want to build your own video-editing system — follow the system-requirements guidelines listed earlier in this chapter when you pick out your components. (Get as far above the minimums as you can afford.)

Some of the most powerful computers built today are designed as gaming systems. Modern computer games require massive amounts of disk space, memory, CPU power, and a great display. So if you see a computer that advertises itself to gamers ("The Ultimate Gaming System — this thing will blast your socks off!"), you can bet this system will probably make a great video-editing computer. Just make sure you get that FireWire option!

Eventually your FireWire cable will fall down behind your desk. Then you'll have to get down on the floor and fish around behind your PC to retrieve the stray cable. Not fun. To address this, I like to have FireWire connectors right on the front of my computer case. If you are ordering a computer, contact the builder to find out if this feature can be added. If you are building your own, check your local PC parts retailer for a front plate kit for your FireWire connectors.

Choosing Video Gear

So you have a fantabulous new computer that is ready to edit video at blazing speeds. Don't worry; you're not done spending money just yet; you still have a lot of cool — and really important — gear left to buy. Some of the gear covered in the next few sections is pretty mandatory — a camera, for instance. Video can be kind of hard to record without a video camera. Other gear — video decks, audio recorders, and capture cards — may be less mandatory, depending on your needs and budget.

Cameras

No single piece of gear is more precious to a budding videographer than a good video camera. Most modern video cameras are actually *camcorders*, because they serve as both a camera and a recorder. Older video cameras connected to separate VCR units on which to record video. Often these VCR units were hung by a strap from the videographer's shoulder. Bulky.

When buying a new camcorder, go digital. The quality of digital video is higher, and it is a lot easier to transfer video from a digital camcorder into a computer. And these days you don't have to take out a second mortgage to afford a digital camcorder — they start at less than $500.

See Chapter 4 for more information on digital video formats, as well as a comparison of digital video versus analog video.

Of course, if you *want* to spend a lot of money, plenty of high-end camcorders are available as well. The best digital camcorders have three *charged coupled devices* (CCDs) — the eyes in the camera that actually pick up light and turn it into a video image. These include the Canon GL1 and XL1, and the Sony DCR-VX2000. These cameras provide superior color and resolution, as well as features that the pros like such as interchangeable lenses and high-quality microphones. Be prepared to spend $2,500 to $5,000 for these high-end digital camcorders.

When you're shopping for a new digital camcorder, check the following:

- ✔ **Audio?** Most digital camcorders can record 16-bit stereo audio. Don't accept anything less.

- ✔ **Batteries?** If the camcorder has a built-in, non-removable battery, run away! Get a camera with replaceable, rechargeable batteries. Buy extra batteries when you buy your camcorder.

- ✔ **FireWire?** This interface is also called IEEE-1394 or i.Link by some camera manufacturers. FireWire allows you to quickly copy video into your computer.

✔ **Manual controls?** Auto focus and automatic exposure controls are great, but as you get more serious about shooting video you may want more control over these features. The easiest manual focus and exposure controls are ones that are manipulated by a ring around the lens body. Small knobs or slider switches on the side of the camera are more difficult to use.

✔ **Storage media?** Make sure that tapes are affordable and widely available. MiniDV is now the most common recording format, and tapes are affordable and easy to find.

✔ **Zoom?** You'll see "400X ZOOM" splashed across the side of the camera. Such huge numbers usually express *digital* zoom, which is (in my opinion) virtually useless. Check the fine print next to the digital zoom figure and you should see a figure for *optical* zoom. Optical zoom is something you can actually use, and most mass-market digital camcorders offer around 10X to 25X optical zoom.

When you start spending over $2,000 for a camcorder, some people begin to look at you differently. They don't think you're crazy; they think you're a "professional." Actually, true "professional" videographers are shooting the 11:00 O'clock News with cameras that start at $20,000. So there you are with your $4,000 Canon XL1S — not quite a professional, but not exactly a typical consumer either. While I hesitate to slap a label on anyone (I hardly know you!), industry people obsessed with categorizing customers would refer to you as a *prosumer* (a buyer in-between pro and consumer). Don't slap them; you will often see "prosumer" used to describe higher-quality gear in the video world.

Video decks

The first time I heard the term *video deck,* I thought it referred to the deck on a cruise ship where everyone goes to watch movies. Not so. *Video deck* is actually just a fancy term for a *videocassette recorder,* which you may know as a VCR. If you want to talk like a true video geek, however, *video deck* must become part of your lexicon.

Why do you need a video deck? A high-quality deck becomes really useful if you plan to distribute your movies on tape. With the proper electronic connections, you can output a movie directly from your computer to videotape. Also, if you have a deck that uses the same tape format as your camcorder, you can save wear and tear on the camcorder's tape mechanism when you capture video into your computer. Good video decks aren't cheap, however, and a typical VHS VCR will not offer much in the way of quality or-editing capabilities. When looking for a video deck, consider the following:

✔ **Format?** S-VHS decks are good for outputting movies to VHS tape, and provide decent quality. MiniDV decks and other formats are also available from a variety of sources. Some decks even offer both S-VHS and MiniDV in the same unit.

 ✔ **FireWire?** Some newer decks have FireWire connections. As with camcorders, this greatly simplifies the process of interfacing with your computer.

 ✔ **Device control?** You might be able to control the video deck using controls in Adobe Premiere. FireWire greatly simplifies this process, but some decks can use a serial cable for device control as well.

If you're just starting to get involved with video editing, a video deck may seem like an extravagance. But the more time you spend capturing and outputting video, the more useful a good video deck can be.

For some specific video-deck recommendations, check out Chapter 17.

Audio recorders

All modern camcorders have built-in microphones, and most digital camcorders can record decent-quality audio. However, you may find that the built-in audio recording never exceeds "decent" on the quality scale. There are two simple solutions to recording better audio:

 ✔ Use a high-quality accessory microphone.
 ✔ Record audio separately.

If you want to connect a better microphone to your camcorder, the best place to start is with your camcorder's manufacturer (you'll need a *really* long cable — just kidding). Usually accessory microphones are available from the manufacturer. These accessory units make use of connections, accessory shoes, and other features on your camcorder.

Separate sound recorders give you more flexibility, especially if you just want to record audio in a certain location but not video. Many professionals use DAT (digital audiotape) recorders to record audio, but DAT recorders are usually quite expensive. Digital voice recorders are also available, but the amount of audio they can record is often limited by whatever storage is built into the unit. For a good balance of quality and affordability, I recommend one of the new MiniDisc recorders.

Audio quality has a profound effect on the way people perceive a video program. For more on recording great audio, see Chapter 11. For more on MiniDisc recorders, see Chapter 17.

Capture hardware

A digital camcorder and a powerful computer equipped with Adobe Premiere won't do you much good if you can't get video from the camcorder into the computer. For this you need capture hardware, so-called because it captures audio and video into your computer.

FireWire (IEEE-1394) devices

FireWire is a high-speed interface developed by Apple and first released in 1996. "FireWire" is actually Apple's trademarked name for the technology officially known as IEEE-1394, named for the international standard to which it conforms. Sony and a few other companies call the interface "i.Link." All DV-format camcorders have a FireWire interface. Although Apple originally developed FireWire with digital video in mind, the IEEE-1394 interface is also used by other devices including external hard drives, still cameras, and scanners.

A FireWire interface makes capturing digital video really easy. You just connect a cable between the FireWire port on your computer and the FireWire port on your camcorder, and then capture video using Premiere. It's easy because all Premiere really has to do is copy digital video from the camcorder onto your hard drive.

All new Macintosh computers come with FireWire ports. Many new Windows-based PCs do as well, but you need to double-check. You should see a 6-pin FireWire port that resembles Figure 2-2. If you don't see one, you can purchase a FireWire expansion card from many electronics retailers. Installing a FireWire card in your PC has three indispensable requirements:

  ✔ Windows 98 Second Edition (SE) or higher
  ✔ A vacant expansion slot in your computer
  ✔ PC hardware expertise

If you aren't familiar with expansion slots and don't have experience with hardware upgrades, consult a professional PC technician. If your computer is still under warranty, don't even *look* at a screwdriver until you've reviewed the warranty terms to determine whether — and how — upgrades should be performed.

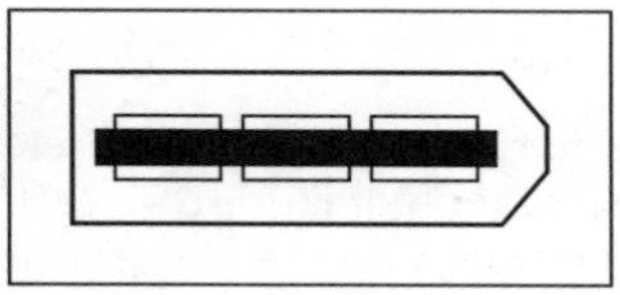

Figure 2-2:
The
FireWire
port on your
computer
should look
something
like this.

Analog video-capture devices

Analog video is a bit trickier to get into your computer, because it must first be digitized. Capture cards are available to help you do this bit of magic (they tend to be expensive), but if you don't already have Adobe Premiere, you may find that one cost-effective way to buy a high-end analog capture card is to get one that already comes bundled with Premiere. Pinnacle's DV500+ is an excellent analog capture card which includes Adobe Premiere as part of the package deal.

Don't tell Adobe I said so, but if you shop around you can often find the Pinnacle DV500+ with Premiere for *less* than what Adobe normally charges for Premiere all by itself! Just double-check the version of Premiere that comes with the capture card; a card that has been sitting in a warehouse for a while might come with an older version of Premiere.

For light-duty usage, a good solution may be a video display adapter card that also includes composite or S-Video inputs. The ATI All-In-Wonder cards serve as display adapters, and they also include composite video inputs/outputs. Some All-In-Wonder cards even have built-in FireWire ports.

What is a video display adapter? The display adapter is the component in your computer that generates a video image for the monitor. The monitor cable usually plugs directly into the display adapter.

A video-capture card isn't the only way to get analog video into your computer. Various external capture devices also exist, such as the Canopus ADVC-100 or Dazzle Hollywood DV-Bridge. You can usually connect analog video hardware to these external devices using composite or S-Video connectors. The device digitizes the video and then transfers the video to your computer via a FireWire port. If you don't feel like tearing open your computer and dealing with expansion cards, this is a great way to capture analog video.

Chapter 3

Preparing Adobe Premiere

● ●

In This Chapter

▶ Getting comfortable in your workspace

▶ Tweaking program settings

▶ Customizing windows in Premiere

▶ Installing plug-ins for Adobe Premiere

● ●

*I*f you've been using computers for a while, you have probably gotten used to just opening a program and getting right to work. If you need to type a memo, you launch your word processor, type a few paragraphs, and click Print. If you want to peruse the Internet, you launch your Web browser and start clicking away at links. But Adobe Premiere might be a bit of a switch for you, because you can't just open the program and start making a movie. Some preparation is in order when you start working in this program.

Why does Adobe Premiere need to be set up before you can use it? The main reason is that Premiere is an advanced program that can work with many different kinds of video. Premiere accommodates a variety of editing styles, and you can configure Premiere to use your preferred style. Premiere also offers some options that you should also review to ensure that your movie comes out right. This chapter helps you configure Premiere for editing, take charge of important program settings, and get familiar with some useful options.

Setting Up Your Workspace

Look around at the workspace in your office, or wherever it is you plan to use Adobe Premiere. You probably have the computer set up a certain way, the mouse is in your favorite spot, and a ring on the desktop reminds you where you normally place your coffee cup. You have everything just where you like it and it works.

If you aren't familiar with using the window and palette controls in Adobe Premiere, turn back to Chapter 1 and take a grand tour of the program.

When you launch Adobe Premiere, it presents a virtual workspace on the screen. Just like the physical workspace around your desk, you can customize Premiere and set up its workspace just the way you like it. You can move windows around, close some items, and open others. Premiere offers a couple of preset workspaces. The first time you launch Premiere you will be asked which workspace you want to use (If you aren't sure, pick the A/B Editing workspace). Whenever you are working in Premiere, you can select a preset workspace by choosing Window⇨Workspace from the menu bar, and then choosing one of the four predefined workspaces (described in the following sections). You can switch back and forth between workspaces whenever you want. For example, if you're editing in the Single-Track Editing workspace and decide it's time to work on audio, you may find it easier to simply open the Audio workspace as opposed to manually opening the various elements you'll need for audio work.

You can create your own custom workspaces and save them for future use. To do so, choose Window⇨Workspace⇨Save Workspace, give your custom workspace a descriptive name, and then click OK or press Enter. Your custom workspace joins the others on the list in the Window⇨Workspace menu. To reload the workspace later, just choose it from the menu!

The A/B Editing workspace

Premiere's A/B Editing workspace is a good place to start for simple projects. To make sure that you are looking at the A/B Editing workspace, choose Window⇨Workspace⇨A/B Editing. As you can see in Figure 3-1, this workspace includes the Project window, the Monitor, the Timeline, and several palettes. Unique elements of the A/B Editing workspace include:

- ✔ **Single View Monitor:** This Monitor displays the frame at the current location of the edit line in the Timeline. In the A/B Editing workspace, the Monitor only shows one panel, as shown in Figure 3-1.

- ✔ **Video 1A/B tracks:** The Video 1 track is divided into three separate tracks: Video 1A, Transition, and Video 1B. This is unique because in other workspaces, Video 1 appears as a single, integrated track.

If you have used other mass-market video editing programs (such as Apple iMovie, Ulead VideoStudio, or Windows Movie Maker), the A/B Editing workspace may seem familiar. In A/B Editing mode, you simply drag clips from the Project window directly to the Timeline. You may also find that the relationships between video clips and transitions are easier to visualize in A/B Editing.

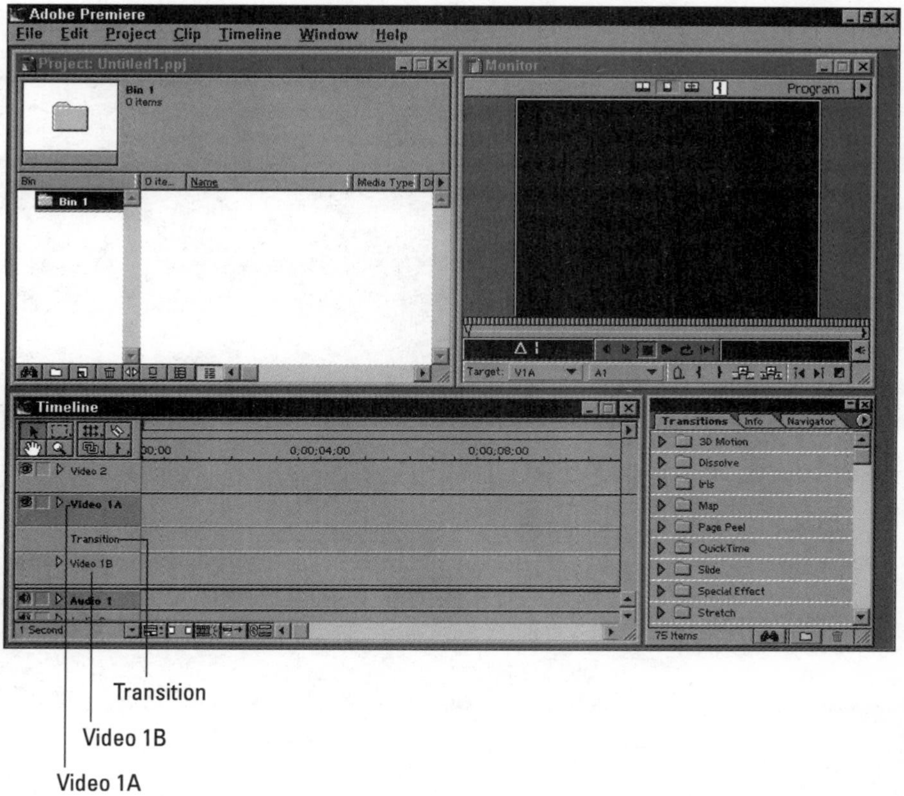

Figure 3-1:
The A/B
Editing
workspace
is a good
place to
perform
simple edits.

Transition

Video 1B

Video 1A

The Single-Track Editing workspace

The A/B Editing workspace is swell, but many experienced editors find that it doesn't make the most efficient use of screen space. Many experienced editors prefer the Single-Track Editing workspace. Check it out now by choosing Window⇨Workspace⇨Single-Track Editing. You should see a workspace similar to Figure 3-2. Key features include:

✔ **Dual View Monitor:** One Monitor pane shows the source clip. This is where you decide which portions of a clip you actually want to edit into the Timeline. The other Monitor pane shows the program that you are actually assembling in the Timeline. You may find that being able to see both clips simultaneously makes editing clips into the Timeline a lot easier.

✔ **Single video tracks:** All clips and transitions in a track appear as one. This view not only makes more efficient use of screen space, but I also find it easier to work with because you don't have to alternate clips between A and B tracks. The track view can easily be expanded to an A/B view.

Drag clips here first.

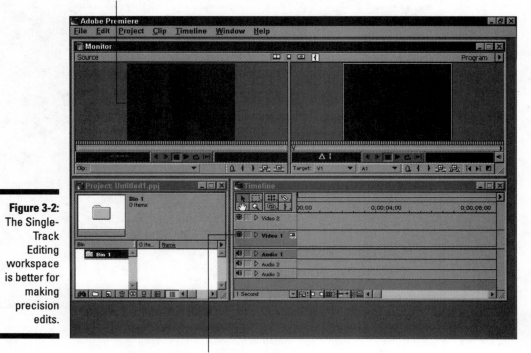

Figure 3-2:
The Single-
Track
Editing
workspace
is better for
making
precision
edits.

Single-track view can be expanded.

Although you can still drag clips into the Timeline if you want to, Single-Track Editing accommodates a different editing style. To really take advantage of this workspace, you first drag a clip from the Project window to the Monitor. Then you can use the Monitor to set precise in and out points on the clip before you edit it into the Timeline.

For more information on getting clips ready for editing into the Timeline, see Chapter 7.

The Effects workspace

Another preset workspace provided by Premiere is the Effects workspace. This workspace has a single view Monitor (like A/B Editing) and a single-track Timeline (like Single-Track Editing). Palettes are arranged so as to give you easy access to audio and video effects. As you switch from clip to clip, the Effects Controls palette changes to reflect the effects applied to each respective clip, or the available effects in the current Timeline track.

Effects are cool, and Premiere lets you apply lots of them. To begin using effects in Premiere, see Chapter 10. Audio effects are covered in Chapter 11.

The Audio workspace

Video is so exciting that it's easy to forget how important a good soundtrack is in a movie project. If you want your project to make a positive impression, then you'd better put some time into editing your audio. Premiere provides the Audio workspace to help you get it done. Although you can edit audio in any workspace, the Audio workspace is custom tailored specifically for audio work. The Audio workspace (shown in Figure 3-3) includes:

✔ **Single-view Monitor**

✔ **Single-track Timeline**

✔ **Audio Mixer** for controlling your audio tracks

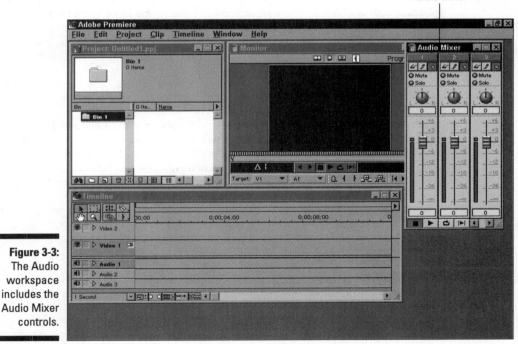

Figure 3-3:
The Audio workspace includes the Audio Mixer controls.

With the Audio Mixer, you can tailor the overall level of your audio to fit your video, as well as mix the levels of individual audio tracks. So (for example), if you have a dialog track that goes with some video, and a musical soundtrack that should play in the background, you can control how loud or quiet the music is relative to the dialog.

Adjusting Program Settings

Adobe Premiere offers a plethora of settings, and you could easily spend a day or two trying to sort through them all. Some settings are immediately relevant to your work; some won't be used until you perform more advanced work. The next few sections show you some key settings that help you make more-effective use of Premiere on a daily basis.

Setting up your scratch disks

I hear some of you scratching your heads. "What in the Wide, Wide World of Sports is a scratch disk?" The *scratch disk* is the disk where you store all of your video stuff. When you capture video onto your computer, you capture it to the scratch disk. Likewise, when you want to preview transitions, time-lines, effects, and various edits, the they must be *rendered*. Rendering is where the transitions or effects are actually applied to the clips. The rendered clips are stored as preview files on the scratch disk. The scratch disk is your Premiere storage place — your video data bucket, so to speak.

If your computer has just one big hard drive, then you won't necessarily have a separate scratch disk. Your scratch disk will actually be a folder on your main hard drive. But if you can get a separate hard drive to use exclusively as a Premiere scratch disk, I recommend it. Because big and fast hard drives are so cheap these days, there is almost no reason to *not* have a separate scratch disk.

A scratch disk must be not only big, but fast. I recommend a 7200rpm IDE drive at the very least, or if you can afford it, a SCSI drive. If your drive isn't fast enough, you'll drop frames during rendering and when you try to output video to tape. See Chapter 2 for more on selecting hard drives.

You can choose different scratch disks and folders for different types of files. Premiere will always use whatever location you specify. To set up your scratch disks, follow these steps:

1. **On the Premiere menu bar, choose Edit⇨Preferences⇨Scratch Disks and Device Control.**

The Preferences dialog box appears, as shown in Figure 3-4.

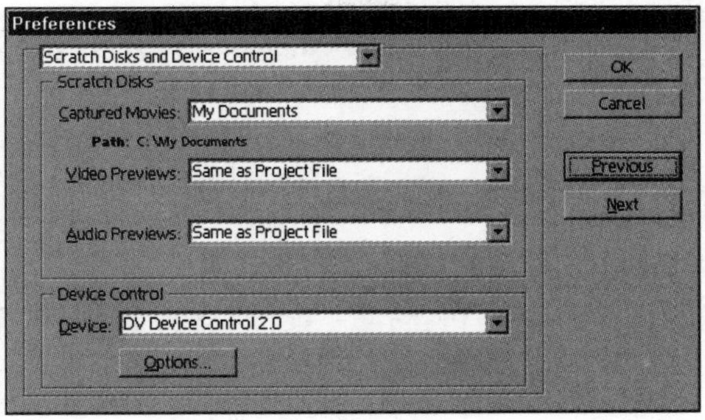

Figure 3-4:
Configure
your storage
space using
the Scratch
Disks
settings.

[Preferences dialog box showing:

Scratch Disks and Device Control

Scratch Disks
Captured Movies: My Documents
   Path: C: \My Documents
Video Previews: Same as Project File
Audio Previews: Same as Project File

Device Control
Device: DV Device Control 2.0
   Options...

OK   Cancel   Previous   Next]

2. **Use the Captured Movies menu to adjust the scratch disk setting for clips that you capture using Premiere.**

   When you capture movies from a camera, video deck, or other source, this is where the video files are stored. The default location on a Windows PC is "My Documents." On a Macintosh, the default location is the Adobe application folder on the hard drive where you installed Premiere. To choose a different location, choose Select Folder from the menu. When a standard Browse (Windows) or Finder (Macintosh) dialog box appears, use it to navigate to and select a new disk and folder.

3. **Choose a scratch disk for video previews from the Video Previews drop-down menu.**

   When you want to preview part of your project or the whole thing, Premiere must render a preview file. The default location for these preview files is "Same as Project File," which as the name suggests is the folder where your Premiere Project (.PPJ) file is saved. You can select a different folder if you wish.

4. **Choose a scratch disk for audio previews from the Audio Previews drop-down menu.**

   Audio must also be rendered before it can be previewed.

5. **Click OK when you are done adjusting your Scratch Disk settings.**

If your computer is on a network, you will be able to choose network drives on other computers when you set up your scratch disks. However, I strongly recommend against using network drives as scratch disks. Most networks are not fast or reliable enough to adequately handle large video files without dropping frames and causing other problems.

Customizing other options

You can customize what happens when you first start Premiere. Right now you probably see the Load Project Settings dialog box every time you start Premiere. If you wish something else would happen on startup instead, try this:

1. **Launch Premiere, and click Cancel to close the Load Project Settings dialog box if it appears.**

2. **Choose Edit⬦Preferences⬦General and Still Image.**

   The General and Still Image Preferences dialog box appears, as shown in Figure 3-5.

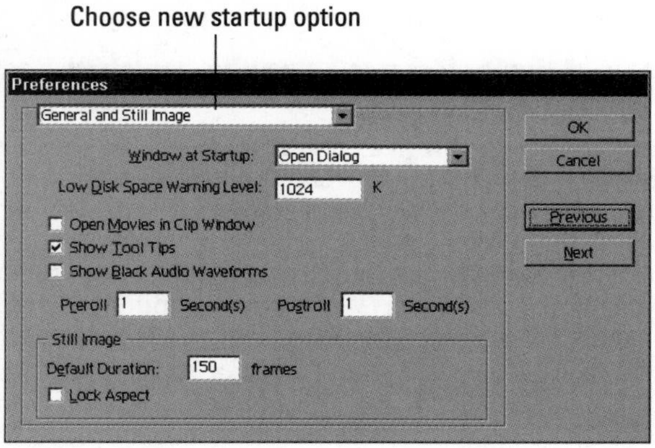

Choose new startup option

Figure 3-5:
Use the
General and
Still Image
page of the
Preferences
dialog box
to change
what
happens
when
Premiere
starts up.

3. **In the Window at Startup drop-down menu, choose None if you don't want any dialog boxes or windows to appear when you first start Premiere.**

   Other "Window at Startup" options include the following:

   • Choose Open Dialog if you want the Open Project dialog box to open at startup.

   • Choose New Project if you want the New Project Settings dialog box to appear at startup.

While you have the Preferences dialog box open, open the menu at the top of the dialog box and choose Auto Save and Undo. You should now see a group of Auto Save options. If you place a check mark next to "Automatically Save Projects," Premiere automatically saves your work every five minutes (or you can choose another interval).

Auto Save can work in conjunction with the very cool Project Archive feature. When you set Premiere to automatically save your work periodically, and you have numbers listed next to "Maximum Files in Archive" and "Maximum Project Versions," Premiere then saves a different version of your project every time it autosaves — which can really help you out if you want to go back to an earlier version of the project. The archive files are saved in the same folder as your main .PPJ (project) file, so opening an archived version is as easy as choosing File⇨Open.

Because .PPJ files are small, you can safely use the Project Archive feature without eating up a lot of disk space. In the Preferences dialog box, you set how many versions you want saved. When the specified limit is reached, the oldest version is deleted in favor of the new one.

Finally, open the menu at the top of the Preferences dialog box again — and this time, choose Titler. The Titler options appear, as shown in Figure 3-6. Here you can choose a specific Startup Template for when you first launch the Titler, and you can choose which characters to use for font and style samples. But the most important options here are the two check boxes:

✔ **Show Safe Title Margins** — Virtually all TVs overscan the video image. *Overscan* means that some of the video image is actually cut off at the edges of the screen. When designing video for TV viewing, you must take overscan into account. The title's *safe margin* is actually a border that appears on the video image. If you keep your titles inside that border, the words shouldn't get cut off by overscan. Even if you're only developing video for the Web or other digital source, I recommend that you keep the title's safe margins on at all times.

✔ **Show Safe Action Margins** — Action can usually be shown closer to the edge of the screen than titles, so the safe margins for action are closer to the edges of the video image than are the safe margins of titles. You may find that setting safe margins for actions isn't very useful when you're designing titles (unless you have animated objects or graphics in your titles).

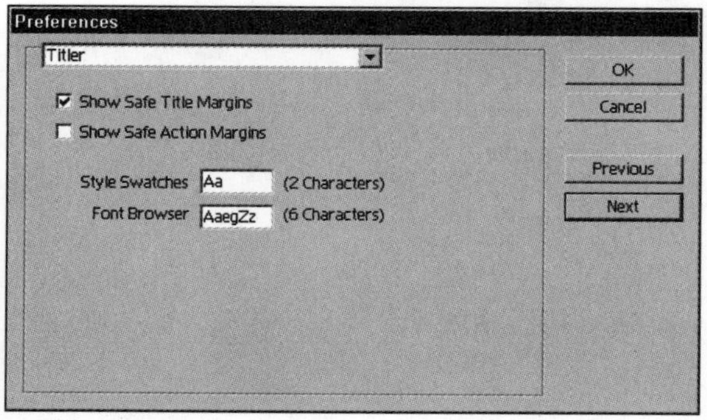

Figure 3-6:
Use the
Preferences
dialog box
to control
default
settings for
the Titler.

Setting online preferences

Adobe wants to help ensure that you have the latest and greatest version of Premiere. The company frequently releases updates and makes them available to you for free download online. The only catch is that you have to actually remember to check for those updates, unless you tell Premiere to automatically check for you. To get that automatic machinery in place, follow these steps:

1. **From the Premiere menu bar choose Edit⇨Preferences⇨Online Settings.**

   A small Adobe Online Preferences dialog box appears, as shown in Figure 3-7.

2. **From the Check for Updates drop-down menu, choose an interval at which you would like Premiere to check for updates.**

   You can tell Premiere to check for updates daily, weekly, monthly, or never.

3. **To check for updates right now, click Updates.**

   Premiere will go online (if your computer has an Internet connection setup and active) and check for updates on the Adobe Web site. If updates are available, they will be downloaded and instructions on-screen will help you through the installation process.

4. **When you're done fiddling with online settings, click OK to close the dialog box.**

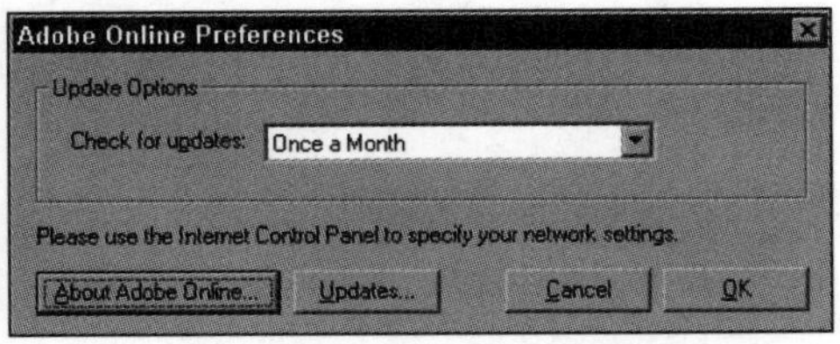

Figure 3-7:
Use this dialog box to tell Premiere to automatically check for updates online at specific intervals.

Adobe Online Preferences

Update Options

Check for updates: Once a Month

Please use the Internet Control Panel to specify your network settings.

About Adobe Online...   Updates...   Cancel   OK

Resetting Premiere preferences

Sometimes the only way to move forward is to go back to the beginning. So it is with software programs. In our eagerness to play around with program settings, we sometimes wind up making mistakes that we can't figure out how to fix. If you ever become unhappy with the way you've set up Premiere, or you simply want all of the various program settings to return to the defaults that you started with, delete Premiere's preferences file.

Adobe Premiere stores all of your setting changes and customizations in a preferences file. On a Windows system, this file is called `Premiere 6.5 Prefs` and is located in the folder `C:\WINDOWS\Application Data\Adobe\Premiere`. On a Macintosh, the file is called `Premiere 6.5 Preferences File`

and is located in the folder `Adobe:Premiere 6.5`. You can delete this file, but make sure Premiere is closed before you delete it. Alternatively, you may want to simply move the file to another folder, or rename it. The next time you open Premiere, a new preferences file will be created with the same default settings you had when you first installed the program.

Another thing you can do with your Preferences file is copy it to other machines. If you get a new computer and want to migrate Premiere over to the new machine, you can copy your preferences file over after Premiere has been installed on the new system. Then you won't have to spend a lot of time re-creating all your preferences.

Customizing Premiere's Windows

As an individual (just like everyone else), you probably like to personalize the software you use to make it better suit your needs. We don't all have the same work habits, and what works for me may not be ideal for you. The programmers at Adobe realized that your idea of the perfect working environment may not be the same as theirs — so they've given you quite a bit of control over Premiere's windows. You can even customize some keyboard commands.

Changing the Project window

The project window is kind of like Premiere's filing cabinet. All files that you use in your project are stored in the Project window. By default, files are displayed in a basic list, with various details about each file displayed. I usually find this to be the most useful display mode for Premiere, but there are alternative views that can be useful. To customize the Project window in Premiere, choose Window⇨Window Options⇨Project Window Options. The Project Window Options dialog box appears, as shown in Figure 3-8.

At the top of the Project Window Options dialog box you'll see a menu that lets you select the basic view mode for the Project window. The default mode is List View, and Figure 3-8 shows the options for List View. Here you can specify which fields are displayed in List View. For example, if you want the file path or reel name to be shown — or you don't need the log comment taking up screen space — you can add or remove check marks next to the fields listed under List View as you see fit. Each field that has a check mark next to it will appear in the Project window when List View is the display mode.

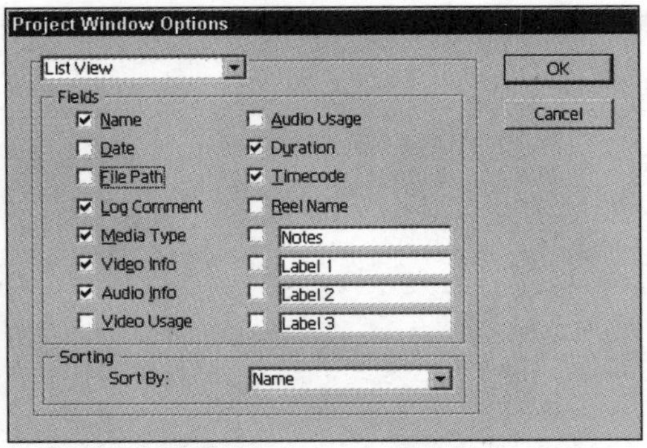

Figure 3-8:
Use this
dialog box
to customize
the Project
window.

Project Window Options

List View

Fields
☑ Name   ☐ Audio Usage
☐ Date   ☑ Duration
☐ File Path   ☑ Timecode
☑ Log Comment   ☐ Reel Name
☑ Media Type   ☐ Notes
☑ Video Info   ☐ Label 1
☑ Audio Info   ☐ Label 2
☐ Video Usage   ☐ Label 3

Sorting
Sort By: Name

OK
Cancel

You can specify which field is used to sort clips if you use the Sort By menu at the bottom of the Project Window Options dialog box — though personally I find that sorting clips by name is the most useful approach. If you want to sort clips by other criteria — Media Type, for example — I recommend that you create separate bins for different types of media instead.

If you want to create bins in the Project window to help organize your material, see Chapter 6.

Two other display modes are available for the Project window. These are Icon View and Thumbnail view. In these two view modes, clips are displayed as icons rather than as items in a list. For video and still-image clips, the icon shows an actual image of the clip. Thus you can identify exactly what is in the clip simply by looking at it. Icon View simply displays a bunch of icons (as shown in Figure 3-9); Thumbnail View displays a list of icons as well as some clip details.

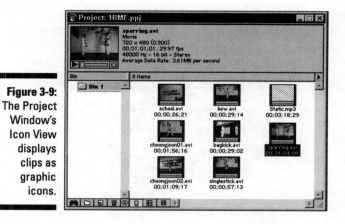

Figure 3-9:
The Project
Window's
Icon View
displays
clips as
graphic
icons.

Modifying the Timeline

Throughout this book, I show the Timeline with default view settings. However, you can set some extremely useful view options by choosing Window➪Window Options➪Timeline Window Options. Doing so opens (surprise) the Timeline Window Options dialog box, as shown in Figure 3-10.

In the Timeline Window Options dialog box, take a look at the options under Track Format. Here you can specify how tracks appear in the Timeline window. The four choices are

- ✔ **All frames:** The whole track appears as a series of frames. This view can be helpful if you want to view a visual representation or storyboard of the whole video program, as shown in Figure 3-11. I don't recommend using this option during normal editing, however, because (as you can see in Figure 3-11) the separations between clips can be tough to see.

- ✔ **In point, file name, and out point:** The first frame of the clip, the file name, and the last frame of the clip are shown. This option can be extremely helpful because you can quickly see how each clip starts and ends, plus you can still see the clip's file name.

- ✔ **In point and file name:** The first frame of the clip and the file name are shown. Use this option if you don't have quite enough screen real estate to display both the in and out point frames. The visual clue provided by having the first frame shown is especially useful if many of your clips have the same file name because they came from the same source clip.

✔ **File name:** Just the file name of the clip is shown. This is the default view option, and makes the most efficient use of screen space.

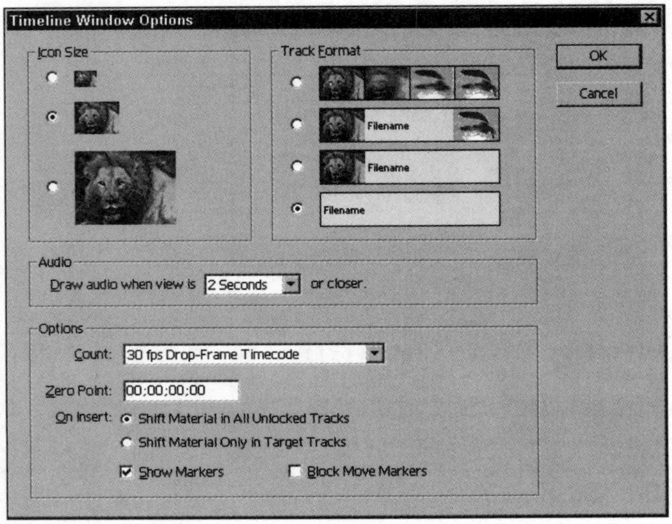

Figure 3-10:
Customize
the
appearance
of your
Timeline in
the Timeline
Window
Options
dialog box.

Figure 3-11:
The All
Frames
view option
provides
a visual
representa-
tion of your
project in
the Timeline,
but clip
separations
can be
difficult to
identify. Can
you tell
where one
clip ends
and another
begins?

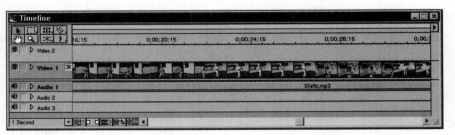

Other options in the Timeline Window Options dialog box allow you to change the size of icons and specify when audio waveforms are drawn. You can also change the timecode format of the Timeline using the Count menu, although I recommend against adjusting the timecode here. You should generally stick with the timecode specified in the project settings when you create a new project. In the Zero Point field you can specify a different starting timecode for your Timeline if you wish. This may be useful if you are creating a project that will later become part of another, bigger project. The On Insert radio buttons allow you to change the Shift Track Option. Finally, with the two check boxes at the bottom of the Timeline Window Options you can specify whether markers are shown in the Timeline or whether Timeline markers should move when you move a block of clips.

For more on managing settings such as timecode format for a new project, see Chapter 5. To find out about the Shift Track Option, markers, or other Timeline editing tools, see Chapter 8.

Adjusting the Monitor

No, this section doesn't show you how to use all those little buttons on the front of your computer's monitor (sorry). Instead, I'll show you how to adjust Premiere's Monitor window. To do so, choose Window⇨Window Options⇨ Monitor Window Options. The Monitor Window Options dialog box appears, as shown in Figure 3-12. Options in this dialog box are divided into three categories:

- ✔ **Source Options:** These options control the Source side of the Monitor window when you are working in Dual Pane mode. The Count menu lets you specify the timecode format for source footage and the Zero Based check box lets you specify that the Timecode will start at zero. I recommend against changing these settings, and instead use the timecode and format that is already native to the source footage.

- ✔ **Safe Margins:** Here you can control the size of the safe margins for action and for titles. If your program will be viewed on broadcast-style TV screens, make sure your action and titles remain inside these respective margins. The margins are expressed as a percentage of the overall screen area.

  I recommend *against* changing the margins from the default settings (10 percent for the Action Safe Margin and 20 percent for the Title Safe Margin).

- ✔ **Trim Mode Options:** These settings let you control the appearance of the video image when trimming or previewing clips. During some Timeline editing tasks (such as Ripple Edits) you can view frames affected by your edits in the Monitor in Trim Mode. In the Monitor Window Options dialog box, you can control how the Monitor appears during Trim Mode.

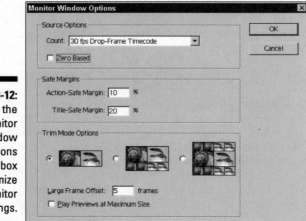

Figure 3-12:
Use the
Monitor
Window
Options
dialog box
to customize
Monitor
settings.

For more on using the Monitor window and switching between Single and Dual Pane modes, see the "Setting up your workspace" section earlier in this chapter. To find out what Trim Mode is and how it works, see Chapter 8.

Mixing up the Audio Mixer

When you're working on a movie project, don't forget about the audio portion of the program as well. Premiere provides you with a special Audio Mixer window to help you control the audio levels of the various audio tracks in your project. And just like other windows in Premiere, the Audio Mixer can be customized. To begin customizing the Audio Mixer, choose Window➪ Window Options➪Audio Mixer Window Options. The Audio Mixer Window Options dialog box appears, as shown in Figure 3-13.

The first group of options is pretty self-explanatory. You can choose to display both the master fader and individual track faders, just the track faders, or just the master fader.

The second group of options is a bit more complicated. The Automation Write Options deal with how adjustments to audio levels are automatically applied to clips as you adjust controls in the Audio Mixer while playing the Timeline. The four options are:

✔ **Touch:** Changes to the audio levels only occur when you actually touch (with the mouse) the controls. When you release a control, it snaps back to the original position.

✔ **Latch:** Changes to the audio levels occur as you touch the controls, but unlike the Touch option, the controls don't snap back to the previous setting when you release the mouse button.

✔ **Write:** Audio levels are set to whatever the current positions of the controls are.

✔ **Write/Touch:** This option is similar to the Write option, but Premiere automatically switches to the Touch option after using the Write option.

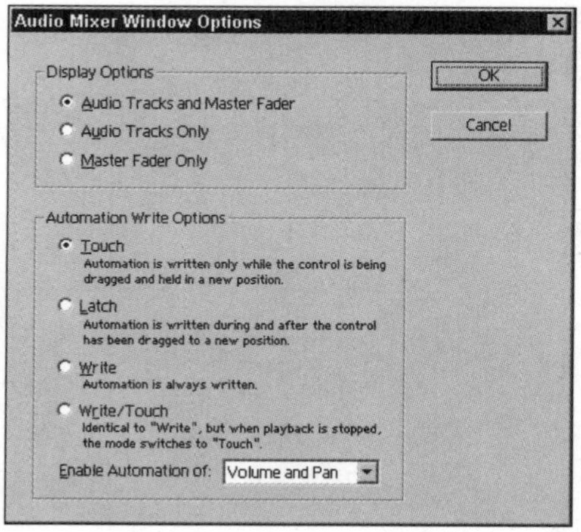

Figure 3-13:
Adjust
settings for
the Audio
Mixer
window
here.

Audio Mixer Window Options

Display Options
- ⦿ Audio Tracks and Master Fader
- ○ Audio Tracks Only
- ○ Master Fader Only

OK
Cancel

Automation Write Options
- ⦿ Touch
  Automation is written only while the control is being dragged and held in a new position.
- ○ Latch
  Automation is written during and after the control has been dragged to a new position.
- ○ Write
  Automation is always written.
- ○ Write/Touch
  Identical to "Write", but when playback is stopped, the mode switches to "Touch".

Enable Automation of: Volume and Pan ▾

Finally, the Enable Automation Of menu at the bottom of the Audio Mixer Window Options dialog box lets you specify whether automation is applied to volume, pan (*pan* is the balance of stereo audio from left to right), or both volume and pan.

For more on working with audio in your Premiere projects, see Chapter 11.

Using keyboard commands

Adobe Premiere follows the same basic design paradigm as most other modern software programs. Premiere's workspace is designed as a GUI (*graphical user interface,* often pronounced "gooey") which means that program elements are laid out graphically. You navigate program windows and execute editing commands using the mouse to click on buttons, drag-and-drop items, and choose menu items. There is almost nothing you can't do in Premiere with a mouse.

Still, don't throw away that keyboard just yet. Many Premiere users find that the mouse just doesn't have enough buttons to quickly perform some important actions. Thankfully, many common commands are accessible by using keys on the keyboard. To view some of the most common keyboard commands in Premiere, choose Window⇨Show Commands (sorry, you'll have to use the mouse for this one). The Commands palette appears, as shown in Figure 3-14. This palette lists 17 commands, along with their associated keyboard commands.

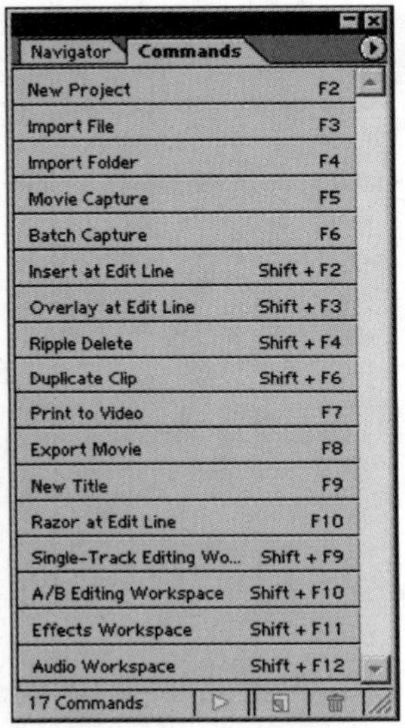

Figure 3-14:
View common keyboard commands by using the Commands palette.

Navigator \ Commands	
New Project	F2
Import File	F3
Import Folder	F4
Movie Capture	F5
Batch Capture	F6
Insert at Edit Line	Shift + F2
Overlay at Edit Line	Shift + F3
Ripple Delete	Shift + F4
Duplicate Clip	Shift + F6
Print to Video	F7
Export Movie	F8
New Title	F9
Razor at Edit Line	F10
Single-Track Editing Wo...	Shift + F9
A/B Editing Workspace	Shift + F10
Effects Workspace	Shift + F11
Audio Workspace	Shift + F12
17 Commands	

Commands listed in the Commands palette can be modified, and you can create your own keyboard commands as well. To modify a command:

1. **In the Commands palette, click the Palette Menu button and choose Button Mode to deselect that option.**

   The Palette Menu button is the right-pointing arrow in the upper-right corner of the palette.

2. **Click a command in the Commands palette to select it.**

3. **Open the Palette Menu again and choose Command Options.**

   The Command Options dialog box appears, as shown in Figure 3-15.

4. **If you want to modify the name of the command, type a new name in the Name field.**

I recommend against making radical changes to command names because it might make getting help or technical support more difficult later on. (Minor changes should be okay.)

5. **Open the Function Key drop-down menu and choose a new function key to use for the command.**

   Only unused function keys will be listed.

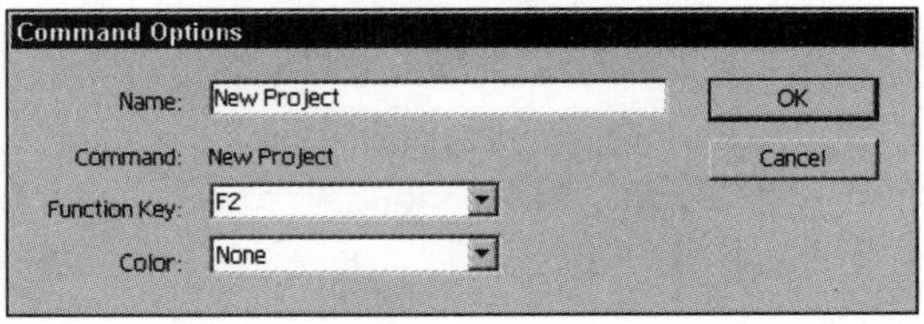

Figure 3-15:
Use the Command Options dialog box to change the name and function key used for various commands.

You can also add new keyboard commands. To do so, choose Add Command from the Commands palette menu, and specify a name and function key for your new command. Then, use your mouse to select a menu item from Premiere's menu bar. The menu item you choose should now be listed next to Command in the Command Options dialog box.

Installing Premiere Plug-Ins

One of the things I really like about Adobe software — from the ubiquitous Acrobat Reader all the way up to Premiere — is that they design their programs so capabilities can be added through the use of plug-ins. Some third-party software companies get pretty creative with the features they add. Plug-ins for Premiere can add new effects, transitions, export options, advanced titling options, and more. Adobe provides a list of select plug-ins for Premiere online at

www.adobe.com/products/plugins/premiere/main.html

I've tested a bunch of really cool third-party plug-ins for Adobe Premiere. I feature several of them in Chapter 16.

When you obtain a Premiere plug-in, installation instructions *should* be provided by the publisher. Ideally, the plug-in will come with a setup program or installer that takes care of everything for you. However, many plug-in publishers assume that you know a thing or two about how Premiere is installed and configured on your system. All plug-ins for Adobe programs are stored in a "plug-ins" folder somewhere on your hard drive. When you obtain a new plug-in, you will often be expected to copy the plug-in file to that folder manually. On a Macintosh, the folder should be

```
Adobe:Premiere 6.5:Plug-Ins
```

On a PC running Windows, the folder will usually be

```
C:\Program Files\Adobe\Premiere 6.5\Plug-ins
```

Make sure that Premiere is completely closed *before* you install a new plug-in. On a Macintosh, double-check your Finder menu to make sure that Premiere is not still active in the background.

Margins aren't just for handwriting assignments anymore . . .

I don't know about you, but every time I hear the word "margins," the voice of my second-grade handwriting teacher starts ringing in my head. As you know, when you write or type on paper it is important to leave margins around the edge of the page. Margins greatly enhance the appearance and readability of the page.

Margins are even more important when you work with video. Virtually all television sets have a problem called *overscan*. In a standard CRT (cathode ray tube) television screen, an electron gun at the back of the picture tube projects an image on the front of the tube, which is the part that we look at when we watch TV. Some of the video image is almost always projected beyond the edge of the viewable area of the tube, however, meaning that the extreme edges of the image are actually cut off. Some TVs overscan worse than others, and if you're working on a video project that will be viewed on TV screens, you must take overscan into account.

If your video will only be viewed on computer monitors, overscan will not be a problem.

Margins in Premiere help you ensure that important parts of your video image aren't cut off due to overscan. Professional video editors generally recommend that important action not appear in the outer 10 percent of the video image, and titles not appear in the outer 20 percent of the image. To display the Action-Safe and Title-Safe Margins in Premiere's Monitor window, open the Monitor window menu by clicking the right-pointing area in the upper-right corner of the Monitor. Then choose Safe Margins for Source Side or Safe Margins for Program Side, as needed. I recommend that, at a minimum, you display the safe margins on the Program side of the Monitor. You will now have white lines in the Monitor window which show the location of the Action-Safe and Title-Safe margins. Make sure that action and titles stay inside these margins.

Figure 3-16 shows what the Premiere plug-ins folder looks like on a Windows PC. Again, carefully read the documentation that comes with the plug-in (there might be a Readme file) for specific installation instructions. Once you place the plug-in file in this folder, it should be available the next time you open Premiere. For example, if the plug-in adds a new transition, the transition should appear in the Transitions palette when you restart Premiere.

One more thing: Since version 6.0 of Premiere came out, some Adobe After Effects plug-ins can be used with Premiere as well. In Windows, After Effects plug-ins usually have the .AEX extension. If you have a Premiere-compatible After Effects plug-in, it should go in a subfolder of the main Plug-ins folder called AEFilters (refer to Figure 3-16).

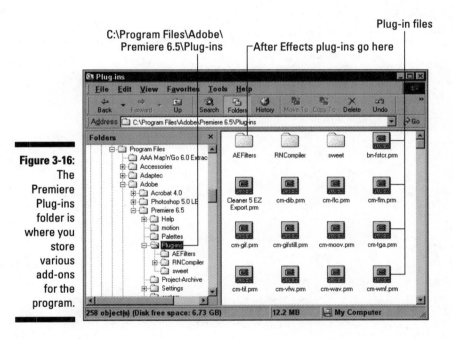

Figure 3-16:
The Premiere Plug-ins folder is where you store various add-ons for the program.

Part II
Beginning a Video Production

The 5th Wave — By Rich Tennant

"What do you mean you're updating our Web page?"

In this part . . .

Every journey must have a first step. When your journey involves moviemaking, your first step should be to familiarize yourself with the techniques and concepts of video creation and editing. This part begins by introducing you to the fundamentals of video production, a full understanding of which is crucial to creating successful movies.

Once you understand the basics and have shot some video footage, you start working with movie projects in Adobe Premiere — and transfer video from your camcorder into your computer.

Chapter 4

A Crash Course in Video Production

In This Chapter

▶ Understanding digital video basics

▶ Comparing digital video formats

▶ Comprehending codecs

▶ Evaluating the various editing methods

▶ Getting the shots for a great video

The reels in the Bell & Howell projector began to turn as the bulb blinked on. On the far wall of the darkened living room, the image of a boy appeared. He was holding a shovel, and piles of snow sat all around him. With the rhythmic ticking of the shutter as a soundtrack, the boy silently flung a shovelful of snow. He then looked up and grinned. Suddenly, a reel in the projector jammed and the image froze. For an instant the boy and his shovel were frozen in time, and then just as suddenly the image shriveled away as the bulb's heat melted through the plastic film. "Oops!" exclaimed my grandfather as he switched off the bulb. "Keith, go get me some tape so I can splice this."

A lot has changed since Grandpa filmed my dad shoveling snow in 1959. The movies he shot on his old 8mm film camera had to be processed by a film developer, who wrapped the film around a metal reel and enclosed it in a disk-shaped film can. A special film projector was needed for display, and edits had to be performed with a razor blade and cellophane tape. Shooting the simplest home movie was a complicated and expensive undertaking.

The first great revolution in personal movie-making equipment was the magnetic videotape. Tapes were reusable, they didn't need to be processed like film, and common televisions could be used for playback. Home movies became simple and affordable, but typical consumers found that editing those tapes was still a burdensome process. Thankfully, the second great movie-making revolution has come, because digital video and personal computers make editing a snap. If you're new to digital video, this chapter introduces you to the technology and shows you how it makes video editing accessible to almost anyone with a computer and a digital camcorder. This chapter also introduces you to video technologies and concepts to help you make more effective use of Adobe Premiere.

What Is DV?

DV is an abbreviation for *digital video*.

Oh, you want a more detailed explanation? No problem. Computers, as you probably know, aren't very intelligent. They don't understand the serene beauty of a rose garden, the mournful song of a cello, or the graceful motion of an eagle in flight. All computers really understand are ones and zeros. And yet, we force computers to show us pictures, play music, and display moving video. In effect, infinitely variable sounds and pictures must be converted into the language of computers: ones and zeros. This conversion process is called *digitizing*. Digital video is (you guessed it) video that has been digitized.

To fully understand the difference between analog data and digital data, suppose you want to draw the profile of a hill. An analog representation of the profile (Figure 4-1) would follow the contour of the hill perfectly, because analog values are infinitely variable. However, a digital contour of that same hill would not be able to follow every single detail of the hill, because, as shown in Figure 4-2, digital values are made up of specifically defined individual bits of data.

Figure 4-1:
Analog data is infinitely variable.

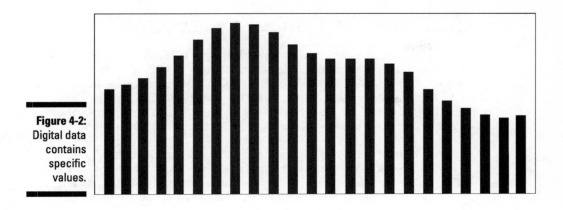

Figure 4-2:
Digital data
contains
specific
values.

Comparing analog and digital video

It could be said that a digital recording will always be theoretically inferior to an analog recording because the analog recording can contain more values. But the truth is that major advances in digital technology mean that this really doesn't matter. Yes, a digital recording must have discrete values, but modern recordings have so many discrete values packed so closely together that human eyes and ears can barely tell the difference. In fact, casual observation often reveals that digital recordings usually seem to be of higher quality than analog recordings. Why?

One of the problems with analog recordings is that they are highly susceptible to deterioration. Every time analog data is copied, some of the original data is lost. This phenomenon is called *generational loss,* and can be observed in that dark, grainy copy of a copy of a copy of a wedding video that was first shot over ten years ago. But digital data doesn't have this problem. A one is always a one, no matter how many times it is copied, and a zero is always a zero. Likewise, analog recordings are more susceptible to deterioration after every playback, which explains why your *Meet the Beatles* LP pops, hisses, and has lost many of its highs and lows over the years.

Whether you are editing analog or digital material, always work from a copy of the master and keep the master safe. When adding analog material to your project, the fewer generations your recording is from the original, the better.

When you consider the implications of generational loss on video editing, you begin to see what a blessing digital video really is. You will constantly be copying, editing, and recopying content as you edit your movie projects, and with digital video, you can edit to your heart's content, confident that the quality won't diminish with each new copy you make.

Understanding video fundamentals

Before getting into a detailed description of what video *is,* take a look at what video *is not.* Video is not film. What's the difference? In film, an image is typically captured by the chemicals on the film. In modern video, an image is captured by a *charged coupled device* (CCD) — a sort of electronic eye — and then the image is recorded magnetically on tape. Many films today are actually shot using video, even though they are output to and distributed on film.

Avoid embarrassment! If you show a movie project on video, don't refer to it as a "film." Some film geeks can get pretty sensitive about terminology, and the term "film" usually refers to a movie that is actually delivered on film, even if it was originally shot using video equipment. If you are heard calling your video a film, the geeks might scoff.

How does video work?

Little Jenny picks a dandelion on a sunny afternoon. She brings the fluffy flower to her lips, and with a puff, the seeds flutter gently away on the breeze (they land in the neighbor's immaculate yard and spawn dozens more of the unappreciated yellow flowers). As this scene unfolds, light photons bounce off Jenny, the dandelion stem, the seeds, and anything else in the shot. Some of those photons pass through the lens of your camcorder. The lens focuses the photons on transistors in the CCD. The transistors get excited, and the CCD converts this excitement into data, which is then magnetically recorded on tape for later playback and editing. This process, shown in Figure 4-3, is repeated approximately 30 times per second.

Most mass-market DV camcorders have a single CCD, but higher quality cameras have three CCDs. In such cameras, individual CCDs capture red, green, and blue light, respectively. Multi-CCD cameras are expensive (typically over $2000), but the image produced is near-broadcast quality.

The prehistoric ancestors of camcorders (portable video cameras of about 20 years ago) used video pickup tubes instead of CCDs. Tubes were inferior to CCDs in many ways, particularly in the way that they handled extremes of light. With video pickup tubes, points of bright light (such as a light bulb) bled and streaked across the picture, and low-light situations were simply too dark to shoot.

Decrypting video standards

A lot of new terms have entered the videophile's lexicon in recent years. NTSC. PAL. HDTV. These terms identify broadcast television standards — which are vitally important for anyone who plans to edit video because your cameras, TVs, and tape decks probably conform to only *one* broadcast standard. Which standard is for you? That depends upon where you live:

- ✔ **NTSC** — *National Television Standards Committee*. Used primarily in North America, Japan, and the Philippines.

- ✔ **PAL** — *Phase Alternating Line*. Used primarily in Western Europe, Australia, Southeast Asia, and South America.

- ✔ **SECAM** — *Sequential Couleur Avec Memoire*. This category actually covers several similar standards used primarily in France, Russia, Eastern Europe, and Central Asia.

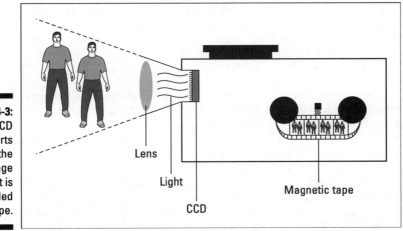

Figure 4-3:
The CCD converts light into the video image that is recorded on tape.

Lens

Light

CCD

Magnetic tape

Adobe Premiere supports all three major broadcast formats. When you begin a project, you should always adjust the project settings to the correct format. See Chapter 5 for more on setting up a new project.

What you need to know about video standards

The most important thing to know about these three broadcast standards is that they are *not* compatible. In other words, if you try to play an NTSC-format videotape in a PAL video deck, the tape won't work, even if both decks use VHS tapes. This is because VHS is merely a physical tape format and not a video format.

Some nice-to-know stuff about video standards

The video standards differ in two primary ways. First, they have different frame rates. The frame rate of video is the number of individual images that appear per second, thus providing the illusion that subjects on the screen are moving. Frame rate is usually abbreviated *fps* (frames per second). Second, the standards use different resolutions. Table 4-1 details the differences.

Table 4-1	Video Standards	
Standard	*Frame rate*	*Resolution*
NTSC	29.97 fps	525 lines
PAL	25 fps	625 lines
SECAM	25 fps	625 lines

A video picture is usually drawn as a series of horizontal lines. An electron gun at the back of the picture tube draws lines of the video picture back and forth, much like the way the printer head on your printer moves back and forth as it prints words on a page. All three video standards listed in Table 4-1 are *interlaced.* This means that the horizontal lines are drawn in two passes rather than one. Every other line is drawn on each consecutive pass, and each of these passes is called a *field.* So on a PAL display, which shows 25 fps, there are actually 50 fields per second.

Noninterlaced displays are also common. Modern computer monitors, for example, are all *noninterlaced,* meaning that all the lines are drawn in a single pass. Some HDTV (High Definition Television) formats are noninterlaced, while others are interlaced.

What was that about HDTV?

Speaking of HDTV, a full accounting of all the HDTV formats would almost fill a book by itself. Resolution in HDTV is measured in pixels (like a computer monitor) rather than horizontal lines (like NTSC and PAL). Resolutions for HDTV formats range from as low as 640 x 480 pixels up to 1920 x 1080. Although 640 x 480 may sound low if you have been around computers for a while, it's still pretty good compared to traditional television displays. Frame rates for HDTV range from 24 fps noninterlaced, up to 60 fps (interlaced or not).

Because of all the uncertainty surrounding HDTV, I recommend against developing video for specific HDTV formats until a single format emerges as a standard. Instead, develop video for your local broadcast format (NTSC, PAL, or SECAM) and assume (hope?) that your audience members have converters on their high-definition TVs.

The many aspects of aspect ratios

Different moving picture displays have different shapes. The screens in movie theaters, for example, look like long rectangles, while most TV screens are almost square. The shape of a video display is called the *aspect ratio.* The following two sections look at how aspect ratios affect editing in Adobe Premiere.

Image aspect ratios

The aspect ratio of a typical television screen is 4:3. This means that for any given size, the display is four units wide and three units high. To put this in real numbers, measure the width and height of a TV or computer monitor that you have nearby. If the display is 32 cm wide, for example, you should notice that it's also 24 cm high. If a picture completely fills this display, the picture is also said to have a 4:3 aspect ratio.

Different numbers are sometimes used to describe the same aspect ratio. The 4:3 aspect ratio is sometimes expressed as 1.33:1. Likewise, the 16:9 aspect ratio is sometimes expressed as 1.78:1.

A lot of movies are distributed on tape and DVD today in *widescreen* format. The aspect ratio of a widescreen picture is usually (but not always) 16:9. If you watch a widescreen movie on a 4:3 TV screen, you will see black bars at the top and bottom of the screen. This format is popular because it more closely matches the aspect ratio of the movie-theater screens for which films are usually shot. Figure 4-4 illustrates the difference between the 4:3 and 16:9 aspect ratios.

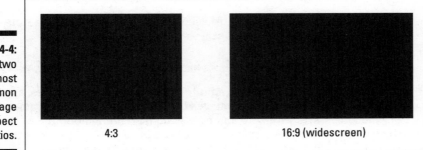

Figure 4-4: The two most common image aspect ratios.

4:3   16:9 (widescreen)

A common misconception is that 16:9 is the aspect ratio of big screen movies. In fact, various aspect ratios for film have been used over the years. Some movies have an aspect ratio of over 2:1, meaning that the image is more than twice as wide as it is high! But for most films, 16:9 is considered close enough. More to the point, it's just right for you because if your camcorder has a widescreen mode, its aspect ratio is probably 16:9. Adobe Premiere fully supports 16:9 media.

Pixel aspect ratios

You may already be familiar with image aspect rations, but did you know that pixels can have various aspect ratios too? If you have ever worked with a drawing or graphics program on a computer, you're probably familiar with pixels. A pixel is the smallest piece of a digital image. Thousands — even millions — of uniquely colored pixels combine in a grid to form an image on a television or computer screen. On computer displays, pixels are square. But in standard video, pixels are rectangular. In NTSC video, pixels are taller than they are wide, and in PAL or SECAM pixels are wider than they are tall.

Pixel aspect ratios become an issue when you start using still computer graphics in projects that also contains standard video. If you don't prepare the still graphic carefully, it could appear distorted when viewed on a TV.

For more on preparing still graphics for use in movie projects, see Chapter 6.

Understanding timecode

A video image is actually a series of still frames that flash rapidly on the screen. Every frame is uniquely identified with a number called a *timecode*. The location and duration of all edits that you perform on a movie project use timecodes for reference points, so a basic understanding of timecode is critical. You'll see and use timecode almost every time you work in Adobe Premiere. Timecode is normally expressed like this:

```
hours : minutes : seconds : frames
```

The fourteenth frame of the third second of the twenty-eighth minute of the first hour of video is identified as:

```
01:28:03:13
```

You already know what hours, minutes, and seconds are. Frames, as stated earlier, are the individual still images that make up video. The frame portion of timecode starts with zero and counts up depending upon the frame rate of the video. In PAL video, frames are counted from 00 to 24 because the frame rate of PAL is 25 fps. In NTSC, frames are counted from 00 to 29.

"Wait!" you exclaim. "Zero to 29 adds up to 30 fps, not 29.97."

You're an observant one, aren't you? As mentioned earlier, the frame rate of NTSC video is 29.97 fps (refer to Table 4-1). NTSC timecode actually skips the frame codes 00 and 01 in the first second of every minute, except every tenth minute. Work it out (you can use a calculator), and you see that this system of reverse leap-frames adds up to 29.97 fps. This is called *drop-frame* timecode. In Premiere and most other video editing systems, drop-frame timecode is expressed with semicolons (;) between the numbers instead of colons (:).

Why does NTSC video use drop-frame timecode? Back when everything was broadcast in black and white, NTSC video was an even 30 fps. For the conversion to color, more bandwidth was needed in the signal to broadcast color information. By dropping a couple of frames every minute, there was enough room left in the signal to broadcast color information, while at the same time keeping the video signals compatible with older black and white TVs.

Analyzing DV Tape Formats

A variety of DV tape formats exist for almost any budget. By far the most common format today is MiniDV, but many others exist. Most alternatives are very expensive, however, and are oriented towards video professionals. I describe the most common formats in the following sections.

MiniDV

MiniDV is quickly becoming the standard format for consumer digital video-tapes. Oh, who am I kidding? For all practical purposes, MiniDV *is* the standard DV tape format. Virtually all digital camcorders sold today use MiniDV, which means that blank tapes are now easy to find and reasonably affordable. If you're still shopping for a camcorder and are wondering which format is best for all-around use, MiniDV is it.

MiniDV tapes are small, and they're more compact than even audiocassette tapes. Small is good because smaller tape-drive mechanisms mean smaller, lighter camcorders. Tapes come in a variety of lengths, the most common length being 60 minutes.

All MiniDV devices use the IEEE-1394 FireWire interface to connect to computers, and the DV codec is used to compress and capture video. (*Codecs* are compression schemes — codec is a shortened form of *compressor/dec*ompressor.) Codecs are described later in this chapter in the "Understanding Codecs" section. The DV codec is supported by virtually all FireWire hardware and video editing software, including Adobe Premiere.

Other consumer-grade formats

Not so long ago, MiniDV tapes were expensive and difficult to find. Several manufacturers began to offer alternative formats for digital camcorders, and many of those alternatives are still available. Perhaps the most common alternative to MiniDV is Digital8. Sony created Digital8, as well as the cameras that record DV video on Hi-8 videotapes (which are about the size of audio-cassette tapes). Digital8 camcorders are available from both Sony and Hitachi. A 120-minute Hi-8 tape can store 60 minutes of Digital8 video.

Because Hi-8 is a popular format for analog camcorders, Hi-8 tapes have been affordable and widely available for several years. In the last year or so, the price of MiniDV tapes has come down enough to make Digital8 camcorders less advantageous. Nothing is wrong with Digital8 camcorders; I have an older one (a Sony DCR-TRV103), and it works great. Like MiniDV camcorders,

Digital8 camcorders use the DV codec. Plug it into your FireWire port and the computer won't know the difference. It's just that the future of DV recording is MiniDV, not Digital8.

Various other recording formats have appeared on the mass market. Some camcorders use a built-in CD-RW (Compact Disc-Recordable/reWritable) drive for storage, but the capacity is usually small (20 minutes is a typical limitation) and the camcorder is often bulky. Still others use propriety or built-in recording media. Any common DV format can be used with Adobe Premiere, but unless you have a special need, I recommend that you avoid the whiz-bang formats and stick with MiniDV.

Always check the price and availability of blank media before you buy any camcorder. If blanks are unavailable or too expensive, your camcorder could become virtually useless.

Professional-grade formats

Do you have $20,000 burning a hole in your pocket? You could spend that sum very quickly on professional-grade video equipment. Wonderful though MiniDV may be for general-purpose use, it does present some shortcomings when used in a professional environment. Professional grade formats offer several advantages over MiniDV:

✔ Pro-grade tapes are usually more robust than MiniDV, which means that they can withstand more shuttling and other editing operations.

✔ Professional formats usually include outputs that aren't included on many MiniDV camcorders. In addition to the FireWire, S-Video, and RCA-style outputs usually found on MiniDV, pro-equipment often includes component video and Serial Digital Interface (SDI) outputs.

✔ A few really expensive digital cameras can shoot at 24 fps, which is the frame rate for film.

✔ Audio-video synchronization is often more precise on professional formats.

Many professional-grade formats are actually derivations of MiniDV. The DVCPro format from Panasonic and the DVCAM format from Sony are both based on the MiniDV format, but they offer more robust assemblies and tracks that are better suited to heavy-duty editing. Sony also offers the Digital Betacam format, which is based upon the vaunted Betacam SP analog format. Older pro-digital formats included D1, D2, D3, and D5. These formats also offered robust design, but the video resolutions were lower than the newer MiniDV-based formats.

The bottom line: If you're a video hobbyist or amateur videographer, MiniDV remains a perfectly adequate format, especially if you aren't operating on a professional-grade budget.

Analog formats

Analog video formats have a lot of history, but they're fading quickly from the scene. A major portent of the death of analog came in late 2001, when Sony announced that it would discontinue its beloved Betacam SP format. Betacam SP was long preferred among video professionals, but Sony opted to drop the format because digital equivalents offer virtually the same quality for far less money.

Because analog video has been around for so long, countless formats exist. You've probably seen these formats around, and you may have even owned (or still own) a camcorder that uses one. Besides the generational-loss problems of analog video, analog formats usually provide fewer horizontal lines of resolution. Compare this to MiniDV formats, which usually provide at least 400 resolution lines. Spend a couple thousand dollars and you can get a MiniDV camcorder like the Canon XL1 or Sony DCR-VX2000 that offers over 500 lines. Table 4-2 provides a brief overview of common analog formats.

Table 4-2		Analog Video Formats
Format	*Resolution Lines*	*Description*
VHS	250	Your basic garden-variety videotape; VHS camcorders are bulky.
S-VHS	400	A higher-quality incarnation of VHS, but the tapes are still big.
VHS-C	250	A compact version of VHS
8mm	260	Smaller tapes mean smaller camcorders.
Hi-8	400	A higher-quality version of 8mm
¾-inch Umatic	280	Bulky analog tapes once common in professional analog systems; a higher-quality version offers 340 lines.
Betacam	300	Sony's professional analog format based on Betamax (remember those?)
Betacam-SP	340	A higher-quality version of Betacam

You can use analog video with Adobe Premiere, but you need a video card (such as the Pinnacle DV500+ card), that can digitize the video. Analog capture devices are discussed in Chapter 2.

Understanding Codecs

A digital video signal contains a lot of data. If you were to copy uncompressed digital video onto your hard drive, it would consume 20MB (megabytes) for every second of video. Simple arithmetic tells us that one minute of uncompressed video would use over 1GB. Even with a 60GB hard drive, you would have room for only about 50 minutes of uncompressed video, assuming that big drive was empty to begin with. Dire though this may seem, storage isn't even the biggest problem with uncompressed video. Typical hard drive busses and other components in your computer simply can't handle a transfer rate of 20MB per second, meaning that some video frames will be dropped from the video.

To deal with the massive bandwidth requirements of video, digital video is compressed using compression schemes called *codecs* (*c*ompressor/ *dec*ompressor). The DV codec, which is used by most digital camcorders, compresses video down to 3.6MB per second. This data rate is far more manageable, and most modern computer hardware can handle it. When you capture DV video from a camcorder using a FireWire interface, a minute of video consumes just over 200MB of hard drive space. Again, most modern computers can manage that.

Why do codecs matter to you? Adobe Premiere enables you to choose from a variety of codecs when you output the video that you edit. If you capture analog video from a capture card, you'll need to choose a codec for the captured video. Logically enough, the more your video is compressed, the more quality you lose. So consider the following issues when you choose a codec:

- ✔ **Is the movie intended for Internet playback?** Most Internet users still have pretty limited bandwidth. At the beginning of 2002, it was estimated that 85 percent of Internet users have dial-up connections with speeds slower than 50 Kbps (kilobits per second). If you're outputting for the Internet, you generally want to use higher compression, or you may choose to provide several levels of compression for various bandwidths.

- ✔ **Is the movie intended for CD-ROM or DVD playback?** Most CD-ROM drives also have serious bandwidth limitations, so you need to use a codec that uses a high compression ratio. If you are outputting for DVD, you need to use the MPEG-2 codec, because that is the compression scheme DVD players use.

- ✔ **Are you outputting back to tape?** If so, your own output hardware is your primary concern.

See Chapter 14 for recommendations on specific codecs to use when out-putting video for various formats.

Comparing Editing Methods

Editing video projects with a program like Adobe Premiere is pretty easy, but this wasn't always the case. Video (and audio, for that matter) is considered a linear media because you view it in a linear manner through time. A still picture (which you take in all at once) is a nonlinear medium; so is a Web site, where you can jump randomly from page to page. You edit linear media (such as video) by using one of two basic methods — linear and (surprise!) nonlinear editing. Each method is described in the following sections.

Linear versus nonlinear editing

My grandfather is a tinkerer. Over the years, he has tinkered with wood, old lawn mowers, and even 8mm film. Not content to simply shoot home movies and then watch them as developed, Grandpa would actually edit his source footage into interesting films. He performed edits by cutting the 8mm film with a razor blade and then splicing in new scenes, using cellophane tape (Scotch tape) to hold the splices together.

The process described above is what professional video editors call *linear editing,* and all motion pictures were edited this way in the past. Video, too, was once edited linearly, and until recently, linear editing was the only option available for home video users. Consider the process of dubbing video from a camcorder onto a tape in a VCR. If there is a scene on the camcorder tape that you want to leave off the VHS tape, you might pause recording on the VCR until that scene has passed. This process is another form of linear editing, because you perform all of your edits in order, or along a timeline for the final program.

Linear editing is terribly inefficient. If you dub a program and then decide to perform an additional edit, subsequent video usually has to be redubbed. What is the alternative? *Nonlinear editing,* of course! As the name implies, nonlinear edits can be performed in any order; you don't have to edit material in a specific order. Nonlinear editing is made possible by the miracle of the personal computer and programs like Adobe Premiere. Suppose that you have a program that includes Scene 1 followed by Scene 2. But then you decide that you want to squeeze another scene — Scene 3 — in between Scenes 1 and 2. In Adobe Premiere, you simply place Scene 3 in the Timeline between Scenes 1 and 2 (shown in Figure 4-5), and Premiere automatically moves Scene 2 over to make room for Scene 3 (shown in Figure 4-6). Imagine

trying to perform this kind of edit by shuttling tapes in a pair of video decks —
take a moment to wince — and you realize what a blessing a nonlinear editor
(NLE) like Premiere really is.

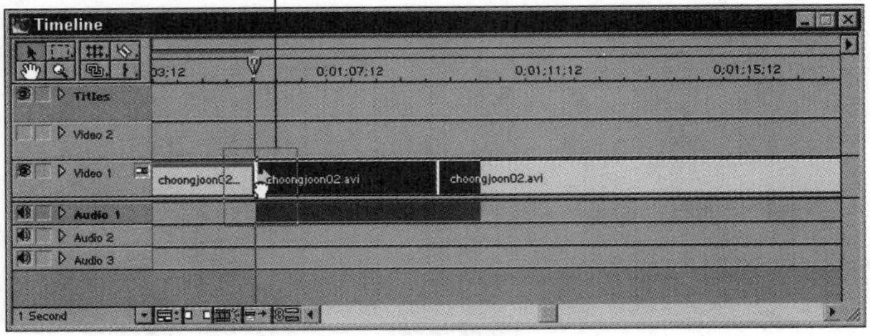

Drop a clip.

Figure 4-5:
To insert
a scene
between
two existing
scenes, just
drop the
new scene
in the
appropriate
place on the
Timeline.

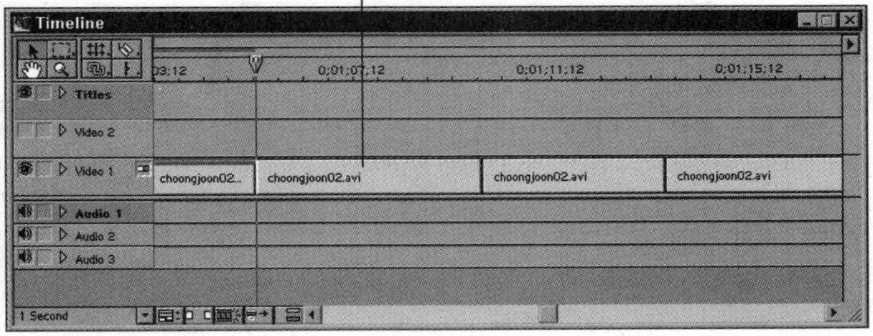

Inserted clip.

Figure 4-6:
When you
perform an
insert edit,
Premiere
automati-
cally shifts
subsequent
material in
the Timeline.

Online versus offline editing

As mentioned previously, video takes up a lot of bandwidth. You need fast
hardware to handle it, and big hard drives to store it. This is especially true if
you're digitizing analog video or capturing uncompressed digital video. If
storage space is limited, you may want to capture a lower-quality version of
the footage on which to perform your edits. Premiere uses timecode to identify the locations and durations of your edits, meaning that those edits can be
applied to the full-quality footage later on. This style of editing, where you do
most of the work on lower-quality footage, is called *offline editing*. Premiere
even lets you create an *edit decision list* (EDL), which is a text file that can be
shared with other video editing systems.

Find out more about edit decision lists and other advanced export options in Chapter 14.

Conversely, when you perform *online editing,* you perform your edits on the original material (or at least, a full-quality copy of the original). Most of your editing in Adobe Premiere will, in fact, be online editing, particularly if you work with DV-format video. As mentioned earlier, the DV codec compresses video down to a data rate of 3.6MB per second. This data rate is manageable enough that it makes offline editing unnecessary. Offline editing is most common when working with film or uncompressed video.

Shooting Great Video

Throughout the years, editors have been called upon to create movies that are worth watching. But ultimately, there is only so much magic that a video editor can wield. If you want to make a great movie, you need to start with great video footage. And if you don't think "great" video footage is possible given your equipment and talents, perhaps you can at least improve your techniques somewhat. The following sections give you some simple tips that can help you shoot video like the pros.

Plan the shot

Camcorders are so simple to use these days that they encourage seat-of-the-pants videography. Just grabbing your camcorder and hastily shooting the UFO that happens to be flying overhead is fine, but for most other situations, some careful planning will provide better quality. You can plan many aspects of the shot:

- ✔ **Make a checklist of shots that you need for your project.** While you're at it, make an equipment checklist too.

- ✔ **Survey the shooting location.** Make sure passersby won't trip over your cables or bump the camera.

- ✔ **Talk to property owners or other responsible parties.** Make sure you have permission to shoot, and identify potential disruptions.

- ✔ **Bring more blank tapes and charged batteries than you think you'll need.**

Compose the shot

Like a photograph, a great video image must be thoughtfully composed. Start by evaluating the type of shot you plan to take. Does the shot include people, landscapes, or some other subject? Consider what kind of tone or feel you want to achieve. Figure 4-7 illustrates how different compositions of the same shot can affect the overall tone. In the first shot, the camera looks down on the subject. Children are shot like this much too often, and it makes them look smaller and inferior. The second shot is level with the subject and portrays him more favorably. The third shot looks up at the subject and makes him seem important, almost larger than life.

Figure 4-7:
Composition
greatly
affects
how your
subject is
perceived.

Panning effectively

Another important aspect of composition is *panning*, or moving the camera. A common shooting technique that snapshot enthusiasts use with home camcorders is to pan the camera back-and-forth, up-and-down, either to follow a moving subject or to show a lot of things that don't fit in a single shot. This technique is called *firehosing*, and is usually not a good idea. Practice these rules when panning:

- ✔ **Pan only once per shot.**

- ✔ **Start panning slowly, gradually speed up, and slow down again before stopping.**

- ✔ **Slow down!** Panning too quickly — say, over a landscape — is a common mistake.

- ✔ **If you have a cheap tripod, you may find it difficult to pan smoothly.** Try lubricating the tripod's swivel head. If that doesn't work, limit tripod use to stationary shots. Ideally you should use a higher-quality tripod with a fluid head for smooth panning.

- ✔ **Keep the camera level with the horizon.** A tilting horizon is very disorienting.

- ✔ **If you're shooting a moving subject, try moving the camera with the subject, rather than panning across a scene.** This reduces out-of-focus issues with the camera lens, and it also helps to keep the subject in frame.

Using (not abusing) the zoom lens

Most camcorders have a handy zoom feature. A zoom lens is basically a lens with an adjustable focal length. A longer lens — also called a *telephoto* lens — makes far-away subjects appear closer. A shorter lens — also called a *wide-angle* lens — allows more of a scene to fit in the shot. Zoom lenses allow you to adjust between wide angle and telephoto.

Because the zoom feature is easy to use and fun to play with, amateur videographers tend to zoom in and out a lot. I recommend that you avoid zooming during a shot as much as possible. Overuse of the zoom lens disorients the viewer, and it creates focal and light problems whether you're focusing the camera manually or using auto focus. Some zoom lens tips include the following:

✔ **Avoid zooming whenever possible.**

✔ **If you must zoom while recording, zoom slowly.** You may need to practice a bit to get a feel for your camera's zoom control.

✔ **Consider repositioning the camera instead of using the zoom lens to compose the shot.** Wide-angle lenses have greater *depth of field*. This means that more of the shot is in focus if you're zoomed out. If you shoot subjects by zooming in on them from across a room, they may move in and out of focus. But if you move the camera in and zoom the lens out, focus will be less of a problem.

Light the shot

Light can be subdivided into two basic categories: good light and bad light. Good light allows you to see your subject, and it flatters your subject by exposing details that you want shown. Shadows aren't completely eliminated, but the shadows don't dominate large portions of the subject either. Bad light, on the other hand, washes out color and creates lens flares — the reflections and bright spots that show up when the sun shines across the lens — and other undesired effects. Consider Figure 4-8. The right side of the subject's face is a featureless white glow because it's washed out by intense sunlight. Meanwhile, the left side of the face is obscured in shadow. Not good.

How do you light your shots effectively? Remain ever aware of both the good light and the bad. If you don't have control over lighting in a location, try to compose the shot to best take advantage of the lighting that is available. More lighting tips include:

✔ **Bounce intense lights off a reflective surface.** Light reflecting from a surface, such as a white sheet or foil screen, is more diffused, providing more flattering lighting than shining bright light directly on the subject.

✔ **Use multiple light sources of varying intensity.** Light on the front of the subject brings out facial details, while light from above and behind highlights the subject relative to the background.

✔ **Watch for backlight situations like the one shown in Figure 4-9.** Try to put extra light on the foreground subject, avoid bright backgrounds, or increase the camera's exposure control. Some cameras have an automatic backlight compensation feature, though as you can see on the right side of Figure 4-9, sometimes the result isn't much better.

✔ **Shield your lens from bright light sources, particularly the sun.** Intense light can reflect on the lens glass and cause flares that only show up later on video. If your camera lens doesn't have a black hood, you can use your hand or black tape to make a temporary shield (check the viewfinder to ensure that your shield doesn't appear in the shot).

✔ **Check your camera's documentation.** Your camcorder might include built-in features to help you deal with special lighting situations, such as sporting events or a sun-washed beach.

✔ **Use lens filters.** A neutral density filter, for example, reduces light in bright outdoor settings and makes colors appear more vivid. A polarizing filter controls how reflective surfaces (like water or glass) appear.

Figure 4-8: Improper lighting spoils this shot.

Shoot the shot

Perhaps the most important tip I can give you before you shoot your video is this: Know your camera. Even the least-expensive digital camcorders available currently are packed with features that were wildly advanced (and expensive) just a few years ago. Most digital camcorders include image stabilization, in-camera effects, and the ability to record 16-bit stereo audio. But these advanced features won't do you much good if they aren't turned on or configured properly. Spend a few hours reviewing the manual that came with your camcorder, and practice using every feature and setting.

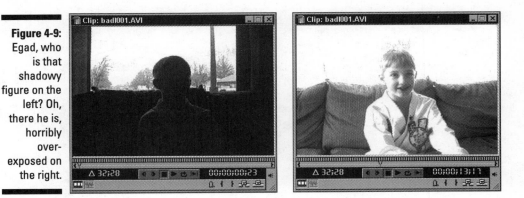

Figure 4-9:
Egad, who is that shadowy figure on the left? Oh, there he is, horribly over-exposed on the right.

Keep the camcorder manual in your gear bag when you hit the road. It may prove an invaluable reference when you're shooting on location. Also, review the manual from time to time; no doubt some useful or cool features are lurking that you forgot all about. If you've lost your manual, check the manufacturer's Web site. You might be able to download a replacement manual.

Virtually all modern camcorders include automatic exposure and focus control. But no matter how advanced this automation may seem, it's not perfect. Learn how to use the manual exposure and focus controls on your camera (if it has them) and practice using them. If you always rely on auto focus, you will inevitably see the lens "hunting" for the right setting during some shots. This will happen a lot if you shoot moving subjects. If your camera has a manual focus mode, you can avoid focus hunting by turning off auto focus. Also learn how to use the manual exposure control (also called the *iris*). This will ultimately give you more control over the light exposure on your video.

Chapter 5

Starting and Managing Your Movie Projects

In This Chapter

▶ Getting your project started

▶ Tweaking the project settings

▶ Collecting information about a project

*S*oftware companies like to create names for program elements that are meant to be analogous to something in "real" life. For example, if you want to delete a file you put it in the *Trash* (Macintosh) or the *Recycle Bin* (Windows). When you want to check your e-mail, you look in your *Inbox*. Sometimes the names they choose work, and sometimes they don't. I used to have an Internet service that had pages named *Runway* and *Boardwalk*. One of them was a page of search engines, and the other a Web directory. Which was which? I forgot all the time.

Adobe probably could have gotten more creative with the names given to parts of Premiere. Thankfully, they picked a few words that worked and stuck with them. When you work on a movie project, for instance, that project is called a (drum roll, please) *project*. It doesn't get much simpler than that, folks. This chapter is all about projects in Adobe Premiere. I show you how to create new projects, modify existing projects, and manage the various projects that you have.

Starting Your Project

When you first launch Adobe Premiere, you probably see the Load Project Settings dialog box shown in Figure 5-1. This dialog box also appears if you choose File➪New Project. Before you can start working on a project, you need to tell Premiere what *kind* of project it is. Are you working with material from a digital camcorder? Are you capturing video from an analog source? Or are you working with video that you got from a CD-ROM or the Internet?

In Figure 5-1, you can see that a list of presets appears on the left side of the dialog box. Each preset contains settings tailored to various different kinds of projects. To start a new project using one of the presets, simply choose the desired preset from the list and click OK.

Choose a preset

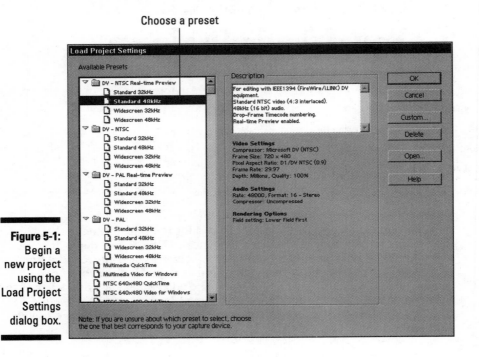

Figure 5-1:
Begin a
new project
using the
Load Project
Settings
dialog box.

The obvious question becomes, "Which preset should I choose?" This depends on the type of video that you're working with. My recommendations are

- ✔ **DV - NTSC:** If you're working with video from a digital camcorder that uses the NTSC broadcast standard, use one of these presets. I recommend 48 kHz sound unless your camcorder was set to record 32 kHz (12-bit) sound. Only choose the Widescreen setting if you shot the material using your camcorder's widescreen (16:9 aspect ratio) feature.

- ✔ **DV - PAL:** These presets are used just like the DV - NTSC presets, except that your video equipment uses the PAL broadcast standard.

- ✔ **Multimedia:** This preset is often used with video that is captured from a CD-ROM or the Internet. This type of video is generally of lower quality and is not suitable for tape playback. The QuickTime format includes MPEG files, and the Video for Windows format (not available with the Mac version of Premiere) includes AVI files.

- ✔ **NTSC 640 x 480:** Use these options with video that is already digitized, or if your analog capture device uses this screen size.

- ✔ **NTSC 720 x 480:** These options are most often used with analog video capture. This screen size more closely approximates the actual size of NTSC video, after the rectangular shape of the video pixels is taken into account.

- ✔ **PAL QuickTime or Video for Windows:** Use these if you're working with PAL-format video in MPEG or AVI format.

If you aren't sure whether you should choose NTSC or PAL, see Chapter 4 for more on broadcast video standards. See Chapter 13 for more on using Premiere's Real-time Preview feature.

For the DV presets (NTSC or PAL) you'll notice that you can choose from ones that have "Real-time Preview" enabled or those that don't. The real-time presets have Premiere 6.5's new Real-time Preview setting enabled. This enables you to view some transitions and effects without first building a preview or render file. If your computer has at least a 1-GHz processor (Windows PC) or a 500-MHz G4 (Macintosh) you should be able to take advantage of Real-time Previews. If your computer is slower, you may find that effects and transitions don't play smoothly using Real-time Preview. Experiment. If you have playback problems with Real-time Preview, you should still be able to get work done the old-fashioned way (rendering).

You can set your own options for a project by clicking the Custom button. Here you can create custom presets, which will then be available in the Presets menu the next time you create a new project. Custom presets are covered in the "Creating your own presets" section later in this chapter.

Saving a project

Saving a project in Premiere is pretty straightforward. Just choose File➪Save from the menu bar and you're done. If you want to save the project with a different name, choose File➪Save As, and if you want to save a copy, choose File➪Save a Copy.

You probably could have figured out how to save a project on your own, so why this section? One of the interesting things about Premiere is that although video files tend to be very large, project files are actually quite small. Indeed, the project file for a 30-minute movie may be smaller than 50 kilobytes (KB). This is because the project file doesn't contain any actual audio or video. But the project file *does* contain

- ✔ Edit points and keyframes that you create.
- ✔ Pointers to the original source clips.

   ✔ Information about effects that are applied to the project.

   ✔ The layout of Premiere windows and palettes from the last time that you
      worked on the project.

Because Premiere project files are so small, it's a good idea to frequently
save backup copies of a project. This way, you can easily go back to an
earlier version of your project if you don't like some of the changes that
you've made.

You can tell Premiere to automatically save a new version of your project
while archiving old versions every few minutes or so. See Chapter 3 for more
on using Premiere's auto save and archiving feature.

So where *are* all the big files? Not only do the source files for your audio and
video take up a lot of disk space, but whenever you render some of your work
for playback or output, huge render files are created as well. (By the way,
rendering is the process of building preview files for video.) All these big files
live on your *scratch disk*. Your scratch disk might simply be your main hard
drive, or you may have a hard drive dedicated solely to video storage. (See
Chapter 3 for more information about scratch disks.) On a Macintosh, the
default scratch disk for audio and video that you capture is

```
Adobe:Premiere 6.5
```

On a Windows PC, the default scratch disk is

```
C:\My Documents\Adobe\Premiere
```

When you render preview files in Premiere, they are stored in the `Adobe`
`Premiere Preview Files` subfolder of the default scratch disk folder.

Before you start deleting files out of the scratch disk folder or the preview
folder, make sure that you don't need those files anymore. If you delete a
video file from the scratch disk, for example, any projects that use that file
become incomplete. And if you delete preview files, you have to spend long
minutes or hours re-rendering those previews if you ever need them again.

Opening an existing project

Premiere gives you a lot of ways to open a project that you've been working
on. The easiest way may be to simply browse to the Premiere Project File
(.PPJ) using My Computer or the Mac Finder and then double-clicking it.
Alternatively, you can

   ✔ Launch Premiere, choose File➪Open Recent Project, and then choose a
      project from the list that appears.

✔ Launch Premiere, choose File➪Open and navigate to the .PPJ file using the tried-and-true Open File dialog box.

✔ Drag a project file and drop it on the Premiere program window (Premiere must already be open for this to work).

✔ In Windows, choose Start➪Documents and select a Premiere project from the list, if the one that you want appears.

✔ On your Mac, choose Apple menu➪Recent Documents and select a Premiere project from the list, if the one that you want appears.

Adjusting Project Settings

When you start a new project, it is vitally important that you choose the correct project settings right from the start. However, you may still find that you need to adjust some settings as you work. Or you may find that none of the presets provided with Premiere exactly match the type of work you usually do. In that case, you can either modify project settings when the project is open, or better yet, you can create your own presets.

Modifying settings for your project

You can review the current settings for your project at any time using the Settings Viewer. This is a handy little tool, and if you are having some strange video problems that you can't quite track down, you may want to spend a few minutes looking over your settings. To open the Settings Viewer in Premiere, choose Project➪Settings Viewer. The settings in the Capture, Project, and Export columns should be as identical as possible. As you can see in Figure 5-2, I'm working on a lower-quality project, which I intend to export for Internet use.

As you review the Settings Viewer, double-check the following:

✔ **Compressor:** Generally the compressor should be the same for all items, though you might ultimately use a different compressor for export.

✔ **Frame Size:** Notice that in Figure 5-2 all my frame sizes are 720 x 480 pixels.

✔ **Frame Rate:** At the very least, your project and export settings should be the same. In some cases, your source clip will have a higher frame rate than the project. This is okay because Premiere converts the video to the lower frame rate when you render the project.

✔ **Pixel Aspect Ratio:** If the pixel aspect ratios differ, your video may look distorted. In Figure 5-2, notice that the Export Settings show square pixels, but the other settings show NTSC (0.9) pixels. If I only plan to export the movie directly back to tape, this isn't a problem because for export to tape the Export Settings are not used.

✔ **The pull-down menu:** Notice that the third column in the Settings Viewer has a pull-down menu. Open this menu and check the settings for each and every item you see listed. Things you find listed in the menu include source clips, title clips, black video, color bars and tone, counter leaders, and anything else that happens to be in the currently open Bin in the Project window.

If multiple items are listed, check all of them.

Figure 5-2:
The Settings Viewer helps you identify possible video problems.

	Capture Settings	Project Settings	CP landscape.avi ▼	Export Settings	OK
Video					Load...
Mode:	DV /IEEE1394 Capture	Microsoft DV AVI	Microsoft DV AVI	Microsoft DV AVI	
Compressor:	Microsoft DV (NTSC)	Microsoft DV (NTSC)	Microsoft DV (NTSC)	Microsoft DV (NTSC)	
Frame Size:	720 x 480	720 x 480	720 x 480	720 x 480	
Frame Rate:	29.97 FPS	29.97 FPS	29.97 FPS	29.97 FPS	
Depth:	Millions	Millions	Millions	Millions	
Quality:	100 %	100 %	100 %	100 %	
Pixel Aspect Ratio:	D1 /DV NTSC (0.9)	D1 /DV NTSC (0.9)	D1 /DV NTSC (0.9)	Square Pixels (1.0)	
Audio					
Sample Rate:	48000 Hz	48000 Hz	48000 Hz	32000 Hz	
Format:	16 bit – Stereo	16 bit – Stereo	16 bit – Stereo	16 bit – Stereo	
Compressor:	Uncompressed	Uncompressed	Uncompressed	Uncompressed	
Render					
Field Settings:	Lower Field First	Lower Field First	Unknown	Lower Field First	

ⓘ For optimal performance, Capture Settings, Project Settings and Clip Settings should be identical.

If you find that you need to change some settings, first close the Settings Viewer. Then choose Project➪Settings and choose a settings category that you need to modify. When you have the Project Settings dialog box open, you can jump between categories using a pull-down menu at the top of the dialog box. The five categories of settings are briefly described in the following sections. Specific project settings are discussed where appropriate throughout this book.

If you have a collection of unique settings that you like to use, I recommend you click the Save button before closing the Project Settings dialog box. If you save your settings, they will be available as a preset in the Load Project Settings dialog box that appears when you first open Premiere.

General settings

The General Settings dialog box is where you set general options for your project. Here you can choose from one of three basic editing modes in

Windows, or two basic editing modes on a Macintosh. The mode chosen here is what the Timeline will use — meaning that anything you add to the Timeline will be nipped and tucked to fit that mode.

The Timeline is where you actually assemble your movie program, so I usually recommend that you choose a mode that matches the content you're importing or capturing for the project. You can always reduce the quality during export if you wish. The modes are DV Playback, QuickTime, and Video for Windows (the latter is not available on a Mac). In general, leave the Timebase and Time Display options alone. The DV Playback mode should be used if you're working with video from a digital camcorder.

Video settings

The Video Settings dialog box, shown in Figure 5-3, should match the source video that you're working with. The settings and options here depend largely on the editing mode chosen under General settings. The compressor (or *codec*) is what will be used when building Timeline previews. Other settings — depth, frame size and aspect ratio, frame rate, and pixel aspect ratio — usually match your final product.

You can control the picture quality of Timeline previews using the Quality setting. Because this setting only affects previews, you can safely choose a lower quality in order to save preview-rendering time. If your previews don't play smoothly, try reducing the data rate listed in the Video settings dialog box.

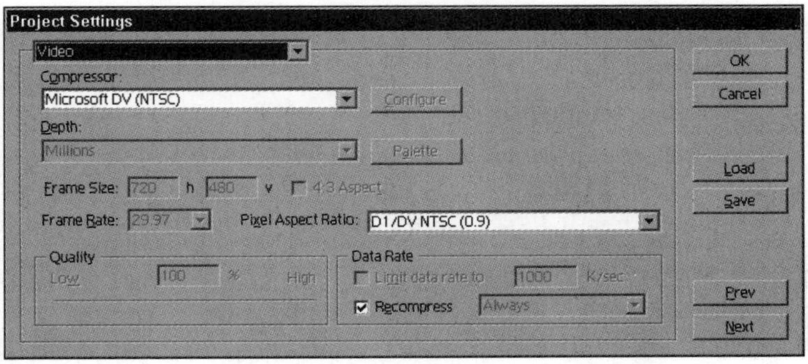

Figure 5-3:
Try to match
the video
settings
with the
source
video that
you're
working
with.

Audio settings

As with video settings, audio settings vary depending upon the type of source material that you're working with. If you're working with a DV camcorder, you must capture audio at the same data rate at which it was recorded on the camcorder (usually 48000 Hz and 16-bit stereo). Other audio settings to review include the following:

✔ **Interleave:** This setting determines how much audio is stored in your computer's memory at any given time for preview. If audio breaks up during Timeline previews, reduce the time interval listed in the Interleave drop-down menu. A shorter interleave time will put less demand on your computer's resources.

✔ **Enhanced Rate Conversion:** This setting allows you to balance audio quality with rendering time for audio previews. The choices are Off (adequate quality, quicker rendering), Better (better quality, slower rendering), and Best (best quality, slowest rendering).

✔ **Use Logarithmic Audio Fades:** Select this option to allow audio fades that sound more natural to the human ear. Audio fades that happen on a logarithmic scale (as opposed to a linear scale) sound more natural because it more closely matches how the human ear hears sounds. Like all good options, this one increases rendering time.

✔ **Create audio preview files:** If you hear pops or other errors in your audio, it means that Premiere is taxing your computer's audio resources. In that case, reduce the numbers listed here. If you only have one or two audio tracks in your program — say, one is an actor's voice and the other is background music — Premiere can usually preview that audio for you in real time. But as you add more audio tracks on top of each other, Premiere pushes your system's resources to the limit to play these real-time previews. The strain often rears its ugly head as loud pops in the audio, but you can reduce the strain by telling Premiere to render audio preview files instead of previewing the audio from memory in real time. This setting allows you to specify how many audio tracks are allowed to play in real time without a render file.

For more on working with audio in your Premiere projects, see Chapter 11.

Keyframe and rendering settings

When you want to preview the work you've done in Premiere's Timeline, you must first render it. Rendering is the process of creating a preview file on the hard drive. Even with a very fast computer, rendering can take a really long time. To speed things up, you can tell Premiere not to render certain things when you build a Timeline preview. In particular, you can tell Premiere to ignore audio effects, video effects, and audio rubberband controls. (Audio *rubberbands* are controls that you click and drag up or down on an audio track to control the volume of the audio clip. Rubberbands can also be used to adjust audio between left and right channels.)

As the name suggests, the Keyframe and Rendering dialog box also lets you set keyframe options. The term *keyframes* is actually used for a couple of different things in Premiere. First of all, keyframes are used to adjust effects. Most effects that come with Premiere are adjustable, and you use keyframes to tell Premiere when to make those adjustments. Effect keyframes are described in Chapter 10.

These effect keyframes are not what the Keyframe and Rendering dialog box controls. Some video codecs use keyframes at specific intervals as part of the compression scheme. For example, rather than saving ten consecutive frames, the codec might create just two keyframes that are ten frames apart. During playback, the codec then extrapolates changes between those keyframes. These compression keyframes are what the Keyframe and Rendering dialog box controls. Keyframes are used by some codecs but not others, so the keyframe options in the Keyframe and Rendering dialog box may or may not be available, depending upon the codec you chose in Video dialog box.

Review the following options in the Keyframe and Rendering dialog box:

- ✔ **Optimize Stills:** If your project has a lot of still images, choose this option to reduce rendering time. Optimizing stills could cause some playback problems, however. If you encounter glitches or other problems when the stills play, disable Optimization again.

- ✔ **Frames Only at Markers:** Choose this if you only want to render frames that you have marked in the Timeline.

- ✔ **Preview (Macintosh only):** If you're really impatient and you want to take advantage of Premiere's Real-time Preview feature (see Chapter 13), choose To Screen from the Preview menu. If you want to render preview files before playing effects, choose From Disk. If you have a capture card or DV device that you want to preview your video on, choose To Hardware.

- ✔ **Real Time Preview (Windows only):** If you want to preview effects, transitions, and other edits without first having to build a preview or render file on the hard drive, place a check mark next to this option.

- ✔ **Fields:** As described in Chapter 4, broadcast video is interlaced. This means that each frame of video actually consists of two fields. One field contains every other horizontal line of video resolution. Your capture card might recommend a "field dominance" setting which tells you what to choose here. Otherwise, leave this setting alone.

- ✔ **Keyframe Options:** Some codecs use keyframes as reference points during compression. If the codec you're working with uses keyframes, I recommend that you place a check mark next to Add Keyframes at Markers and Add Keyframes at Edits.

Capture settings

The Project Settings dialog box shown in Figure 5-4 gives you some control over the capture process, which is where you capture video from your camcorder or video deck. You can, for example, choose whether you want to capture audio, video, or both. In some cases, you may decide that you don't want to capture audio along with the video that you captured. You can also force Premiere to report dropped frames during capture, or even abort capture

if frames are dropped. As you capture video, if something on your computer —
the processor, the memory, your hard drive, or another component — can't
work fast enough to keep up with the video, some frames might get dropped
out of the captured video. Dropped frames are disastrous to video quality
because not only will the video image be jerky, your audio probably won't be
synchronized properly with the video either. I strongly recommend that you
keep both the Report Dropped Frames and the Abort on Dropped Frames
settings enabled.

Dropping frames during capture is a common problem and is often difficult to
troubleshoot. For more on capturing video and preventing dropped frames,
see Chapter 6.

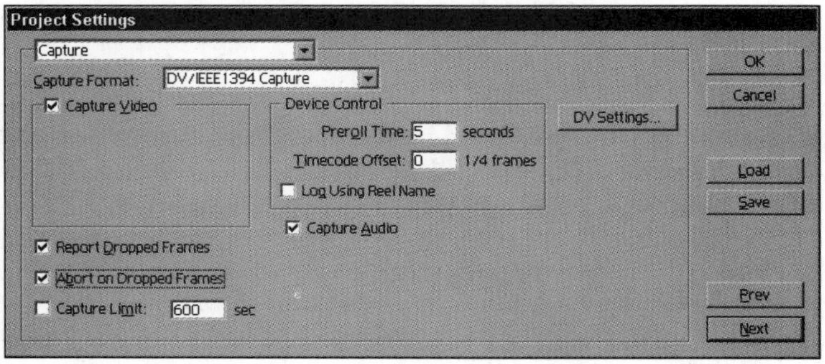

Figure 5-4:
Choose
capture
settings that
match what
you're
capturing.

You should start with the Capture Format drop-down menu. If you are
capturing video from a DV camcorder or another source of DV video using
your FireWire port, use the DV/IEEE 1394 Capture option in the Capture Format
menu. If you're capturing analog video, use the setting recommended by your
capture card's documentation. Most analog capture cards come with special
software that installs card-specific options in this Capture Format menu.

The Device Control section of the Capture settings allows you to set Preroll
Time. Most tape decks and camcorders need a bit of a running start in
order to get the tape mechanism up to speed and all the little gears turning
properly before video can be safely captured. For this reason, Premiere
usually rewinds the tape a few seconds before the point at which it starts
to capture. This process is called preroll, and a good preroll time is at least
five seconds. Without adequate preroll, Premiere can't capture the video
properly. Inadequate preroll is why Premiere usually can't capture the first
five seconds or so on a tape. Keep preroll in mind when you shoot video.

You should usually keep the Timecode Offset option set at zero quarter-frames.
Timecode Offset is one of those really advanced settings that should only be
adjusted if the timecode on your video deck or camcorder doesn't exactly

match the captured timecode of the video. If you encounter this, you can enter amounts here to calibrate your deck with a quarter of a frame. With most DV hardware, this won't be a problem.

If you're capturing DV video and you have trouble with dropped frames during capture, open the Capture Settings dialog box and click the DV Settings button. Remove the check marks next to the Preview Video on Desktop and the Preview Audio on Desktop options under During Capture. This reduces the processing load on your system because the computer doesn't have to generate a preview in addition to successfully capturing the content.

Creating your own presets

Although the built-in project settings that come with Premiere are pretty versatile, they must appeal to a broad range of users. This means that while one of the preset groups of settings might come close to meeting your needs, there are still some settings that you change. Rather than manually changing all these settings every time you start a new project, Premiere lets you save your own presets for future use. When you have your project settings the way you like them, follow these steps:

1. **Open the Project Settings dialog box by choosing Project⇨Project Settings⇨General.**

   Review the various pages of the Project Settings dialog box to ensure that all the settings are just as you want them.

2. **On any page of the Project Settings dialog box, click the Save button.**

   The Save Project Settings dialog box appears.

3. **Give your preset a descriptive name in the Name field, such as "XL1 Widescreen" or "Intel Web cam."**

4. **Type a brief description of the preset in the Description box.**

5. **If the preset will always be used with a specific piece of capture hardware, select the Include Device Control Settings checkbox.**

6. **Click OK.**

After you save your custom settings, whenever you open the Load Project Settings dialog box, your saved preset appears in the list.

Documenting a Project

When I write a book like this one, I spend a lot of time reading and re-reading what I wrote. One of the things I like to do is print chapters out and read them on paper without all the various editorial notes. I have found that no matter how many times I read something on my computer screen, the words always "sound" a little different to me when I'm sitting in the living room and reading them from paper.

You might find it helpful to review your movie editing work from a different perspective as well. Premiere provides you with a couple of tools that help you document your editing work and, if you wish, print that work on paper. These tools are as follows:

- **Edit Decision List (EDL):** EDLs are used in professional video editing environments to document and share editing information across various platforms. The EDL contains information about edits that were performed, and reel names and timecode are used to identify the location of each edit on the original source material. EDLs can be complicated to read, but they also provide detailed information about all of the edits that you have performed. To generate an EDL, choose File➪Export Timeline➪EDL and choose an EDL format (such as Generic EDL).

- **Exported file list:** If you simply want a list of the files used in a project, choose File➪Export Timeline➪File List. Give the list a name and choose a location in which to save it. A file list looks similar to Figure 5-5. This list can be helpful if you're having export problems because one or more source files are missing. It should also be used if you plan to move a project onto a new system. You can use the exported file list as a checklist to ensure that you move all the files that are needed for your project.

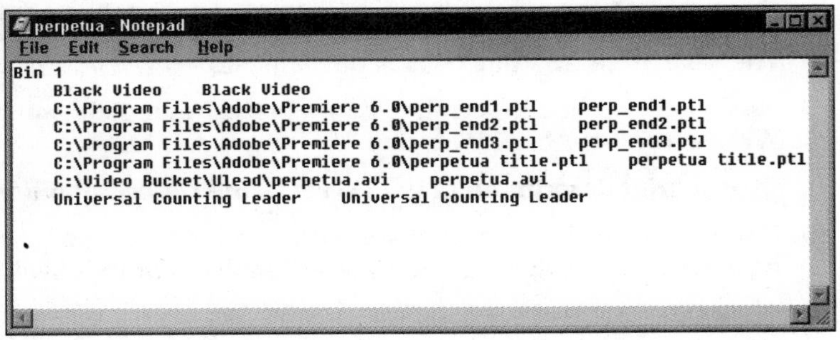

Figure 5-5:
A project file list can help you troubleshoot problems associated with missing source files.

```
perpetua - Notepad                                              _ □ ×
File   Edit   Search   Help
Bin 1
    Black Video       Black Video
    C:\Program Files\Adobe\Premiere 6.0\perp_end1.ptl     perp_end1.ptl
    C:\Program Files\Adobe\Premiere 6.0\perp_end2.ptl     perp_end2.ptl
    C:\Program Files\Adobe\Premiere 6.0\perp_end3.ptl     perp_end3.ptl
    C:\Program Files\Adobe\Premiere 6.0\perpetua title.ptl     perpetua title.ptl
    C:\Video Bucket\Ulead\perpetua.avi     perpetua.avi
    Universal Counting Leader     Universal Counting Leader
.
```

Edit Decision Lists tend to be complex and are usually specific to a particular video editing system. For more on producing, reading, and using EDLs, see Chapter 14.

Chapter 6

Capturing, Importing, and Managing Media

In This Chapter

▶ Capturing media to edit

▶ Importing media from other sources

▶ Organizing media into the stuff of movies

*I*f you think Adobe Premiere is fun now, just wait until you actually have some material to edit in this amazing program. Actually, don't wait. Let's start gathering some media into Premiere right now, shall we? No time like the present, I always say.

This chapter guides you through the process of capturing audio and video using Premiere, whether you're capturing video from a digital camcorder, analog camcorder, or another source. This chapter also shows you how to import various types of media, and you'll get some help with the task of organizing your media.

Capturing Media

Most of my movies begin life as concepts floating around in the gray matter of my brain. A cartoonish light bulb appears overhead, and before I know it I'm shooting video, editing it in Premiere, and sharing my grand production with anyone fortunate enough to be in the room at that moment. That "editing it in Premiere" step can be broken down into three basic phases:

✔ Import

✔ Edit

✔ Output

Obviously, before you can edit your project, you need something to edit. You can get source material into Premiere by importing existing files or by capturing media from an external source (the most common example of which is a digital camcorder). The following sections show you how to capture audio and video in Premiere. I cover importation of video files, still graphics, music, and other media later in the chapter.

Setting up your hardware

This is the part of the book where I'm supposed to show you a simple line art diagram of a camcorder connected to a computer by a cable. If only it were that easy. Preparing your computer for video capture can actually be a complicated process, and you must approach this process carefully to achieve success.

The next couple of sections describe a lot of ways to make your computer perform better during capture. These same techniques can also be used to increase performance during editing, rendering, and output too!

The first thing to go is memory . . .

Whether you're capturing DV video using FireWire or analog video using a video capture card, video capture puts very high demands upon your computer. The processor, RAM, and hard drive in particular must be able to work fast in order to capture video without dropping frames (where frames go missing from the video because the computer couldn't keep up with the video stream) or causing other problems. As you prepare to capture video, follow these basic guidelines:

- Close all applications except Premiere. This includes utility programs and even antivirus programs. Temporarily disabling antivirus programs will greatly increase the performance of your system.

- Defragment your hard drive. Use a defragmenting tool built into your operating system, or use a third-party hard-drive maintenance utility. Frequent defragmentation is doubly important for Windows Me, because experience has shown that the overall performance of Windows Me is greatly affected by the state of the hard drive.

- Restart your computer. This is especially important for Windows 98/Me systems, which tend to have memory management problems that can only be resolved with a restart.

- Disable your screen saver if you have one, as well as those fancy desktop-beautification schemes.

✔ Take control of virtual memory. On your Mac, disable virtual memory using the Memory Control Panel unless you have less than 256MB of physical RAM. In Windows, manually configure virtual memory to be twice the size of physical RAM. This process can be complicated, so before you adjust memory settings I recommend that you pick up a book that provides memory-management procedures for your particular operating system.

✔ On a Macintosh, allocate 96MB of RAM to Premiere.

✔ Adjust your power-management settings so your monitor and hard drives won't shut down in the middle of a long capture job. Power or energy management settings are Control Panel items on both Macintosh and Windows systems.

✔ Temporarily disable unneeded memory-resident items that are not directly related to video capture or vital operating system functions. Unneeded items include antivirus programs, Internet programs, and system monitors. On a Macintosh, you can safely disable printing and Internet-related extensions and control panels. In Windows, memory-resident programs can often be disabled using System Tray icons, as shown in Figure 6-1. Right-click each icon and choose Close or Disable for as many of them as possible.

Adobe Premiere is such an advanced program that covering everything you need to know about it in this book is difficult. Providing detailed instructions on how to control memory, disable extensions, and manage other aspects of your computer's operating system is simply not possible. I strongly urge you to pick up a book that covers your operating system in detail, such as *The iMac For Dummies, Mac OS 9 For Dummies, Mac OS X For Dummies, Microsoft Windows Me For Dummies, Windows 2000 Professional For Dummies,* or *Windows XP For Dummies.* (Whew! I think that covers just about all of them.)

Figure 6-1:
You can usually disable Windows antivirus software by using a System Tray icon.

Right-click each icon and close or disable if possible.

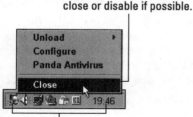

Windows System Tray

Configuring DV hardware

Configuring your computer for video capture may not be easy, but at least configuring DV hardware is. Along with high video quality, simplicity is one of the main strengths of DV. The most common way to capture video from a DV camcorder or video deck is to use a FireWire (IEEE-1394) port on your computer. You should also tell Premiere what specific piece of DV hardware you're using. Follow these steps:

1. **Connect your DV camcorder or deck to your FireWire port using an appropriate cable.**

2. **Turn on the device. If you're capturing from a camcorder, turn it on to VTR (video tape recorder) mode, not camera mode.**

3. **Launch Premiere. If Premiere was already open, you may need to quit and then restart the program to ensure that your DV hardware is recognized by the program.**

4. **Choose a DV preset that matches the type of video you plan to capture.**

   For more on choosing a good preset for your project, see "Starting Your Project" in Chapter 5.

5. **In Premiere, choose File➪Capture➪Movie Capture.**

   The Movie Capture window appears.

6. **On the left side of the Movie Capture window, click the Settings tab to bring the tab to the front.**

7. **Click Edit under Capture Settings.**

   The Capture Project Settings dialog box appears. If the Capture settings area is blank, see the troubleshooting tips at the end of this section.

8. **In the Capture Project Settings dialog box, click the DV Settings button.**

   The DV Capture Options dialog box opens, as shown in Figure 6-2.

   I recommend unchecking both Preview options under the During Capture heading. Previewing audio and video takes up processing power and RAM, so disabling these two frees up more system resources for capture. You should still be able to preview audio and video using your external video monitor or the LCD display on your camcorder.

9. **Click OK twice to close the dialog boxes.**

10. **Click Edit under Preferences on the Settings tab of the Movie Capture window.**

    The Scratch Disks and Device Control Preferences dialog box appears, as shown in Figure 6-3.

Uncheck these two items.

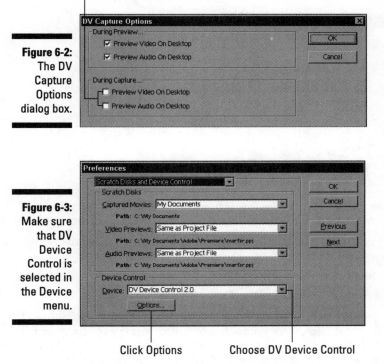

Figure 6-2:
The DV
Capture
Options
dialog box.

Figure 6-3:
Make sure
that DV
Device
Control is
selected in
the Device
menu.

Click Options   Choose DV Device Control

11. **Make sure that DV Device Control 2.0 is selected in the Device menu, and then click the Options button.**

    The DV Device Control Options dialog box appears, as shown in Figure 6-4. If DV Device Control is not selected in the Device menu, Premiere will not be able to automatically control your camcorder.

12. **Choose the video standard, brand, and model that correspond to your capture device in the menus provided.**

    A specific model may or may not be available in the Device Model menu. If you're not sure what to choose, check your camcorder's documentation or click the Go Online for Device Info button. This will open a Web page at Adobe with information about your camcorder or similar devices. In the Timecode Format menu, I generally recommend accepting the default setting. If your video standard is set to NTSC, you'll normally use Drop-Frame format. If your standard is PAL, Non Drop-Frame is the only option.

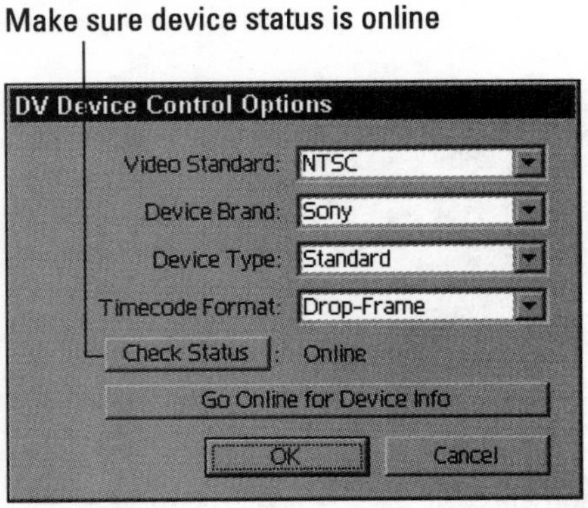

Make sure device status is online

Figure 6-4:
Configure
your DV
device for
use with
Premiere.

13. Make sure that Online is displayed next to the Check Status button in the DV Device Control Options dialog box, as shown in Figure 6-4.

If the status is Offline, click the Check Status button. If the status is still Offline after several clicks, close Premiere and then reopen it.

14. Click OK to close the DV Device Control Options dialog box, and then click OK again to close the Preferences dialog box.

If you got hung up on lucky Step Number 13, there is probably something wrong with your DV device, your computer, or both. This is especially true if you were able to locate the brand and model of your device in the menus. If your device wasn't specifically listed, it simply may not be supported by Premiere. Check the documentation that came with the device (or the manufacturer's Web site), and find out what the recommended procedure is for capturing video. If your device was listed and still registers as offline, follow these troubleshooting tips:

✔ Close and restart Adobe Premiere. While you're at it, go ahead and restart your computer too. Make sure that the camcorder's power is turned on *before* you restart Premiere.

✔ Double-check the physical connection to your computer. Is the FireWire cable properly installed and secure?

✔ Check to see whether any device drivers need to be installed. The device manufacturer's documentation may provide information about this. In Windows, open the System icon in the Control Panel and click the Device Manager tab. (DV devices are most often listed under "Imaging Device," as shown in Figure 6-5.) If the power is on, the device is connected, and you can't find it in the Device Manager, the software device driver is not properly installed or there is a physical problem with a component.

While you're here, make sure that your 1394 Bus Controller (your FireWire port) is OHCI-compliant and configured properly. A yellow exclamation mark means the item is *not* configured properly on your system. To correct this problem, consult the documentation or technical support that came with the FireWire controller card or your computer.

✔ Does the DV device recognize the FireWire connection? The display may show an indication such as "DV IN" if the connection is detected.

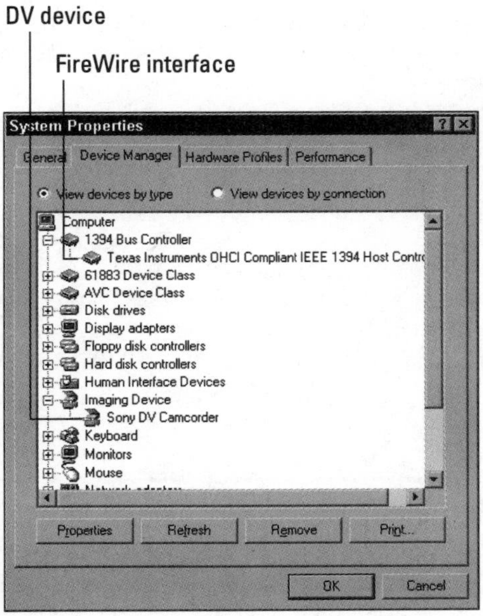

DV device

FireWire interface

Figure 6-5: Use the Device Manager to make sure your hardware is functioning properly with your computer.

Configuring analog hardware

Although digital video seems to be the wave of the future, there are still a lot of great analog video devices out there. To capture analog video you must have a device that can digitize analog video into a digital format for computer editing. This device may be a video capture card that is installed in your computer, or it may be an external device which connects to your computer using a FireWire or SCSI interface. Adobe Premiere comes free with many higher-quality capture devices.

If you're interesting in some really cool capture devices for analog video, check out Chapter 17. One external capture device that I feature there is the Canopus ADVC-100, which plugs into your FireWire port and can capture a wide variety of analog formats.

Understanding device control

Remember that movie *Back to the Future* where Christopher Lloyd's character controlled a toaster, a coffeepot, a dog-food dispenser, and various other appliances with his computer? Yes, it really has been almost two decades since that movie came out, and no, we still don't control our coffee machines or refrigerators with computers. However, thanks to a technology called *device control* we can control camcorders and video decks with our computers. (It's a start.)

Device control is one of the most accurately named technologies to come along in quite some time. It allows you to control your devices using a computer. For example, if your DV camcorder is connected to your FireWire port, you can start playing the tape in that camcorder by clicking the Play button in Adobe Premiere. Cool, huh?

Not only is device control cool, it's useful. When you capture video, synchronization between the computer and the videotape player is crucial. It also allows Premiere to access and use the Timecode recorded on the tape. This is important if you plan to capture batches of video. Batch captures use timecode to identify where to start and stop, and thanks to device control Premiere's batch capture feature can automatically play, fast forward, rewind, and stop the tape as needed to capture the desired batches of video.

Most DV camcorders and decks allow device control. Commands for device control are shared through the FireWire cable. Some professional-grade analog decks also offer device control, but it usually requires a separate serial cable connected between the computer and the playback device. Device control also requires a deck that accurately records and uses timecode.

Okay, McFly, now that you understand device control, let's start capturing some video!

Before you do anything else, read the documentation that came with your capture hardware. That documentation no doubt contains specific instructions for capturing video. You may be able to adjust color and video quality during capture. Your capture card or device might even have come with separate software for capturing video. If your card came with its own capture software, you may want to use it for video capture rather than Premiere — especially if you have trouble capturing with Premiere. Just make sure that the captured video is of a quality and format that you can use in Premiere.

Before you use Adobe Premiere to capture analog video, configure your hardware as follows:

1. **Connect your analog camcorder or deck to your capture device. Connect all cables as described in the documentation.**

2. **Turn on the device. If you're capturing from a camcorder, turn it on to VTR mode, not camera mode.**

3. **Launch Premiere.**

   If Premiere was already open, you may have to quit and then restart the program to ensure that your capture hardware is recognized by the program.

4. **Choose a preset that matches the type of video you plan to capture.**

For analog video, you normally use a QuickTime Capture preset, though in Windows you can also use a Video for Windows preset.

For more on choosing a good preset for your project, see "Starting Your Project" in Chapter 5.

5. **In Premiere, choose File⇨Capture⇨Movie Capture.**

The Movie Capture window appears.

6. **On the left side of the Movie Capture window, click the Settings tab to bring the tab to the front.**

7. **Click Edit under Capture Settings.**

The Capture Project Settings dialog box appears. Review the settings listed here and adjust them in accordance with the documentation for your capture hardware. Each capture card is different, so reviewing the documentation that came with the card and following the instructions found there is critical.

8. **Click OK to close the Project Settings dialog box.**

Capturing with the Movie Capture window

It's hard to believe that you are this many pages into a chapter titled "Capturing, Importing, and Managing Media" and so far you have not captured, imported, or managed any media at all. The only thing you have managed to do is get ready for capture. Getting ready to capture is no small matter, though. In fact, *preparing* to capture is the most challenging part of the process.

If you have jumped ahead and plan to just plug in your camcorder and start capturing without much preparation, you may experience troubles — particularly dropped frames. If you experience trouble during capture, check out the preceding pages of this chapter. (I won't tell a soul.)

Once your hardware is configured and ready for capture, follow these steps to identify video that you want to capture and then capture it:

1. **Connect all the necessary cables, turn on your hardware, launch Premiere, choose a preset, and perform all the other preparatory steps described earlier in this chapter.**

2. **In Premiere, choose File⇨Capture⇨Movie Capture.**

The Movie Capture window appears as shown in Figure 6-6.

3. **On the Settings tab, review the Capture Settings and Preferences and adjust as necessary (again, these subjects are covered earlier in this chapter).**

4. **Click the Logging tab on the right side of the Movie Capture window to bring the tab to the front.**

5. **If you have device control, click Play in the capture window. If you don't have device control, press the Play button on your playback device. The video should play in the viewer window.**

If you don't have device control, skip Steps 6, 7, 8, and 9 in this section.

Review settings

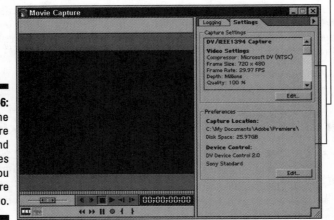

Figure 6-6:
Review the capture settings and preferences before you capture your video.

6. **Use the controls located beneath the viewer section of the Movie Capture window to review the tape. Use the Frame Back and Frame Forward buttons to identify the exact frame at which you want to start and finish capturing.**

Figure 6-7 details the various playback controls.

7. **When you find the spot where you want to start capturing, click the Set In button — located beneath the viewer of the Movie Capture window — to set an in point (you can also click the Set In button on the Logging tab).**

The timecode listed next to In on the Logging tab should now match the timecode shown under the viewer window.

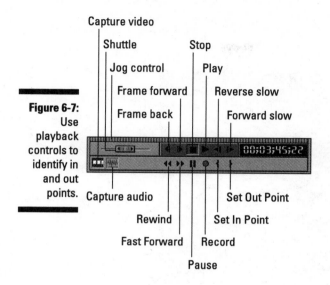

Figure 6-7: Use playback controls to identify in and out points.

Capture video
Shuttle
Jog control
Frame forward
Frame back
Stop
Play
Reverse slow
Forward slow
Capture audio
Rewind
Fast Forward
Pause
Record
Set In Point
Set Out Point

8. **Locate the place where you want to stop capturing and click the Set Out button either under the viewer or on the Logging tab.**

    The timecode next to Out on the Logging tab should match the timecode under the viewer (see Figure 6-8).

9. **Note the duration of your capture. As you can see in Figure 6-8, the duration of my capture is 21 seconds and 14 frames.**

10. **If you have device control and you want to capture the video right now, click Capture In/Out on the Logging tab.**

    Device control rewinds the tape in your playback device as needed and capture the video. If you have set up Premiere so that video and audio are not played on the computer during capture, the viewer screen is black during capture. An indicator at the top of the viewer window tells you how many frames have been captured, as well as how many frames have been dropped (hopefully, the dropped frames figure remains at zero).

    If you don't have device control, rewind the tape to just slightly before the point where you want to begin capture. Click the Record button beneath the viewer in the Movie Capture window and press the Play button on your playback device. When you want to stop capturing, click the Stop button in the Movie Capture window and then press Stop on your playback device.

When the capture job is done, a dialog box asks you to name the file and provide a comment if desired. Once saved, the file appears in your Project window. If you expand your Project window so it looks like the one shown in Figure 6-9 (or just scroll using the scroll bar at the bottom of the window), you can read a lot of information about your clip.

Out point timecode

In point timecode

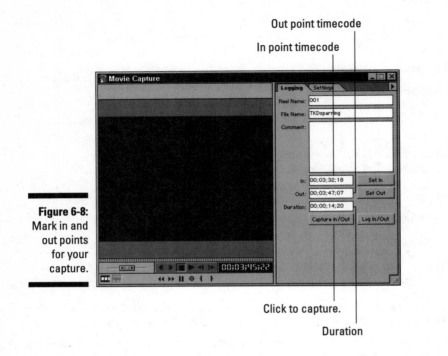

Figure 6-8:
Mark in and
out points
for your
capture.

Click to capture.

Duration

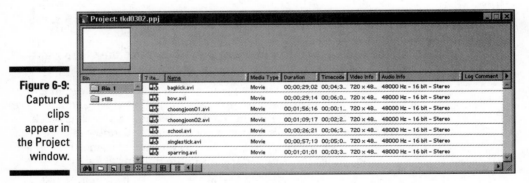

Figure 6-9:
Captured
clips
appear in
the Project
window.

Eek! I dropped a frame!

Of all the capture problems mentioned in this chapter, by far the most common — as well as the hardest to troubleshoot — is dropped frames. If you're capturing NTSC video from a DV camcorder, for example, Premiere captures 29.97 frames per second (fps). If something in the computer gets choked up, it may miss, or *drop,* one or more frames during capture. Dropped frames create unacceptable quality problems for captured clips in Premiere.

If you finish capturing a clip and a Properties dialog box like the one shown in Figure 6-10 appears, that is a bad sign. Review the statistics in this dialog box. If you see a line that says, `This movie appears to have DROPPED FRAMES`, then you almost certainly dropped frames during capture.

TIP

Timecode breaks on the tape can confuse Premiere into thinking it dropped frames when it really didn't. Timecode breaks often occur when you reuse tapes by recording new footage over old. When the end of the new footage is reached, the timecode may change and thus confuse Premiere. If you have been reusing tapes — not something I recommend — you might want to consider this as a possible cause of dropped frames reports.

Determining the cause of dropped frames can be challenging; however, I have found that the most common cause is that the hard drive couldn't maintain the required data rate during capture. As you can see in Figure 6-10, the average data rate for my capture was 2.51MB per second. For DV, the data rate *should* read 3.61MB per second. Common causes include:

✔ Programs other than Adobe Premiere were open during capture.

✔ The hard drive has not been defragmented recently.

✔ Another computer was trying to access the hard drive over your network (if you have one) during capture.

If you would like a visual illustration of "what happened" that caused the dropped frames, click the Data Rate button at the bottom of the clip's Properties dialog box. A graph similar to Figure 6-11 appears. The upper graph in Figure 6-11 represents a successful capture, and the lower graph indicates a capture with problems. Each vertical line in the graph represents a frame of video. They should all be red. Gaps indicate dropped frames. The white data rate line should be even for DV material, but other codecs might have a variable data rate.

So what can you do about dropped frames? Start by methodically re-preparing your computer for capture as described earlier in this chapter. Close unneeded programs, defragment your hard drive, buy more RAM, or consider upgrading your drives. If your capture card came with its own capture software, you may want to try using that software to capture, and then import the captured clips into Premiere for editing.

Capturing audio

Up to this point I have talked primarily about capturing video, as well as the audio that is recorded along with most video. You can also capture audio all by itself. You may want to capture just the audio that was recorded on your videotape, or you may want to capture audio from an audio CD in your CD-ROM drive.

This is bad.

A clue to the cause.

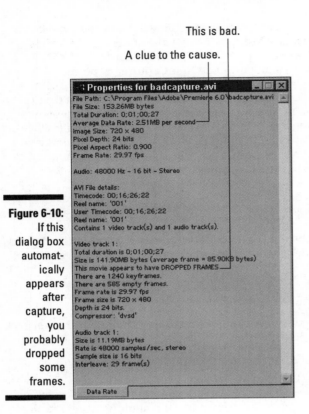

Figure 6-10:
If this dialog box automatically appears after capture, you probably dropped some frames.

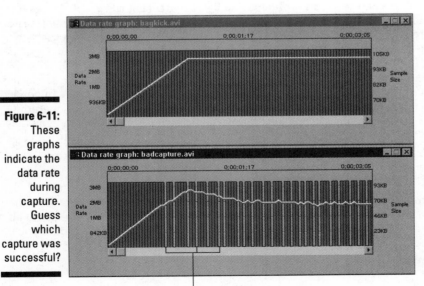

Figure 6-11:
These graphs indicate the data rate during capture. Guess which capture was successful?

Gaps indicate dropped frames.

The method you use depends on the audio source and your computer. If you're capturing audio from a videotape in your camcorder or video deck, follow the instructions given earlier in this chapter for capturing video. However, in the Capture Movie window click the Capture Video button to place a red slash through it. This results in only audio being captured.

If you're capturing audio from another source in Windows, you must use an external audio-recording program. The Windows Sound Recorder records WAV files, which can easily be used in Premiere. To record audio, follow these steps:

1. **In Premiere choose File⇨Capture⇨Audio Capture.**

2. **The first time you choose Audio Capture, you are asked to browse your computer and select a program that can capture audio.**

   If you want to use the Windows Sound Recorder, browse to the file SNDREC32.EXE in the C:\WINDOWS folder.

3. **Use the external program to record your audio.**

   Make sure that you adjust quality settings to the correct levels. CD audio is usually recorded with a sample rate of 44,100 Hz, in 16-bit stereo. Check the documentation for the software for details on controlling the recording process and saving the files.

Unfortunately, you're likely to have a tough time copying CD audio if you use only the tools provided with Windows. Copy protection schemes in Windows Media Player and the Sound Recorder prevent you from capturing music directly from an audio CD in your CD-ROM drive. I recommend that you find a program which can copy CD audio to MP3 format. Visit a Web site such as Tucows (www.tucows.com) that provides downloadable Windows software and look for programs that can encode or "rip" MP3 audio from music CDs.

Capturing audio in the Macintosh version of Premiere is a lot easier. On your Mac, follow these steps:

1. **In Premiere choose File⇨Capture⇨Audio Capture.**

2. **Choose Audio Capture⇨Sound Input.**

3. **Choose a source for your audio from the Source menu.**

4. **Choose quality settings that match your audio.**

   Remember that CD audio is usually recorded with a sample rate of 44,100 Hz with 16-bit stereo.

5. **Click OK to close the Settings dialog box.**

6. **Click Record.**

CD audio is also a lot easier to record on a Mac. Indeed, all you have to do in Premiere is choose File➪Open and select tracks directly from the audio CD in your CD-ROM drive. Before you open the CD audio, click Properties in the Open dialog box and adjust quality settings as appropriate.

Capturing stop-motion video

I know what you're thinking. The term *stop-motion* seems to make about as much sense as *jumbo shrimp*. But in the world of video, stop-motion refers to motion pictures that are created from a series of still shots. If you've ever seen a "claymation" holiday special or a time-lapse film of a flower blooming, then you have seen stop-motion video. Premiere can capture stop-motion video from either a DV or analog source.

If the stop-motion video was captured on a camera and is already assembled into a video format, you can simply import it as regular video. The steps described here assume that you wish to capture individual frames using Premiere, including images that were captured in still format by a video camera.

To capture stop-motion video using Premiere, do the following:

1. **Connect your capture device to your computer, turn it on, and start Premiere.**

2. **Choose File➪Capture➪Stop Motion.**

   A Stop Motion capture window appears, and a Stop Motion menu is added to the Premiere menu bar as shown in Figure 6-12.

3. **Choose Stop Motion➪Capture Options.**

4. **In the Stop Motion Options dialog box, choose a capture type.**

   In Windows, choose "Still Image" if you just want to capture a single image, "Manual Capture" if you want to manually capture a series of stills, or "Time Lapse" if you want to take a capture at regular intervals. On a Macintosh, choose "Manual Recording" for manual stop-motion capture or "Time Lapse" for automatic captures at regular intervals.

5. **Review and adjust the remaining settings as you see fit.**

   Some settings may or may not be available depending upon the type of capture you're performing. You might be able to adjust the size of the capture images, or set intervals for automated captures. You can also set a maximum number of frames that will be captured, a useful setting if you plan to automate the capture and don't want to have to remember to come back and turn the process off when enough material has been captured. Click OK when you're done adjusting the settings.

Stop Motion menu

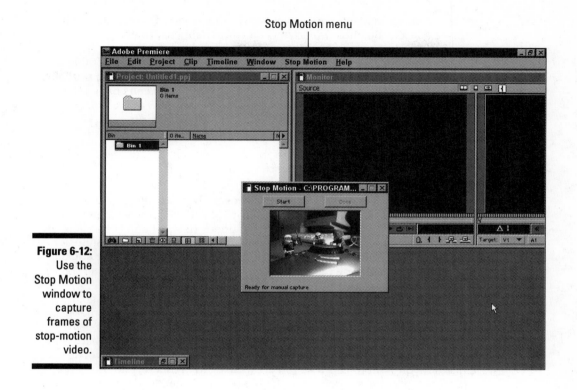

Figure 6-12:
Use the
Stop Motion
window to
capture
frames of
stop-motion
video.

6. **In the Stop Motion window, click Capture or Start depending upon the type of capture you're performing.**

   If you're doing manual stop-motion capture (as I'm doing in Figure 6-13), click Step each time you want to capture another frame. Click Done when you're done.

Figure 6-13:
Click Step
each time
you want to
capture
another
frame.

I have captured 30 frames so far.

Once you're finished, you have a video file (the format depends upon the capture source you chose) that you can use in a movie project.

Stop-motion animation requires a lot of frames. Remember that NTSC video plays back at almost 30 frames per second. For many uses you can probably get away with 15 frames per second. Once captured, you can change the speed of a clip by selecting the clip in the Project window and choosing Clip➪Speed.

Doing batch captures

After you have shot some video, your next step is probably to determine which portions of the video are worth keeping and which ones aren't. You probably want to use that clip that just happens to show a UFO zooming by in the background, but you probably don't want to use the five minutes of video you "shot" when you forgot to turn the camcorder off before sticking it in your camera bag (don't feel bad, it happens to everyone eventually).

Determining which video you want to keep is time-consuming enough, but then you have to go back and actually capture all that material. To make this all go a heck of a lot easier, I recommend you automate the process using Premiere's batch capture feature. Here's how it works: You shuttle back and forth through your tape, noting the timecode for in and out points for the clips that you want to capture. You create a log in Premiere, and then Premiere uses that log to automatically shuttle the tape back and forth to perform the captures for you. The next few sections show you exactly how.

To perform batch captures you must have a capture device with device control. This is because Premiere must be able to operate the playback controls on the device during batch capture, and Premiere must be able to accurately read the timecode from the tape.

Logging clips

The first step in performing batch captures is to log the clips that you actually want to capture. To log clips, follow these steps:

1. **Open the Movie Capture window by choosing File➪Capture➪Movie Capture.**

2. **Review your Capture Settings and Preferences on the Settings tab of the Movie Capture window, and then click the Logging tab to bring it to the front.**

3. **Use the playback controls under the viewer in the Movie Capture window to identify a clip that you want to capture. Move to the exact frame at which you want to begin.**

4. **On the Logging tab, click Set In.**

   The current timecode should now appear in both the In and Out boxes.

5. **Use the playback controls to move to the exact frame at which you want to stop capture and click Set Out.**

   The timecode for the out point should now appear in the Out box. The duration of the capture is also noted.

6. **Click Log In/Out.**

   A File Name dialog box appears as shown in Figure 6-14. By clicking the Log In/Out button, you add the logged clip to a batch list, as opposed to a regular capture where you set in and out points and simply click Capture In/Out.

7. **Enter a file name and a log comment if desired. Click OK when you're done.**

   The logged clip is added to a batch list.

8. **Repeat steps 3 through 7 for each clip on the tape that you want to log.**

Figure 6-14:
Provide a file name for the logged clip, and enter a log comment if you wish.

Working with batch lists

Once you have logged some clips that you want to capture, you have a batch list similar to the one shown in Figure 6-15. I recommend that you save your batch list for future use. To save it, click in the Batch Capture window (Figure 6-15) to make it active and choose File⇨Save. Give the batch list a name that is similar to the tape or reel name to which it corresponds. You can open the batch list later if you wish by choosing File⇨Open and navigating to the batch list file you want to open.

You can use the Batch Capture window to manage and edit your batch lists in a variety of ways. Here are some tips for working with batch lists:

✔ To select a clip for capture, make sure it has a diamond next to it in the far left column as shown in Figure 6-15. By default, any uncaptured clip has a diamond next to it. If you don't want to capture a certain clip, remove the diamond by clicking on it. Once a clip is captured, a black check mark will appear next to it in the batch list. If a red X appears next to the clip, that means Premiere experienced a problem when it tried to capture that clip.

✔ Click the Sort By In Point button to sort all clips by the in point. This can be handy if you have skipped around on the tape a bit while logging clips.

✔ To manually add an item to the list, click Add New Item. Enter relevant information about the new item in the Clip Capture Parameters dialog box that appears.

✔ To delete an item from the batch list, select it and click the trash icon in the lower-right corner.

✔ Click Record to capture all clips that have a diamond next to them.

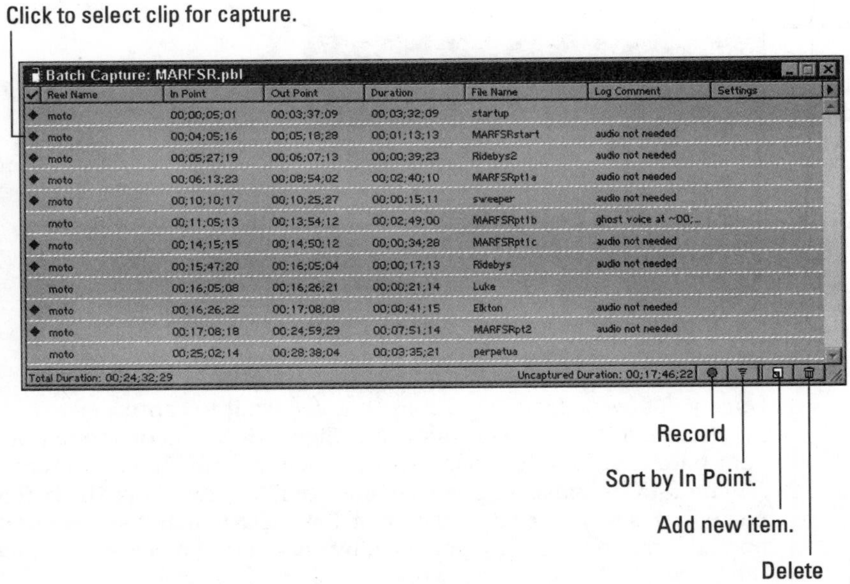

Click to select clip for capture.

Figure 6-15:
Use batch
lists to
automate
capture
jobs.

✔ Reel Name	In Point	Out Point	Duration	File Name	Log Comment	Settings
◆ moto	00;00;05;01	00;03;37;09	00;03;32;09	startup		
◆ moto	00;04;05;16	00;05;18;29	00;01;13;13	MARFSRstart	audio not needed	
◆ moto	00;05;27;19	00;06;07;13	00;00;39;23	Ridebys2	audio not needed	
◆ moto	00;06;13;23	00;08;54;02	00;02;40;10	MARFSRpt1a	audio not needed	
◆ moto	00;10;10;17	00;10;25;27	00;00;15;11	sweeper	audio not needed	
moto	00;11;05;13	00;13;54;12	00;02;49;00	MARFSRpt1b	ghost voice at ~00;...	
◆ moto	00;14;15;15	00;14;50;12	00;00;34;28	MARFSRpt1c	audio not needed	
◆ moto	00;15;47;20	00;16;05;04	00;00;17;13	Ridebys	audio not needed	
moto	00;16;05;08	00;16;26;21	00;00;21;14	Luke		
◆ moto	00;16;26;22	00;17;08;08	00;00;41;15	Elkton	audio not needed	
◆ moto	00;17;08;18	00;24;59;29	00;07;51;14	MARFSRpt2	audio not needed	
moto	00;25;02;14	00;28;38;04	00;03;35;21	perpetua		

Total Duration: 00;24;32;29   Uncaptured Duration: 00;17;46;22

Record

Sort by In Point.

Add new item.

Delete

I find that printed batch lists can be extremely handy as I work. To print the list, simply choose File⇨Print. Then you'll have a hard copy reference to all the clips on a reel or tape, including timecodes. Keep the list with that tape for future reference.

Importing Media

There is no doubt in my mind that all the video you record with your camcorder is indescribably perfect just the way it is. But, if I may be so bold, wouldn't it be *even better* if you enhanced it a bit with some music, or perhaps some illustrative stills? Good, I'm glad you agree. Premiere can import all kinds of media, even video that has been produced by another application. Supported formats include:

- AI — Adobe Illustrator graphic
- AIFF — Audio Interchange File Format
- ASF — Microsoft Advanced Streaming Format *(Windows only)*
- AVI — Audio/Video Interleave, also called Video for Windows
- BMP — Bitmap still graphic *(Windows only)*
- DV — Digital video format
- FLC/FLI — Autodesk Animator animation
- FLM — FilmStrip
- GIF — Graphics Interchange Format image
- JPEG — Joint Photographic Experts Group image
- MPEG — Motion Picture Experts Group movie
- MP3 — MPEG Layer-3 audio
- MOV — QuickTime movie
- PICS — Pixar animation
- PICT — Macintosh image format
- PCX — PC Paintbrush image *(Windows only)*
- PSD — Adobe Photoshop document
- SND — Macintosh sound format *(Macintosh only)*
- Sound Designer I/II — An audio composition and editing tool *(Macintosh only)*
- TGA — Targa bitmap graphic
- TIFF — Tagged Image File Format
- WAV — Windows sound format *(Windows only)*
- WMA — Windows Media Audio *(Windows only)*
- WMV — Windows Media Video *(Windows only)*

Any of the formats in this list can be imported into Premiere and used in your projects. Of all these formats, you may find that still graphics are among the most common. You also usually have more control over stills than audio or video formats. Because of this, the next section shows you how to prepare still graphics for use in Premiere. Once you've done that, you can move to the next section, which describes how to actually import files (stills or not).

Preparing stills for your movie

You're probably pretty accustomed to seeing images that have a 4:3 aspect ratio. Your computer's monitor most likely has a 4:3 aspect ratio. Most still photos that you take have a 4:3 aspect ratio. And of course, most TVs have a 4:3 aspect ratio. So dropping a 4:3 digital photo into a DV-based video project should be easy, right? Not really.

If you don't know the answer to the above question, I suggest that you spend some time in Chapter 4. There you'll find some important fundamentals about working with video, including screen and pixel aspect ratios.

Before you insert a still image into a video project, you must also consider pixel aspect ratio. Digital graphics usually have square pixels; video usually has rectangular pixels. The frame size of NTSC video is usually 720 x 480 pixels. Do the math and you'll find that this does not work out to 4:3 (it's actually 3:2). However, it still appears to have a 4:3 aspect ratio because NTSC video pixels are slightly taller than they are wide. To account for this, adjust the image size of your stills before you import them into Premiere. For NTSC video, your images should be 720 x 534 pixels before importing them into Premiere. For PAL video, the images should be 768 x 576 pixels before import. To adjust the size of an image using Adobe Photoshop (an excellent image editing program that comes free with Premiere):

1. **Open the image and save it as a Photoshop document (PSD) before performing any edits.**

   Photoshop documents can be imported directly into Premiere.

2. **In Photoshop, choose Image⇨Image Size.**

   The Image Size dialog box appears.

3. **In the Image Size dialog box, remove the check mark next to Constrain Proportions, as shown in Figure 6-16.**

4. **In the Pixel Dimensions section of the Image Size dialog box, enter 720 (NTSC) or 768 (PAL) in the Width field and 534 (NTSC) or 576 (PAL) in the Height field. For both fields, choose Pixels from the accompanying drop-down menus.**

   Don't concern yourself with the Print Size section. You only use that when printing still graphics out on paper.

5. Click OK, and then save and close the image.

After you click OK in the Image Size dialog box, your still image will probably look distorted somewhat. Don't worry; once the image is imported into an NTSC or PAL video program it will look right.

Adobe Premiere comes with a version of Photoshop on the program disk, so if you have Premiere, you also have a great image editing program!

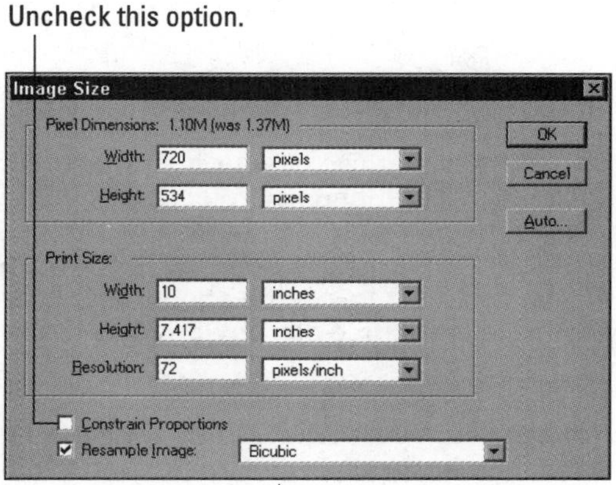

Uncheck this option.

Figure 6-16:
Adjust the size of your still before importing it into a video project.

Importing stills and other fun stuff

Importing still graphics, audio files, and other neat things into Premiere is really easy. If you're importing a still image into a project that is based on NTSC or PAL video, first adjust the image size as described in the previous section. Then follow these steps:

1. In Premiere, choose File⇨Import⇨File. You can also import an entire folder if you wish, or a Premiere project.

2. Browse to the file that you want to import.

Note that "All Format Types" is selected in the Files of Type menu by default. If you only want to search for files of a certain type, choose the desired type from this menu.

3. Click Open. The imported file appears in your Project window.

If the file you want to import doesn't show up in the Import window — and you're certain that you're looking in the correct folder — the file may be of a type that isn't supported by Premiere. See my list of supported file types earlier in this chapter.

Organizing Your Media

When we think of Adobe Premiere we think mainly of video, but this is truly a multimedia-rich program. Be it audio, video, still graphics, or even text, you'll no doubt work with many different kinds of media in Premiere. You'll wind up using files from all over your computer, and possibly even your network. Keeping track of all this media can be a challenge, but Premiere can help. This section shows you how to manage your media.

Managing source clips

Premiere does its best to make efficient use of your disk space. For example, suppose you import a song into three different projects. Does this mean you have three separate copies of that song on your hard drive? No, in all three projects Premiere points to the same source file. While this is an efficient way to do business, it also means you must be careful about moving or deleting source files. If you move or delete a source file, any projects that point to that source file can't access it.

Where does Premiere store all your source files? They are stored on your scratch disk. To determine the location of your scratch disk, choose Edit➪Preferences➪Scratch Disks and Device Control. The Scratch Disks and Device Control Preferences dialog box appears as shown in Figure 6-17. Paths are given for your scratch disks for captures and previews. Using this information you can browse your hard drive using Windows Explorer or the Mac Finder and identify large source files that are taking up a lot of disk space. In particular, check for the following:

- ✔ **Adobe Premiere Preview Files folder** — This folder is located in your scratch disk folder for Video Previews. Rendered preview files are stored here, subdivided into folders labeled by project. If you see a folder for an old project that you're not working on anymore, you can probably save a lot of disk space by deleting its Preview Files folder. Just keep in mind that if you ever want to work on that project again, you'll have to sit through the rendering process all over again as the preview files are recreated.

- ✔ **Project-Archive folder** — This folder contains archived back-up copies of project files (PPJ). These usually don't take up much space, but you can safely delete archives for older projects. Before deleting archives, make sure that the original project files are backed up on a CD-R or floppy disk.

✔ **Capture files** — When you capture media, it ends up on your scratch disk. Some of that media, particularly video files, takes up a lot of space. You can save a lot of that space by deleting old AVI and QuickTime video files, but make absolutely certain that none of the files you delete are needed by current projects. Projects always link back to the original source file, so if you delete a source file, any projects that used it will now have missing media. You should also make sure that you still have the original source tapes for the media in a safe place.

✔ **Project files and batch lists** — These files don't use up much space, and I generally recommend against deleting them. One simple way to "back up" batch lists is to simply print them out. I usually print out batch lists, fold them into little squares (batch list origami can be a great way to express yourself), and then stick them in the plastic tape case with the original source tape to which the batch list corresponds.

Scratch disk paths

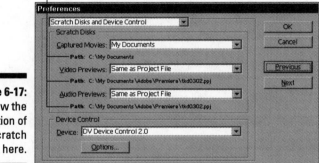

Figure 6-17:
Review the location of your scratch disk here.

For more on using and configuring scratch disks, see "Setting Up Your Scratch Disk" in Chapter 3.

Using the Project window

As you work in a project, any media that you import or capture are added to your Project window. The Project window is usually pretty small, but if you expand the window, as shown in Figure 6-18, you'll see a lot more information about your clips. (You can expand the Project window by clicking-and-dragging on the lower-right corner of the window.) Key features of the Project window — all shown in Figure 6-18 — include:

 ✔ Use bins to organize material. Bins work like folders on your hard drive, and you can create your own bins by clicking the New Bin button. Click-and-drag items to move them into bins.

 ✔ Click Create Item to quickly create a title, black video, bars and tone, or other element.

 ✔ Use the view controls to switch between Icon view, Thumbnails view, and Details view.

 ✔ Customize the view by choosing Window⇨Window Options⇨Project Window Options. Select columns to list and adjust other view options.

 ✔ In Details view, click a column head to sort clips by that heading.

 ✔ Click an item to view it in the preview area of the Project window. Click Play to play audio or video clips.

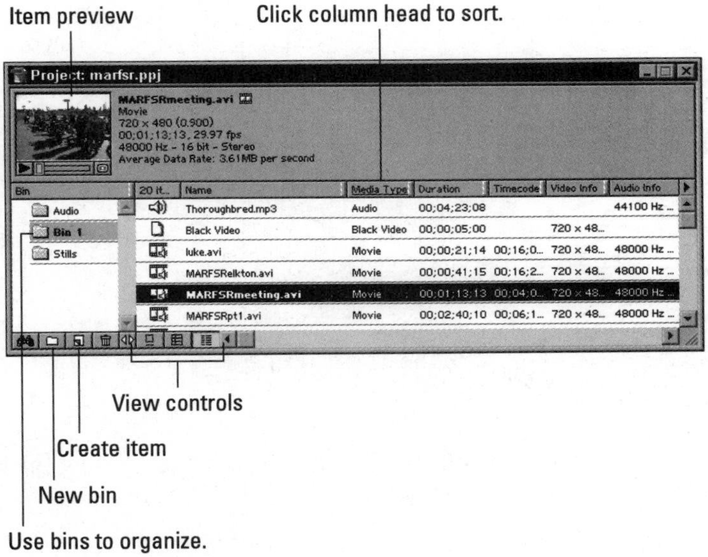

Item preview

Click column head to sort.

Figure 6-18:
Use the
Project
window to
manage
media in
Premiere.

View controls

Create item

New bin

Use bins to organize.

Part III
Editing in Premiere

The 5th Wave — By Rich Tennant

THE NEW HOLLYWOOD

CUT! PASTE!

In this part . . .

With Adobe Premiere, you have chosen one of the world's greatest video-editing programs. Just a couple of years ago, the editing capabilities offered in Premiere were only available on professional-grade systems that cost hundreds of thousands of dollars.

Part III explores Premiere's editing capabilities. You get a chance to edit clips, assemble them into a project using the Timeline, and then add some transitions, special effects, and audio.

Chapter 7

Editing Clips

● ●

In This Chapter

▶ Getting the skinny on your clips

▶ Working with markers and in and out points

▶ Tweaking your clips till they squeak

▶ Undoing mistakes

● ●

*I*n the American economy, the basic currency is the dollar. The light-year is used to express interstellar distances, and in video editing, the basic unit of measure is the clip. Chunks of audio, video, or even still graphics are all referred to as *clips* when you work in a nonlinear video editing program. Of course, unlike dollars or light-years, there is no specific standard which defines a clip, but short or long, clips are your basic unit of measure when working in Adobe Premiere. This chapter introduces you to the details of your clips and shows you how to work with them in your projects.

Getting to Know Your Clips

Clips that you capture or import into Premiere all wind up in the Project window (see Chapter 6 for more on capturing and importing clips). Clips come in many shapes and sizes, so to speak. Types of clips include:

- ✔ Video clips
- ✔ Audio clips
- ✔ Still graphics
- ✔ Titles
- ✔ Color matte (a solid-colored clip)
- ✔ Black video
- ✔ Bars and tone (used to calibrate sound and color on video equipment)
- ✔ Universal counting leader (a countdown that helps synchronize audio and video)

You can generate any of the last five items in this list by clicking the Create Item button at the bottom of the Project window.

For more on working with titles, see Chapter 12. See Chapter 13 for information on when and how to use bars and tone, black video, and counting leaders.

Analyzing clip details

You can learn a lot about a clip in the Project window. To view a brief summary, click on a clip. The clip is loaded into the preview area in the upper-left corner of the Project window, as shown in Figure 7-1. You'll also see a summary of the clip's length, frame size, audio quality, and data rate as appropriate. This summary appears just to the right of the preview window.

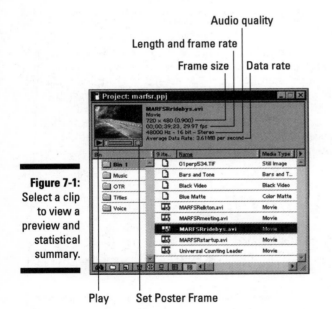

Figure 7-1: Select a clip to view a preview and statistical summary.

If you require even more information about a clip, select it in the Project window and choose Clip⇨Properties. A Properties dialog box opens, containing more detailed information than you likely need to know about the clip. These details can help you troubleshoot problems that you may be experiencing with that clip.

Playing clips

When you select a clip in the Project window, a preview of it appears in the tiny preview window in the upper-left corner. If the clip is audio or video, you can play it by clicking the Play button underneath the preview window. You can move to specific parts of the clip using the slider next to the Play button.

Setting a new poster frame

By default, the first frame of the clip appears in the preview. The frame that first appears in the preview window is called the *poster frame*, but there's no rule that says the first frame of a clip must be the poster frame. You may find that a frame further along in that clip is actually more descriptive of the actual contents of the clip. To set a new poster frame, follow these steps:

1. **Click on a clip to load it into the preview window.**

2. **Click the Play button to play the clip, and click the Stop button when you get to the spot you want to set as the new poster frame.**

3. **Click the Set Poster Frame button (see Figure 7-1).**

   Now, whenever you select that clip, the new poster frame appears in the preview window. Of course, when you click the Play button, the clip returns to the first frame to begin playback.

Playing clips in the Monitor window

As you can see, the clip previews provided in the Project window are pretty small. If you get tired of squinting, you may want to load the clip into the Monitor window to preview it. Follow these steps to play your clip in the Monitor window:

1. **Switch to Single-Track Editing mode by choosing Window⇨ Workspace⇨Single-Track Editing.**

   The Monitor window appears and switches to Dual View, if it wasn't like that already.

2. **Click-and-drag a clip from the Project window and drop it in the left pane of the Monitor window, as shown in Figure 7-2.**

3. **Use the playback controls at the bottom of the Monitor window (Figure 7-3) to preview the clip.**

The Monitor window offers buttons and tools for controlling playback at various speeds. Some of these buttons — Play, Stop, Pause — you're probably familiar with from years of using VCRs, tape decks, and CD players. Other controls may be new. Figure 7-3 details the Monitor's playback controls.

Drag a clip from here.   Drop the clip here.

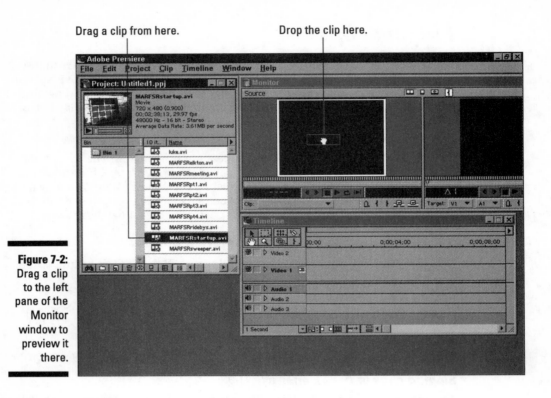

Figure 7-2:
Drag a clip
to the left
pane of the
Monitor
window to
preview it
there.

Some of the controls shown in Figure 7-3 are described throughout this chapter and in Chapter 8. Take a close look at the playback controls right now by loading a clip into the Monitor and clicking the Play button. Somewhere in the middle of the clip, click the Stop button. Now you can play with some controls that help you identify specific frames in a clip:

✔ Click the Frame Forward button. The clip moves forward by one frame. You can also press the right arrow key on your keyboard to move forward one frame at a time.

✔ Click the Frame Back button. The clip moves back a frame. You can also control the Frame Back function by pressing the left-arrow key.

✔ Place the mouse pointer directly on the Frame Jog control. Click and drag the jog control back and forth. Jog controls have been common on professional video equipment for years because they provide precise control as you move through video frame by frame. Notice that the clip frames jump forward or back as you move the Frame Jog control.

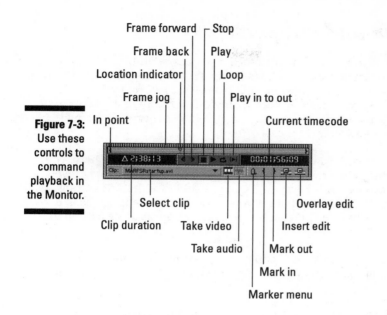

Figure 7-3:
Use these
controls to
command
playback in
the Monitor.

Frame forward — Stop
Frame back — Play
Location indicator — Loop
Frame jog — Play in to out
In point — Current timecode
Select clip — Overlay edit
Clip duration — Insert edit
Take video — Mark out
Take audio — Mark in
Marker menu

To be honest, I have a difficult time manipulating the jog and frame forward/
back controls with a mouse, even a high-quality optical mouse. I much prefer to
control these functions using a multimedia controller, such as the Contour
Design ShuttlePRO. A multimedia controller connects to your computer and
has special buttons and knobs to make moving about and controlling playback
easier. The ShuttlePRO's ergonomic design and dial control for frame jogging
ultimately save me time, frustration, and wrist movement. I feature this useful
device in Chapter 17.

The Ins and Outs of In and Out Points

In a perfect universe, there would be peace on Earth, everyone would dine on
free Bubble UP and rainbow stew, and every clip of video would start and end
at exactly the right time. Alas, this world is not quite perfect just yet. But at
least in the case of video, you can provide the illusion of perfection by using *in
points* and *out points*. In and out points — more generally known as *markers* —
are critical in video editing because they let you control which portions of a
clip appear in the video program and which portions don't appear. So get your
silver spoon ready as the following sections serve up steps for perfecting your
clips by using in points, out points, and other markers.

Setting in and out points

Setting in points and out points on a clip is pretty easy, and Premiere gives you several different methods to choose from. I strongly recommend that you set in and out points on a clip *before* you insert it into a project's Timeline. For this process, I recommend using the Single-Track Editing workspace (Window➪Workspace➪Single-Track Editing), because it provides a dual-pane Monitor window that I find easier to work with.

Although I recommend using the Single-Track Editing workspace here, you can set in and out points for clips using the A/B Editing workspace as well (Window➪Workspace➪A/B Editing). If you're working in the A/B Editing workspace, double-click a clip in the Project window. The clip opens in a new window with the same playback and marker controls as described in this section.

The in point is the spot where the clip begins playing in the project. In general, you should not set the in point at the very beginning of the clip if you can avoid doing so.

The main reason for not setting the in point at the very beginning of the clip is to facilitate transitions. Suppose that you want to apply a transition to the beginning of a clip. The transition you choose is a Cross Dissolve, and you set it to last for one second — as the previous clip fades out and the new clip fades in. In the Timeline, this edit might resemble Figure 7-4. To facilitate this Cross Dissolve transition, the two adjacent clips must overlap each other for the duration of the transition (one second). The transition requires an additional half-second of lead-out/in material on each clip beyond where the original in and out points were marked.

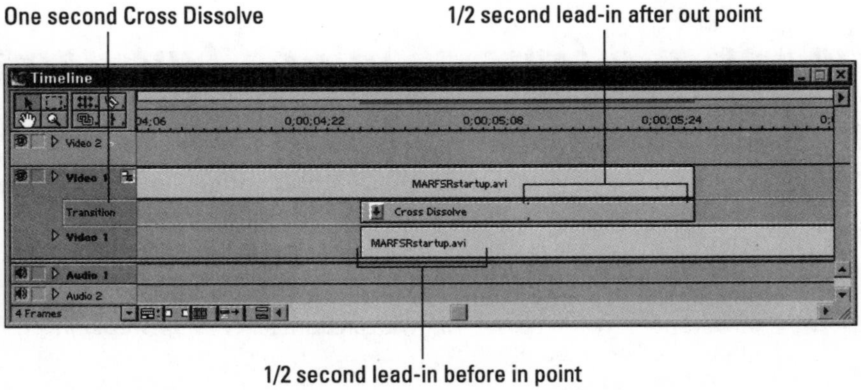

One second Cross Dissolve   1/2 second lead-in after out point

Figure 7-4:
Transitions often require lead-in material before the marked in point of the clip.

1/2 second lead-in before in point

An out point is, of course, the spot where you want to stop using the clip. Like in points, out points should not be set at the very end of a clip.

When you locate the place where you want to set an in or out point, Premiere provides several methods for setting these points (refer to Figure 7-3 for control locations):

✔ In the Monitor, click-and-drag the In Point and Out Point markers. This method is not very precise.

✔ Click the Mark In or Mark Out buttons.

✔ Press I (in point) or O (out point) on your keyboard.

After you've marked in and out points on a clip, the duration of your marked clip portion appears in the Clip Duration field in the Monitor window, as shown in Figure 7-5.

There is a marker on the current frame.

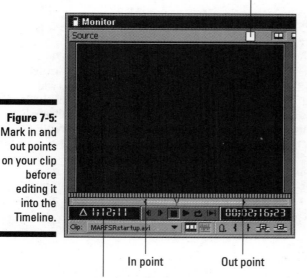

Figure 7-5:
Mark in and out points on your clip before editing it into the Timeline.

In point   Out point

Duration of marked segment

Using other markers

In points and out points usually get all the attention in books like this, but you can use many other markers in your clips as well. Different markers include:

- ✔ **In and out points for just audio or video tracks:** Use these if you want audio and video to go in or out separately. Figure 7-6 shows that I edited a clip into the Timeline so that the Audio In point starts well before the Video In point.

- ✔ **Numbered markers:** Use numbered markers for later reference. I like to use these to mark the location of visual events, which I will later match with an audio soundtrack.

- ✔ **Unnumbered markers:** If you only want to mark a single spot in the clip, add an unnumbered marker. As you can see in Figure 7-5, the Monitor window provides an indicator when there is a marker at the current frame.

You can also use the Marker menu at the bottom of the Monitor window (Figure 7-3) to move through a clip using markers. Open the Marker menu, choose Go To, and select a marker from the menu. You instantly move to that marker. The Go To feature is especially handy if you have a hardware multimedia controller, because you can usually jump from marker to marker by pressing a single button.

Deleting markers

After going through all the trouble to set in points, out points, and various other markers, why would you want to go and delete them? You may want to delete markers for various reasons. You may change your mind about the location of in and out points or about whether you want to use the clip altogether. Or, after you edit a clip into the Timeline, you may want to clear current in and out points so that you can select a new portion of that clip to use.

To delete an in or out point, simply click the button for the Marker menu (refer to Figure 7-3), choose Clear from the menu, and then select an option. You can clear individual markers, all markers of a given type, or all markers in the current clip.

Modifying Clips

What *is* a clip, really? When you see a list of clips in the Project window, you're looking at references to actual files on your hard drive. When you set markers on clips or perform edits, you're actually editing the references in Premiere, and not the original source file. This is important, because it leaves the original source file undisturbed for future use. It also saves storage space because you don't have multiple copies of the same material all over your hard drive.

Video in point

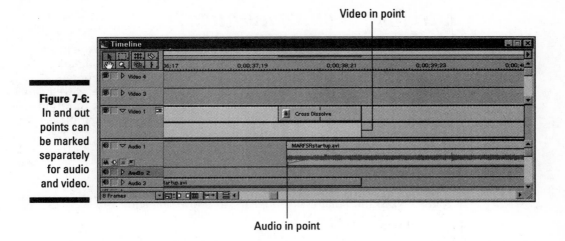

Figure 7-6:
In and out
points can
be marked
separately
for audio
and video.

Audio in point

Copying clips

Usually each clip in the Project window refers to a separate file, but there's
no rule that says you can't have multiple clips which all refer to the same
source file. For example, suppose you capture several minutes of video all in
a single clip, but in Premiere you plan to pick and choose various portions of
that clip for use in different locations in a project. You may find it handy to
create subclips for each segment that you want to use. Follow these steps to
create a duplicate clip of a portion of the original clip:

1. **Open a clip by dragging it from the Project window to the Monitor
   and mark in and out points on the clip.**

2. **With the Monitor window active, choose Edit⇨Duplicate Clip.**

   The Duplicate Clip dialog box opens, as shown in Figure 7-7.

3. **Type a name for the clip.**

   If you have more than one project open, you can also choose a location
   for the duplicate clip.

4. **Click OK.**

   The new clip duplicate now appears in the project window.

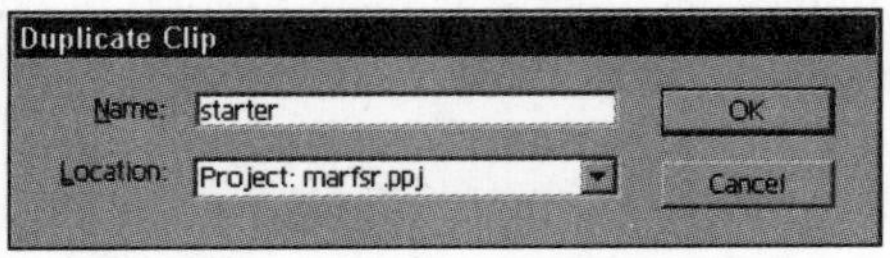

Figure 7-7:
Name your
duplicate
clip here.

Controlling a clip's duration

The duration of a clip is determined by the length of time between the in and out points for the clip. For audio or video clips, I recommend that in most cases you only adjust the duration of the clip by setting in and out points. However, you can change the duration by entering a numeric value as well. While this often isn't a good idea for video, you often set a numeric duration value for still clips. The duration of a still clip determines how long it plays when inserted in a movie. To adjust the duration of a clip, follow these steps:

1. **Select a clip in the Project window.**

2. **Choose Clip⇨Duration.**

   The Clip Duration dialog box appears, as shown in Figure 7-8.

3. **Enter a new duration for the clip.**

   Clip duration is expressed in the same format as timecode, so it should be read as

   ```
   hours;minutes;seconds;frames
   ```

4. **Click OK when you're done.**

The clip in Figure 7-8 is set to play for exactly five seconds.

You can also adjust a clip's duration in the Timeline. See Chapter 8 for more on working with clips in the Timeline.

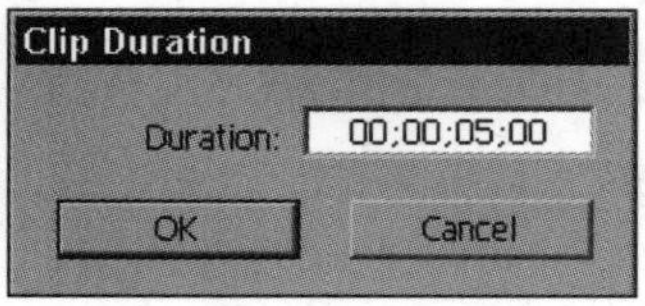

Figure 7-8:
Set the duration of your clip using numeric values.

Clip Duration

Duration: 00;00;05;00

OK   Cancel

Speeding up (or slowing down) your clips

Besides adjusting the duration of a clip, you can also adjust the speed at which it plays. Speed adjustments can give you a fast motion or slo-mo effect. Before you dismiss speed adjustment as gimmicky, consider some useful applications of this feature:

✔ You can adjust the length of the clip without reshooting it. If you have a specific period of time in your project that a clip must fill, but the clip is shorter than the gap, slow the clip down slightly.

✔ You can use speed adjustments to correct too slow or too fast shots. If you're not happy with the speed at which the camera pans across a scene — say, across a landscape — adjust the speed of the clip to speed up or slow down the pan as desired.

✔ You can use speed adjustments to change the mood or feel of a shot. If an action scene doesn't seem quite as exciting as you would like, speed it up just a bit. Conversely, if two lovers are running across a grassy field at sunset toward each other's embrace, slow the speed down a bit to increase the drama.

✔ You can create interesting voice effects by adjusting playback speed. A faster speed makes the voice sound small and wacky (like Alvin and the Chipmunks), and a slower speed makes the voice sound large and ominous (like Darth Vader).

Just be aware of the potential negative effects of speed adjustment. While moderate speed adjustments to video may be imperceptible to the eyes of most viewers, even slight speed adjustments to audio tracks will be immediately obvious. Also, if you slow a video clip down too much, the motion could become jerky.

To be on the safe side, I recommend that you make a duplicate copy of a clip before adjusting its speed. Follow the steps provided earlier in this chapter for copying clips.

Adjusting the speed of a clip is pretty easy:

1. **Select a clip on which you want to adjust the speed.**

   You can choose a clip in the Project window, or one that has already been edited into the Monitor. Again, I recommend that you work with a duplicate of the original.

2. **Choose Clip⇨Speed.**

   The Clip Speed dialog box appears, as shown in Figure 7-9.

3. **Enter a new percentage number in the New Rate field.**

   To make the clip play at double its original speed, enter **200** percent. To make the clip play at half its original speed, enter **50** percent. The duration of the clip is adjusted automatically, based on your percentage change.

   Alternatively, if you want to speed up or slow down the clip to make it fit a specific time period, click the New Duration radio button and enter the desired duration. The clip's speed is automatically adjusted to fill the specified gap.

4. **Click OK to close the Clip Speed dialog box.**

5. **Play the clip to preview your speed changes.**

If you find that the speed changes you chose were too extreme, enter more moderate percentages to make finer adjustments. If you're filling a specific gap, you may need to adjust in and out points on the clip to lessen the extremity of the changes. Fortunately, clip speed is a pretty fun thing to experiment with!

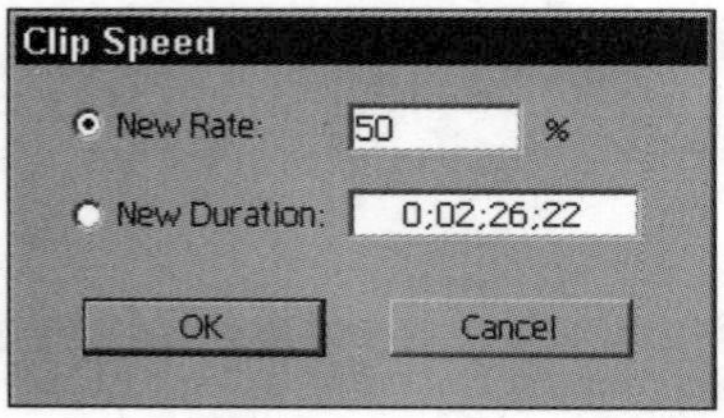

Figure 7-9:
Adjusting
the speed of
your clips
can be more
than just a
gimmick.

"Oops!" Undoing Mistakes

Don't feel bad; everyone makes a mistake once in a while. For some of us, making mistakes is a way of life! Adobe Premiere understands that you might make a goof occasionally, and like any good computer program, it's forgiving.

"I feel like I keep making the same edits over and over. . . ."

Do you ever feel like you keep repeating yourself? Do you find yourself performing the same redundant tasks? Do you often feel like you do the same thing over and over? Before you form any habits that might lead to a repetitive stress injury, you may want to see if you can adjust a setting in Adobe Premiere that might save you a lot of repeated effort.

Take still graphics, for example. If you use a lot of stills in your movie projects, you may find that you to adjust the duration repeatedly for each still — by the same amount almost every single time. Adobe Premiere has a default duration for still graphics, and you can adjust that default if you want. To do so, choose Edit⇨Preferences⇨ General and Still Image. The default duration for a still image is 150 frames, which works out to about five seconds in NTSC video. Simply enter a new number in the Default Duration box, remembering the frame rate of the video that you work with.

Premiere incorporates the Undo feature beloved by computer users the world over. If you make a mistake, you can quickly undo it by choosing Edit⇨ Undo. The Edit menu lists the last action that was performed next to Undo so that you know exactly what it is that you're undoing. If you don't like using the Edit menu, you can also quickly undo an action using the keyboard shortcut Command+Z (Macintosh) or Ctrl+Z (Windows).

Did you change your mind again? Perhaps that "mistake" wasn't such a bad thing after all. If you want to redo the mistake that you just undid, choose Edit⇨Redo.

If you aren't sure about a change, you can use the Undo and Redo commands to toggle back and forth between project states.

Adjusting Undo levels

Thankfully, Premiere lets you undo more than one mistake. Anyone who has been using Adobe software for a while probably remembers the bad old days when you could only undo one action in programs like Photoshop and Illustrator. Premiere offers up to 99 levels of Undo, although by default only the last 15 actions can be undone. The following steps adjust the levels of the Undo command:

1. **Choose Edit⇨Preferences⇨Auto Save and Undo.**

2. **Enter a new number in the Levels of Undo field.**

   The number must be between 1 and 99.

3. **Click OK.**

Before you adjust the Undo levels, keep in mind that each level of Undo uses up some memory. Thus, I recommend that you not bump the levels too far beyond 15 unless you're really, really fond of the Undo feature and don't mind a significant performance hit. A bunch of "undos" stored in memory can really tax your system's resources while providing little value. (Who on earth ever undoes the last 99 actions anyway?)

Another good disaster-averting feature of Premiere is the Project Archive feature. This feature automatically saves a backup copy of your project every five minutes or so, allowing you to quickly go back in time to an earlier version of your project. See Chapter 3 for more on adjusting and using the Project Archive feature.

Using the History palette

One of the things I really like about the interface design in Adobe software is the use of floating palettes. Palettes provide quick access to powerful features, yet they're easy to show or hide as needed. One of the more useful palettes is the History palette, shown in Figure 7-10. To open the History palette, choose Window⇨Show History.

Click for menu

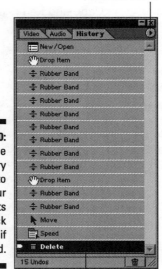

Figure 7-10:
Use the
History
palette to
review your
recent edits
and go back
in time if
needed.

Most recent edit

If you see Hide History in the Window menu, it means the History palette is already open somewhere. If you don't see it, the palette may be hidden behind another window. The History palette lives on the same floating palette window as the Navigator and Info palettes.

The History palette shows you edits that you have made in order. The most recent edit is at the bottom of the list. To move back in history, simply click an item on the palette. When you click an item, that action and all actions that came after it are undone. If you want to clear the history, click the right-facing arrow in the upper-right corner of the History palette and choose Clear History.

Chapter 8

Working with the Timeline

In This Chapter

▶ Finagling your clips into the Timeline

▶ Using markers in the Timeline

▶ Creating storyboards for your projects

Hungry? Me too. Let's visit your favorite restaurant, shall we?

```
[transit to restaurant]
```

Hey, nice place. What is it you like best about this restaurant, anyway? Sure, the location is good, the atmosphere is pleasing, and the staff is cordial, but ultimately it's what goes on back in the kitchen that determines how favorable your dining experience will be.

You can think of the Timeline as Adobe Premiere's "kitchen" — you carefully choose ingredients for your project and then blend them together in the Timeline until you've cooked up a movie worth serving to your audience. How effectively you use the Timeline determines whether your productions are fine video delicacies or half-baked episodes. This chapter shows you how to use Premiere's Timeline for editing your movie projects. Put on your apron and let's get cooking!

For now I'll assume that you're familiar with the basics of moving around in the Timeline. If not, check out the "Timeline Grand Tour" in Chapter 1.

Editing Clips into the Timeline

First things first: Make sure you've used the Monitor window to edit clips and mark the in points and out points of your video (Chapter 7 explains how). Once you've completed that process, you can start editing your marked clips into the Timeline where your project will actually be assembled. The following sections show you how to edit clips into the Timeline and then help you figure out what to do with those clips once they're there.

Although most of my examples assume you're working in the Single-Track Editing workspace, the same basic techniques apply to the A/B Editing workspace as well. (Workspaces are covered in more detail in Chapter 3.) For example, in the Single-Track Editing workspace you mark your in and out points in the Monitor window. In the A/B Editing workspace, you end up double-clicking a clip and marking in and out points in an unlabeled window that (coincidentally) looks exactly like the Monitor.

Inserting clips

You've probably already discovered that a lot of work in Adobe Premiere is performed by simply dragging-and-dropping items onto new locations. And so it is when editing clips into the Timeline. You can drag clips from the Monitor window or the Project window directly into the Timeline. As you can see in Figure 8-1, I am dragging a clip to the Timeline after marking in and out points in the Monitor.

In and out points marked in monitor

Drag from here

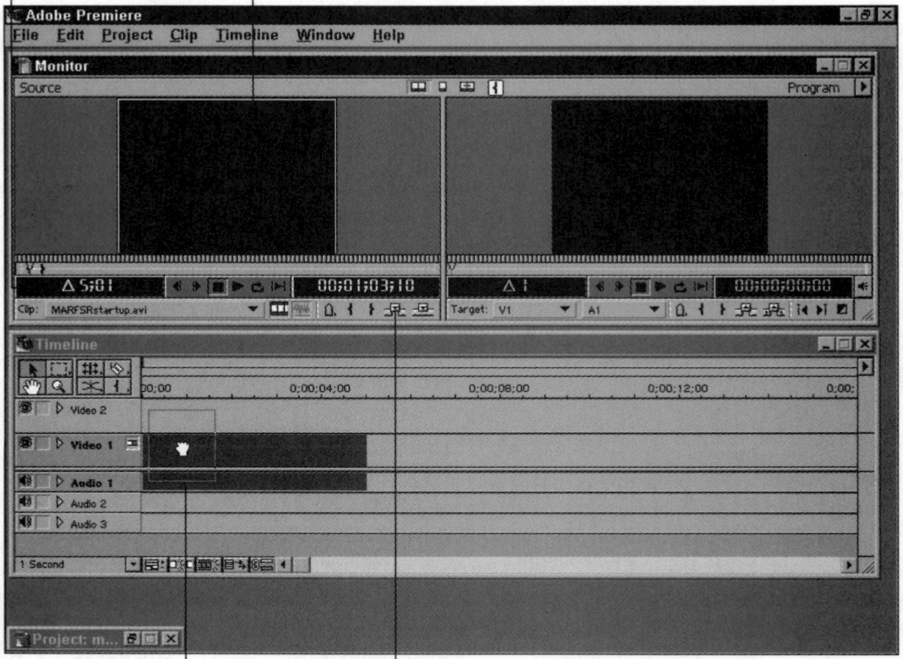

Figure 8-1:
Inserting
clips into
the Timeline
is a simple
drag-and-
drop action.

Drop here   Insert button

If you want, you can also insert a clip by clicking the Insert button (see Figure 8-1) in the Monitor. The clip is inserted into whichever track is currently active (the *active track* in the Timeline is slightly darker than the others) at the current location of the Edit line. This method is not the easiest; I don't normally recommend it unless you really, *really* don't like to drag-and-drop.

Once you've edited a clip into the Timeline, two things change in the appearance of your screen:

✔ **The contents of the Timeline appear in the Monitor.** If you're working in the Single-Track Editing workspace, the Timeline will appear in the right pane of the Monitor as shown in Figure 8-2.

✔ **The clip appears in the Timeline.** Notice that a horizontal line divides the various tracks in the Timeline. Above the line are video tracks, and below the line are audio tracks. In Figure 8-2 you can see that the clip I added to the Timeline has both audio and video (it's camcorder footage, so the audio and video were recorded together).

Timeline preview

Figure 8-2:
The right pane of the Monitor window shows the Timeline.

Audio track

Video track

Inserting a second clip after the first one is easy. Just drag-and-drop it as you did the first clip. But what if you want to insert a clip in between two that are already there? No problem! Just drop the new clip between the existing clips, as shown in Figure 8-3. The right-pointing arrow indicates that subsequent content in the Timeline is shifted automatically to accommodate the inserted clip. (How painless can it get?)

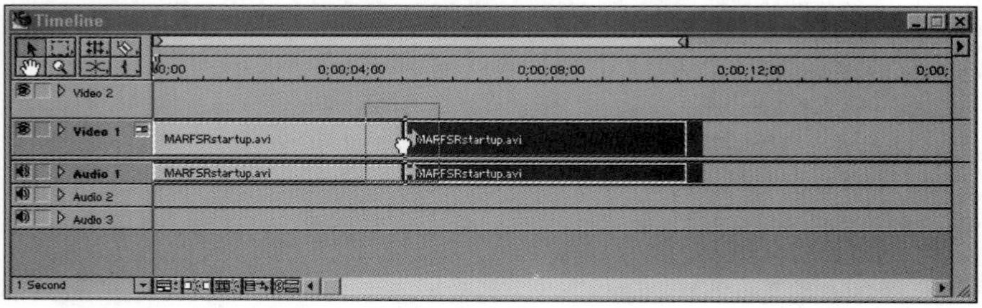

Figure 8-3:
A new clip
is about to
be inserted
between
two existing
clips.
Subsequent
content will
automati-
cally shift
over to
make room.

Controlling Timeline options

If you look closely at the bottom of the Timeline window, you see a row of tiny buttons. The purpose of these obscure tools may not be immediately apparent. The Timeline controls, identified in Figure 8-4, are as follows:

- **Zoom Level menu.** Zoom in or out on your Timeline using the Zoom Level pop-up menu. Zoom in to see more Timeline details, or zoom out to see more of your program at once. Increments in the Zoom Level menu range from 1 Frame up to 8 Minutes.

- **Track Options Dialog Box.** You use this dialog box to manage the tracks in your Timeline. (Tracks are described in greater detail later in this chapter.)

- **Toggle Snap to Edges.** When you insert a clip into the Timeline, you may notice that as you drag the clip towards a spot it seems to "snap" into place. This feature, called Snap to Edges, may make some editing tasks slightly easier — but you may find it a bit of a pain when you're trying to perform precision edits. The Toggle Snap to Edges button turns this feature on and off.

- **Toggle Edge Viewing.** You can move in or out points in the Timeline by clicking-and-dragging on the edges of clips. With Toggle Edge Viewing enabled, the new edge of the clip appears in the Monitor.

✔ **Toggle Shift Tracks Options.** When you perform an edit in one track, the Toggle Shift Tracks Options button lets you decide whether all tracks will shift as a result of your edit, or only the track in which you performed the edit.

✔ **Toggle Sync Mode.** When you edit a clip into the Timeline that contains both audio and video, the audio and video tracks for that clip are normally locked, or *synced* (movie slang for "synchronized"), to each other. Use the Toggle Sync Mode button to turn this locking on and off.

Figure 8-4:
Use these
controls to
set basic
Timeline
options.

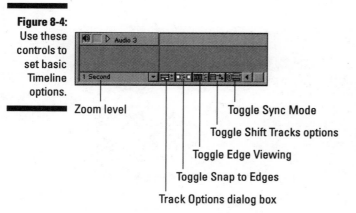

Zoom level

Toggle Sync Mode

Toggle Shift Tracks options

Toggle Edge Viewing

Toggle Snap to Edges

Track Options dialog box

Overlaying clips

In a previous section you saw how to insert clips into the Timeline. You can insert clips into any available track, although normally you will start by editing clips into the first video or audio track. If you just want a series of clips to appear one after the other, you could edit all of them into a single track. But in other cases you may want to overlay clips over one another. Overlaying has a variety of applications, including:

✔ If you want titles to appear over a video image, you overlay a title clip over a video clip.

✔ If you want to briefly show a clip in the middle of another longer clip, you can overlay it and switch back and forth between clips. For example, the long clip might show a figure skater gliding across an ice rink while the short overlaid clip provides a close-up of the skater's face.

✔ Combine multiple clips into one scene in a process called *compositing*. Compositing is often seen on TV when a meteorologist appears to stand in front of a moving weather map. The meteorologist is actually standing in front of a blue or green screen, and the weather map is composited in with special editing equipment.

Compositing is a big subject, and although this section provides the basics on overlay edits, you can read a lot more about compositing in Chapter 9. And speaking of stuff that is covered elsewhere, see Chapter 12 for more on titles.

Until now you've mainly been editing video in the Video 1 track of the Timeline (or audio into Audio 1, if that's all you're working with). But when you perform overlay edits, you will start using other tracks, that is, Video 2, Video 3, Audio 2, and so on. These tracks are called *overlay* or *superimpose* tracks. To perform an overlay edit, just drag-and-drop a clip to an overlay track. The result may look something like Figure 8-5.

Overlaid video

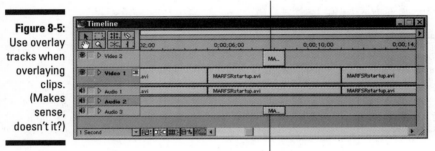

Figure 8-5:
Use overlay tracks when overlaying clips. (Makes sense, doesn't it?)

Overlaid audio

In the Timeline shown in Figure 8-5, I have overlaid a one-second clip over an existing clip by adding the one-second clip to the Video 2 track. The one-second-long clip in Video 2 will replace one second of the video in Video 1. One interesting thing to note is that when you insert a clip into Video 2 (as I have done in Figure 8-5), the audio that goes with that video is placed in track Audio 3. This is because Audio 2 is usually reserved for a primary soundtrack, such as music or narration.

Moving clips

Once you have some clips in the Timeline, it's time to actually do something with them. Probably one of the most common things you'll do is simply move clips around. Moving a clip is so easy that you've probably already figured out how: You simply click-and-drag clips to new locations. You can drag clips back and forth in a track, or drag them to a different track altogether.

If you're trying to move a clip at very small increments, you may get frustrated by the tendency of clips to snap to the nearest adjacent clip edge when you get close. Click the Toggle Snap to Edges button at the bottom of the Timeline to disable the snap-to-edges feature.

Other methods for "moving" a clip exist. Some clip movements can affect the in and out points of clips, adjacent clips, or the duration of the program in the Timeline. Table 8-1 outlines the four basic types of edits.

Table 8-1	Edit Types		
Edit Type	*Description*	*Clip Duration*	*Program Duration*
Roll edit	Drag the edit line between two clips to change the out point of one and the in point of another.	Changed	No change
Ripple edit	Drag the edit line to change the in or out point on one clip without affecting other clips.	Changed	Changed
Slip edit	Drag the clip to change the in and out points of that clip.	No change	No change
Slide edit	Drag a clip to change the in and out points of adjacent clips.	No change	No change

Each of the edits described in Table 8-1 is easy to perform and is described in the following sections. To select one edit type or another, you use the Edit tool on the Timeline toolbar. Click-and-hold on the Edit tool to open up a menu of edit types, as shown in Figure 8-6, and then click one of the tools to choose it.

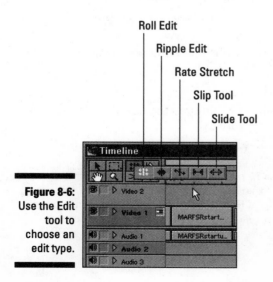

Roll Edit

Ripple Edit

Rate Stretch

Slip Tool

Slide Tool

Figure 8-6:
Use the Edit
tool to
choose an
edit type.

The Rate Stretch tool is described later in this chapter under "Changing the Speed of Clips."

Performing roll edits

No, this isn't the sort of edit you do while attempting aerobatics in a plane. As mentioned in Table 8-1, a *roll edit* adjusts the out point of one clip and the in point of the adjacent clip. The duration of each clip is changed, but the duration of the overall program stays the same. In Figure 8-7, you can see that I have rolled the out point of Clip A and the in point of Clip B.

Figure 8-7:
A roll edit changes the duration of adjacent clips without affecting the overall program.

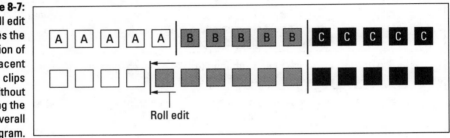

When you perform a roll edit, remember that the amount you "roll" the edit line is limited by the amount of source material still available for the clip that is being lengthened. To perform a roll edit, follow these steps:

1. **Choose the Roll Edit tool in the Timeline toolbar.**

2. **Hover the mouse pointer over the edit point between the clips you want to roll**

   The mouse pointer changes to a vertical line with arrows pointing both left and right.

3. **Click-and-drag the edit point.**

   The Monitor window will change to show you the new in and out points of the rolled clips, as shown in Figure 8-8.

Performing ripple edits

No hip waders required. Honest. A *ripple edit* differs from a roll edit by modifying only one clip instead of two adjacent clips. The result of editing the in or out point on only one clip is that the length of the whole program will change. In Figure 8-9, I have rippled the out point for Clip B, thereby shortening the whole program.

Figure 8-8:
The Monitor
displays
your new
in and out
points as
you perform
a roll edit.

Figure 8-9:
A ripple edit
changes
the duration
of a single
clip and the
overall
program.

A ripple edit relies on extra material in the source clip only if your ripple edit extends the clip. To perform a ripple edit, follow these steps:

1. **Choose the Ripple Edit tool in the Timeline toolbar.**

2. **Hover the mouse pointer over the edit point of the clip you want to ripple.**

   The mouse pointer changes to a bracket facing towards the affected clip as shown in Figure 8-10.

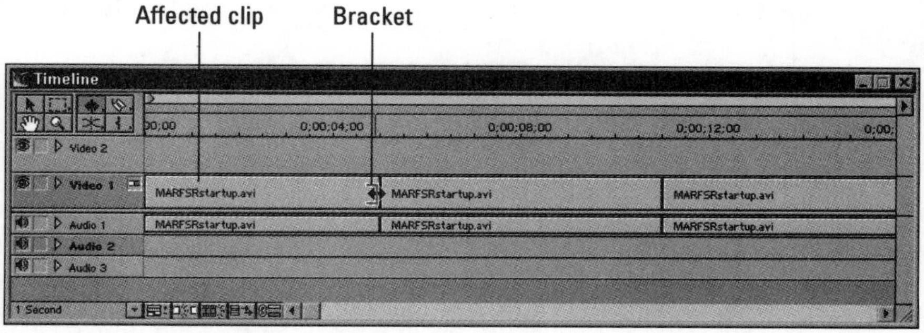

Figure 8-10:
The mouse
pointer
indicates
which clip
will be
rippled.

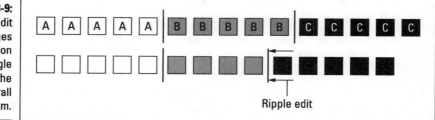

3. **Click-and-drag the edit point.**

The Monitor window changes to show you the new in or out point of the rippled clip.

Performing slip edits

No, this isn't where you put in a banana peel and a pratfall. A *slip edit* simply slips the in and out points of a clip to a different place on the Timeline, without changing the duration between those points. Adjacent clips aren't affected, nor is the duration of the overall program. To perform a slip edit, follow these steps:

1. **Choose the Slip Edit tool in the Timeline toolbar.**

2. **Hover the mouse pointer over the clip you want to slip.**

The mouse pointer changes to a double-headed arrow between two vertical lines.

3. **Click-and-drag the clip.**

As you can see in Figure 8-11, the Monitor window changes so that four frames are shown. The left frame shows the out point of the previous clip, the right frame shows the in point of the following clip, and the two middle frames show the new in and out points of the clip you're slipping.

Performing slide edits

No trombone required. A *slide edit* is, in fact, the opposite of a slip edit. As you slide a clip back and forth, its in and out points remain unchanged, but the in and out points of *adjacent* clips change to accommodate the clip you're sliding. As you can see in Figure 8-12, as Clip B slides to the right, Clip A lengthens, Clip C shortens, and the overall duration of the program is unchanged.

As with roll edits, a slide edit requires that extra source material be available on the clip that is being lengthened. To perform a slide edit, follow these steps:

1. **Choose the Slide Edit tool in the Timeline toolbar.**

2. **Hover the mouse pointer over the clip you want to slide.**

The mouse pointer changes to a double-headed arrow that crosses two vertical lines.

3. **Click-and-drag the clip.**

The Monitor window changes so that four frames are shown similar to the slip edit shown in Figure 8-11. However, during a slide edit the center two frames remain static, the left frame shows the new out point of the previous clip, and the right frame shows the new in point of the following clip.

Deleting blank space with Ripple Delete

It's virtually inevitable that you'll wind up deleting a clip from the Timeline. When you do so, a gaping hole is left in the Timeline where that clip used to be. You could fill in the space by dragging each subsequent item in the Timeline over, but this can be time consuming, and if you've done a lot of advanced edits, you could make a mistake. Another solution might be to find an alternate clip that can be used to fill the vacancy left in the Timeline. If all else fails, you could insert a black matte with the word "Intermission" splashed across it. Then your audience will think you meant to leave the space blank. Yeah, it's so crazy it might just work. . . .

The only problem with an "Intermission" placard is that really good intermission music can be difficult to choose. Better yet, use a ripple edit to automatically delete the blank space left over in the Timeline — and automatically shift all subsequent material over. To do so, simply click the undesired void to select it and then choose Timeline➪Ripple Delete. In Windows, you can also right-click the void and choose Ripple Delete from the menu that appears.

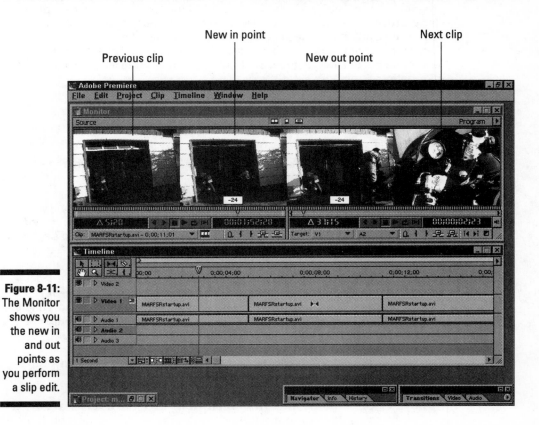

Previous clip

New in point

New out point

Next clip

Figure 8-11: The Monitor shows you the new in and out points as you perform a slip edit.

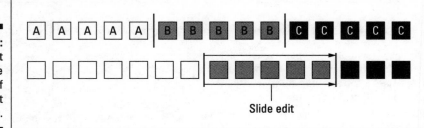

Figure 8-12:
A slide edit changes the duration of adjacent clips.

Slide edit

Replacing frames with three- and four-point edits

Another edit technique exists which I haven't talked about yet. "Replace" is a common editing technique in various computer programs. In word processing programs, for example, you can choose Edit⇨Replace and replace an old text string with a new one. Premiere also allows you to replace material, and you do it using traditional video editing techniques called *three-* and *four-point edits*. Suppose you want to replace some frames in your Timeline with a few new frames from a new source. To do that, you need at least three pieces of information:

- ✔ The in point on the source clip for the new material.
- ✔ The in point for the spot in the Timeline where you want to start replacing material.
- ✔ An out point on either the source clip or Timeline so the length of the replacement is defined.

If you perform an edit using these three bits of information, each one corresponding to an in point or an out point, you perform a *three-point edit*. Premiere automatically figures out where a fourth out point should be, based on the duration given by the one out point you've already defined (either on the Timeline or in the source clip).

 You can, of course, define all four points if you want — thus making it a *four-point edit* — and if the marked durations on the source clip and Timeline don't match, Premiere helps you resolve the difference. (More about that in a minute.)

For the moment, sticking to three points is a good idea. To perform a three-point edit, follow these steps:

1. **Switch the Monitor window to Dual view (click the Dual View button at the top of the Monitor window) so the Program is shown on the right side and the Source is shown on the left.**

Remember, the Source side of the Monitor shows the source clip that you are getting ready to add to the Timeline (but haven't added yet); the Program side of the Monitor shows the actual program that is already assembled in the Timeline.

2. **Drag a clip from the Project window and drop it on the Source side of the Monitor to load the new source clip.**

3. **Mark in points for the source clip and the program using the marker controls at the bottom of each side of the Monitor window.**

4. **Mark an out point on either the source clip or the program.**

   If you have a specific portion of the Timeline that you want to replace, mark the out point on the program. If you have a specific portion of the source clip that you want to edit in, mark the out point on the source.

5. **Click the Overlay button on the source side of the Monitor.**

If you do a four-point edit and the durations don't match, you'll see the Fit Clip dialog box, as shown in Figure 8-13. If you see this dialog box, you have three options:

✔ **Change Speed.** The speed of the source clip is adjusted to fit the marked duration on the Timeline.

✔ **Trim Source.** The out point of the source clip is adjusted so the durations match. This option is only available if the marked source clip is longer than the marked duration in the Timeline.

✔ **Cancel.** Click this if you want to go back and change the in and out points you marked.

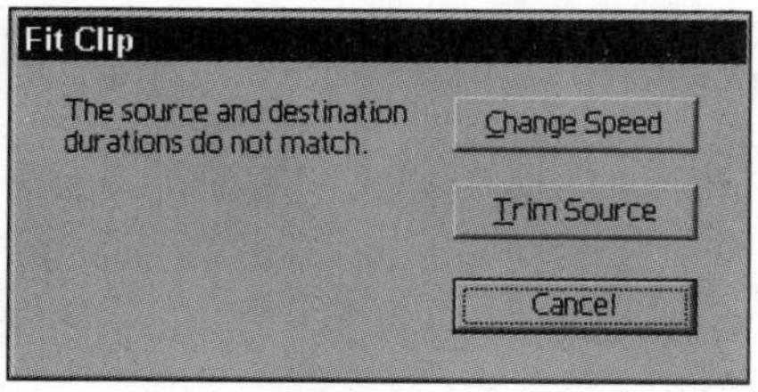

Figure 8-13:
This dialog box appears if the durations don't match during a four-point edit.

Selecting clips

If you've been following along with this chapter from the beginning, you've probably noticed that we've been working with only one clip at a time. You can, however, select and work with multiple clips in the Timeline, portions of clips, portions of multiple clips, multiple portions of clips, select clipped portions of multiple selected clipped clips . . . er, ah, well, you get the idea.

The Timeline's selection tools can be found in the upper-left corner of the Timeline toolbar, as shown in Figure 8-14. The lone arrow is the very basic Selection Tool, and when it's active you select individual clips by (surprise) clicking them. When you click anywhere on a clip, the whole clip is selected. If you click a video track that is locked to an audio track (or vice versa) both portions of the clip are selected. You can tell when a clip is selected because it has a dotted border that moves slowly like a line of marching ants (or, yes, the lights around a movie marquee).

Additional selection tools are available using the button just to the right of the Selection Tool arrow button. Click-and-hold the button to make a menu of buttons appear as shown in Figure 8-14. Selection tools in this menu include

- ✔ **Range Select Tool.** Use this tool to click-and-drag a box around a range of clips you want to select. Even if you only draw the box over a portion of a clip, the entire clip is selected. The Range Select Tool only selects clips in tracks that you draw the box over.

- ✔ **Block Select Tool.** Use this tool to select only the portions of clips that you click-and-drag a box over. The Block Select Tool selects material in all tracks (top to bottom) when you draw a box.

- ✔ **Track Select Tool.** When you click a clip, that clip is selected — along with all subsequent clips in that track. Track contents that precede the clip on which you click will not be selected.

- ✔ **Multitrack Select Tool.** When you click a clip, that clip is selected — along with all subsequent clips in *all* tracks. Program contents that precede the clip on which you click are not selected.

Selection Tool

Range Select Tool

Block Select Tool

Track Select Tool

Multitrack Select Tool

Figure 8-14:
Use these
selection
tools in the
Timeline.

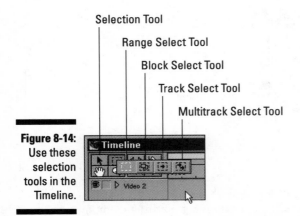

Using virtual clips

You may find that you reuse certain complex sequences on a regular basis. For example, you might create a sequence that is used as an elaborate transition between major scenes. The sequence may contain in points, out points, transitions, audio tracks, and other edits, and you may not want to recreate all the same edits from scratch several times in the same project. Instead, you can quickly copy portions of the Timeline by creating a *virtual clip* — which you can do by following these steps:

1. **Add clips to the Timeline and perform any other edits you want to use in the virtual clip.**

2. **Choose the Block Select Tool in the Timeline and draw a box around the clips that you want to copy.**

   Remember, the Block Select Tool only selects portions of a clip, not the whole clip.

3. **Position the cursor inside the box you just drew.**

   The pointer becomes a double-sided arrow above two small rectangles (see Figure 8-15).

4. **Click-and-drag on the selection and drop it on a new location in the Timeline.**

   A virtual clip, containing all the same content and edits, is created, as shown in Figure 8-15.

Selected block   New virtual clip

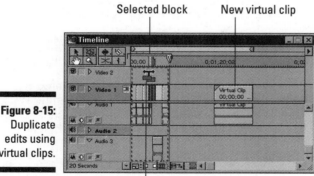

Figure 8-15: Duplicate edits using virtual clips.

Virtual Clip cursor

You may find it easier to select portions of the Timeline if you adjust the zoom level. In Figure 8-15, I am using a 20-second zoom increment so I can see more of the project at once.

Freezing frames

At the risk of getting an old J. Geils Band song stuck in your head, consider the freeze frame. You can actually "freeze" video so that the video stops and a single frame appears on screen. Adobe Premiere allows you to freeze frames of video and keep them on screen. Here's how:

1. **Move the edit line in the Timeline to the frame you want to freeze.**

   You may need to use Frame Forward and Frame Back buttons at the bottom of the Monitor window to find the exact frame that you want to freeze.

   An even easier way to move forward or back one frame at a time is to use the left and right arrow keys on your keyboard. Press the left arrow to move one frame back, and press the right arrow to move forward a frame.

2. **Click the clip to make sure it is selected and choose Clip⇨Set Clip Marker⇨0 (Poster Frame).**

   A small clip marker icon should now appear on the clip in the Timeline.

3. **Choose Clip⇨Video Options⇨Frame Hold.**

   The Frame Hold Options dialog box appears.

4. **Place a check mark next to Hold On and choose "Marker 0" from the menu.**

   Note that you can freeze a clip on the in point or out point as well.

5. **If the frame comes from interlaced video (NTSC or PAL DV video *is* interlaced) place a check mark next to the Deinterlace option.**

   This will prevent flickering when the frame appears on screen.

6. **Click OK to close the dialog box.**

After you have set frame hold options for a clip, you will need to render the work area to preview your change. To do this, choose Timeline⇨Render Work Area. The clip will still play for the original duration that you specified, except that only the poster frame that you chose in Step 2 will appear.

Changing the speed of clips

If you watched much TV in the 1970s you probably remember a series called *The Six Million Dollar Man*. It revolved around a former test pilot named Steve Austin (Lee Majors) who after a horrific plane crash was rebuilt using cybernetic enhancements (we assume that those enhancements cost about $6 million). The cybernetics gave Steve super strength and speed, abilities he used to fight crime and battle the forces of evil. Several times each episode Steve Austin would run somewhere. When they showed him running, they would not show a blur and a cloud of dust, but rather we would see the hero running . . . in slow motion.

Video technology has progressed a great deal since the '70s, but few computer-generated effects would provide the same dramatic effect as slo-mo video and some well-crafted music. Changing the speed of your own clips in Adobe Premiere is simply one of the most effective (yet overlooked) visual effects you can apply to video. You can adjust the speed of clips in the Timeline to create your own fast- or slow-motion effects. To adjust the speed of a clip in the Timeline, follow these steps:

1. **Select a clip in the Timeline for which you want to adjust the playback speed.**

2. **Choose Clip⇨Speed.**

   The Clip Speed dialog box appears as shown in Figure 8-16.

3. **Enter a new percentage in the New Rate field.**

   If you want to slow the clip down, enter a rate that is below 100%. If you want to speed it up, enter a rate above 100%. Leave the New Duration field alone for now.

4. **Click OK.**

   The clip will need to be rendered after the speed has been adjusted.

You may need to experiment a bit with the rate that you choose. In Figure 8-16 I have made a relatively minor speed change because I only want to speed the clip up a small, almost imperceptible amount.

 You can also adjust speed by changing the duration of a clip. This may be useful if you know you have a specific amount of time that the clip must fill. Choose Clip⇨Duration to adjust duration.

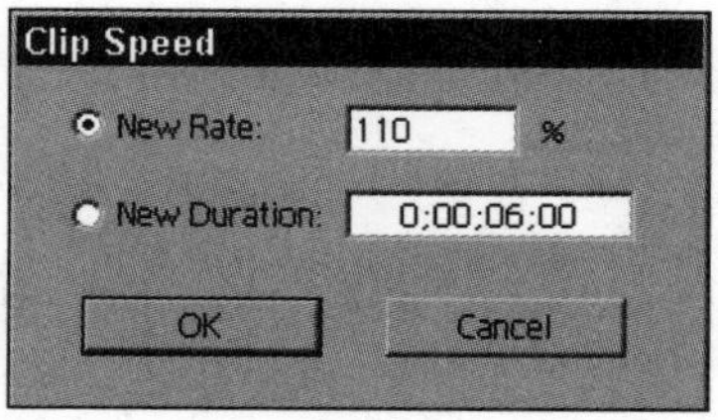

Figure 8-16:
Adjust the
playback
rate of the
clip to
change its
playback
speed.

Clip Speed

◉ New Rate: 110 %

○ New Duration: 0;00;06;00

[OK] [Cancel]

Working with tracks in the Timeline

By now you've probably noticed all those different tracks in the Timeline. There are video tracks, audio tracks, and even transition tracks if you're viewing the Timeline a certain way. Now that you've probably spent a lot of time editing clips into the Timeline, let's take a closer look at those tracks that you've been using.

Adjusting track views

The current appearance of your tracks varies depending upon which workspace you're using. Figure 8-17 shows the default track view in the A/B Editing workspace, as well as the default view in the Single-Track Editing workspace.

One of the reasons I generally prefer the Single-Track Editing workspace is that I can quickly expand the view of single-tracks so they resemble A/B tracks. You do this by clicking the Track Mode button (see Figure 8-17). This button is not available in the A/B Editing workspace.

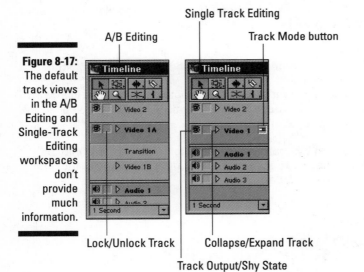

Figure 8-17:
The default track views in the A/B Editing and Single-Track Editing workspaces don't provide much information.

I like to expand the track mode when I am fine-tuning transitions. Other useful buttons found on most tracks include

✔ **Track Output/Shy State.** Click this button to effectively "hide" the track from the project. When an eye (video tracks) or speaker (audio tracks) appears in this button, the track is active in the project.

Slicing and dicing with the Razor tool

In Chapter 7, I compared clips to currency, because a clip is the basic unit of measure in Adobe Premiere. Something you often need to do with currency is change it into smaller denominations. For example, if you want to buy a soft drink from a vending machine, a $20 bill will probably be too large. Likewise, you'll sometimes find that you need to make change (so to speak) with clips in Premiere. Premiere gives you a simple little tool that lets you quickly turn one large clip in the Timeline into many smaller ones. This tool is called the Razor, and is located in the Timeline toolbar as shown here.

The Razor tool comes in handy more often than you might think. For example, suppose you want a clip to freeze in the middle of playback. You can set a poster frame and then choose Clip➪Video Options➪Frame Hold to freeze the clip, but this freezes the entire clip (see the section titled "Freezing Frames" earlier in this chapter). What if you want the clip to play normally up until the point where it reaches the poster frame? The solution is to slice the clip in two at the point where you want to freeze playback. Set your poster frame at the place where you want to freeze the video by placing the Edit line on the desired point and choosing Clip➪Set Clip Marker➪0 (Poster Frame). Then click the Razor tool to select it. When you hover the mouse pointer over a clip, the pointer turns into a razor blade. Hover the mouse pointer directly over the poster frame and click once to slice the clip. Now you'll have two clips instead of just one. Leave the first clip — the one before the poster frame — alone so that it plays normally. On the second clip — the one that comes after the poster frame — adjust the Frame Hold settings so that the clip holds on the poster frame. Now, your video will play normally until it gets to that poster frame, at which time it will freeze.

- ✔ **Lock/Unlock Track.** Click here to place a padlock in the button and lock the track. A locked track cannot be edited. Click it again to unlock it.

- ✔ **Collapse/Expand Track.** Click this arrow to spin it down and expand the view of the track. Many tracks have additional options for controlling effects, keyframes, and transparency. When the audio tracks are expanded, you see a waveform of the audio and you can control the fading of that clip.

Adding and renaming tracks

You can put as many as 99 video tracks and 99 audio tracks into the Adobe Premiere Timeline, though it is difficult to imagine what one might do with that many. When it comes to Timeline tracks, however, it's better to have too many than not enough, however, so I'm certainly not complaining. If you need more tracks in your Timeline than those already present, you can add them by following these steps:

1. **Choose Timeline⇨Track Options.**

   The Track Options dialog box opens as shown in Figure 8-18.

2. **To add a track, click Add.**

   The Add Tracks dialog box appears.

3. **In the Add Tracks dialog box, enter the number of audio and video tracks you want to add.**

   The number of tracks that are still available is listed.

4. **Click OK to close the dialog box.**

You can also delete or rename tracks using the Track Options dialog box. To rename a track, select it from the list in the Track Options dialog box and click Name. In the Name Track dialog box that appears, type a new name for the track and click OK. As you can see in Figure 8-18, I have named my Video 3 track "Copyright" because it will contain a small copyright notice overlaid across the entire project. Other changes include renaming Video 2 "Titles" and Audio 2 "Music track." You can pick whatever names you find helpful.

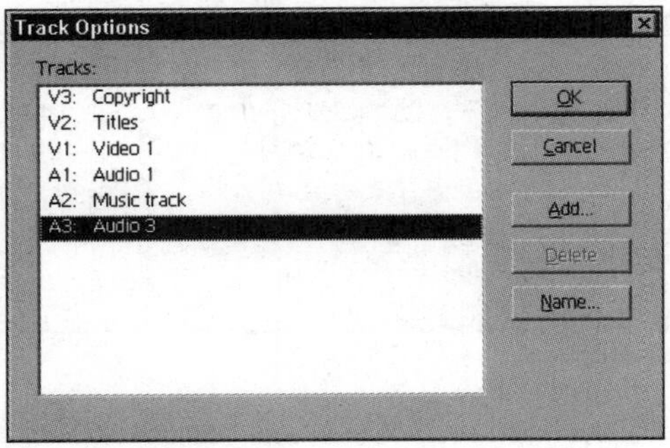

Figure 8-18:
Use the Track Options dialog box to add, delete, and rename tracks.

Track Options

Tracks:

V3: Copyright
V2: Titles
V1: Video 1
A1: Audio 1
A2: Music track
A3: Audio 3

OK
Cancel
Add...
Delete
Name...

Using Markers in the Timeline

Markers can be extremely helpful as you work in the Timeline. You can use markers as reference points for key events, visual indicators as you edit, or cues for events such as Web links or chapter references. Any markers that were added to a source clip before it was added to the Timeline will also appear in the Timeline. Markers that are added only to the Timeline, however, will not be added to the source clips. Timeline markers appear on the Timeline ruler, as shown in Figure 8-19.

For more on using clip markers, see Chapter 7.

Adding markers to the Timeline

Markers can serve various purposes. In Figure 8-19, I have added a Timeline marker to indicate where a specific visual event occurs. I used that marker as a reference when I later edited in some audio that needed to align with that marker. To add a marker to the Timeline:

1. **Move the edit line to the exact location where you want to place a marker. If necessary, use the Frame Jog or Frame Forward/Frame Back buttons in the Monitor to move frame by frame to the correct location.**

2. **Choose Timeline⇨Set Timeline Marker⇨and choose a marker from the menu that appears.**

The marker will now appear on the Timeline ruler. Pretty easy, huh? If you ever want to get rid of a marker, simply choose Timeline⇨Clear Timeline Marker⇨ and sentence one of the listed markers to the electronic ether.

Timeline marker

Marker from source clip

Timeline ruler

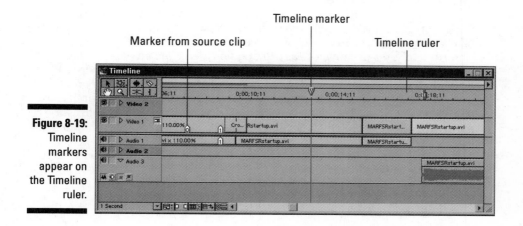

Figure 8-19: Timeline markers appear on the Timeline ruler.

Moving around with markers

Moving around in the Timeline is perhaps my favorite use of Timeline markers. As I'm working through a project I often say to myself, "I will probably want to come back to this point." That's my cue to create a marker. Eventually I have a collection of markers that I can use to quickly jump back and forth in the project. There are several methods for moving around in the Timeline using markers:

- Choose Timeline➪Go to Timeline Marker➪ and then choose a marker.

- On the keyboard, press Command+Shift+Up arrow (Mac) or Ctrl+Shift+Up arrow (Windows) to move to the first marker in the Timeline. Substitute the down arrow to move to the last marker in the Timeline.

- In Windows, right-click the Timeline ruler, choose Go to Timeline Marker➪ and select the marker to which you want to jump.

Creating a Storyboard

As much as I am involved with computer technology, you might be surprised to see how my creative process gets started. When I am brainstorming a new book, I sit down in a comfortable chair — sometimes in a lawn chair out back, sometimes in a waiting area while my kids take Taekwondo lessons — with a tablet of paper and a pen. There's just something about ink on a dead tree that helps me concentrate.

When you start working on a movie project, you may find that you need to take a simpler approach as well when you start brainstorming the movie. Unfortunately, it's usually not easy to doodle video clips on paper unless you're a skilled illustrator — but most of us would agree that Premiere can be a bit, shall we say, *complicated* at times. Fortunately, Premiere does provide an excellent and (most importantly) simple tool to help you plan and brainstorm a project — the *Storyboard*. You can use a Storyboard to conceptualize an entire project, or just a small portion of one. To create a new Storyboard

1. **In Premiere, import or capture the video source clips that will make up the bulk of your project.**

2. **Choose File➪New➪Storyboard.**

   A Storyboard window appears.

3. **Drag a clip from the Project window to the Storyboard.**

   A poster frame for the clip appears, along with the clip's name and duration. A poster frame is simply a representative frame (usually the first frame) of the clip.

Using Timeline markers for fun and profit

Perhaps the greatest revolution in home multimedia entertainment that is happening right now involves DVDs. The Digital Versatile Disc is quickly becoming *the* standard for mass-market video distribution. After a few minutes spent watching a movie on DVD, it's easy to see why so many folks are eager to abandon their rattling old VHS tapes.

One of my favorite DVD features is the ability to quickly jump from scene to scene with the click of a button. No more do we have to wait for a tape to cue forward or back when we want to skip to a specific scene. But when you click that button, how does the DVD player know where the next scene is? Someone who helped prepare that movie for DVD spent some time creating chapter references at key intervals in the program. Premiere lets you create your own chapter references in your projects. Chapter references will not only be useful if you decided to output your movie to DVD but also if you're distributing it online in QuickTime format. The Apple QuickTime Player supports chapter references as well.

To create chapter references in your Timeline, first create markers at the desired locations for the references. Then, double-click a marker. The Marker dialog box appears. Enter a name and/or number for the chapter reference in the Chapter field. Click OK when you're done.

Another excellent use of markers is to create keyframes. Most codecs (those are the compression/decompression schemes used to compress video for export) use keyframes to efficiently compress video. Rather than save 30 individual frames for one second of video, many codecs save two keyframes — one keyframe shows the first frame of that one second of video, and the second keyframe shows the frame at the end. The codec then extrapolates the difference between those two keyframes during playback.

Most codecs automatically set keyframes at specific intervals (once every 30 frames, for example). However, you can specify additional keyframes in certain circumstances. For example, suppose you have a clip that contains a relatively still subject. Then, suddenly, some action explodes onto the scene. If you place a keyframe at the very beginning of the action, most codecs will be able to compress the clip more efficiently. To do so, first set a Timeline marker at the desired frame. Later, when you export the movie, click Settings in the Export Movie dialog box, click Next until you see the Keyframe and Rendering settings, and place a check mark next to the Add Keyframes at Markers option. Note that this option will only be available if the export codec supports keyframes.

4. **Continue to drag clips into the Storyboard. Click-and-drag clips to new locations to change the order in which they appear.**

Eventually, what you have on-screen starts to look like an illustrated storyline. Then you know you have a Storyboard that provides a basic concept of how your project will come together, similar to Figure 8-20.

5. **To save the Storyboard, choose File⇨Save.**

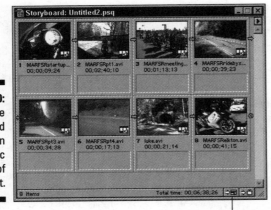

Automate to Timeline

At this point, you aren't worried about details like audio, in and out points, transitions, and the like. You can use the Storyboard merely as a visual planning aid — or even to form the foundation of a new project. Just click the Automate to Timeline button at the bottom of the Storyboard to automatically edit the clips into a Timeline. (Of course, you'll have to edit the details, but this is one good way to get started.)

Chapter 9

The Fine Art of Transitioning and Compositing

• •

In This Chapter

▶ Getting from one scene to another via transitions

▶ Seeing through the use of transparency

• •

Movie editing per se is nothing special, really; anyone with two VCRs and a cable can dub desirable bits of video from one tape to another. But fine-tuning your edits frame by frame, applying your own soundtrack, and adding special effects — now, *that* is special. Adobe Premiere gives you the capability to do all that and more. If you've followed along in previous chapters — capturing video onto your computer's hard drive, sorting through clips, picking out the parts you want to use, and assembling those clips in the Timeline — then you're ready for the next step in your video editing adventure.

One of the first things you'll probably want to do to dress up your project is to add some fancy transitions between scenes. Next, you might want to add some graphics to your video, or possibly even superimpose one clip on top of another. This chapter shows you how to apply these common types of edits to your projects.

Using Transitions in the Timeline

One of the trickiest aspects of movie editing (for me, anyway) is making clean transitions between clips. Sometimes the best transition is a simple, straight cut from one clip to the next. Other times you need a fancy transition — say, one that rotates the image from the old clip in an ever decreasing radius, like a vortex spinning, spinning towards the center until, a tiny black dot at the center of the screen, it disappears entirely. Most of your transitions probably fall somewhere in between.

You may find it easier to work in the A/B Editing workspace when working with transitions, because it provides a separate transition track for the Video 1 track. To open this workspace, choose Window⇨Workspace⇨A/B Editing. Alternatively, from the Single-Track Editing workspace, you can click the Track Mode button on the Video 1 track to split that track into two halves plus a transition track.

Using the Transitions palette

If you're new to video, you may be surprised by how many different transitions are possible between two clips. Some simple video editing programs only do two kinds of transitions — either straight cut or a fade from one clip to the next. But Adobe Premiere offers so many options that it can be difficult to choose. Premiere 6.5 comes with 75 transitions already built in, and you can add even more by using third-party plug-ins.

Premiere stores all its transitions in the Transitions palette (shown in Figure 9-1), which you can view by choosing Window⇨Show Transitions. Transitions are divvied up into 11 folders, and you can create new folders by clicking the New Folder button. (This capability can be handy if you want to create a "Favorites" folder and move your favorite transitions to that single new folder.)

Click to expand tree.

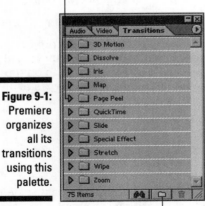

Figure 9-1: Premiere organizes all its transitions using this palette.

New folder

Adding a transition to your project

The software designers at Adobe must really like drag-and-drop, because as with so many other editing actions in Premiere drag-and-drop is the best way to apply a transition. Simply choose a transition and drag it directly from the Transitions palette to the desired spot on the Timeline. In Figure 9-2, you can see what this looks like when using a single-track Timeline. In Figure 9-3, you can see how it looks in a split-track Timeline.

Before you can apply a transition between clips, each clip must have some unused frames for use in the original source clip; if a transition will last one second, the preceding clip must have at least one half-second of trailing material, and the following clip must have one half-second of leading material. Keep this in mind when you set the in and out points as you edit clips into the Timeline.

Drop here.   Drag transition from here.

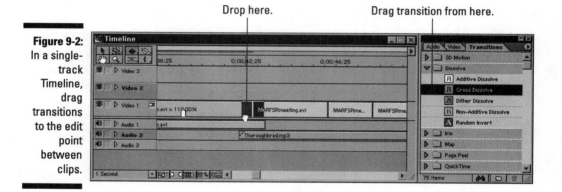

Figure 9-2:
In a single-
track
Timeline,
drag
transitions
to the edit
point
between
clips.

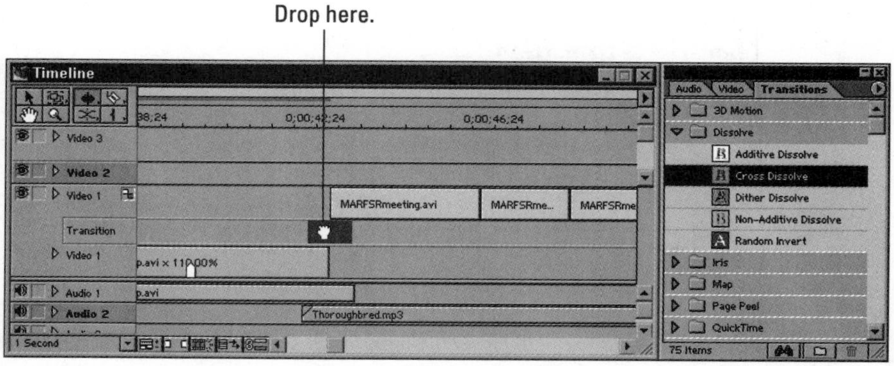

Drop here.

Figure 9-3:
In a split-
track
Timeline,
drag
transitions
to the
Transition
track.

When you add a transition to the Timeline, the in and out points of adjacent clips are automatically extended to facilitate the transition. This change won't be immediately apparent in a single-track Timeline, but you'll see it in a split-track Timeline. Consider Figure 9-4 and compare it to Figure 9-3. Note that in Figure 9-3, one clip ended abruptly as the next one began. But now that the transition has been added, you can see in Figure 9-4 that the same clips now appear to overlap.

Also notice that when you apply a transition, a red line appears at the top of the Timeline under the work area bar. The red line means that the transition (and possibly the adjacent clips) need to be *rendered* — created as a preview file on the hard drive — before you can preview them. When a portion of the Timeline is rendered, a green line appears in place of the red. (Rendering is covered later, in the section called "Previewing transitions.")

Red here means rendering is required.

Work area bar   Overlap

Figure 9-4:
With a
transition in
place, clips
now appear
to overlap
each other
in the
Timeline.

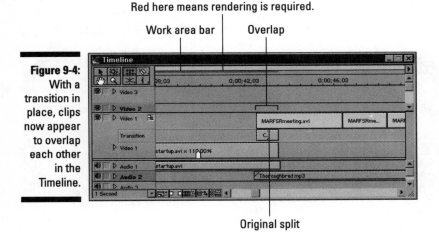

Original split

Choosing a transition

Premiere 6.5 comes with 75 transitions built in, and you can install even more transitions from third-party software vendors. With so many transitions available, it can be difficult to choose just the right one. Frankly, I end up using the Cross Dissolve transition about 90 percent of the time, if not more. But there are a lot of other cool transitions to choose from. I suggest that you spend some time playing around, applying each one to get a feel for what each transition can do.

You can preview any transition in the Transitions palette by double-clicking it. A window appears showing a basic representation of what that transition does.

The transitions that come with Premiere 6.5 occupy 11 basic categories:

- **3D Motion.** This is a group of 11 transitions that apply various kinds of motion to one clip as it disappears to reveal the next one. Most of the transitions here involve some sort of thing where the exiting clip swings like a door or spins in a spiral.

- **Dissolve.** My favorite transition, the Cross Dissolve, can be found here. It's my favorite not because it is fancy but because it is not. The Cross Dissolve is subtle; one clip blends smoothly into the next. It's softer than a straight cut, and if I want the program to be about what's in the clips and not about a fancy transition, this is the one I choose. Cross Dissolve is just one of five dissolve transitions available with Premiere.

- **Iris.** The seven Iris transitions are all variations on a theme of one clip starting as a point in the middle and growing to fill the screen. Different Iris patterns include circles, squares, stars, diamonds (I know, it's starting to sound like a breakfast cereal!), and more.

- **Map.** The Channel Map and Luminance Map remap colors to create a transition.

- **Page Peel.** The five Page Peel transitions simulate the turning of a page. Use these to transition from your "Once upon a time . . ." screen to the story!

- **QuickTime.** The QuickTime Transition is actually a collection of transitions from which you can choose. When you drop this transition on the Timeline, you get a chance to choose the style of the transition that you want to use. Most QuickTime transitions resemble other Premiere transitions, such as dissolves and wipes.

- **Slide.** This descriptively named group contains 12 transitions, all variations on sliding a clip one way or the other. These subtle transitions are also favorites of mine.

- **Special Effect.** This group contains six advanced and varied transitions. They apply various combinations of color masks and distortions during transitions.

- **Stretch.** The five stretch transitions are pretty cool, even though technically some of them squeeze rather than stretch the clip image during transition.

- **Wipe.** Wipes are a general style of transition that has been around for a while. In a wipe, one clip appears from the edge of the screen and appears to wipe over the previous clip like a squeegee. Premiere includes no less than 17 different wipe transitions.

- **Zoom.** There are four zoom transitions, and as you would imagine they all use a simulated zoom effect during transition.

Controlling transitions

More often than not, you'll probably just plop a transition down on the Timeline and use it as it sits. Sometimes, however, you may want to fine-tune the transition. First of all, you can perform roll and ripple edits on adjacent clips by dragging a transition. When you perform a roll edit, the Monitor window shows you the in and out points on the adjacent clips, as shown in Figure 9-5.

Out point of preceding clip

In point of following clip

Roll edit

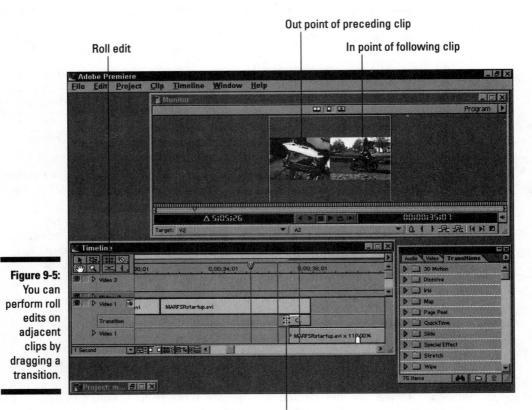

Figure 9-5:
You can
perform roll
edits on
adjacent
clips by
dragging a
transition.

Drag transition

If you don't remember what roll and ripple edits do, see Chapter 8 for complete descriptions of the different kinds of edits.

You can also modify the duration of a clip. The default duration for most clips is one second, but you can make the transition shorter or longer if you want (and if there is enough extra material in the source clips). To adjust the duration of a transition, click on the transition you plopped down on the

Timeline and choose Clip⇨Duration. The Clip Duration dialog box appears as shown in Figure 9-6. Enter the desired duration (in timecode format) for the transition.

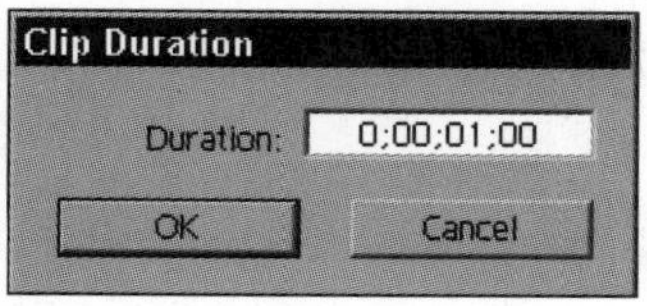

Figure 9-6:
The default
duration
for most
transitions
is one
second.

Clip Duration
Duration: `0:00:01;00`
OK   Cancel

Finally, most transitions also have specific attributes you can adjust — in no more than two steps:

1. **Double-click a transition that you have added to the Timeline.**

   A dialog box similar to the one shown in Figure 9-7 appears. The *A* monitor represents the outgoing clip; the *B* monitor represents the incoming clip.

2. **To view the actual source clips instead of the A and B simulations, place a check mark next to "Show Actual Sources."**

Remember, 75 different transitions come with Premiere, all with different settings to adjust, so your dialog box may not look like Figure 9-7 (unless you just happen to be using the Tumble Away transition). Here are some shoot-from-the-hip suggestions for adjustments you can often make:

- To adjust the start and end points for the transition's action, try using the sliders under the monitor windows.

- Many transitions can have a border around the action. Use the border thickness slider to change how thick the border is; click the color swatch to open the Color Picker and choose a new color.

- The sequence of your transition can be adjusted by clicking the blue arrow button. Using this control, you can make the transition run from Clip B to Clip A, even though B appears after A on the Timeline.

- Reverse the direction of the transition by clicking the F or R button.

- For directionally oriented transitions, change the path of travel by using the directional arrows.

- You can sometimes smooth the appearance of a clip by clicking the anti-alias button.

Again, each transition is different. Play around a bit to find the transitions and combinations of settings that work best for you!

When you are choosing a color in the Color Picker, watch out for a yellow triangle with an exclamation point in the upper-right corner of the window. If you see the warning icon, it means that the color you chose won't appear properly on video equipment in your area (NTSC or PAL). In that case, your best option is to choose a different color.

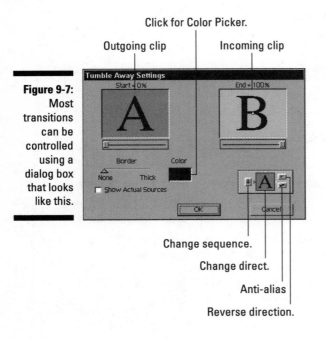

Click for Color Picker.

Outgoing clip

Incoming clip

Figure 9-7: Most transitions can be controlled using a dialog box that looks like this.

Change sequence.

Change direct.

Anti-alias

Reverse direction.

Using a default transition

Premiere knows that a lot of people are like me and have one type of transition that they use most of the time. It just so happens that my favorite transition — the Cross Dissolve — is the default transition in Premiere. (Sorry — it's just so useful I can't resist it.) The default transition is especially handy if you want to quickly apply a transition without having to open the Transitions palette. The default transition can be used in several ways:

✔ You can move the edit line in the Timeline to the place where you want to apply the default transition, as shown in Figure 9-8, and click the Add Default Transition button in the Monitor.

✔ In a split-track Timeline, you can hold down Ctrl+Alt+Shift (Windows) or Command-Option-Shift (Mac) and click the Transition track on which you want the transition to appear.

✔ In the Project window, you can select all the clips you want to edit into the Timeline, and then choose Project➪Automate to Timeline. Place a check mark next to the "Use Default Transition" option. (You can also click the Automate to Timeline button at the bottom of a Storyboard window.)

See Chapter 8 for more on creating and using storyboards.

You can change the default transition if you want. To set a new default transition, first open the Transitions palette (Window➪Show Transitions) and click the transition you want to use to select it. Click the Transitions palette menu (it's the little right-pointing arrow in the upper-right corner of the palette; see Figure 9-9) and choose Set Selected as Default. In the Default Effect dialog box that appears, set a default duration and alignment, if applicable.

Position edit line.

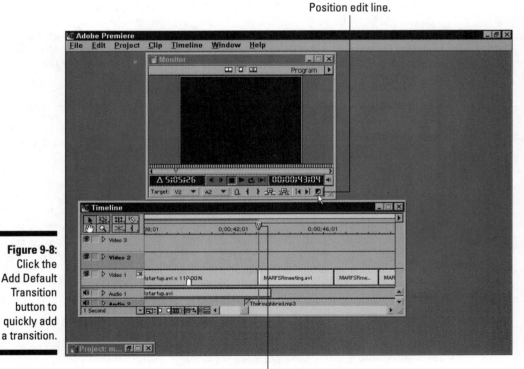

Figure 9-8: Click the Add Default Transition button to quickly add a transition.

Add Default Transition

Click to open menu.

Figure 9-9:
Use the palette menu to set a new default transition.

Previewing transitions

Transitions add a great deal of complexity to a video image; for this reason, a transition must be rendered before you can preview it. When you place a transition on the Timeline, a red bar appears above it on the Timeline, as shown back in Figure 9-4. If you try to preview the transition without rendering it, the transition's effect simply won't appear. There are two ways to render the transition so that you can preview it:

- In Windows, right-click in the work-area bar and choose Render Work Area from the menu that appears.
- On a Macintosh or in Windows, choose Timeline⇨Render Work Area.

One thing to note is that when you choose to render the work area, Premiere renders the *whole* work area. A lot of your Timeline probably doesn't need to be rendered, but any unrendered areas are rendered when you choose this command. If all you need to render in the work area is a single transition, the process takes mere seconds. If long clips with effects or speed changes need to be rendered, you could be waiting a few minutes. In that case, a progress bar appears on-screen to tell you how many frames must be rendered — and approximately how long it will take.

Using Transparency

Over the years, we have come to expect sophisticated illusions in our entertainment — starships flying into a space battle, lovers standing on the bow of a long-gone ocean liner, or a weatherman standing in front of a moving weather-satellite graphic — and if you ever wanted to create some of your own, now you can: Adobe Premiere is fully capable of creating such effects.

One of the great spells you can cast in the magic of moviemaking involves *compositing*. When you composite clips, you combine portions of two or more clips to make a video image that would otherwise be difficult or impossible to capture. Consider a movie where an actor appears to be hanging by his fingertips from the fiftieth floor of a skyscraper as cars move like ants on the streets far below. Did the producers risk the actor's life and force him to hang from a tall building? Not likely — think of the insurance costs! — they probably shot him hanging from a prop in a studio and then superimposed that image over a shot taken from an actual skyscraper.

Fundamental to the process of compositing is the careful layering of images. Using Premiere, you can superimpose up to 99 separate video tracks upon one another. Each track contains part of the final image; by making parts of each track either opaque or transparent, you can create a convincing illusion of three-dimensional space.

See Chapter 8 for more on creating new tracks and adjusting their view.

Adjusting the opacity of a clip

Video clips in Premiere can vary between transparent and opaque. One of the most basic superimposition effects is to make a clip less opaque — that is, more transparent. The more transparent clip becomes a ghostlike image superimposed over the more opaque image behind it. You can change the opacity of an entire clip, or change it gradually throughout a clip. To adjust the opacity of a clip, follow these steps:

1. **Add a clip to the Video 1 track in the Timeline.**

   Clips in the Video 1 track should not be made transparent, so you might think of Video 1 as the background layer. When you layer additional clips over it and make them transparent, the background clip on Video 1 should show through.

2. **Add a clip to a superimpose track in the Timeline**

   Video 2 and any higher-numbered tracks are all considered *superimpose tracks* because they are the ones you use to superimpose images over a primary or background image. You can think of the video tracks in the Timeline as layers on top of each other. If you superimposed 99 tracks (the maximum number of tracks allowed by Premiere) on top of each other, Track 99 would be the very top layer and opaque areas of that track would cover all other tracks.

   Once you have added a clip to a superimpose track, the superimposed clip should appear directly above the background clip in Video 1, as shown in Figure 9-10.

3. **Select the clip that you want to make more transparent.**

4. **Click the arrow to expand the track view, as shown in Figure 9-10.**

5. **Click the Display Opacity Rubberbands button to display the red opacity rubberband under the clip.**

6. **Click and drag on the opacity rubber band to adjust opacity throughout the clip.**

   As you drag the rubberband down, the clip becomes more transparent. As you drag it up, it becomes more opaque.

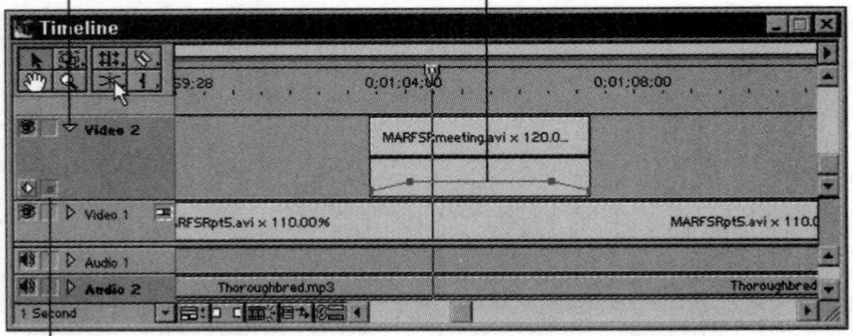

Expand track.   Click to adjust.

Figure 9-10:
Use the
opacity
rubber band
to adjust
opacity
throughout
a clip.

Display Opacity Rubberbands.

As with transitions, adjustments to a clip's opacity cannot be previewed until that clip is rendered. Choose Timeline⇨Render Work Area to render the clip.

Using keys

In the previous section you adjusted the opacity of a clip to make the entire image transparent or semi-transparent. But what if you only want parts of the image to become transparent while other parts of the image remain fully opaque?

You've probably heard of a video technique called *bluescreening,* often used in special-effects shots in movies, or during the evening news when a meteorologist must appear in front of a moving weather map. In actuality, the announcer is standing in front of a blue screen — Why clash? Because you're not supposed to see that color.

Here's how the blue screen becomes a weather map: Video-editing software uses a *key* — a setting that recognizes the special shade of blue and defines it as transparent. Because the wall behind the announcer is the only thing painted that shade of blue, it "disappears." In effect, the image of the meteorologist has been placed on a virtual "glass slide" and superimposed electronically over the image of the weather map. Pretty slick, eh?

Of course, if the meteorologist happens to wear a tie or blouse that matches the "transparent" color, you could see chunks of the weather map "right through" the person. (Oops . . .) That's why this section of the book shows you how to use different kinds of keys to define transparent areas in your video image.

Understanding the key types

Although the example just given — a key that recognizes a blue screen behind a meteorologist — is extremely common, it isn't the only kind of key available to you in Premiere. In fact, Premiere provides 14 different kinds of keys for you to use:

- **Chroma:** This key enables you to key out a specific color or range of similar colors. With some fine-tuning you can use this key with almost any clip. In Figure 9-11, I have applied a chroma key to the clip on the left to create the *superimpose* effect shown on the right.

  As you can see in the figure, I've made everything *but* the banner text and logo transparent. When I place this clip on top of another clip, the image on the bottom clip "shows through" the transparent sections of the top clip.

- **RGB Difference:** This key is similar to the chroma key, but with fewer options. This key works best when the background and subject contrast strongly.

- **Luminance:** Luminance is just a fancy word for color, and this key eliminates darker colors from an image.

- **Alpha Channel:** Use this key on images that already have an alpha channel in them. As you know, most computer images are made up of blocks of color. Some image formats allow you to define no color at all for some blocks, meaning that some portions of the image are empty (as opposed to containing a filler color such as white). This transparency is defined using an *alpha channel*. In Premiere, you'll often encounter alpha channels when you import Photoshop documents (.PSD) that have transparent areas. Without applying this mask, the transparent area of the image will be rendered as white in the video image.

- **Black Alpha Matte:** This matte keys out the alpha channel and black background layers.

- **White Alpha Matte:** This matte keys out the alpha channel and white background layers.

- **Image Matte:** This key uses a second still image to create transparency. When you use this key, you choose an image (such as a flower) to provide the basic shape for the key.

✔ **Difference Matte:** This matte enables you to key out the areas of two images that match each other.

✔ **Blue Screen:** Use this key when you have shot video with the subject in front of a blue screen. The blue screen must be well lit and brilliant for this key to be effective. Shadows cast by the subject onto the screen will cause this key to be less effective.

✔ **Green Screen:** This key works just like the Blue Screen except it uses (surprise) green instead of blue.

✔ **Multiply:** With this key, transparency is based on bright areas on the video track underneath the superimpose track.

✔ **Screen:** With this key, the transparency is based on dark areas on the video track underneath the superimpose track.

✔ **Track Matte:** Use this matte with a black and white image that moves across the screen. Transparency moves with the image.

✔ **Non-Red:** This key works like the Blue Screen and Green Screen mattes, but it keys out both blue and green screens.

Figure 9-11:
Super-
impose
effects like
this one can
be created
with the
chroma key.

Applying a key

Applying a key to a clip is pretty easy. A key allows portions of one image to be transparent when it is superimposed over another image. Remember, you can only apply a key to a clip in a superimpose track — that is, Video 2 or higher. To apply a key, follow these steps:

1. **Click a clip in a superimpose track to select it.**

2. **Choose Clip⇨Video Options⇨Transparency.**

   The Transparency Settings dialog box appears, as shown in Figure 9-12.

3. **Choose a key from the Key type menu.**

   If the key uses color information, you may need to choose a base color for transparency.

4. **Move the mouse pointer over the image in the Color box, if it is available.**

   The cursor should turn into an eyedropper, as shown in Figure 9-12.

5. **If the key uses a second image as a matte, click Choose; when the Look In (Windows) or Finder (Macintosh) window appears, use it to choose the file on your hard drive that contains the matte image.**

6. **Adjust any other settings that may be available.**

   Each key is different, so experiment a bit with the settings to achieve various effects.

7. **Click OK to close the dialog box. You will need to render the Timeline (Timeline⇨Render Work Area) to preview your change.**

Choose matte.

Choose a key.

Pick color.

Preview effect.

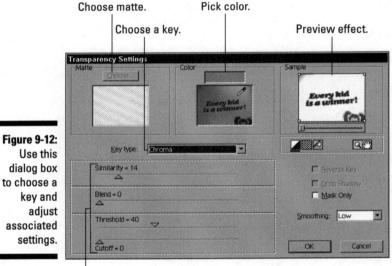

Figure 9-12:
Use this
dialog box
to choose a
key and
adjust
associated
settings.

Adjust settings.

Creating a matte

Some of the keys available in Premiere use matte images to define transparent areas. You can create your own mattes by using a graphics program such as Adobe Photoshop (which comes with Adobe Premiere), and you can create some mattes within Premiere itself. You can create mattes for a variety of purposes:

✔ A solid, brightly colored matte can help you key transparency on another clip. To create a matte of a solid color, choose File⇨New⇨Color Matte. Choose a color for the matte from the Color Picker. If you see a warning that the picture is out of the color gamut for your video format ("Whaddaya *mean* I can't use fluorescent puce there?"), choose another color. Then, place this matte on a track that is under the clip to which you're trying to apply a key. The brightly colored matte will show through to help you identify transparent areas and adjust as necessary. When you've made all the necessary adjustments, just delete the color matte.

✔ To mask out specific areas of an image, create a "garbage" matte and crop out the undesired object. To do this, first create a color matte (this will be your "garbage" matte) or import a background image. Next, select the image that has an object you want to crop out and add it to a superimpose track above the color matte or background image. Select the superimposed clip and choose Clip⇨Video Options⇨Transparency. The Transparency Settings dialog box appears. In the Sample window, click-and-drag the handles on the corners of the image to crop out unwanted portions of the image, as shown in Figure 9-13. The garbage matte or background image in the underlying track should show through. Click OK when you are done.

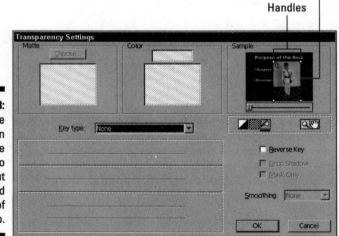

Figure 9-13: Drag the handles in the Sample window to crop out unwanted portions of a clip.

Creating a split-screen effect

Here's another really cool trick you can perform in Adobe Premiere. You can create split-screen effects using selective transparency in a clip. You don't actually use a key to create a split-screen effect, but you do use the

Transparency Settings dialog box. Place a clip in a superimpose track, select that clip, and then choose Clip⇨Video Options⇨Transparency. Choose None for the Key type and then drag the corner handles in the preview window, as shown in Figure 9-14. (For the sake of clarity, the underlying clip is not shown in the figure.) As you can see in the figure, I am creating a basic split-screen effect, though you can also create small squares that float in the middle of the video image. This is very similar to the garbage matte concept shown in Figure 9-13, except in this case I used two video images.

Drag handles.

Figure 9-14: Use the Transparency Settings dialog box to create a split-screen effect.

Once rendered, your split-screen effect can be previewed in the Timeline. You may need to play around a bit to get the alignments right. Figure 9-15 shows the results of the split-screen effect I created in Figure 9-14.

Figure 9-15: Split-screen effects are easy to create in Premiere!

Chapter 10

Affecting Effects in Your Movies

• •

In This Chapter

▶ Having (and making) a great effect

▶ Fixing flaws in video

▶ Animating your clips

▶ Checking over your effects arsenal

• •

Personal computers capable of editing video have been widely available for several years now, and in the last year or so they've been downright cheap. This — combined with continuing price drops on DV camcorders — has led to an explosion in the number of video-editing programs available. From mild to wild, entry-level to professional, there is a video editor for every need and budget.

Not all video-editing programs are created equal, however. Many editors offer special effects you can apply to your video clips, but few offer the quality and variety available with Adobe Premiere — 79 professional-grade effects. You can add even more from third-party vendors.

Effects can help you clean up your video or add special touches that amaze and astound your audience. One of the really cool things about effects is that you can add effects to (or and remove effects from) any clip you want. Effects do not permanently change your clips, so if you aren't happy with a result you can simply delete that effect. Although this book isn't the place to cover each of Premiere's effects in detail, this chapter does show you the basics of using effects — including the brass-tacks specifics of using several common effects.

Understanding Effects

Adobe Premiere comes with 79 effects built right in. Some of these effects may not seem immediately useful, but you may be surprised in a future project when what seems like the most obscure effect comes in handy. You can get a look at Premiere's effects by choosing Window⇨Show Video Effects. They're organized in 14 categories:

- **Adjust:** These seven effects let you tweak levels of color and light. They can be useful for fixing color- and light-related problems in your video clips.

- **Blur:** These eight effects allow you to soften the outlines of things, simulate disorientation, or suggest speed by "unfocusing" parts of the video image.

- **Channel:** This category includes two effects. The Invert effect inverts colors in a clip. The Blend effect enables you to blend the colors of superimposed clips.

- **Distort:** This folder contains 12 effects that bend, twist, or exaggerate the shape and view of your video.

- **Image Control:** These eight effects change the way color is viewed in your clips. They can remove a color (or range of colors) from a clip, convert a color image to black and white, or adjust the overall tint of the image (useful if, for example, you want to transform an ordinary outdoor scene into an alien landscape).

- **Perspective:** These four effects add a three-dimensional feel to your clips — for example, when you bevel the edges of the video image or create shadows.

- **Pixelate:** These three effects modify the pixels that make up your video image to create some unusual visual coloration and appearances. (Textures, anyone?)

- **QuickTime:** The included QuickTime effects are, for the most part, similar to other effects available with Premiere.

- **Render:** The three render effects allow you to simulate various properties of real light. One of the effects simulates lens flares — momentary bright circles that often occur in video footage when the sun reflects or glares on the lens. Although you probably work hard to avoid *real* lens flares when you shoot video, well-placed *simulated* lens flares can have a dramatic effect, especially if you are depicting a sunrise or sunset. The Lightning effect is especially cool because you can create realistic lightning on-screen.

- **Sharpen:** These three effects perform a variety of sharpening enhancements to an image. Use these effects to sharpen images that appear too soft.

- **Stylize:** These 12 effects create a variety of image modifications. With stylize effects you can simulate video noise, create clip mosaics, add texturized or windswept appearances to the image, and more.

- **Time:** The Echo effect creates visual echoes (or double-image) of a picture. The Posterize Time effect modifies the apparent frame rate of a clip. Use this effect to make it look like you dropped frames during capture or output even if you really didn't.

✔ **Transform:** These 11 effects transform the view of your clip in a variety of ways. The image can be rotated in three dimensions, you can simulate a panning effect, or you can simulate a vertical-hold problem on a TV (you can have a lot of fun with this one; just imagine your friends banging on their TVs trying to figure out why the vertical hold is messed up).

✔ **Video:** These three effects help correct video problems or prepare video for output to tape. You can apply the Broadcast Colors effect to clips when you want to filter out colors that aren't broadcast-legal, or use the Field Interpolate effect to replace missing fields knocked off the screen by interlacing. If you have a clip with many thin lines, the lines may flicker when viewed on a regular TV. Use the Reduce Interlace Flicker effect to soften the image and reduce the flickering problem.

Applying effects

To apply an effect to a clip, you simply drag the effect from the Video Effects palette to a clip. (Choose Window⇨Show Video Effects to open this palette.) You can adjust attributes of an effect using the Effect Controls palette. To reveal this palette, click the clip in the Timeline to select it and choose Window⇨Show Effect Controls. The Effect Controls palette will appear as shown in Figure 10-1. Key features of the Effect Controls palette include:

✔ Each effect applied to a clip will have a separate listing. Click the arrow to expand the view of options for each effect.

✔ To disable an effect, click to remove the tiny *f* next to the effect's title, as shown in Figure 10-1.

✔ To enable keyframing so that the effect can be changed over time, click the Enable Keyframing box, as shown in Figure 10-1.

Effects must be rendered (that is the process where a preview file is generated) before you can preview them in the Monitor. To render an effect, choose Timeline⇨Render Work Area.

Using keyframes

Effects can have a variety of, er, *effects* on clips in Premiere. Video clips can be blurred, recolored, distorted, and more. You can apply an effect as is to an entire clip, or you can set the effect up so it changes over time. To do the latter, however, Premiere needs a way to determine exactly how and when to make such changes. For this purpose the program uses reference points called *keyframes*. If you want an effect to change over time, you use keyframes to specify when those changes occur. Premiere automatically extrapolates how the effect should progress from one keyframe to the next.

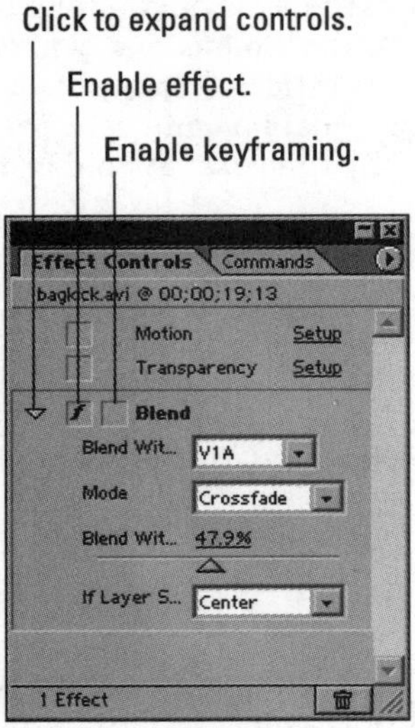

Click to expand controls.

Enable effect.

Enable keyframing.

Figure 10-1:
Control your
effects
using the
Effect
Controls
palette.

Before you apply effects and work with keyframes, you should be familiar with working in the Timeline. Of course, you should also have some clips in the Timeline that you can apply affects to (but you already knew that). See Chapter 8 for more on editing clips in the Timeline.

Once you have applied an effect to a clip, you can adjust that effect using keyframes. To set keyframes, follow these steps:

1. **Locate the clip in the Timeline that has the effect you want to modify.**

2. **Expand the track in which the clip resides by clicking the arrow on the left end of the track (see Figure 10-2).**

3. **Navigate to the frame where you want to set a keyframe using the playback controls in the Monitor and click the Add/Delete Keyframe button to add a keyframe. (The Add/Delete Keyframe button is on the left side of the Timeline, as shown in Figure 10-2.)**

   A check mark on the Add/Delete Keyframe button indicates that a keyframe has been set at the current frame.

4. **Open the Effect Controls palette (Window⇨Show Effect Controls) and adjust the settings to the desired level for that frame.**

   In Figure 10-2, I have applied the Echo effect to a clip. (The Echo effect creates a double, triple, quadruple, or morple image effect, depending upon how many "echoes" I specify) However, I only want the echo to start after the clip has played for a few seconds. Thus, at the first keyframe I set the echo Number to 0; at this frame there won't be any echo effect.

Expand track.   Adjust effect settings.

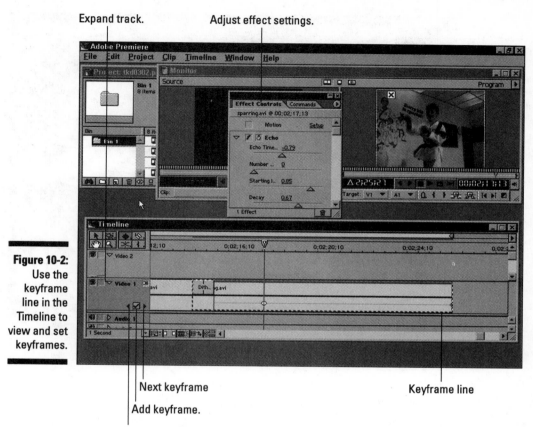

Figure 10-2:
Use the
keyframe
line in the
Timeline to
view and set
keyframes.

Next keyframe   Keyframe line

Add keyframe.

Previous keyframe

Because I don't want there to be any echo effect from the beginning of
the clip up to the keyframe I just set, I also need to go to the beginning
of the clip. By default there are keyframes at the beginning and end of
the clip. So I click the Previous Keyframe button to jump to the beginning of the clip, where I also set the echo Number to 0.

5. **Move to the next frame where you want to set a keyframe and click
   the Add/Delete Keyframe button again.**

6. **In the Effect Controls palette, adjust the settings as desired, as shown
   in Figure 10-3.**

   In Figure 10-3 I have set a new keyframe and changed the echo number
   to 4; by the time playback reaches this frame there will be four echoed
   images. Premiere automatically extrapolates how to linearly adjust the
   effect between the two keyframes.

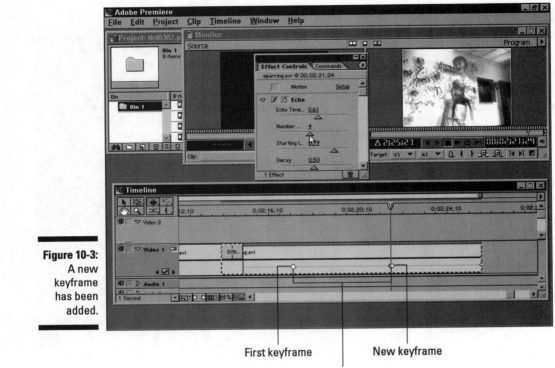

Figure 10-3:
A new
keyframe
has been
added.

First keyframe   New keyframe

Premiere extrapolates the change between here.

7. Set additional keyframes as desired.

Don't forget to use those Previous and Next Keyframe buttons. They
provide an easy way to move from keyframe to keyframe. If you want to
remove a keyframe, simply move to the keyframe and click the Add/
Delete Keyframe button to remove the check mark. When you remove
that check mark you'll notice that the keyframe also magically disappears from the clip.

If you apply multiple effects to a clip, each effect gets its own keyframe. Thus,
if you set a keyframe for one effect, don't assume that it will apply to the
other effects on that clip as well. To view the keyframes for an effect, click
that effect in the Effect Controls palette to select it.

Removing effects

You'll probably change your mind about some of the effects that you apply to
your clips. Don't feel bad; this is perfectly natural. In fact, you'll find that a lot

of time in video editing is spent on good ol' trial and error. You'll try an effect, you won't like it, so then you'll try something else.

To get rid of an effect, click the clip in the Timeline to select it and then choose Window⇨Show Effect Controls to reveal the Effect Controls palette, as shown in Figure 10-4. You have two options for removing effects from a clip:

✔ You can temporarily disable an effect by clicking the little *f* next to the effect's listing in the Effect Controls palette. This can be handy because any settings that you changed for the effect are preserved. With the *f* removed, the clip is disabled and will not be applied to the clip when the Timeline is rendered or output.

✔ You can delete an effect by selecting it in the Effect Controls palette and clicking the Remove Effect button at the bottom of the palette. The Remove Effect button looks like a trash can. (To select an effect, click on its name so that the name becomes bold and the area around the effect appears inset; in Figure 10-4 the "Noise" effect is currently selected.)

Click to disable.

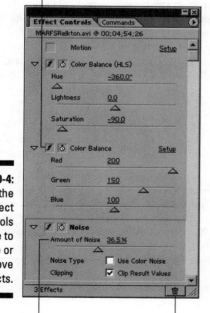

Figure 10-4:
Use the
Effect
Controls
palette to
disable or
remove
effects.

Select an effect.   Remove an effect.

Fixing Imperfect Video

We can't all be perfect. I know I've shot my share of crummy video over the years, and you probably have to. Thankfully, Premiere has some effects that can help you clean up video that might otherwise seem unusable. Specific effects that you might find useful include these:

- **Brightness & Contrast:** Found in the Adjust folder, this effect can be used to brighten poorly lit shots (or take the edge off shots that were lit a little *too* well). In Figure 10-5 I have increased the brightness and contrast to account for what photographers and videographers call a "back-light situation" (where a strong light source in the background causes the subject in the foreground to appear dark) in the original shot. This is not a perfect solution, but at least now the subject's face is not just a dark blur.

- **Gamma Correction:** This effect, which is found in the Image Control folder, adjusts brightness of just the midtones in the video rather than the overall image. This has less effect on shadows and bright areas, making the image appear less washed out.

- **Color Balance:** Perhaps the biggest problem caused by poor lighting is that colors don't appear correctly on screen. A scene that looks okay to the naked eye could turn out unnaturally blue on video if the room contained a lot of diffuse sunlight. You can often achieve surprising improvements by simply adjusting the balance of red, green, and blue colors in the image using the Color Balance effect (also found in the Adjust folder).

If you expect to output your finished movie back to tape, color adjustments you make in Premiere could create colors that can't be displayed on NTSC or PAL video equipment. To correct potential color problems, apply the Broadcast Colors effect in the Video folder *to the entire project* before output.

- **Color Balance (HLS):** This effect (found in the Image Control folder) differs from the standard Color Balance effect because it adjusts color using hue, lightness, and saturation (HLS) rather than red, green, and blue color levels. When used conservatively, this effect can be used to adjust lightness as well as color saturation, although if you start making anything more than minor adjustments with this effect, the colors will start to look unnatural.

Figure 10-5:
The source clip (left) was badly backlit, so brightness and contrast were increased for the clip in the Timeline (right).

Animating Clips

I know what you're thinking when you read this heading. "Why do I need to animate a video clip in which the subjects are already moving?" You may not need to animate the actual subjects in the video, but you can move the video image across the screen. You can move a clip across the screen along a fixed path or a zigzag pattern, you can rotate clips, and you can distort them. Here's how:

1. **Click the clip in the Timeline that you want to animate to select it.**

2. **Choose Clip⇨Video Options⇨Motion.**

   The Motion Settings dialog box appears, as shown in Figure 10-6.

3. **Under Alpha, click to select either Use Clip's or Create New.**

   As the clip moves across the screen, empty portions of the screen will be transparent. This transparent area is called an alpha channel. For most video clips, you'll select "Create New" for the Alpha mode. However, you can choose "Use Clip's" if the clip has it's own alpha channel. You may use this if the image is a still graphic with transparency and you only want the nontransparent graphic to appear on screen.

4. **In the upper-right screen of the Motion Settings dialog box, click on the black horizontal line to set keyframes, and then drag these keyframes to change the path of the clip's motion.**

The black line indicates the path of travel. Click on the black line to create additional keyframes. As you can see in Figure 10-6, I added a keyframe in the middle of the line and dragged it up so the clip will move in an inverted V pattern. Once you have clicked to create a new keyframe, drag it with the mouse to modify the path.

5. **If the moving clip is in a superimpose track, click the Show All box to view underlying tracks in the preview area.**

   The Show All check box is in the center of the Motion Settings dialog box. With Show All checked, the underlying tracks will appear in the background, thus giving you a better idea of how the final video image will appear.

6. **To view outlines of the clip at the start and finish keyframes, click Show Outlines (you'll find it right under the Show All box).**

   Personally, I don't usually find that the outlines are all that useful, although they can help you ensure that the moving clip is completely off-screen before the motion starts and after it ends. If an edge of the clip is still in the Visible Area when it stops or disappears, this flaw will be readily apparent to your viewers.

7. **If the clip is not on a superimpose track, you may want to fill the empty areas of the frame with a specific color. Click the Fill Color box to open the Color Picker and choose a color.**

   The Fill Color box is in the lower-left corner of the Motion Settings dialog box shown in Figure 10-6. If you don't choose a unique fill color and there is no underlying video image, the background will simply be white.

   Watch out for that "out of gamut" warning icon in the Color Picker! If you see the little yellow exclamation mark, choose a different color.

8. **To apply zoom or rotation effects, click on the black line in the upper right window of the Motion Settings dialog box to set keyframes along the path of travel.**

   Zoom and rotation controls are located near the bottom of the Motion Settings dialog box.

9. **To reduce the size of the frame as it moves, move to a keyframe by clicking it in the upper-right window and then reduce the percentage listed next to Zoom near the bottom of the dialog box. To increase the frame size, increase the Zoom level. Adjust additional keyframes as needed.**

10. **To rotate a clip, adjust the Rotation angle at various keyframes.**

    If you refer to Figure 10-6, you can see I have set rotation so the clip rotates in one circle through the path of its movement. To do this, I set the rotation angle at 0 degrees for the starting keyframe. At about one-quarter of the way through the animation, I set the angle at 90 degrees. At the halfway point the rotation angle is 180 degrees, at three-fourths it is 270 degrees, and the ending keyframe is 360 degrees.

11. **Drag the handles in the Distortion box in the bottom-center of the Motion Settings dialog box to distort the shape of the clip at various keyframes.**

    You can combine rotation and distortion to create some interesting effects.

12. **If you want to delay the motion of your clip as it moves across the screen, adjust the Delay control at the bottom of the Motion Settings dialog box.**

    The delay control temporarily stops the clip at the current keyframe for a percentage of the overall playback time based upon what percentage you input.

13. **Click OK to close the Motion Settings dialog box when you are done.**

Although the Motion Settings dialog box can show you a preview of your work, clip animation must still be rendered in the Timeline. To render it, choose Timeline➪Render Work Area.

New keyframes

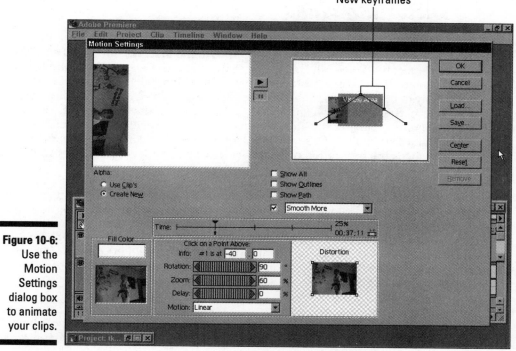

Figure 10-6:
Use the
Motion
Settings
dialog box
to animate
your clips.

One of the things I like to use animation for is to pan across large still images. For example, suppose you have a large graphic of a map, and you want to make it appear that the camera is panning across this map. Place the graphic in your Timeline, open the Motion Settings dialog box, and use the Distortion box in the lower right corner of the dialog box to make the image larger than the viewable area. This is important because to make the panning effect seem realistic the image must seem larger than the screen. Finally, adjust motion settings so that the camera appears to pan across the image, making sure that part of the image always covers the entire viewable area.

Using Other Video Effects

Lots of other effects are available with Premiere, and I couldn't possibly describe them all here. Rather than provide a brief overview of many effects, the following sections show you a detailed approach to using a few common effects. You can adapt the techniques described here when using other effects.

Distorting video

Adobe Premiere comes with a plethora of effects that you can use to distort your video. Some of the best ones can be found in the Distort and Transform folders of the Video Effects palette. Distortion effects range from mild to wild. You may find that the best way to give your video a custom appearance is to apply multiple effects. Consider the clip in Figure 10-7. I want to distort the view of the road, which I have done with the use of the Pinch effect, found in the Distort folder of the Video Effects palette. The Pinch effect simulates a pinching or pulling of a spot in the video image. In Figure 10-7, the pinch enhances the perception of speed because scenery seems to move through the pinched area at a faster rate.

When you apply the Pinch effect — just drag it from the Video Effects palette and drop it on a clip in the Timeline — the Pinch settings dialog box appears, as shown in Figure 10-8. The bottom of this dialog box shows a representation of the pinch that you are about to apply. You can use the grid to move the pinch point, and move the Amount slider to control the degree to which you will pinch the image. I want an extreme pinch appearance so I have set the slider relatively high.

You can open the Pinch Settings dialog box at any time by clicking Setup next to the Pinch effect in the Effect Controls palette. Use the plus (+) and minus (–) signs in the Pinch Settings dialog box to zoom in or out on the preview window.

Figure 10-7:
The Pinch
effect has
been used
to distort the
view of this
video clip.

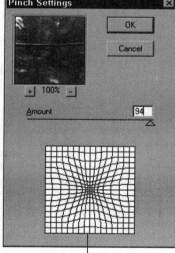

Figure 10-8:
Use this
dialog box
to control
the Pinch
effect.

Set pinch point here.

Now, to really make things tricky, several seconds into the clip I want to zoom in on the image and reduce the pinch effect. To do this, I first apply the Camera View effect (located in the Transform folder) to the clip. The Camera View effect contains, among other things, a zoom effect. Next, I add two keyframes to the clip. Between those keyframes the zoom level will go from the default level (10) to a more zoomed-in level (6). I also change the keyframes at the beginning and end of the clip to match these settings. Finally, I also create keyframes for the Pinch effect so that it diminishes as the camera view zooms in. Figure 10-9 shows the keyframes that I created.

Pinch effect

New keyframes

Figure 10-9:
You can
apply
multiple
effects to
a clip and
control them
separately
with
keyframes.

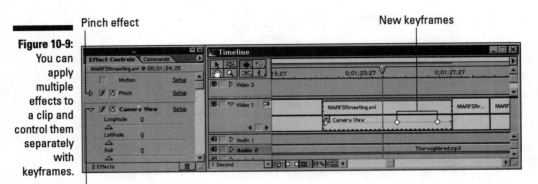

Camera View effect

Disorienting your audience

Suppose a subject in a movie is sick or disoriented. What is the best way to communicate this to the audience? You could have someone in the movie say, "Hey, you don't look well. Are you sick?" and then the unwell person can stumble and fall down. That may be effective, but an even better way to convey a feeling of illness or confusion is to let your audience see through the subject's blurry and disheveled eyes.

You can begin by shooting some footage as if from the view of the subject. Hand-hold the camera and let it move slightly as you walk. You probably don't need to exaggerate the movement, but the camera shouldn't be tripod-stable either. As you shoot, pan across the scene — but not too quickly — as if the subject were looking around the room. Occasionally you may want to dip the camera slightly left or right so the video image appears to tilt. A tilting video image has a strong disorienting effect on the viewer.

Now that you have some footage to work with, you can perform the real magic in Premiere. One effect that can provide a feeling of illness or disorientation is Camera Blur (found in the Blur folder). Use keyframes to adjust camera blur throughout a clip, as if the subject's vision were moving in and out of focus. Another good one is Ghosting (also in the Blur folder). Ghosting produces ghost images of moving objects. Similar to ghosting is the Echo effect, found in the Time folder, which is used in Figure 10-10. Echo gives you a bit more control over the number and timing of echoed images.

Working in the Golden Age of Cinema

Motion pictures have been around for well over a century now, and you may want to use some "old" footage in your movie projects. Thankfully, creating footage that looks old does not require a trip to some dank film vault deep

Figure 10-10:
The Echo
effect can
be used to
disorient the
viewer.

beneath a Hollywood movie studio. You can simulate an old-fashioned look with your own video. To simulate old video

- ✔ Pay attention to your subjects and the scene. Cowboys of the Old West didn't carry cell phones in their pockets, for example, or drive sport utility vehicles. Remove objects from the scene that don't fit the period you are trying to simulate.

- ✔ Remove color from the clip. Perhaps the easiest way to convert a color image to grayscale is to use the Black & White filter in the Image Control folder, although I prefer to use the Color Balance (HLS) effect. Adjust the saturation level to –100 and the clip will be essentially grayscale. One advantage of using the Color Balance (HLS) effect is that you can use keyframes to change the effect in the middle of a clip. It also enables you to use some color to simulate a sepia tone look to your video. First, apply the Color Balance (HLS) effect and set the Saturation to –100. Next, apply the Color Balance effect from the Adjust folder and set Red to 200, Green to 150, and Blue to 100 (the default level). The video image will now have a yellowish tint that resembles some old film.

Grayscale is just a fancy way of saying "black and white." Technically grayscale is a more accurate term, because "black and white" video images are actually made using various shades of gray.

- ✔ "Weather" the video image. Film tends to deteriorate over time, so if you're trying to simulate old footage you should simulate some of that deterioration. Use the Noise effect to add some graininess to the video image.

- ✔ Reduce audio quality and if possible use a mono setting. Audio recordings made 75 years ago did not use 16-bit stereo sound. To reduce quality, reduce the sampling rate of the audio when you export your movie (see Chapter 14 for more on movie export settings). Alternatively, you may want to go for the "silent movie" effect and not record any audio at all. Just use an appropriate musical soundtrack and title screens for dialog.

✔ Speed up the clip. Older film often plays back at a faster speed, so speed up the clip by selecting it, choosing Clip➪Speed, and increasing the "New Rate" percentage in the Clip Speed dialog box that appears.

When you're done making all these changes, your Effect Controls palette may look pretty full. In Figure 10-11 you can see that I have applied the Color Balance (HLS), Color Balance, and Noise effects to a clip.

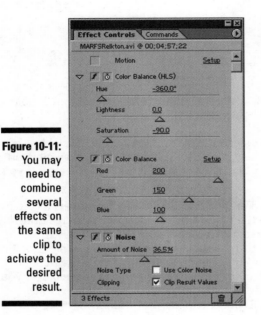

Figure 10-11:
You may need to combine several effects on the same clip to achieve the desired result.

Flipping video

Do you ever wish you could produce a mirror image of a video clip, or maybe rotate it and change its orientation on the screen? Such modifications are easy to make with Premiere. Effects that you can use to flip video can be found in the Transform folder of the Video Effects palette. These effects include two classics:

✔ **Horizontal Flip:** This effect flips the video left to right, as shown in Figure 10-12.

✔ **Vertical Flip:** This effect flips the video top to bottom.

When flipping video, watch out for letters and numbers that appear in the frame. Backward letters will stick out like sore thumbs (or rude gestures) when your audience views the movie.

Using effects from older versions of Premiere

If you have used earlier versions of Adobe Premiere — particularly version 5 or earlier — you may be wondering where some of your old effects have gone. When Premiere 6.0 was released in 2001, many older Premiere effects were replaced with effects from Adobe After Effects. The "official" recommendation is of course that you start using the new effects. However, I know how difficult it can be to break old habits, especially when it comes to software.

Once you get used to something, you don't want to change. If you want to continue to use these old effects (which Adobe considers obsolete), open the Video Effects palette menu (it's the little right-pointing arrow in the upper-right corner of the palette) and choose Show Hidden. Your Video Effects palette will now have a new folder named Obsolete. There you will find 23 old effects that Adobe has deemed obsolete.

Figure 10-12:
The Horizontal Flip effect was applied to the clip on the left and — *voilà!* — suddenly you're on the left and riding in England.

Adding Web links to movies

The term *multimedia* is used pretty loosely these days, although few types of media are as "multi" as the movies you can create with Premiere. Not only can your movies contain audio, video, and still graphics, but they can also include links to the World Wide Web. Of course, for the link to work, your audience must be watching the movie on a computer that can connect to the Internet. Also, the movie needs to be output in a format that supports Web links, such as QuickTime. Web links can be handy if you want a specific Web page to open during or after playback. To create a Web link:

1. **Move the edit line in the Timeline to the point at which you want the link to be activated.**

2. **Choose Timeline⇨Set Timeline Marker and choose a numbered or unnumbered marker.**

   A marker appears on the Timeline ruler.

3. **Double-click the marker.**

   The Marker Properties dialog box appears, as shown in Figure 10-13.

4. **In the URL field, type the complete URL (Uniform Resource Locator) for the link target**

   The URL is the Web address for the site that you want to open. To be safe, it should include the `http://` part of the address. Consider the URL that you enter here carefully. Does it point to a page that will still be online several months or even a year from now? Consider how long users might be viewing copies of your movie.

5. **Click OK to close the dialog box.**

Test your Web link in the final output format! If it works, the desired Web page should open in a Web browser. Some formats (like QuickTime) support Web links, but some don't.

Be really, really careful when you type the address for your Web URL. Exact spelling and syntax is crucial or else your Web link will be broken, and that will create a bad impression with your audience. Furthermore, because most Web servers run a UNIX-based operating system, everything after the `.com` part of the Web address is probably case-sensitive.

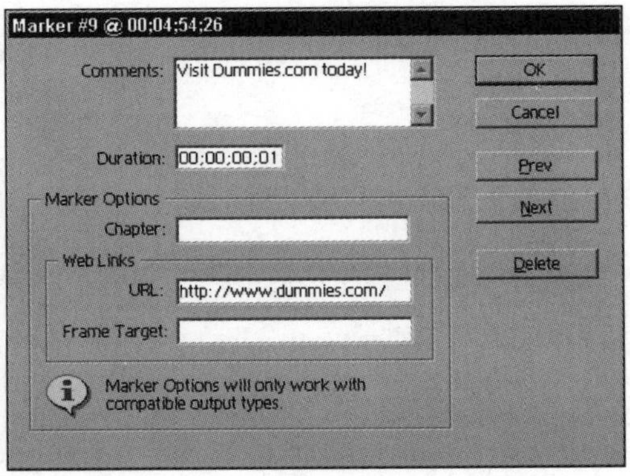

Figure 10-13:
Timeline
markers can
link to World
Wide Web
addresses.

Marker #9 @ 00;04;54;26

Comments:	Visit Dummies.com today!

Duration: 00;00;00;01

Marker Options
Chapter:
Web Links
URL: http://www.dummies.com/
Frame Target:

OK
Cancel
Prev
Next
Delete

Marker Options will only work with compatible output types.

Chapter 11

Working with Audio

In This Chapter

▶ Digging into audio

▶ Listening to audio clips

▶ Tweaking audio in the Timeline (not illegal in most states)

▶ Making the best use of audio effects

*O*f all the various aspects of a video program, audio is typically the easiest to overlook. We tend to think of movies as a visual art form, but it turns out that the audible portion of a movie is nearly as important as what happens on screen. In fact, a lot of video experts will tell you that while audiences tend to be forgiving of flaws and mistakes in a video image, they find poor-quality audio almost immediately noticeable and offputting.

To tell the truth, I'd love to dedicate more than one chapter to audio; it's a big subject. But I think this chapter can cover the essentials — a brief look at just what audio is, followed by a hands-on delve into actually editing audio in Adobe Premiere.

Understanding Audio

Consider how audio affects the feel of a video program. Honking car horns on a busy street; crashing surf and calling seagulls at a beach; a howling wolf on the moors; these are sounds that help us identify a place as quickly as our eyes can, if not quicker. If a picture is worth a thousand words, sometimes a sound in a movie is worth a thousand pictures.

What is audio? Well, if I check my notes from high school science class, I get the impression that audio is produced by sound waves moving through the air; human beings hear those waves when they make our eardrums vibrate. The speed at which a sound makes the eardrum vibrate is the *frequency*. Frequency is measured in kilohertz (kHz), and one kHz equals one thousand vibrations per second. A lower-frequency sound is perceived as a lower pitch or tone, and a higher-frequency sound is perceived as a high pitch or tone. The volume or intensity of audio is measured in *decibels* (dB).

Understanding sampling rates

For over a century, humans have been using analog devices (ranging from wax cylinders to magnetic tapes) to record sound waves. As with video, digital audio recordings are all the rage today. Because a digital recording can only contain specific values, it can only approximate a continuous wave of sound; a digital recording device must "sample" a sound many times per second; the more samples per second, the more closely the recording can approximate the live sound (although a digital approximation of a "wave" actually looks more like the stairs on an Aztec pyramid). The number of samples per second is called the *sampling rate*. As you might expect, a higher sampling rate provides better recording quality. CD audio typically has a sampling rate of 44.1 kHz — that's 44,100 samples per second — and many digital camcorders can record at a sampling rate of 48 kHz. The sampling rate for your project is one of the things you will have to determine when you create a new project in Premiere.

Delving into bit depth

Another term you'll hear bandied about in audio editing is *bit depth*. The quality of an audio recording is affected by the number of samples per second, as well as the amount of information in each of those samples. The amount of information that can be recorded per sample is the bit depth. More bits equal more information. Many digital recorders and camcorders offer a choice between 12-bit and 16-bit audio; choose 16-bit whenever possible.

Making sound audio recordings

Recording great-quality audio is no simple matter. Professional recording studios spend thousands, even millions, of dollars to set up acoustically superior sound rooms. I'm guessing you don't have that kind of budgetary firepower, but if you are recording your own sound, you can get pro-sounding results with Premiere if you follow these basic tips:

- **Use an external microphone whenever possible.** The built-in microphones in modern camcorders have improved greatly in recent years, but they still present problems. They often record undesired ambient sound near the camcorder (such as audience members) or even mechanical sound from the camcorder's tape drive. If possible, connect an external microphone to the camcorder's mic input.

- **Eliminate unwanted noise sources.** If you *must* use the camcorder's built-in mic, be aware of your movements and other things that can cause loud, distracting noises on tape. Problem items can include a loose lens cap banging around, your finger rubbing against the mic, wind blowing across the mic, and the *swish-swish* of those nylon workout pants you wore this morning.

✔ **Try to minimize sound reflection.** Audio waves reflect off any hard surface, which can cause echoing in a recording. Hanging blankets on the walls and other hard surfaces will significantly reduce reflection.

✔ **Obtain and use a high-quality microphone.** A good mic isn't cheap, but it can make a huge difference in recording quality.

✔ **Watch for trip hazards!** In your haste to record great sound, don't forget that your microphone cables can become a hazard on scene. Not only is this a safety hazard to anyone walking by, but if someone snags a cable, your equipment could be damaged as well. If necessary, bring along some duct tape to temporarily cover cables that run across the floor.

For more on picking a good microphone as well as other cool toys for your movie productions, check out Chapter 17.

Acquiring music and stock audio

Few things can spice up a movie project like a musical soundtrack. People respond emotionally to music, and you can use that fact to great advantage in your projects. Music is pretty easy to insert in a project in Premiere, but the tricky part is obtaining the rights to use some music. Realistically, if you're making a video of your daughter's birthday party, and you only plan to share that video with yourself and perhaps a grandparent or two, Kool and the Gang probably don't care if you use the song "Celebration" as a musical soundtrack. But if you start distributing that movie all over the Internet, or, even worse, you start selling it, you could have a problem that involves the band, the record company, and lots and lots of lawyers.

The key to using music legally is licensing. You can license the right to use just about any music you want, but it can get expensive. Licensing "Celebration" for your movie project (for example) could cost hundreds of dollars or more. Fortunately, more-affordable alternatives exist. Numerous companies offer CDs and online libraries of stock audio and music, which you can license for surprisingly affordable fees. If you use audio from such a resource, make sure you read the licensing agreement carefully. There may be restrictions on how many copies you may distribute, how much money you can charge, what formats you may offer, or other restrictions.

Adobe Premiere comes with a cool little program called SmartSound QuickTracks. This program provides high-quality, royalty-free music for your projects. See Chapter 16 for more on using SmartSound QuickTracks.

Playing Audio Clips

To begin editing an audio clip, double-click it in the Project window. The audio clip will open in its own viewer window, as shown in Figure 11-1. If the clip is audio-only (no picture), an audio waveform will be displayed.

Before you can edit audio, you must have some audio to edit. See Chapter 6 for more on capturing and importing clips.

Audio waveform   Volume toggle

Figure 11-1:
Double-click
an audio
clip to
preview it in
a viewer
window like
this one.

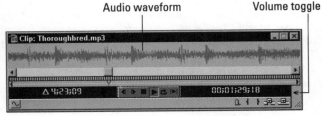

You can set in and out points on audio just as you do with video clips. The audio viewer window also includes a basic volume control (see Figure 11-1). Click the volume control toggle once to mute the sound, click it again to play the sound quietly, and click it again to play at full volume. Once you are ready to edit the audio clip into the Timeline, simply click-and-drag it from the viewer window to the desired audio track on the Timeline.

Working with Audio in the Timeline

The designers of Premiere thought that audio was such an important part of a movie project that they provided a workspace specifically tailored to audio. To open the Audio Editing workspace, choose Window⇨Workspace⇨Audio. One of the primary features of the audio workspace is the Audio Mixer window shown in Figure 11-2. The Mixer includes mixing controls for each audio track, as well as master controls for the project. Audio tracks in the Timeline are listed by number in the Audio Mixer. Figure 11-2 shows an Audio Mixer that is open in a project that has three audio tracks. If the project had four audio tracks, you would see an additional column of controls.

If you don't see the MASTER controls or other tracks, you may need to click-and-drag the edge of the Mixer window to expand it.

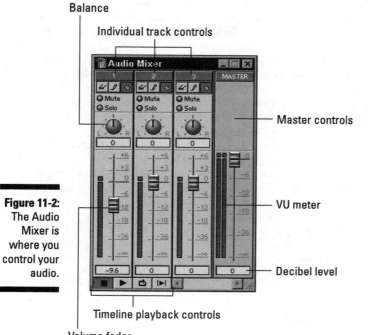

Balance

Individual track controls

Master controls

VU meter

Decibel level

Figure 11-2:
The Audio
Mixer is
where you
control your
audio.

Timeline playback controls

Volume fader

As you play your Timeline, you'll notice that your audio registers on the VU (volume unit) meter for the corresponding track. You can also use the Audio Mixer to control which audio tracks play and which ones don't. To mute a track, click the Mute button in the Audio Mixer for that track. The Mute indicator should turn red to indicate that it is muted.

If you only want to play one of the audio tracks, click its Solo button in the Audio Mixer. The Solo button for that track will turn green, and the Mute button for every other track will turn red. Click the Solo button again to turn it off.

Adjusting volume

I like to use a lot of different audio tracks in a project. If possible, I try to insert each new audio element on a different track. This gives greater flexibility when making adjustments to things such as volume. Different bits of audio get recorded at different levels, and you may find that one audio clip is too loud while another is not loud enough. You can adjust the volume for a track by using the Volume sliders in the Audio Mixer. Simply click-and-drag the slider to adjust the volume.

The volume of audio in video projects is measured in volume units (VU). Premiere's Audio Mixer includes VU meters that may appear similar to the volume meters on a tape deck or other recording device you've used before. If you've ever recorded audio on tape using an analog tape deck, you probably made sure that the audio levels got above 0 and into the red once in a while, but that average volume was below 0. But when you are working with digital audio, 0 is the maximum volume level you can have before distortion occurs. That's why if you look at the Audio Mixer in Figure 11-3, you'll notice that the VU meter scales stop at 0.

When adjusting volume for a track, keep an eye on its VU meter in the Audio Mixer. If the meter reaches 0, then you'll probably get audio distortion in the final program. If 0 is reached, the red indicator at the top of the VU meter will light up as shown at the top of the VU meter for track 3 in Figure 11-3. The indicator will remain lit until you click Play again.

Besides watching for audio peaks that are above 0, you should also keep an eye on the average audio levels. The VU meter will dance up and down quite a bit as you play the project, but you should adjust the volume control so that the average levels are between –12 and –18 on the VU meter.

Red here is bad.

Figure 11-3: The Audio Mixer warns you of potential audio distortion.

Adjusting audio balance

You can also adjust balance in the Audio Mixer. In a stereo channel you have a right channel and a left channel. You can use the balance knobs at the top of the Audio Mixer to adjust this balance. Simply turn the balance knob left or right. If you turn the knob all the way to the left, audio will only be sent to the left channel, and thus will only come out of the left speaker on a system with stereo audio. Moving the audio from one channel to another is also referred to as *panning*.

You can also adjust panning in the Timeline. Follow these steps:

1. **Click the arrow to expand the view of the audio track in the Timeline.**

2. **Click the blue Display Pan Rubberbands button, as shown in Figure 11-4.**

   The blue pan rubberband will appear across the clip's waveform in the Timeline.

3. **Place the mouse pointer over the rubberband and click-and-drag it up to pan left or down to pan right.**

   In Figure 11-4, I am panning the sound of a motorcycle engine to the left channel as the motorcycle rides off the left side of the screen.

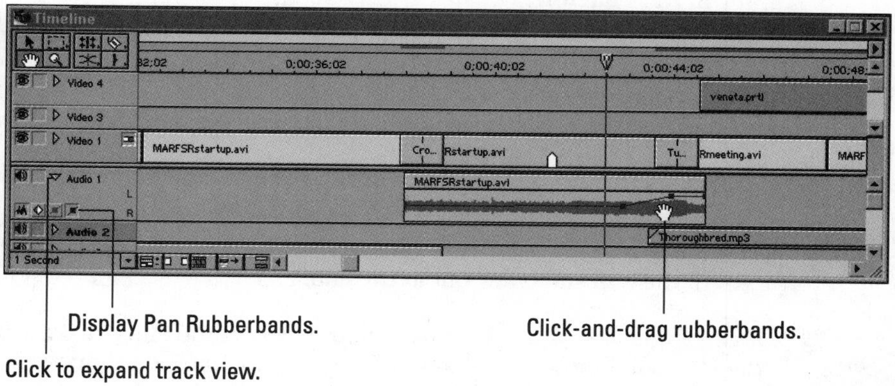

Figure 11-4:
Use the
blue pan
rubberband
to adjust
panning in
the Timeline.

Display Pan Rubberbands.

Click-and-drag rubberbands.

Click to expand track view.

A couple of other audio balance adjustments you can make include:

✔ Muting one channel or the other by selecting the clip and choosing Clip⇨Audio Options⇨Mute Left or Mute Right.

✔ Swapping the left and right audio channels by selecting the clip in the Timeline and choosing Clip⇨Audio Options⇨Swap Channels.

Adjusting audio gain

Sometimes it makes perfect sense to adjust the volume of an entire track. Other times you may just want to adjust the volume of an individual clip. To do that, you adjust that clip's *gain,* which is just a fancy word for "volume."

You can adjust the overall gain for an entire clip, or you can adjust gain variously throughout a clip. To adjust the gain of the whole clip at once:

1. **Select the audio clip in the Timeline and choose Clip⇔Audio Options⇔Audio Gain.**

   The Audio Gain dialog box appears.

2. **Enter a new percentage. A higher percentage increases gain, and a lower percentage decreases gain.**

   Alternatively, click Smart Gain to have Premiere automatically adjust gain so that the loudest portion of the clip is at the maximum safe level.

3. **Click OK to close the dialog box.**

In addition to adjusting the overall gain of an audio clip, you can also adjust gain at individual points within the clip. Here's how:

1. **Click the arrow on the left side of the audio track to expand its view in the Timeline.**

2. **Click the red Display Volume Rubberbands button, as shown in Figure 11-5.**

   The red volume rubberband appears across the clip's waveform in the Timeline.

3. **Place the mouse pointer over the rubberband and click-and-drag it up to increase gain or down to decrease gain.**

   In Figure 11-5, I adjusted gain so that the sound fades in at the beginning of the clip and fades out at the end.

If you adjust the gain rubberbands up on any audio clips, make sure you play the clip using the Audio Mixer and keep an eye on the VU meter for that track. See the "Adjusting volume" section earlier in this chapter for more on setting good audio levels.

Cross-fading audio

One of the most common reasons for adjusting gain on a clip (at least, in my experience) is to fade a clip in as it begins and out as it ends. In fact, if you look at the volume rubberband in Figure 11-5, you'll see that I have done exactly that with an audio clip. Fading in and out is usually barely perceptible to the viewer, but it takes a distinct "edge" off the transition as a loud noise starts or stops. And when you transition between video clips, fading the audio from the first clip out as the new clip fades in greatly improves the feel of the transition, even if the video portions of the clips do not fade in or out.

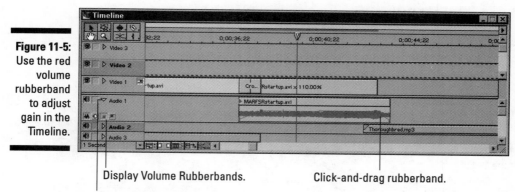

Figure 11-5:
Use the red
volume
rubberband
to adjust
gain in the
Timeline.

Display Volume Rubberbands.   Click-and-drag rubberband.

Click to expand track view.

Premiere makes the process of fading between clips easy with the help of the
cross-fade tool in the Timeline. To cross-fade audio clips, those clips must
overlap. Thus, you may find it easier to unlink clips in which audio and video
are linked (see the next section). You can perform a ripple edit on unlinked
audio clips to make them overlap each other. Once you've done that, cross-
fading is easy:

For more on ripple edits, see Chapter 8.

1. **Click the Cross-Fade tool in the Timeline toolbar.**

2. **Click on the audio clip that you want to fade out.**

3. **Move the cursor over the audio clip that you want to fade in.**

   The cursor should change to the cross-fade icon.

4. **Click on the second audio clip. Premiere will automatically adjust
   gain so that the clips are cross-faded, as shown in Figure 11-6.**

Linking audio and video

When you insert a clip into the Timeline that contains both audio and video,
the audio and video tracks for that clip are usually linked together. If audio
and video clips are linked together, you'll notice that when you click on one
in the Timeline they both become selected. Usually this is handy, but sometimes you may want to unlink the two and edit them individually. To unlink
audio and video for a clip, select that clip in the Timeline and choose
Clip⇨Unlink Audio and Video. Clips in the Timeline are color-coded based on
their linked status:

 ✔ **Green:** Audio and video clips are linked.

 ✔ **Yellow:** A video clip with no linked audio.

 ✔ **Blue:** An audio clip with no linked video.

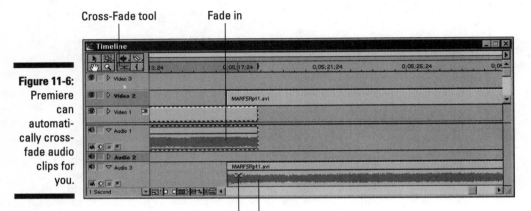

Figure 11-6:
Premiere
can
automatically cross-fade audio
clips for
you.

Cross-Fade tool Fade in

Cross-Fade icon Fade out

Using Audio Effects

Adobe Premiere comes with a pretty substantial collection of audio effects. Some of these effects can be used to make audio seem distorted or surreal, while other effects simply help you repair problems within an audio track. Premiere's audio effects live on the Audio Effects palette (shown in Figure 11-7), which you can reveal by choosing Window➪Show Audio Effects. Audio effects that come with Adobe Premiere 6.5 include the following:

 ✔ **Highpass:** Removes lower frequencies from the audio.

 ✔ **Lowpass:** Removes higher frequencies from the audio.

 ✔ **Notch/Hum Filter:** Removes sound at a frequency you specify. This effect can be used if the audio clip has a constant hum.

 ✔ **Auto Pan:** Automatically pans audio balance from left to right as the clip plays.

 ✔ **Fill Left/Right:** Moves the audio completely to the left or right channel, depending on which direction you choose.

 ✔ **Pan:** Controls pan (balance) within a clip.

 ✔ **Swap Left & Right:** Swaps the left and right channels.

 ✔ **Boost:** Boosts weaker sounds.

- **Compressor/Expander:** Compresses or expands the dynamic range of the clip. This effect works similar to gain, but you can adjust lows without affecting highs, or vice versa.

- **Noise Gate:** Removes unwanted background noise during quiet parts of the clip.

- **Bass & Treble:** Provides control over base and treble in the clip.

- **Equalize:** Adjusts audio tone much like a stereo equalizer.

- **Parametric Equalization:** Similar to the Equalize effect, but offering a bit more control.

- **Chorus:** Makes a single voice or instrument sound like a chorus.

- **Flanger:** Similar to the Chorus effect, but with a bit of a psychedelic twist.

- **Multi-Effect:** Provides a combination of chorus and echo effects.

- **Echo:** Echoes the clip. Echoes the clip.

- **Multitap Delay:** Provides a combination of advanced delays and rhythms. Each delay effect is called a *tap,* and you can uniquely control up to four taps with this effect.

- **Reverb:** Makes the audio sound as if it's being played in a large hall or room.

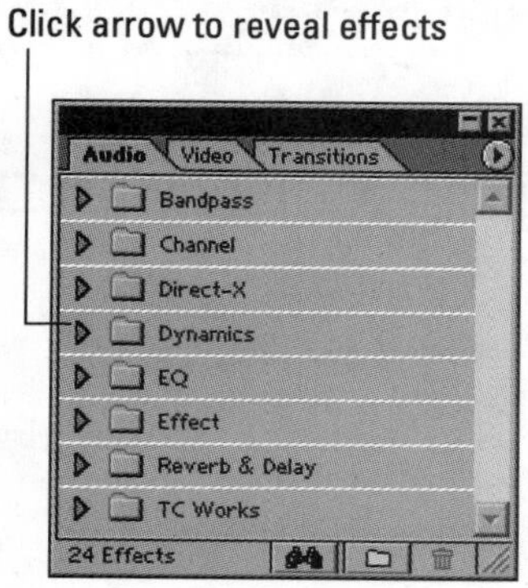

Click arrow to reveal effects

Figure 11-7:
Premiere
comes with
quite a few
useful audio
effects
already
built in.

A complete course on how to use each effect would take up nearly another whole book (each effect differs considerably from the others). Some general instructions are in order, however: To apply an audio effect to a clip, simply drag it from the Audio Effects palette and drop it onto your clip in the Timeline. Depending on which filter you chose, the Effect Controls palette appears (as shown in Figure 11-8), allowing you to make adjustments and settings. To adjust the effect controls for a clip at any time, select that clip in the Timeline and choose Window➪Show Effect Controls.

Visually editing audio

The audio waveforms that Premiere displays in audio tracks may seem like just squiggly lines that are fun to look at, but they can also serve an important purpose. Audio waveforms allow you to edit audio with your *eyes*. It sounds crazy, I know, but it's true. Those squiggly lines actually provide visual clues to sounds occurring in the clip. When you are doing frame-by-frame editing on a project, such precise data can be invaluable.

Consider the Timeline in the figure following. The clip in track Audio 3 contains a sound effect that I want to synchronize with a visual event in the video clip in Video 1. As you can see in the figure, I placed a marker on the Timeline at the location of the visual event. The waveform in Audio 3 shows quite clearly where the sound begins, so all I have to do is line up the Timeline marker with the desired spot on the waveform.

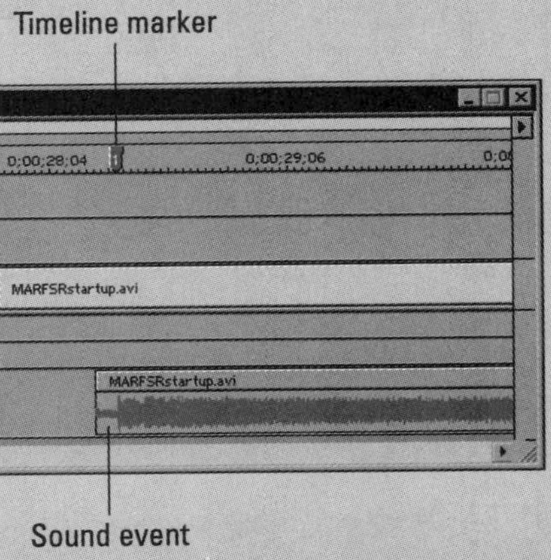

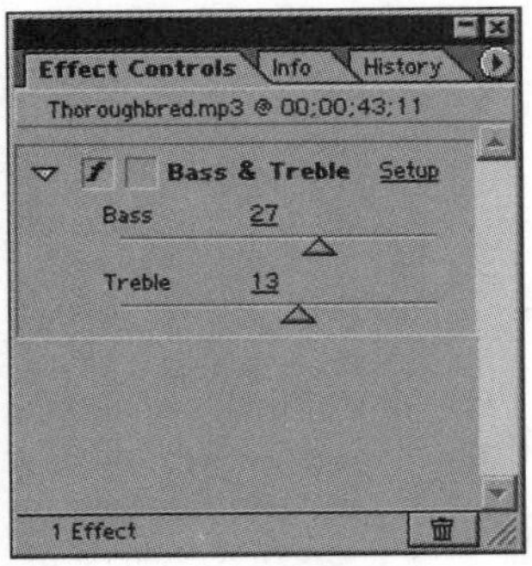

Timeline marker

Sound event

Figure 11-8:
Use the Effect Controls palette to adjust audio effect controls.

Part IV
Wrapping Up
Your Project

The 5th Wave   By Rich Tennant

THE SCARLET LETTER

©RICHTENNANT

17th CENTURY | 20th CENTURY

ADULTERY | ANALOG

In this part . . .

Any chef will tell you that presentation is key to the success of any fine meal. And so it is with movie projects. Once you have edited your movie, you must prepare it for distribution, whether your audience is a few friends and family on the Internet, or a local broadcast outlet.

This part shows you how to wrap up your project and get it ready for distribution. You start by adding titles to your project so viewers know the name of your movie and who is responsible for it. Then you actually finalize the project and output it for distribution.

Chapter 12

Giving Credit with Titles

In This Chapter

▶ Titling your project in Premiere

▶ Creating, adding, and tweaking titles

n their rush to get to the pictures, folks who are new to video editing often overlook the importance of good audio. The same could also be said of titles — the subject of this chapter. Titles — the words that appear on-screen during a movie — are critically important in many different kinds of projects. Titles tell your audience the name of your movie, who made it, who starred in it, who paid for it, and who baked cookies for the cast. Titles can also clue the audience in to vital details — where the story takes place, what time it is, even what year it is — with minimum fuss. And of course, titles can reveal what the characters are saying if they're speaking a different language.

Adobe Premiere has always included tools to help you make titles for your movies. Version 6.5 of the software includes an all-new titling tool called the Adobe Title Designer. This new tool is more sophisticated and powerful than the previous Titler. This chapter shows you how to use this Adobe Title Designer to create on-screen words for your movie projects.

If you have Adobe Premiere 6.0, your Titler is considerably different from the one shown in this chapter (at least in the way it looks and acts). It's similar enough, however, that you should be able to follow many of the steps given here to get started creating basic titles.

Creating Titles in Premiere

It's easy to think of titles as just words on the screen. But think of the effects, both forceful and subtle, that well-designed titles can have. Consider the *Star Wars* movies, which all begin with a black screen and the sentence, "A long time ago, in a galaxy far, far away . . .." The simple title screen quickly and effectively sets the tone and tells the audience that the story is beginning. And then, of course, you get those scrolling words that float three-dimensionally off into space, immediately after that first title screen. A story floating through space is far more interesting than white text scrolling from the bottom to top of the screen, don't you think?

To begin creating titles for a project, open that project and choose File⇨New⇨Title. The Adobe Title Designer window appears, as shown in Figure 12-1. Before you begin actually creating text, I recommend that you spend some time setting up the view.

Title menu   Title safe margin

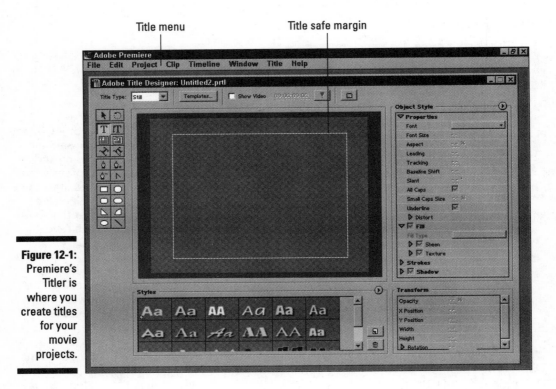

Figure 12-1: Premiere's Titler is where you create titles for your movie projects.

Setting up the Adobe Title Designer view

One of the first things you should do before creating titles is make sure that the Title Safe margin is shown. To do so, choose Title⇨View and make sure that Safe Title Margin has a check mark next to it. A thin line showing the margin should appear in the title area. By default, only the Safe Title Margin is displayed as shown in Figure 12-1. If both the Safe Title Margin and Safe Action Margin are displayed, the outer margin is the Safe Action Margin and the inner margin is the Safe Title Margin. Make sure that none of your titles fall outside the Safe Title Margin.

The Safe Title and Safe Action Margins are especially important if you're producing a movie that will be viewed on TV screens. Most TVs *overscan* the image, which means that they allow some of the video image to be cut off at the edges of the screen. Some TVs overscan worse than others, but anything inside the Safe Title Margin should appear on just about any TV screen with a bit of room to spare. If you place titles outside that margin, you're taking a chance that some text will run off the screen and be unreadable. The Safe Action Margin is a bit bigger than the Safe Title Margin because readability is less important for action in the video image.

If you're creating a title to be superimposed over a video image, I recommend that you display the actual image in the Adobe Title Designer window as you work on the title. Doing so helps you decide exactly where to position the text. In Premiere 6.0, showing a preview image meant importing a sample frame, a time-consuming process. But in the new tool, simply click to place a check mark next to the Show Video option. Video from your current project's Timeline appears. You can move to a specific point in your Timeline by using several methods:

- ✔ Click once on the timecode next to Show Video and then enter a specific timecode to which you want to jump.
- ✔ Click-and-drag left or right on the timecode next to Show Video. The video image jogs back and forth as you drag.
- ✔ Click the Edit Line button (see Figure 12-2). This moves the video to the current location of the Edit Line in the Timeline.

In Figure 12-2, you can see that I have moved to 00;04;22;18 in my Timeline.

Creating text

Once you have the Adobe Title Designer's view set up the way you like it, you can start adding text. From the toolbar on the left side of the Title Designer window, choose either the Horizontal or the Vertical text tool, and then click in the window and start typing. Your text appears on-screen. As you can see in Figure 12-3, the text probably doesn't look exactly the way you want it at first. To begin with, you probably want to move the text after you're done typing it. Click the Move tool and then click-and-drag the text box to a new location. Don't get too picky at this point; you'll probably move the text again later after you adjust some text attributes.

If you don't like the way text wraps to the next line when space runs out, open the Title menu from the Premiere menu bar and remove the check mark next to the Word Wrap option.

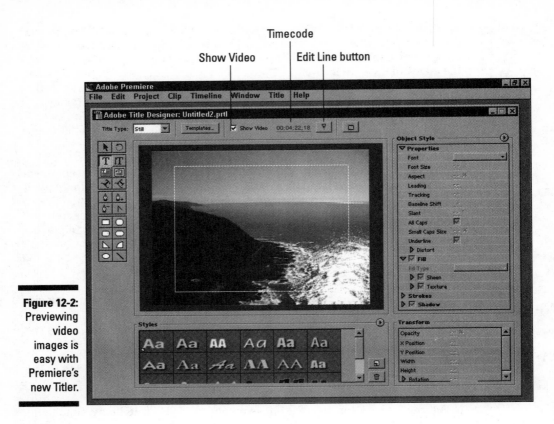

Figure 12-2:
Previewing
video
images is
easy with
Premiere's
new Titler.

Using title templates

Another — even simpler — way to start creating titles is to use one of Premiere's built-in title templates. Premiere 6.5 comes with more than 300 predesigned templates that can save time when you're creating complete titles. To use a title template, click the Templates button in the Adobe Title Designer window. The Templates window appears, as shown in Figure 12-4. To preview a template, click it in the Templates list on the left and then preview it in the upper-right corner of the Templates window. Many designs are available, so you may want to spend some time exploring the choices. If you scroll to the bottom of the list, you'll find folders containing elaborately designed titles that fit a variety of themes. For example, within the Professional folder you'll find a subfolder called Real Estate. Here, you'll find a collection of titles that would work well in, say, a video that features a home you're offering for sale.

Horizontal text

Move tool

Vertical text

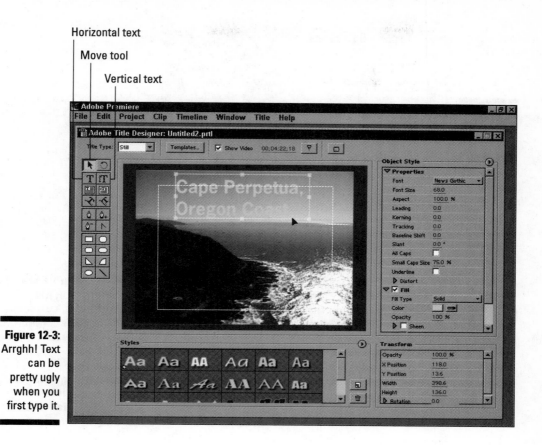

Figure 12-3:
Arrghh! Text
can be
pretty ugly
when you
first type it.

You can use a template even if you have already entered some text in the Title Designer window. Place a check mark next to the Preserve Title Text option to preserve the text you've already entered. When you are ready to apply a template to a title, select the template in the list on the left and click Apply. The Templates window will disappear and the template you chose will be applied in the Adobe Title Designer window.

Setting text properties

Whether you use a template for your title or not, you'll probably want to adjust the attributes of the text in your titles to make them more to your liking. For example, you can pick a font that's consistent with the project's style (as well as easy to read), pick a color that contrasts adequately with the background, adjust the size and scaling of the text, and more. To adjust text properties, click the text object once to select it, and then twirl down the arrow next to Properties in the Object Style menu.

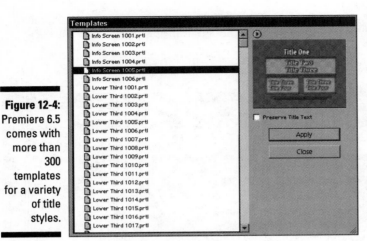

Figure 12-4: Premiere 6.5 comes with more than 300 templates for a variety of title styles.

You may find that selecting a text object in the Adobe Title Designer can be tricky. For example, rather than selecting an existing text object, you may find that clicking creates a new unwanted text object. To avoid this, carefully hover the mouse pointer over the text object that you want to select. Wait until a light rectangle appears around the desired text object; when that rectangle appears, click once to select the text object.

As you can see in Figure 12-5, many of the properties are numeric values. To change these, you can either click once and type a new value, or click-and-drag left or right to adjust the value with the mouse. Some properties — such as Font — have their own submenus. Click the box next to an item to open its submenu; then choose an item from the submenu.

When you've made your choices, click the arrow next to Properties to twirl the options back out of sight. Scroll down the list of items in the Object Style menu (refer to Figure 12-2). You see a few general categories of properties to adjust, including the following:

- ✔ **Properties:** This is where you adjust general text properties such as font, size, and other typographic properties. For example, Leading adjusts the vertical spacing between lines of text, and Kerning fine-tunes the spacing between individual characters. The Distort subgroup of options lets you add vertical and horizontal distortions to your characters for that fun-house-mirror look.

- ✔ **Fill:** Here you set the color and pattern for the text. For basic text you may want to choose "Solid" from the Fill Type menu. Gradient, bevel, and ghost patterns are also available. Choose text colors using color pickers, and adjust the opacity of the text or object. An object that is less than 100 percent opaque is slightly transparent.

↙ **Strokes:** Adjust the appearance of text on various "strokes" of the characters. This requires some experimentation to get just the right effect.

↙ **Shadow:** Use this group of options to apply a shadow to your text, as described in the next section.

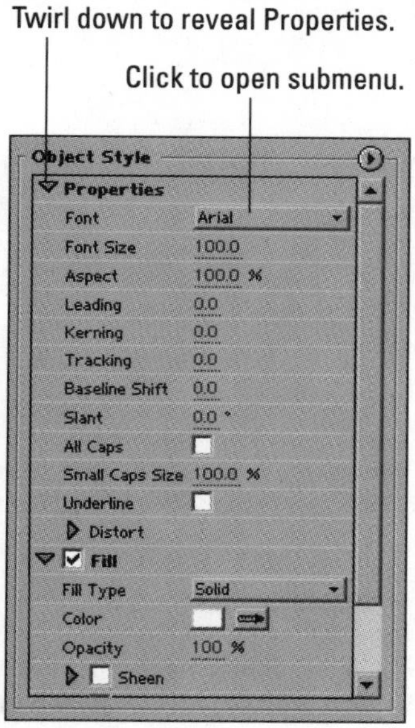

Twirl down to reveal Properties.

Click to open submenu.

Figure 12-5:
Adjust text attributes using the Object Style menu on the right side of the Titler window.

Shadowing text

If you want to apply a shadow to some text, Premiere's Titler provides a great deal of control. To apply a shadow to some text, first click the text in the Adobe Title Designer window to select it. In the Object Style menu, scroll the list and place a check mark next to Shadow. Then twirl down the arrow and adjust attributes of the shadow:

↙ **Color:** Shadows are usually dark. Click the color swatch to open the color picker and choose a color.

↙ **Opacity:** Adjust this to make the shadow somewhat transparent. Some transparency makes the shadow seem more realistic.

↙ **Angle:** Adjust this from 0 to 360 degrees to precisely set the angle of the shadow. The default angle is 273 degrees.

↙ **Distance:** The distance should be greater than 0, but it shouldn't be so great that the text is blurry and difficult to read.

> ✔ **Size:** Adjust the size of the image, but again the shadow shouldn't overpower the text in front.
>
> ✔ **Spread:** Use this to soften or sharpen the shadow's appearance.

A shadow can help offset text from the video image somewhat, as shown in Figure 12-6.

Figure 12-6: Use text shadows to subtly offset text and make it stand out.

Using styles

If a title template seems too fancy and manually adjusting title attributes is too time consuming, try using one of the Adobe Title Designer's predesigned styles. A selection of more than 20 styles is available in the Styles menu at the bottom of the Title Designer window. To use a style, follow these steps:

1. **Use the Text tool to create a text object and enter some text as described previously in this chapter.**

2. **Select a style in the Style menu at the bottom of the Adobe Title Designer window.**

3. **Click-and-drag the style from the Style menu and drop it on the text object.**

   A rectangle should appear around the text object before you release the mouse button to drop the style. Once applied, the text will automatically change to match the style you applied to it.

Styles can be thought of as starting points. Even if one of the styles doesn't exactly match what you need, choosing one that is close can still save you a lot of time. Once you've applied the style, you can always fine-tune attributes such as color, size, and shadows.

Orienting text

Text can be oriented in a variety of ways using the Adobe Title Designer. You've already seen horizontal text, and that's what you're likeliest to use. But you can change the orientation of your text as well. Text can appear

Making effective titles

If you've ever worked in print or Web design, you know some of the general rules for text: Use dark text on light backgrounds; use serif typefaces for large bodies of text; don't use too many different typefaces on a page.

Video has some text rules too, although they differ considerably from print. One of the things you must take into consideration when creating text for video is the effect that interlacing has on your text. Interlacing on NTSC or PAL TV screens causes thin lines to flicker or crawl on-screen. To prevent this headache, make sure that all the lines in your text are thicker than one pixel. Also, avoid using serif typefaces in video. Serif typefaces — such as Times New Roman — have those extra little strokes at the ends of characters, while sans serif typefaces — like Arial — do not. Those little strokes in serif typefaces are often thin enough to cause interlacing flicker. The text you're reading right now uses a sans serif face, while most of the text in the previous section uses a serif face. To be on the safe side, always carefully preview your titles on an external video monitor and check for flickering or other appearance problems.

Text color is another important consideration. In print and on the Web, dark text over a light background is usually best. Adequate contrast is still important, but in video light text usually works better. The best possible combination for video is white text on a dark background. Back in Figure 12-6, you can see that I have used shadowing to create a makeshift dark background behind my light text.

Finally, *always* keep your titles inside the Title Safe margin. Not only does this prevent text from running off the screen on TVs that badly overscan the image, but it also means that your text isn't running right up against the edge of the screen.

vertically on the screen, or on an angle or curve that you define. On the Title Designer toolbar you'll notice several basic text tools:

 Horizontal Text tool

Vertical Text tool

 Path Text tool

The Horizontal and Vertical Text tools are pretty self-explanatory, so I'll assume you can figure those out for now. The Path Text tool is a bit trickier because it allows you to define a path on which your text will appear. To use the Path Text tool:

1. **Click the Path Text tool to select it.**

2. **Move the mouse pointer over the spot where you want the text to** *begin.*

3. **Click and drag the mouse along an angle.**

A text baseline appears with control points at both ends, as shown in Figure 12-7. The angle described by the baseline is the angle that the characters will follow at the beginning of the text.

4. **Move the mouse pointer over the spot where you want the text to *end*.**

5. **Click-and-drag the mouse along another angle.**

As before, a baseline with control points will appear. The angle described by this second baseline will be the angle of the characters at the end of the text. You'll also notice that a curve will appear to connect the two baselines as shown in Figure 12-8. This curve shows the actual path that your text will follow.

6. **Begin typing some text.**

The text should appear along the angle you defined. Adjust text properties as needed.

You may find that you need to move or resize the text. To do so, select the Move tool and drag the text object to a new location. Use the handles at the corners of the text object to resize it. Once you've fine-tuned the text position and properties, your finished result might look similar to Figure 12-9. In the figure I have curved some text so that it follows the subject's physical action.

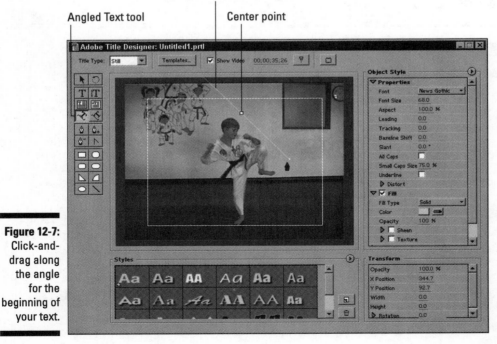

Angled Text tool

Text baseline shows angle.

Center point

Figure 12-7:
Click-and-drag along the angle for the beginning of your text.

Drag adjustment handles to change curve.

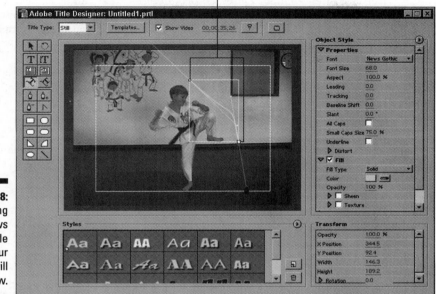

Figure 12-8:
A curving
path shows
the angle
that your
text will
follow.

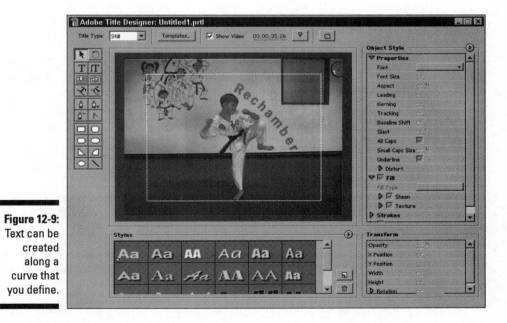

Figure 12-9:
Text can be
created
along a
curve that
you define.

Animating text

Titles are often animated in video productions. Text can fly onto the screen, crawl along the bottom like a stock ticker, or scroll from bottom to top as you roll the credits at the end of your movie. You can animate text using one of two methods:

- ✔ Animate the title clip in the Timeline using Premiere's animation tools. (For more on animating titles and other clips in the Timeline, see Chapter 10.)
- ✔ Use the animation tools built into the Adobe Title Designer.

The second method is the less complex of the two, so it's a good general choice. To create animated titles using the Adobe Title Designer, follow these steps:

1. **In Premiere, choose File⇨New⇨Title.**

2. **In the Title Type menu, choose Roll or Crawl.**

   Rolling titles roll from the bottom to the top of the screen, and crawling titles crawl from right to left.

3. **Create text objects for your titles.**

   If you're creating a rolling title, you can scroll down in the title area to add more titles. If you're creating a crawling title, you can scroll right.

4. **Open the Title menu on the Premiere menu bar and choose Roll/Crawl Options.**

   The Roll/Crawl Options dialog box appears.

5. **If you want the rolling or crawling title to begin off screen, select the Start Off Screen option. If you want the title to end out of view, choose the End Off Screen option.**

6. **If you want the title to remain static for a while before it starts to roll or crawl, enter a time in frames in the Pre-Roll field.**

   If you enter 15 in the Pre-Roll field, the title will appear on screen for 15 frames before it starts to roll or crawl off the screen. This field is not available if you choose the Start Off Screen option.

7. **If you want the title to roll or crawl on screen and then stop, enter a time in the Post-Roll field.**

   Like Pre-Roll, Post-Roll is measured in frames.

8. **If you want the title to gradually increase speed as it starts to move or gradually decrease as it stops, enter times in the Ease-In and Ease-Out fields.**

   Like Pre-Roll and Post-Roll, Ease-In and Ease-Out are expressed in frames. If you enter an Ease-In time of 15 frames, the title will start moving slowly and gradually build up to full speed within 15 frames.

9. **Click OK when you are done to close the Roll/Crawl Options dialog box.**

Although you can scroll in the work area of the Adobe Title Designer to see your entire title, you cannot preview the actual roll or crawl in the Title Designer. This is because Premiere dynamically adjusts the speed of the roll or crawl based on the length of the clip in the Timeline. The entire title will roll or crawl past whether you have the title set to play for five seconds or five minutes in the Timeline. Obviously, the more time you give the title to play the slower it will roll by.

Adding graphics to titles

Besides text, Adobe's Title Designer also enables you to draw some basic graphics and shapes in your titles. The drawing tools can serve a variety of useful purposes including:

✔ Draw a line under some text, thus making the text stand out a bit more on the screen. This is often done when identifying a speaker or subject on-screen (see Figure 12-10).

✔ A solid-colored box behind your text can help when the colors in the video image make it difficult to create adequate contrast between words and the background image.

The drawing tools can be found in the toolbar of the Title Designer window. Their functions are pretty self-explanatory; simply click a tool and then click-and-drag the shape on-screen. Use the Object Style menu to adjust colors and other attributes of the objects you draw. In Figure 12-10, for example, I have drawn a line between two rows of text. To create the line, I actually drew a narrow rectangle and then changed the fill color to the desired color (green, though you can't see that in the monochrome image shown here).

Figure 12-10: Subtle graphics can greatly improve the readability of text.

TIP

Notice that the two lines of text and the horizontal line in Figure 12-10 have little leading between them (*leading* is the vertical spacing between the lines). If you're creating a similar title, you'll probably want to keep the objects pretty tight together as well. Remember that small gaps on the computer screen become vast gulfs on a big TV screen.

You may want to adjust several other attributes of your graphics as well. When you select a graphic object using the Move tool, the Title menu (located up on the main Premiere menu bar) provides access to a couple of important options:

✔ **Arrange.** If some objects in a title will overlap other objects (say, for example, you want text over a background graphic), you'll need control over which objects are arranged on top of others. To move an item forward or back relative to other objects in the title, select that item and choose Title⇨Arrange and select an option from the submenu that appears. In Figure 12-11 I created a black background graphic for the text and chose Send to Back from the Arrange menu to ensure that the graphic was behind everything else in the title.

✔ **Opacity.** By default, all graphics you create in a title are opaque, which means you can't see through them. You can reduce the opacity of graphic objects, thereby making them more transparent. To adjust opacity, select a graphic object and choose Title⇨Transform⇨Opacity. Enter a percentage less than 100 to make the object less opaque. In Figure 12-11, I placed a black oval behind the text. An opaque black oval looked like a heavy black blob, but by reducing opacity to 50 percent, the background oval has now gained some subtlety. It still helps the text stand out, but it doesn't completely blot out the action that is going on behind it either.

Figure 12-11:
A slightly transparent black oval provides emphasis for the text without completely obscuring the action in the video image.

Adding Titles to Your Project

Once you have created titles in the Titler window, adding them to your project is pretty simple. When you're done creating a title, choose File⇨Save to name and save the title as a file on your hard drive. The title then appears in your Project window and resides in whatever bin happened to be open when you saved the title. To help keep things organized, I recommend that you create a special bin just for titles (call it "Titles" or something similarly creative), and store all your titles there.

Adding titles to the Timeline

To add a title to a project you basically just drag it from the Project window to a video track on the Timeline. But wait! Don't do it quite yet. There are a few things to double-check before you actually get started. To add a title to the Timeline, follow these steps:

1. **Click the Toggle Shift Tracks Options button on the Timeline to disable it.**

   You should see only one arrow on the button when it is disabled.

2. **Create a new video track specifically for titles.**

   To do so, you click the Track Options Dialog button on the Timeline, click Add in the Track Options dialog box, and add one video track. Give the new track a name ("Titles" or whatever, though "Whatever" takes longer to type). Click OK to close the Track Options dialog box.

3. **Drag the title from the Project window and drop it on the title track in your Timeline, as shown in Figure 12-12.**

   As with still graphics and many other elements, the default duration for a title is five seconds.

4. **Fine-tune your title to fit the needs of your project.**

   - **To change the duration of your title:** Select the Slide Edit tool and then click-and-drag the edge of the title clip to increase or decrease its duration.

   - **To fade a title in or out:** Expand the title track and use the Opacity rubber bands to control opacity.

Create a title track

Expand track

Slide Edit tool

Use Opacity Rubberband to fade out

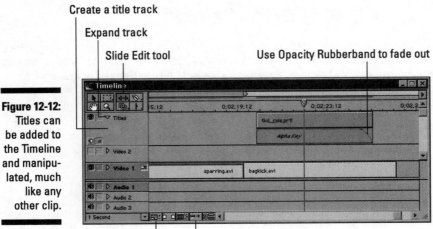

Figure 12-12:
Titles can be added to the Timeline and manipulated, much like any other clip.

Disable Shift Tracks option

Track Options dialog box

Importing titles from other programs

Adobe's Title Designer isn't your only option for creating titles for Premiere projects. Many other software publishers offer programs that do nothing but generate titles. And of course, many graphics and illustration programs offer elaborate ways to create titles as well. Some designers like to create titles in Adobe Illustrator or Photoshop and then import their creations into Premiere. This is fine, but for best results, be sure to define any areas of the file that you don't want to show up on-screen (say, the background) as transparent. In Photoshop, for example, a title file would probably have two layers:

  ✔ **Background:** This layer is transparent.

  ✔ **Layer 1:** This layer has the actual title.

Save the file as a Photoshop (.PSD) document, and then import that document directly into Premiere. When you're asked which layers you want to import, choose Merged Layers.

When you add the Photoshop title to your Timeline, select it and choose Clip➪Video Options➪Transparency. In the Transparency Settings dialog box, choose Alpha Channel from the Key type menu. The title should now appear correctly in the project.

Previewing titles

Previewing your titles is critical; presenting a movie with a half-obscured (or otherwise mangled) title is like slipping on a banana peel right before you want to quote Shakespeare. A word to the wise: Preview the timing of the appearance and disappearance of the titles, and review the positioning of your titles as action takes place behind the text.

Consider, for example, the image in Figure 12-13. It shows the same video clip and title that was shown back in Figure 12-11, but this time we're looking at a different frame. By comparing the two figures you can see that the subject moves his leg during the clip. Fortunately, the title was created so that it doesn't interfere with any of the action in the clip.

Figure 12-13: Make sure that action on the shot doesn't conflict with your titles.

Titles that come from the Adobe Title Designer are generated in much the same way that black video or bars and tone are generated — automatically. Because of this, titles must be rendered before you can preview them, unless you're using Premiere's Real-time Preview feature (see Chapter 13 for details). To render your titles in the Timeline, choose Timeline➪Render Work Area. Fortunately, titles render pretty quickly so it shouldn't take long before your preview is ready. After a few adjustments (and/or a few moments to gaze admiringly at your work), you can rest assured that your movie will make a competent entrance.

Chapter 13

Finalizing the Project

In This Chapter

▶ Getting a sneak preview of the Timeline

▶ Adding some finishing touches to your movie

I don't know about you, but I have a really hard time finishing a movie project. Some clip always lasts a few frames too long, or an effect keyframe isn't in exactly the right spot, or a title font isn't exactly what I wanted. There's always *something* — no matter how miniscule — that could be improved upon. Moviemaking is like that. But at some point, you have to give up tweaking your masterpiece and decide that it is "good enough."

Before you can actually stick a fork in your movie and call it done, you have a few tasks to do to finalize the movie and get it ready for output. You should sit back and preview the whole thing, of course, and also add elements to the beginning and end of the movie to prepare it for broadcast or delivery. Finally, you need to make sure that the project is rendered and ready for output. This chapter helps you put the finishing touches on your project.

Previewing the Timeline

I could start and end this section by simply telling you to click Play on the Program side of the Monitor to preview the Timeline. As an "oh-by-the-way," I could also mention the need to *render* effects, speed changes, transitions, and some other edits before you can preview them (unless, that is, you have real-time previews enabled, which is described in the following section). Rendering can take a long time, even with a fast computer, so I like to render as I go. Any portion of your Timeline that has to be rendered — but isn't yet — shows a red line under the Work Area bar, as shown in Figure 13-1. A green line means the section needed to be rendered but you already rendered it. To render unrendered portions of the Timeline, choose Timeline⇨Render Work Area.

TIP

If large sections of your Timeline need to be rendered, the process will take a while; this would be a good time to refill your coffee cup or get some lunch.

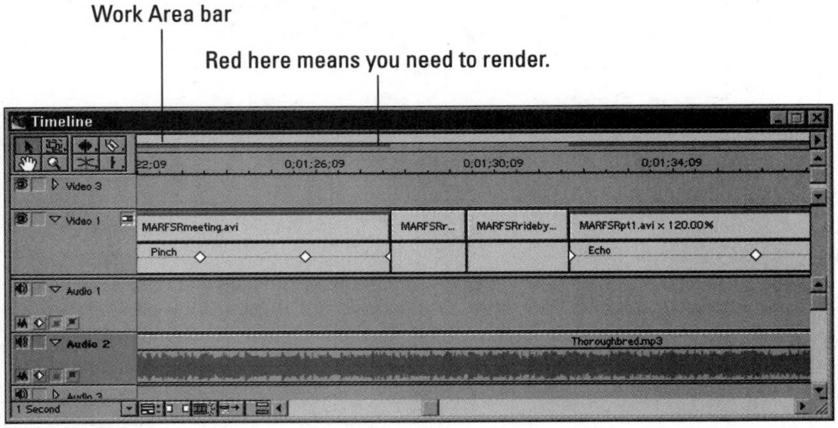

Work Area bar

Red here means you need to render.

Figure 13-1:
The Work
Area bar at
the top of
the Timeline
shows you
whether
the project
must be
rendered.

Previewing your project in real time

One new capability added to Premiere 6.5 is real-time previews. You can pre-view many transitions, effects, and other changes without having to render your work beforehand. If you are working with DV-based source material, you may have noticed some "Real-time Preview" presets in the Load Project Settings dialog box. These "Real-time" presets differ from the regular presets by only a single setting (which you can change any time you want anyway). To enable real time previews in any DV-based project:

1. **Open the DV project and choose Project⇨Project Settings⇨Keyframe and Rendering.**

   The Project Settings dialog box appears, displaying the Keyframe and Rendering options.

2. **In Windows, place a check mark next to Real Time Preview. On a Macintosh, choose To Screen in the Preview menu.**

3. **Click OK to close the dialog box.**

Pretty easy, huh? When you have real-time previews enabled, simply press the Enter (Windows) or Return (Macintosh) key. The Timeline will start to play, and most transitions and effects should play properly even if they aren't rendered. The effectiveness of real-time previews depends heavily on your hardware. If your computer isn't powerful enough to play some effects in real time, you may see dropped frames or other playback glitches. In that case, you either have to buy a faster computer or simply render the Timeline before you preview it.

Even if you don't have real-time previews enabled in your current project, you may still be able to do a quick preview anyway. Press Shift+Enter (Windows) or Shift+Return (Macintosh) to do a quick real-time preview.

Casting a critical eye upon your project

Of course, there's more to previewing your project than simply rendering the Timeline and clicking Play. Consider carefully what you are actually previewing when you play the Timeline. Here are some ways to get the most out of previewing your project:

- **Watch the whole program from start to finish**. You may be tempted to periodically stop playback, reverse, and repeat sections, perhaps even make tweaks to the program as you run it. This is fine, but to get a really good "feeling" for the flow of the project, watch the whole thing start to finish — just as your audience will. Keep a notepad handy and jot down quick notes if you must.

- **Watch the program on an external television monitor.** If you plan to export your movie to tape, previewing on an external monitor is crucial. (See the next section in this chapter for a more detailed explanation.)

- **Have trusted third parties review the project.** Moviemakers and writers are often too close to their creations to be totally objective; an "outside" point of view can help a lot. Though I worked hard to write this book (for example), my work was reviewed by various editors and their feedback was invaluable. Movie projects benefit from a similar review process. Even if you want to maintain strict creative control over your project, feedback from people who were not involved with creating it can help you see it afresh.

Speeding up your renders

As you've probably noticed, rendering can take a really, really long time. When the Timeline workspace is being rendered, a Building Preview dialog box appears, showing you (roughly) how far the render process has come and how long it has yet to run. This dialog box can provide more information if you click the arrow on the Building Preview window to expand it, as shown in Figure 13-2.

Click to expand.

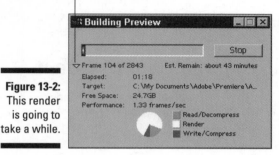

Figure 13-2:
This render
is going to
take a while.

If you want to speed up the process a bit, you can adjust certain render settings to reduce the overall time it takes. This may be useful if you want to do a basic preview of the project but you don't have to see every transition or effect. Follow these steps:

1. **Open your project in Premiere if you haven't done so already (in Premiere, choose File➪Recent Projects and select your project from the submenu that appears) and choose Project➪Project Settings➪Keyframe and Rendering.**

   The Keyframe and Rendering page of the Project Settings dialog box appears, as shown in Figure 13-3.

2. **Place check marks to ignore audio and video effects as appropriate.**

   Effects will not be rendered if you choose to ignore them here.

3. **Place a check mark next to the "Optimize Stills" option.**

   With this option enabled, still images are used far more efficiently. You should not enable this option if you encounter playback problems with stills, or if you have a capture card preset that specifies a stills setting.

4. **Click OK to close the dialog box.**

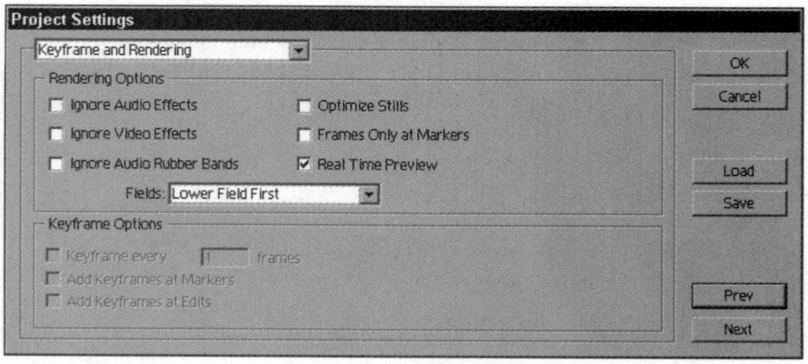

Figure 13-3:
Set options
here to
adjust how
previews
are
rendered.

As mentioned earlier in this chapter, if you select the Real-time Preview option, Premiere will attempt to simply preview the project from RAM instead of rendering a preview file. Just keep in mind that edits must still be rendered before you can export the movie, even if you have enabled the Real-time Preview option. The Real-time Preview setting has no effect on the speed of the actual rendering process.

Previewing on an external monitor

Even if you expand Premiere's Monitor window to a really big size, it still probably won't be as large as some of the displays that your audience is likely to use. A larger external monitor reveals camera movements and other flaws that might not be obvious on your computer screen. But even more important is color. Your computer monitor uses the RGB (red-green-blue) color space to generate color, but television screens generate colors differently. It is virtually impossible to properly preview the colors of your project on a computer monitor.

How you connect an external monitor to your computer varies depending on your hardware. If you have a video card with analog outputs, you should be able to connect your external monitor to those outputs. If you're really on a tight budget, you could connect your digital camcorder to your FireWire port, set the camera to VTR mode, and connect a monitor to the analog outputs on your camcorder. Sure, you'll have a mess of cables strewn all over the place, but this method should be effective.

If you preview your Timeline on an external DV device, the preview playback in the Monitor window probably won't play back at full quality.

Also, configure Premiere to play the Timeline on your external monitor. Here's how:

1. **In your project choose Project⇨Project Settings⇨General.**

   The General page of the Project Settings dialog box appears.

2. **Click the Playback Settings button.**

   The Playback Options dialog box opens, as shown in Figure 13-4.

3. **Choose the appropriate playback options.**

   If you choose the Playback on Camcorder/VCR option, you can disable Playback on Desktop. Disabling desktop playback may be useful if you are having problems with dropped frames during playback.

4. Choose Scrub options for audio and video.

Scrubbing is the process of slowly moving back and forth through video as if you were pulling or scrubbing a tape over the playhead in a tape deck. The Scrub options here control whether individual frames appear on the external monitor as you move frame by frame through the Timeline during editing. I generally recommend you leave the two scrubbing options enabled unless your external playback is running through a device that doesn't handle frame-by-frame scrubbing well, in which case you can disable scrub output to the external device.

5. Click OK when you are done.

Analog playback equipment varies greatly, so you should check the documentation for your video card and devices for specific information on video playback.

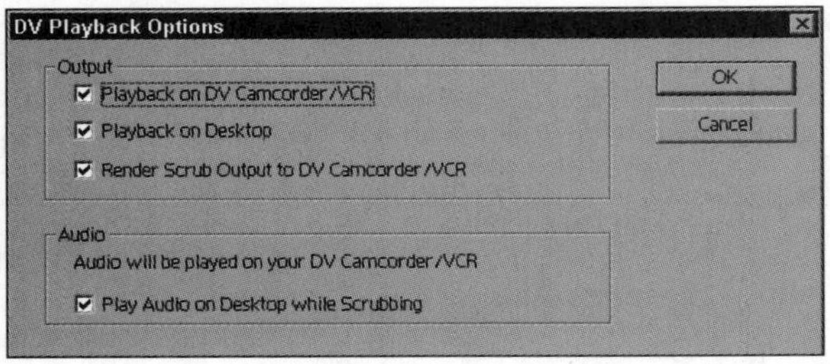

Figure 13-4:
Use the
Playback
Options
dialog box
to control
playback
options for
your
external
monitor.

Adding Final Video Elements

Movies and videos usually have a few elements that you may take for granted if you've never worked with professional video before. Some elements are tools that broadcast engineers normally use to adjust video equipment. These include counting leaders and color bars and tone. A third element that we'll discuss in the following sections seems like nothing at all: black video.

Creating a leader

Have you ever seen one of those spinning countdowns at the beginning of a video program? It's called a counting leader and is used by video engineers to ensure that the playback speed is correct and that audio and video is synchronized. The leader counts down from eight, and when it reaches two, a

Previewing video with your camcorder

If you aren't able or don't feel like connecting an external monitor to your computer, you could simply use your camcorder. (It's better than nothing!) However, there are some very important reasons why your camcorder is not the ideal preview monitor. First of all (and most obviously), the displays on camcorders are very small. Small details and problems may not show up very well on the tiny LCD screen or viewfinder of your camcorder.

There is another problem with previewing video on a camcorder that people don't often consider. This problem involves *interlacing*. If you'll be exporting your movie to videotape, you can assume that most of your audience will be watching the movie on standard TV screens. NTSC and PAL television displays are interlaced, meaning that each frame is drawn in two consecutive passes or *fields*. Each field contains every other horizontal resolution line. Interlacing is necessary, but it can create some anomalies in your video. Most of these

anomalies involve thin lines. If a subject on-screen is wearing a pinstripe shirt, the pinstripes will appear to crawl or waver on the screen. This is called a moiré pattern. Also, if you have titles or graphics on-screen with very thin lines, those lines may flicker annoyingly on a TV screen.

What do moiré patterns and interlacing flicker have to do with your camcorder? If you preview video on your camcorder's LCD screen, you probably won't see them. This is because the LCD screens on most camcorders are progressively scanned (which means they aren't interlaced, all resolution lines are drawn in a single pass). Your video might have serious problems that simply won't show up on your progressive scanning LCD monitor. The small viewfinder on your camcorder *might* be interlaced (check your camcorder's documentation), so you could try previewing the video through that, but if possible I still recommend that you use a real TV as your external monitor.

---

blip sounds. This blip helps the engineer synchronize the audio with the video. If your project is for use in broadcast or another professional environment, it should have a counting leader at the beginning of the tape.

If you have used Apple's Final Cut Pro or some other video editors, you may be accustomed to adding a SMPTE (Society of Motion Picture and Television Engineers) counter using the Print to Tape dialog box. Alas, Premiere's Print to Tape dialog box does not include a counting leader option, so you'll have to add it to the Timeline.

Premiere can generate a universal counting leader. It is 11 seconds long and must be placed in the Timeline. Ideally, you should plan ahead and leave 11 seconds open at the beginning of the Timeline, although it is possible to insert that time later. To create a counting leader follow these steps:

1. **In your project, choose File⇨New⇨Universal Counting Leader.**

   Alternatively, you can click the Create Item button in the Project window and choose Universal Counting Leader in the dialog box that appears.

Calibrating color with color bars

If you have an external video monitor, you should use color bars to calibrate it. Start by playing the color bars out to the monitor, and then pause playback so that the color bars remain. Next, turn the Color knob on the monitor all the way down and take a look at the PLUGE line (see Figure 13-6). You should see three different shades of black in the PLUGE line. Adjust the brightness knob on the monitor until the middle shade and the left shade appear to be the same. Now adjust the contrast knob up, and then turn it gradually down until the right shade in the PLUGE line is barely visible.

Now you are ready to adjust the color. If your monitor has a Blue Only setting, turn it on. Otherwise you have to use a blue filter, which is available at many photo supply vendors. Adjust the Tint (or Hue) knob until the third bars from the left and right seem to match with the small bars just under them. Then adjust the Color knob so that the outermost bars seem to match the small bars just under them. Turn off the Blue Only setting, and your colors are calibrated. Well done!

2. **Review the settings in the Universal Counting Leader Setup dialog box.**

   In general, I recommend that you maintain the default colors and settings unless you are just creating the leader because you think it looks cool and you'd like to create some custom colors.

   You see two audio options in the Counting Leader dialog box. The first one — Cue Blip on 2 — you should leave enabled unless you are not concerned about audio synchronization. Alternatively, if you're *really* concerned about synchronization, enable the Cue Blip at all Second Starts option. Doing so creates a blip at the beginning of each second during the countdown.

3. **Click OK to close the dialog box.**

   The counting leader is generated, appearing in the Project window when it's ready.

4. **If you have an open block of 11 seconds or more at the beginning of your Timeline, simply drag the Universal Counting Leader from the Project window and drop it in the Timeline.**

If you do *not* have an open 11-second block to accept the counting leader, make one. Follow these steps:

1. **Make sure that the Toggle Shift Tracks Option in the Timeline is enabled.**

2. **Choose the Multitrack Selection Tool and click the first clip in the Timeline.**

   All clips in all tracks of the Timeline should now be selected.

3. **Drag the selection to the right in the Timeline so that slightly more than 11 seconds of blank space is available at the beginning of the project.**

4. **Drag the Universal Counting Leader from the Project window and drop it on Track 1, as shown in Figure 13-5.**

5. **If a blank space appears between the counting leader and the first clip in the Timeline (and it probably will), click the space to select it and then choose Timeline⇨Ripple Delete.**

Your project will now have an 11-second counting leader at the beginning. You'll probably have to render your entire Timeline again to create all new preview files. You should play through the whole Timeline to ensure that all of the clips still play correctly.

For more on editing in the Timeline and working with Timeline options, see "Controlling Timeline Options" in Chapter 8.

Drag leader from here.   Counting leader

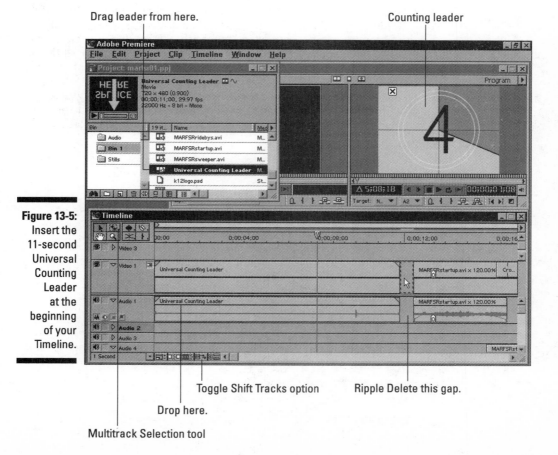

Figure 13-5: Insert the 11-second Universal Counting Leader at the beginning of your Timeline.

Toggle Shift Tracks option   Ripple Delete this gap.

Drop here.

Multitrack Selection tool

Adding bars and tone to the project

Two more important movie elements — especially if you plan to export to a professional broadcast environment — are color bars and a 1 kHz tone. The pattern for color bars, shown in Figure 13-6, is standardized by the Society for Motion Picture and Television Engineers (SMPTE) and can be used to calibrate the colors on a TV monitor. The 1 kHz tone serves to calibrate audio levels. There are two ways to generate bars and tone:

✔ Choose File⇨New⇨Bars and Tone. A five-second long Bars and Tone clip now appears in the Project window. As with the Universal Counting Leader described in the previous section, you can drag the Bars and Tone clip to an empty space at the beginning of the Timeline.

✔ Export the movie by choosing File⇨Export Timeline⇨Print to Video. The Print to Video dialog box has an option that enables you to lay down bars and tone at the beginning of a tape. You can specify how many seconds to show the bars and play the tone.

The bars and tone don't necessarily need to appear for long, although you should consult with the video engineers at the broadcast facility or production house to find out exactly what they want. In some cases they may only need a single frame of bars and tone, but in other cases they may want up to 30 seconds of bars and tone at the beginning of the tape.

Of the two options just described, I recommend using the Print to Video option. With Print to Video you don't have to create empty space at the beginning of the Timeline and possible re-render much of your project.

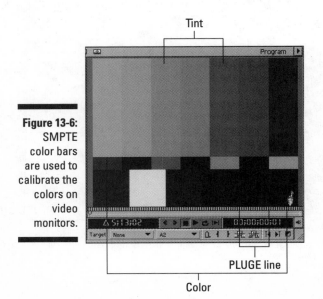

Figure 13-6: SMPTE color bars are used to calibrate the colors on video monitors.

Tint

PLUGE line

Color

Generating black video

Let's talk about nothing for a moment, shall we? By "nothing" I mean black video. Black video is a surprisingly important element for almost any movie project, but it is often overlooked precisely because it seems like there is nothing to overlook. Black video serves several important purposes:

- ✔ At the beginning of a movie, a stretch of black video gives the viewer a chance to get comfortable or "in the mood" after pressing Play. If the movie starts immediately once Play is pressed, the perception of the movie can be abrupt and unsettling for the viewer.

- ✔ At the end of the movie, black video gives the viewer some cushion space to press Stop after the credits stop rolling but before the static at the end of the tape starts. Without a bit of black video at the end of the program, that static could put someone's eye out if they're not expecting it (well, maybe it won't be *that* drastic, but you get the idea).

- ✔ Black video provides splicing room at the beginning of a tape. If you plan to distribute your movie on videotapes, remember that one of the most common mechanical failures on VHS tapes is the tape snapping at the beginning of the reel during rewind. This breakage can be repaired using a razor blade and some scotch tape, but some tape from the beginning of the reel is usually cut off. It would be better if a few seconds of black video were cut rather than the first few seconds of your program. If you're outputting for VHS tape, I recommend at least 60 seconds of black video at the beginning of the tape.

Black video can be generated in one of two ways. You can generate a black video clip in the Project window by choosing File⇨New⇨Black Video. A five-second black video clip appears in the Project window. To change the duration of the Black Video clip, select it in the Project window and choose Clip⇨Duration. The Clip Duration dialog box appears as shown in Figure 13-7. As you can see in the figure, I have changed the duration of my Black Video clip to 60 seconds.

Figure 13-7:
Use the Clip
Duration
dialog box
to change
the duration
of your
black video
clip.

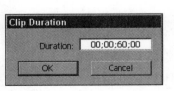

The Clip Duration dialog box uses timecode to specify a clip's duration. If you still aren't comfortable with timecode, see "Understanding Timecode" in Chapter 4.

The second method for generating black video is to use the Print to Video dialog box. If you use Print to Video to export your movie, you can specify how many seconds of black play before the movie starts. The default setting is just one second, but if you are outputting for videotape, bump up the Play Black setting to a more reasonable level (a 60-second interval is about right).

Chapter 14

Sending Your Project to the World

In This Chapter

▶ Catering to digital playback

▶ Setting up for analog playback

▶ Sending the project off for further editing

▶ Exporting just the audio

▶ Tantalizing viewers with exported still images

1 don't know about you, but I have so much fun working on movie projects in Adobe Premiere that I almost forget that other people might want to see my work. After all, sharing your movies is one of the main reasons for editing them in the first place, right?

You can share your completed movies with the world in many different ways. You can put your movies on the Internet, distribute them on CD-ROM (or DVD), or record your movies on videotape. You can also export your work for further editing, whether in another program or at a professional video-editing facility. You can export still images from your video, and even use Premiere to export audio in MP3 or other formats.

This chapter shows you how to share your movie projects with the rest of the world. You'll notice that I have divided the coverage according to some possible ways you may distribute your work. The first section helps you export movies for use in a digital format such as a CD-ROM, a DVD, or the Internet. The second section covers analog formats — in particular, video-tape. Finally, I include sections to help you export for further editing elsewhere, export audio, and export still images.

Exporting for Digital Playback

Until a few years ago, virtually all video was distributed on videotape. Now there are all kinds of options. You can put your movies on the Internet, burn them onto a CD-ROM, or (if you're a traditionalist at heart) put them on tape.

DVD recorders have become affordable in the last year or so, meaning you can even put your movies on DVD without breaking the bank.

Exporting a movie from Premiere for digital playback is pretty easy because, well, if you've been editing it in Premiere, then it's *already* digital. The following sections show you how to output your movie for specific delivery media. But first, a quick look at software players can give you a good working idea of what to consider if you distribute your movie digitally.

If you want to output your movie to an analog format such as videotape, see the next section in this chapter, "Exporting for Analog Playback."

Selecting a player

Distributing your movie digitally actually means distributing it as a file — so you have to make sure your intended audience can open that file. If you're distributing on a DVD, this usually isn't a problem; DVD players have their own built-in software for playing movies. But if you're distributing a movie file on CD-ROM or over the Internet, your audience has to have the right program to play your movie. As the moviemaker, you have three basic choices:

 ✔ Assume that your audience already has the necessary software installed.

 ✔ Direct your audience to download the necessary software from a Web site.

 ✔ Provide your audience with a copy of the necessary software.

The last option can be tricky — if you choose it, you must abide by software-distribution agreements — but if you want the viewing experience to be pleasant for the user, it's worth considering. The following sections describe some common software players for your movies.

Legal stuff has a tendency to change over time, and full details for each player would overflow the available space. Therefore, the following sections provide brief, basic descriptions of the redistribution rights (if any) specified for various software players — but you should carefully review each publisher's respective agreement before redistributing *any* software.

QuickTime

Apple QuickTime (see Figure 14-1) is perhaps the most ubiquitous media player in the personal computer world today, which makes it a good overall choice for your audience. QuickTime is available for Macintosh and Windows systems and is included with Mac OS X. QuickTime can play MPEG and QuickTime media. The QuickTime Player also supports progressive download, where files begin playing as soon as enough has been downloaded to allow continuous playback. The free QuickTime Player is available for download at

```
www.apple.com/quicktime/download/
```

Apple also offers a version of QuickTime called QuickTime Pro. Key features of QuickTime Pro include

- ✔ Full-screen playback
- ✔ Additional media management features
- ✔ Simple authoring tools
- ✔ Advanced import/export options

As an owner of Adobe Premiere, you don't need the extra features of QuickTime Pro; it doesn't do anything that Premiere can't do already. Your audience really doesn't need QuickTime Pro either (unless of course they want to watch movies in full screen.) The standard QuickTime Player should suffice in most cases. QuickTime-format files can be exported from both Macintosh and Windows versions of Premiere, but it is a lot easier on the Macintosh platform because the Mac version of Premiere 6.5 comes with a new tool called the QuickTime File Exporter, a tool that greatly simplifies the QuickTime export process.

Figure 14-1:
Apple's QuickTime is one of the most common and best media players available.

You can license QuickTime for redistribution with your movies. To do so you must fill out and submit a QuickTime licensing agreement. Once Apple has executed the agreement, you may distribute QuickTime in accordance with the license. For more on licensing QuickTime, visit

```
developer.apple.com/mkt/swl/agreements.html
```

RealPlayer

Another very popular media player is RealPlayer from RealNetworks. RealPlayer is available for Macintosh, Windows, and even Unix-based systems. The free RealPlayer software is most often used for RealMedia streaming media over the Internet, though it can also play MPEG-format media as well. Adobe Premiere includes a codec (compressor/decompressor software, see Chapter 4 for more on codecs) for exporting movies in the RealMedia format. To download the RealPlayer in its various incarnations, visit

```
www.real.com/
```

Although RealNetworks does offer a free version of the RealPlayer (pictured in Figure 14-2), you have to look carefully for the "Free RealPlayer" or "Free RealOne Player" links to download it. RealNetworks offers other programs that aren't free of charge but do have additional features. RealNetworks has specialized in the delivery of streaming content, and it offers a variety of delivery options. You can use its software to run your own RealMedia streaming server, or you can outsource "broadcast" duties to RealNetworks.

Free RealPlayer versions can be redistributed in accordance with RealNetworks' Licensing Distribution Program. The exact requirements vary, depending on how you plan to distribute and use the software, but it is generally free. To begin the process of licensing RealPlayer for redistribution, visit

```
forms.real.com/rnforms/resources/licensing/index.html
```

Figure 14-2: RealPlayer is a very popular media player and is often used for streaming media on the Internet.

A complaint often heard about RealPlayer is that the software tends to be intrusive and resource-hungry once installed — and that the program itself collects information about your media-usage habits and sends that information to RealNetworks. Although RealPlayer is extremely popular, consider that some folks out there simply refuse to install RealNetworks software on their computers. Although RealMedia is an excellent format, I recommend that you offer your audience a choice if you plan to use it; include another format such as QuickTime or Windows Media Video.

Windows Media Player

Microsoft's Windows Media Player (version 7 or newer) can play many common media formats. I like to abbreviate the program's name *WinMP* because, well, it's easier to type. WinMP 7 comes preinstalled on computers that run Windows Me or Windows XP. Although the name says "Windows," versions of WinMP are also available for Macintosh computers that run OS 8 (a version of WinMP is included with OS X). WinMP 7 is even available for Pocket PCs and countless other devices! WinMP is available for free download at:

```
www.microsoft.com/windows/windowsmedia/download/
```

WinMP can play video in MPEG and AVI formats. Premiere can output both of these formats, but they're not terribly useful for online applications because they're big and have an appetite for resources. Windows Media Player can also play Windows Media Video (WMV) format, and Premiere can output that as well by using the Advanced Windows Media Plug-in. I like the WMV format because it provides decent quality (for Web movies) with incredibly small file sizes.

You are allowed to redistribute Windows Media Player, but you must complete a Windows Media Licensing Form and receive approval from Microsoft. For information on obtaining and submitting a Windows Media Licensing Form, visit

```
wmlicense.smdisp.net/licenserequest/
```

What are the compelling reasons for choosing WinMP (shown in Figure 14-3) over other players? Choose Windows Media Player as your format if

- **Most or all of your audience members use Windows.** Most Windows users already have WinMP installed on their systems, so they won't have to download or install new software before viewing your Windows Media-format movie.

- **You want the look, but not the expense and complexity, of streaming media.** If you don't want to deal with the hassle of setting up and maintaining a streaming-media server, Windows Media-format files can provide a workable compromise. WinMP does a decent simulation of streaming media with *progressive downloadable video*: When downloading files, WinMP begins playing the movie as soon as enough of it is downloaded to ensure uninterrupted playback.

✔ **You're distributing your movie online and extremely small file size is more important than quality.** The Windows Media format can offer some remarkably small file sizes, which is good if your audience will be downloading your movie over slow dial-up Internet connections. I recently placed a 3:23-long movie online in Windows Media format, and the file size was only 5.5MB (megabytes). Of course, the movie was not broadcast quality. It had 32 kHz stereo audio, a frame size of 320 x 240 pixels, and a frame rate of 15 frames per second (fps). Although the quality was relatively low (compared to, say, DVD), it was superior to the quality offered by other formats, given the file size and length of the movie.

Figure 14-3:
Windows Media Player is required for viewing Windows Media-format movies.

DivX

What's this? I've gone out of alphabetical order! DivX is an increasingly popular video format used primarily for exchanging movies on the Internet. DivX offers an excellent balance of quality and file size. I'm covering the DivX Player last because Adobe Premiere does not offer built-in support for DivX. It is easy enough to produce DivX movies from Premiere, however, so I've taken the liberty of covering it here. Find out more about DivX (or download the software) at

```
www.divx.com
```

The DivX described here should not be confused with DIVX DVDs, which are limited, pay-per-use DVD movies. That particular format, created several years ago by Circuit City and a few other companies, has basically disappeared from the modern video scene.

When you distribute a movie online, you must first consider what player software your audience will have. Although QuickTime, RealPlayer, and Windows Media Player are still the most popular video players on the Web, DivX is quickly gaining ground because people like it. Why?

- ✔ DivX is free and available for Macintosh, Windows, and Unix-based systems (that is, Linux).
- ✔ The DivX Player download is small (less than 3MB).
- ✔ The DivX Player is not absolutely necessary to view DivX movies. If you have the DivX codec installed, many other media players can be used, including WinMP.
- ✔ Users don't have to provide any personal information — not even an e-mail address — to download or use DivX. This really matters to some people.

DivX is both a player (shown in Figure 14-4) and a codec. When you install the software on your computer, it not only installs the DivX Player software but also the DivX codec. The Windows version installs the codec in your System folder, but with the Mac version, you must manually move all the DivX components to your Extensions folder. Once installed, the DivX codec can be used within Premiere during the movie export process, just like any other codec. The DivX software comes in three basic flavors:

- ✔ **DivX:** The basic software package is free and provides the basic tools needed to produce and view DivX movies.
- ✔ **DivX Pro (ad supported):** DivX Pro adds more control over encoding. The advertising-supported version is free, except that you must view advertising while you use the software.
- ✔ **DivX Pro:** If you don't want to view ads, you can pay $30 for the commercial-free version of DivX Pro.

Redistribution agreements are available for DivX, and redistribution is generally free for individuals and independent filmmakers. However, if you are redistributing the software with a commercial product, licensing fees may apply. Review the licensing policies on the DivX Web site before you try to redistribute DivX.

Why choose DivX? First, the quality-versus-file-size balance is quite good. Second, it could be said that the DivX format has the least amount of political "baggage" on the Web. Let's face it, if you start developing movies specifically for Apple or Microsoft software, someone is going to complain and accuse you of being a "Mac freak" or "Windows bigot." And as mentioned previously, plenty of people are off-put by RealNetworks software as well. If you have similar concerns, you may find that DivX is a good baggage-free (for now) compromise.

Figure 14-4:
The DivX
Player is
simple,
free, and
increasingly
popular.

CD-ROM

CD-ROM seems a natural choice for distributing video. Blank discs are cheap — just pennies each, if you buy blank CDs in spindles of 50 or 100 at a time — and they're easy to mail. Recording a movie onto a blank CD is really easy, too. CD-R (Compact Disc-Recordable) drives are widely available, and with software like Roxio's Easy CD Creator or Toast, copying video files onto a CD is a matter of just a few mouse clicks. Still, there are some important issues to consider before you record video onto CD-ROM:

If you have enough free space on the disc, you may want to provide your audience with a copy of the necessary player software. You can add the installer file for the software to the CD-ROM. (See the previous section for licensing information on redistributing player software.)

✔ **Does the audience have the necessary playback software?** In the previous section of this chapter, I showed you several popular media players. Make sure that your audience knows what software they need to view the movie on your CD-ROM.

✔ **Will the movie fit on the CD-ROM?** Most blank CDs hold only 650MB of data. Some claim to hold up to 700MB, although you may find that trying to squeeze more than 690MB onto a disc is risky business (data retrieval becomes unreliable).

▸ **Will the movie play adequately?** CD-ROM drives usually can't read data very quickly (by today's standards, at least). Video requires a high data rate, and some CD-ROM drives might not be able to handle it.

To ensure that your video fits on a CD-ROM and it plays adequately, I recommend that you use either the Cinepak or Sorenson codecs. The Sorenson codec offers greater quality, but it also requires that your audience have a

Compressing video with DivX

If you install the DivX software on your system, you can use the DivX codec when exporting video from Premiere. To do so, export your movie by choosing File⇨Export Timeline⇨Movie. Click the Settings button and choose Microsoft DV as the editing mode. Then click Next to move to Video settings. You should be able to choose the DivX codec from the Compressor menu.

To adjust DivX options, click the Configure button. The DivX codec properties dialog box will appear with several tabs of options. On the

DivX Codec tab, use the Encoding bitrate slider to adjust the bitrate for the movie. A higher bitrate provides higher playback quality but also larger file sizes. In the Variable bit rate mode menu, choose 2-pass for maximum compression (and the longest rendering time). On the General Parameters tab, choose Enable Resize and enter a new frame size if you want to change the frame size for the output movie. Also, choose the All Frames are Interlaced option in the Source Interlace menu if your source material is interlaced.

newer computer with a faster CPU. Cinepak is a better choice if your users have older, slower machines. Cinepak movies play in Windows Media Player, but Sorenson movies don't. The DivX codec works pretty well too, if you and your audience have the DivX software. Follow these steps to output your movie for CD-ROM playback:

1. **Choose File⇨Export Timeline⇨Movie.**

   The Export Movie dialog box appears.

2. **Click the Settings button at the bottom of the Export Movie dialog box.**

   The Export Movie Settings dialog box appears with the General group of options displayed.

3. **In the File Type menu, choose Microsoft AVI or QuickTime.**

   If you're not sure which one to pick, I recommend QuickTime, as shown in Figure 14-5.

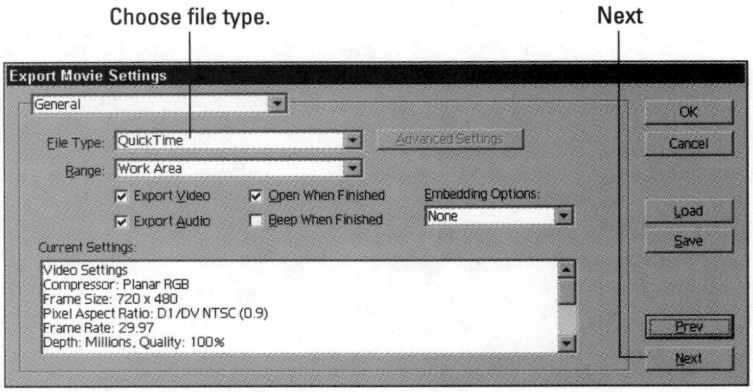

Choose file type.   Next

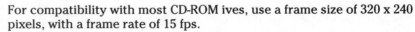

Figure 14-5:
Choose
Microsoft
AVI or
QuickTime
as the file
type for
export.

4. **Click Next to display the Video options.**

5. **In the Compressor menu, choose Cinepak or Sorenson.**

6. **Review and adjust the frame size and frame rate settings as shown in Figure 14-6.**

   For compatibility with most CD-ROM ives, use a frame size of 320 x 240 pixels, with a frame rate of 15 fps.

7. **Click Next to display the Audio options.**

8. **Set the Rate to 22050 Hz.**

   With the Sorenson codec you can leave the format at 16 Bit - Stereo, but for Cinepak you should choose 16 Bit - Mono.

9. **Click OK to close the Export Movie Settings dialog box.**

Choose codec.

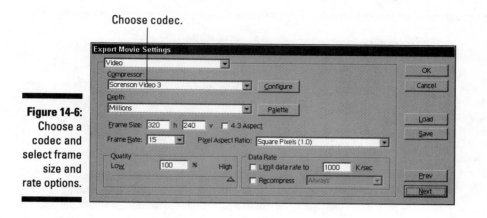

Figure 14-6:
Choose a
codec and
select frame
size and
rate options.

10. **Back in the Export Movie dialog box, choose a location and enter a file name for your movie, and then click Save.**

    The export process may take a while, depending on the length of your movie.

You may need to experiment with settings and codecs to get a pattern that works best for your audience. One problem you may encounter if your source footage is interlaced is that fast-moving portions of your video may appear jagged, as shown in Figure 14-7. To rectify this, you need to deinterlace the movie during export. In the Export Movie Settings dialog box, click Next until you reach the Special Processing settings; then click Modify and select the Deinterlace option.

Deinterlacing with the codec usually won't work well, especially if you changed the frame size of the video image. If you continue to have interlacing problems, use the Field Interpolate effect in the Timeline to deinterlace the problematic clips before export. See Chapter 10 for more on using effects in the Timeline.

World Wide Web

It's hard to believe, but the World Wide Web has been with us for almost ten years now. As for the Internet (of which the World Wide Web is a part), in a few years it reaches middle age. The good folks who built the foundations of the online world envisioned it as an efficient global information exchange, though I doubt they envisioned folks like you and me exchanging full-motion video online. Video, especially streaming video, is at odds with the fundamental design of the Internet for two key reasons:

Creating cross-platform CD-ROMs

When people talk about cross-platform CD-ROMs, they usually refer to a disc that works on both Macintosh and Windows computers. Creating such a disc can be tricky. The main problem is that Windows and the Mac OS use different file system formats for CD-ROM discs. The Mac OS uses a system called HFS (Hierarchical File System) while Windows uses either the ISO-9660 or Joliet file systems. To make a disc fully functional in both operating systems, you must record the CD with both file systems.

I normally don't get involved in the Mac versus Windows debate, but when it comes to creating cross-platform CDs, a Macintosh is the only place to do it right. None of the CD recording software available for Windows can create a proper cross-platform disc. To create a cross-platform disc, I recommend that you use Roxio's Toast (www.roxio.com) on your Mac. If you have an older version of Toast, such as Toast 4 from Adaptec (the former publisher of Toast), that works too.

To create a cross-platform disc using Toast, first create a temporary partition by choosing Utilities⇨Create Temporary Partition. Name the partition in the Create Temporary Partition dialog box that appears. The name you give the partition here is the name that the final disc will have when your users insert it into their computers. Add all your files to the partition. Keep in mind that when Mac users access the disc later, the window size and layout of the icons will be the same as what you specify on your temporary partition. Therefore you should spend a few minutes laying out the partition neatly to make it more presentable. Choose View⇨Clean Up to arrange all the icons in neat rows and ensure that some icons aren't hiding behind others. I usually like to arrange the most important icons at the top of the window and then resize the window so that just the important icons are shown. I also recommend that you position the window in the upper-left corner of the Macintosh desktop. Doing so ensures that all your users can see the whole window, even if they're using an iMac with the display set at 800 x 600 pixels.

Once the temporary partition is set up the way you want it, go back to the Toast window and choose Mac/ISO Hybrid from the format menu, as shown following. Drag and drop the icon for your temporary partition onto where it says "Drop a volume here" in the Toast window.

To configure the Windows side of the disc, click the ISO button in Toast; the ISO9660 dialog box appears. Remove the check mark next to Resolve Aliases and then switch to the Settings tab. Choose Joliet from the Format menu. Back on the Files tab, drag-and-drop the temporary partition icon, as well as any other files unique to Windows users (such as setup files). Also remove any files that Windows users don't need (for example, be on the lookout for files named "Icon," "DesktopPrinters DB," and "OpenFolderListDF," none of which Windows users need). Click Done when you're finished configuring the ISO9660 partition. If you see a warning about file names that don't conform to the Joliet standard, go back to the Files tab and remove any files that have three red exclamation marks next to them.

When you write the disc, you may be tempted to choose the fastest write speed that is supposedly supported by your CD recorder. One thing I've found after several years of burning disc masters is that the faster the recording speed the more likely it is that errors will occur. No matter how fast your CD burner claims to be, I recommend that you record your discs at 1X or 2X speed. The recording process will take longer, but disc errors are far less likely.

Choose Mac/ISO Hybrid

Adaptec Toast™

TOAST 4.1

Mac/ISO Hybrid

Mac: (Drop a volume here)   Data...

ISO: (Drop files and folders here)   ISO...

Total: -

CD Recorder

CRD-R800S
SCSI Bus 0, ID 4   Search

Check Speed...   Write CD...

✔ **Bandwidth:** The overwhelming majority of Internet users still have slow dial-up connections. Video files tend to be large, meaning they take a long time to download. Quality must often be reduced to ensure reasonable download times.

✔ **Packet delivery:** Data is transmitted over the Internet in packets rather than in steady streams. This makes data transfer over the Internet reliable, but not fast.

Interlacing jaggies

Figure 14-7:
Here you can see how interlacing can ruin the image quality when the video is output for digital playback.

Data is broken down into packets before being transmitted over the Internet. These packets can travel over many different pathways to the destination, where they are reassembled in the correct order. Compare this to, say, a radio or television broadcast where data is transmitted in a continuous wave. Packet delivery is very reliable because it does not require a single unbroken connection between the sender and the receiver. Confused? Imagine you want to give your phone number to someone across a crowded room. You could try yelling across the room (a broadcast) but because of all the other noise, the other person might miss a number or two. A more reliable method would be to write your phone number on a piece of paper and send it via messenger to the other person. The paper method would be slower, but at least you know the recipient will get the correct phone number.

So what is the point of all this technical discussion about bandwidth and packets? I bring it up because you must be aware of the potential problems before you start sharing video over the Web. Video for the Web must be highly compressed, the frame size must be reduced, and you must accept some sacrifices in quality.

Video can be distributed over the Internet in one of two ways:

- ✔ **Download:** Users download the entire movie file before it can be viewed.

- ✔ **Stream:** The movie plays as it downloads to the user's machine. Some of the video is buffered (portions of the file are temporarily stored on the user's hard drive) to provide uninterrupted playback. The three predominant formats for streaming video are QuickTime Streaming, RealMedia, and Windows Media Streaming Video. In each case, special server software is required to host streaming media.

Regardless of which distribution method you choose, the export process for the movie from Adobe Premiere is still the same. You export the movie as a file that resides on your hard drive. Whether that file is later streamed or not is determined by whether or not you use streaming server software on your Web server.

If possible, I recommend that you produce several different versions of your movie for the Web. Produce a lower-quality movie for people on slow dial-up connections, and a higher-quality movie for folks with broadband access. You may also want to offer versions for several different players. For example, you could offer a RealMedia version and a Windows Media version.

Using the QuickTime File Exporter

The Macintosh version of Adobe Premiere comes with a handy tool called the QuickTime File Exporter. This tool simplifies the process of exporting movies into QuickTime format. You can export to QuickTime formats from the Windows version of Premiere, but the process is more complicated. If you're using Premiere on a Windows machine, I recommend you use either the Advanced

RealMedia or Windows Media Export options described in the following sections. To export using the QuickTime File Exporter on your Mac, do this:

1. **When your project is ready to export, choose File⇨Export Timeline⇨Movie.**

   The Export Movie dialog box appears.

2. **Click Settings.**

   The Export Movie Settings dialog box appears.

3. **Choose QuickTime File Exporter in the File Type menu.**

4. **Click the Advanced Settings button.**

   The QuickTime File Export Settings dialog box appears.

5. **Make sure that QuickTime Movie is chosen in the Export menu.**

6. **Choose a preset in the Using menu.**

   The Using menu contains a variety of presets based on different bandwidth capabilities for streaming media. The lower the bandwidth you choose, the lower the file size and quality will be.

7. **To review or adjust the specific settings for a given preset, click Options.**

   The Movie Settings dialog box appears, as shown in Figure 14-8. Review the video and audio settings listed in the dialog box. In Figure 14-8, you can see that my current settings will create a movie with a 176 x 144 image size and 22.05 kHz 16-bit audio. Click the Settings buttons to adjust video or audio settings. If you want to specify a different video size, click Size.

8. **If the movie will not be delivered by a streaming server, remove the check mark next to Prepare for Internet Streaming.**

9. **Click OK three times to return to the Export Movie dialog box. Name the file and click Save.**

   If you will be sharing the movie on the Internet or with Windows users, make sure you add the .QT extension to the end of the filename.

Export video with Cleaner 5 EZ

Another export option you may be able to use is Cleaner 5 EZ from Terran Interactive. Cleaner 5 EZ simplifies the process of exporting Web-friendly movies, and it comes with Premiere 6.5 for Macintosh and Premiere 6.0 for Macintosh or Windows. Cleaner 5 EZ is not included with Premiere 6.5 for Windows because it is not compatible with Windows XP or Windows Media 8. You will also find that even if you have Premiere 6.5 for Macintosh, Cleaner 5 EZ will not work if you are running OS X. To export a movie using Cleaner 5 EZ:

1. **If you only want to export a portion of the Timeline, slide the ends of the Work Area bar at the top of the Timeline so that only the desired portion of your project is covered by the bar.**

   You may want to do so if your Timeline includes elements for tape export such as black video or a counting leader.

2. **Choose File⇨Export Timeline⇨Save for Web.**

   The Cleaner 5 EZ window appears as shown in Figure 14-8.

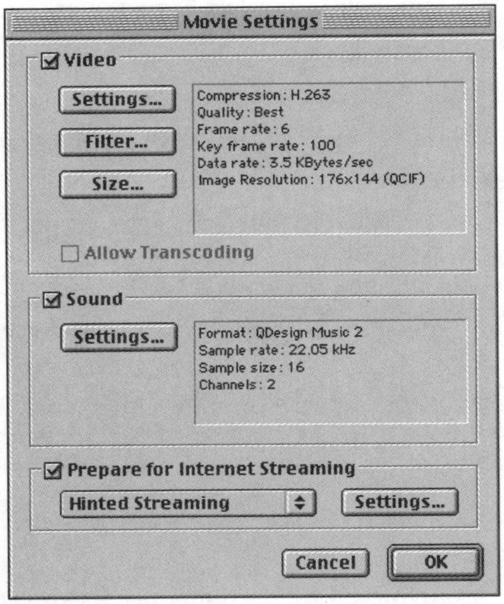

Figure 14-8:
Use the
Movie
Settings
dialog box
to review
and
customize
settings
for your
QuickTime
Movie.

Movie Settings

☑ **Video**

[Settings...] Compression : H.263
[Filter...]   Quality : Best
               Frame rate : 6
[Size...]   Key frame rate : 100
               Data rate : 3.5 KBytes/sec
               Image Resolution : 176x144 (QCIF)

☐ Allow Transcoding

☑ **Sound**

[Settings...] Format : QDesign Music 2
               Sample rate : 22.05 kHz
               Sample size : 16
               Channels : 2

☑ **Prepare for Internet Streaming**

[Hinted Streaming ▲▼] [Settings...]

                        [Cancel] [OK]

If you have Premiere 6.5 for Windows or OS X you will not have a Save for Web option in the Export Timeline submenu. This is because Cleaner 5 EZ does not come with that version of Premiere.

3. **Click the Settings menu to open it.**

   A menu of available export formats appears.

4. **Choose a basic format for export.**

   If you're not sure which one to choose, select QuickTime for now, as shown in Figure 14-9.

   A submenu appears.

5. **In the submenu, choose a secondary export option.**

   If you are using QuickTime Progressive Download, I recommend one of the first three choices in the submenu. These options are Big Movie, Medium Movie, and Small Movie.

Figure 14-9:
Premiere
uses
Cleaner 5 EZ
from Terran
Interactive
to prepare
movies for
the Internet.

Figure 14-9: Premiere uses Cleaner 5 EZ from Terran Interactive to prepare movies for the Internet.

6. **Choose an option in the Export menu.**

   You can export the Entire Project, or you can choose to export only the Selected Work Area. This second option exports only the portion of your Timeline between the in and out points you set back in Step 1.

7. **Click Start.**

   Cleaner 5 EZ from Terran Interactive launches.

8. **Provide a filename for your movie when you are prompted to do so by Cleaner 5 EZ and click OK.**

   Cleaner 5 EZ begins to create your movie. The export process may take a while, depending on the size of your movie and the speed of your computer.

Exporting Advanced RealMedia

Adobe Premiere comes with an Advanced RealMedia Export plug-in that helps you export RealMedia. To view RealMedia, your users must have RealPlayer (or the newer RealOne program). This usually isn't a problem because RealPlayer software is so common as to be virtually ubiquitous. One of the nice things about using RealMedia is that the files can dynamically adjust to various bandwidths. You only have to create one RealMedia file, but the quality that users receive depends on the speed of their Internet connections.

You can use the Advanced RealMedia Export tool to export streaming RealMedia to be used on a RealVideo streaming server, or you can simply export downloadable movie files. To use Advanced RealMedia Export:

1. **If you only want to export a portion of the Timeline, slide the ends of the Work Area bar at the top of the Timeline so that only the desired portion of your project is covered by the bar.**

   You may want to do so if your Timeline includes elements for tape export (such as black video or a counting leader).

2. **Choose File➪Export Timeline➪Advanced RealMedia Export.**

If this is the first time you've used Advanced RealMedia Export, you will be asked to provide your name and e-mail address for registration purposes. You will also be given the opportunity to go online and download the latest version of the RealPlayer software if you don't already have it. Even though Premiere includes Advanced RealMedia Export, it does not include a program that can play RealMedia files, so if you don't already have RealPlayer you should download it. Once you've already registered RealMedia Export, the Advanced RealMedia Export dialog box appears, as shown in Figure 14-10.

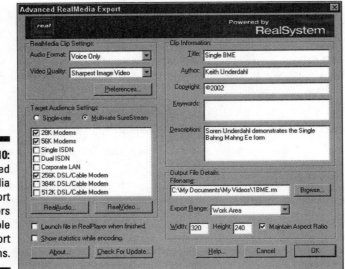

Figure 14-10: Advanced RealMedia Export offers multiple export options.

3. **Choose audio and video quality settings in the RealMedia Clip Settings section.**

   The Audio Format options are self-explanatory, so just choose the one that most closely matches your project. In the Video Quality menu, choose Smoothest Motion for video with little motion, Sharpest Image if there is a lot of fast movement, and Normal Motion for everything in between.

4. **Click Preferences and review the settings found there. In the Preferences dialog box, you get five tabs full of options:**

   - **General:** Specify a rating for your movie and control whether viewers can record your movie or save it to their hard drive.

   - **SureStream:** Set your backward compatibility (I recommend that you choose RealPlayer G2), and choose whether audio or video should be emphasized when bandwidth is limited.

- **Video Filter:** Select filter options. If your video comes from an interlaced source, activate the De-interlace Filter.

- **Video Codec:** Choose a codec. RealVideo 8.0 provides better quality but requires a faster processor on the user's computer. 2-pass Encoding provides more efficient compression, though compression takes a lot longer. If you plan to stream your movie, enable the Loss Protection option.

- **Advanced:** I generally recommend against adjusting the settings on this tab.

5. **Back in the RealMedia Export dialog box, under Target Audience Settings choose Single-rate if you are simply creating a file that people download before viewing, and then choose a quality level under Target Audience Settings**

   When you look at the quality levels, you'll notice that rather than providing details about the actual video and audio quality, all that is listed are Internet connection speeds. It's not terribly informative, I know. The idea is that if the user is viewing the movie as a streaming file, the audio and video quality will be adjusted down to a level that will play adequately at whatever Internet connection speed you specify. Table 14-1 lists the actual settings for each listed quality level. To really get a feel for each quality level, you should preview the file once it's exported. Some experimentation may be necessary.

   Higher quality settings produce larger file sizes.

   If you plan to stream the movie from a RealVideo streaming server, choose Multi-rate and place a check mark next to each quality level for which you want to generate a movie. Again, see Table 14-1 for a breakdown of quality settings.

   Don't underestimate the importance or providing low-quality streams for 56K and 28K modems. By most estimates, more than 80 percent of Internet users still have 50K or slower dial-up connections.

6. **Fill out the Clip Information fields (Title, Author, and such) on the right side of the RealMedia Export dialog box.**

   This information appears in the RealPlayer software as your movie plays.

7. **Enter a filename for your movie in the Filename field.**

8. **From the Export Range drop-down menu, choose whether to export the entire project or just the work area you selected back in Step 1.**

9. **Use the Width and Height fields to adjust the frame size of your movie.**

   If you are exporting a full-size video image, you probably want to reduce the frame size down to 320 x 240 pixels or less.

10. **Click OK.**

    The export process may take a while, depending on the length of your movie and the speed of your computer.

As mentioned in the steps above, Advanced RealMedia Export offers a variety of quality levels to choose from when you export your video. Table 14-1 lists the maximum video quality settings (I've left out audio-only settings from the table) for each available Target Audience Setting. Keep in mind that these are *maximum* levels. The actual quality of audio and video will vary depending upon how efficiently the RealMedia codec is able to compress the media. For example, although the maximum frame rate for the Corporate LAN setting may be 30 fps (frames per second), the actual frame may be less if the Target Bitrate is exceeded. As with all export methods, a thorough preview of your movie is crucial before you actually share it with the rest of the world.

Table 14-1	Advanced RealMedia Export Quality Settings			
Target Audience Setting	*Voice Quality*	*Music Quality*	*Max. Video Frame Rate*	*Target Bitrate*
28K Modem	4 kHz mono	4 kHz mono	15 fps	20 Kbps
56K Modem	4 kHz mono	4 kHz mono	15 fps	34 Kbps
Single ISDN	4 kHz mono	5.5 kHz mono	15 fps	45 Kbps
Dual ISDN	4 kHz mono	5 kHz stereo	15 fps	80 Kbps
Corporate LAN	11 kHz mono	8 kHz stereo	30 fps	150 Kbps
256K DSL/Cable Modem	11 kHz mono	11 kHz stereo	30 fps	225 Kbps
384K DSL/Cable Modem	11 kHz mono	16 kHz stereo	30 fps	350 Kbps
512K DSL/Cable Modem	11 kHz mono	20 kHz stereo	30 fps	450 Kbps

Exporting Windows Media

Another Web-friendly export option available in the Windows version of Adobe Premiere is Windows Media. This export option produces Windows Media Video (WMV), a efficient export format for online media. WMV-format video supports progressive download, which means it starts to play as soon as a sufficient amount of data has been received to ensure continuous playback. To view Windows Media Video, users must have Windows Media Player 7 or higher. Versions of Windows Media Player are available for both Windows and Macintosh systems.

Sadly, Advanced Windows Media Export is not available in the Macintosh version of Premiere at this time.

To export a movie in WMV format, follow these steps:

1. **Choose File⇨Export Timeline⇨Advanced Windows Media.**

   The Windows Media Export Plug-in appears, as shown in Figure 14-11.

2. **Choose a profile from the Profiles list that most closely matches the bandwidth capabilities of your target audience.**

   Unfortunately, the profile definitions are a bit ambiguous because your users are most likely to download WMV files before viewing them anyway. Because the Advanced Windows Media Plug-in isn't quite advanced enough to provide a file-size estimate, you may need to experiment a bit with the Profiles to get a desirable file size. Table 14-2 provides a breakdown of quality settings for each available profile.

3. **Fill out the Properties fields (Title. Author, and so forth) for the movie.**

   This information appears in Windows Media Player as the movie plays.

4. **Provide a filename and choose a destination for the movie file in the Destination field.**

   In Figure 14-11, you can see that I have named my movie file 1BME.wmv, and I will be saving it in the folder C:\My Documents\My Videos.

5. **Click OK.**

   The movie is exported. As with other formats, the export process may take a while.

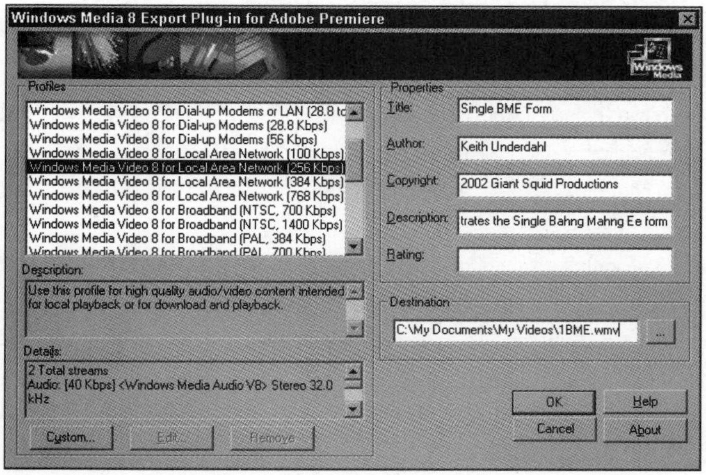

Figure 14-11:
Use the Windows Media Plug-in (Windows version of Premiere only) to export WMV-format video.

The Windows Media Export Plug-in offers a huge variety of Profiles from which to choose, and many of them seem to have similar names. Which Profile is best? Table 14-2 lists the Profiles available in the Windows Media 8 Export Plug-in that comes with Premiere 6.5, and provides basic details on the quality settings used by each Profile. For the sake of simplicity I've left the audio-only (Windows Media Audio) Profiles out of the table. Look through the Profiles and find the one that has the best combination of audio quality, video size, and frame rate for your needs. You may notice that some of the Profiles, such as "Broadband (NTSC, 700 Kbps)" and "Broadband (NTSC 1400 Kbps), seem similar. In such cases, the higher bandwidth Profiles usually provide slightly better video image quality. As with all export options, some experimentation may be necessary on your part to get the quality level and file size you need.

Premiere 6.0 came with version 7 of the Windows Media Export Plug-in instead of version 8, which is shown and described here. If you have Premiere 6.0, your available Profiles will have different (and, thankfully, more descriptive) names.

Table 14-2	Advanced Windows Media Video Quality Settings		
Profile	*Audio Quality*	*Video Size (pixels)*	*Frame Rate*
Color Pocket PCs (225 Kbps)	22.1 kHz stereo	208 x 160	20 fps
Color Pocket PCs (150 Kbps)	22.1 kHz stereo	208 x 260	8 fps
Dial-up Modems or Single-channel ISDN (28.8 to 56 Kbps)	8 kHz mono	176 x 144	15 fps
LAN, Cable Modem, or xDSL (100-768 Kbps)	32 kHz stereo	320 x 240	15 fps
Dial-up Modems or LAN (28.8 to 100Kbps)	8 kHz mono	176 x 144	15 fps
Dial-up Modems (28.8 Kbps)	8 kHz mono	160 x 120	15 fps
Dial-up Modems (56 Kbps)	11 kHz mono	176 x 144	15 fps
Local Area Network (100 Kbps)	16 kHz mono	320 x 240	15 fps
Local Area Network (256 Kbps)	32 kHz stereo	320 x 240	30 fps

Profile	Audio Quality	Video Size (pixels)	Frame Rate
Local Area Network (384 Kbps)	32 kHz stereo	320 x 240	30 fps
Local Area Network (768 Kbps)	44.1 kHz stereo	320 x 240	30 fps
Broadband (NTSC, 700 Kbps)	44.1 kHz stereo	320 x 240	30 fps
Broadband (NTSC, 1400 Kbps)	44.1 kHz stereo	320 x 240	30 fps
Broadband (PAL, 384 Kbps)	32 kHz stereo	352 x 288	30 fps
Broadband (PAL, 700 Kbps)	44.1 kHz stereo	352 x 288	30 fps
Dial-up Modem (No audio, 28.8 Kbps)	none	176x 144	15 fps
Dial-up Modem (No audio, 56 Kbps)	none	240 x 176	15 fps
Fair Quality based VBR for Broadband	44.1 kHz stereo	320 x 240	30 fps
High Quality based VBR for Broadband	44.1 kHz stereo	320x 240	30 fps
Best Quality based VBR for Broadband	44.1 kHz stereo	320 x 240	30 fps

One complaint about the Advanced Windows Media Export tool is that it does not allow you to simply export a selected work area. You can only export the entire Timeline. There are two possible workarounds for this shortcoming:

✔ Export the work area as an AVI file, import that AVI file into a new Premiere project, and then export this new project using the Advanced Windows Media Export tool.

✔ Export the work area as an AVI file and then import it into Windows Movie Maker. Windows Movie Maker is a rudimentary video editing program that comes free with Windows Me and Windows XP. A nice feature of Windows Movie Maker's export process is that it gives you a file-size estimate for your final movie based on the settings you choose.

Neither of these workarounds is ideal, but if you want to create a trimmed-down version of your movie in Windows Media Video format, these are your only options for now.

For more on using Windows Movie Maker, check out *Microsoft Windows Movie Maker For Dummies,* by yours truly.

DVD

You've probably noticed that DVD (Digital Versatile Disc) has become *the* hot method for distributing movies today. However, until recently the process of mastering a DVD movie was complex, and the hardware for recording (a.k.a. *burning*) DVDs was prohibitively expensive. Thankfully, all that is changing. Apple has been at the forefront of affordable DVD production. Apple released an affordable DVD burner in 2001 called the SuperDrive, and by the middle of 2002 you could buy a SuperDrive-equipped Macintosh for less than $2,000. Prices for blank recordable DVD media have also been falling rapidly, with blank discs now available for less than $10 each.

Many other companies have entered the DVD burner fray, and countless drives are now available for both Macintosh and Windows systems for as little as $300. With a DVD burner and the right software you can record your movies onto DVDs, which can then be viewed in nearly any commercial DVD player.

Adobe Premiere 6.5 adds new support for DVD that previous versions didn't have. The exact support varies depending on which platform you use to run Premiere:

- **Macintosh:** Premiere 6.5 for Macintosh integrates with Apple's DVD Studio Pro to encode and author DVDs. Timeline markers created in Premiere can be used as chapter references within DVD Studio Pro. To integrate Premiere with DVD Studio Pro, you must purchase that software from Apple.

- **Windows:** Premiere 6.5 for Windows includes an MPEG-2 encoder, which is the video format used by DVD players. The Premiere 6.5 CD also comes with a program called Sonic DVDit! LE, which enables you to create a DVD interface, create a layout, and author the DVD.

Using Adobe MPEG Export

The MPEG-2 Encoder included with Premiere 6.5 for Windows is pretty slick. Using this tool, you can export video for almost any medium that uses MPEG-2 video — including DVD. To use Adobe MPEG Export, follow these steps:

1. **If you only want to export a portion of the Timeline, slide the ends of the Work Area bar at the top of the Timeline so that only the desired portion of your project is covered by the bar.**

You may want to do so if your Timeline includes elements for tape export such as a long stretch of black video or a counting leader.

2. **Choose File➪Export Timeline➪Adobe MPEG Encoder.**

   The Adobe MPEG Encoder Settings window appears, as shown in Figure 14-12.

   If this is the first time you have ever used the Adobe MPEG Encoder, you will have to activate it. A dialog box will appear giving you the option to activate it via the Internet or telephone. Follow the instructions on-screen to activate the software. Whichever activation method you choose, you'll be given an activation code which must be entered before you can continue using the Adobe MPEG Encoder. Activation is free.

3. **Choose a video standard (NTSC or PAL).**

   If you're not sure which video standard to choose, see "Decrypting Video Standards" in Chapter 4.

4. **Enter a filename and location for the output file in the appropriately named Filename and Location fields.**

5. **If you only want to export the Timeline between the in and out points you set in Step 1, choose Work Area from the Export Range menu. If you want to export the whole project, choose Entire Project from the Export Range menu.**

6. **Click Export.**

   As with other export formats, export may take a while.

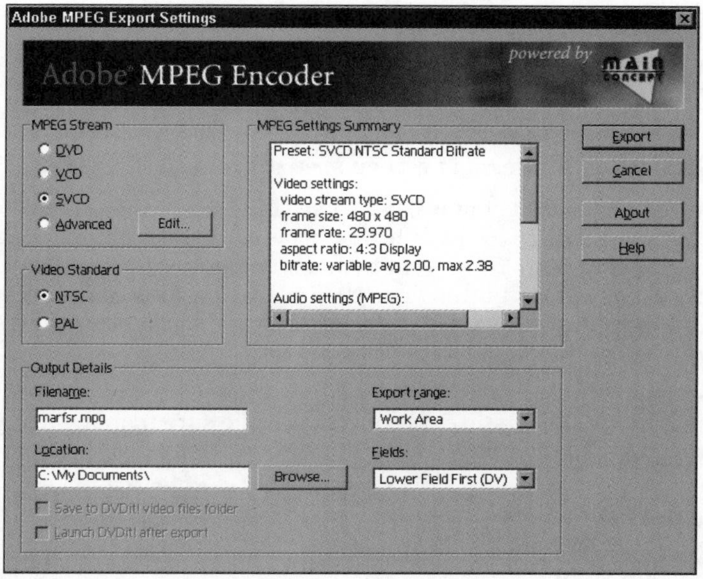

Figure 14-12:
Use the new Adobe MPEG Export feature to export your movies for DVD playback.

Adobe MPEG Export Settings

Adobe MPEG Encoder   *powered by* **main** CONCEPT

MPEG Stream
○ DVD
○ VCD
◉ SVCD
○ Advanced   Edit...

MPEG Settings Summary
Preset: SVCD NTSC Standard Bitrate

Video settings:
video stream type: SVCD
frame size: 480 x 480
frame rate: 29.970
aspect ratio: 4:3 Display
bitrate: variable, avg 2.00, max 2.38

Audio settings (MPEG):

Export
Cancel
About
Help

Video Standard
◉ NTSC
○ PAL

Output Details
Filename:
marfsr.mpg

Location:
C:\My Documents\   Browse...

Export range:
Work Area

Fields:
Lower Field First (DV)

☐ Save to DVDit! video files folder
☐ Launch DVDit! after export

The Adobe MPEG encoder exports an MPEG-2 file. You can then use DVD authoring software to put the MPEG-2 file in a DVD layout and author the DVD. Premiere 6.5 includes a simple DVD authoring tool called DVDit! LE, described in the next section.

Using DVDit! LE

Adobe Premiere 6.5 for Windows comes with a DVD authoring tool called DVDit! LE. It can be found in the DVDit! LE folder on your Premiere installation disc. Once installed, you can launch DVDit! LE using the desktop icon created during setup. When you create a new project, you'll be asked to choose a TV Standard (NTSC or PAL) and a video format. If you're creating a DVD, choose MPEG2 (DVD-compliant). The DVDit! LE interface appears, as shown in Figure 14-13. Follow these basic steps to create the project:

1. **Click the Media button at the bottom of the Theme panel.**

   The Theme panel switches to the Media list, which at this point is probably empty.

2. **Click Theme to open the Theme menu and choose Add Files to Theme.**

   A Look In dialog box opens.

3. **Browse to the folder that contains your MPEG-2 file and open the file.**

   The file appears in your Media list.

4. **Click the Backgrounds button to bring the list of backgrounds to the front, and then drag one of the backgrounds to the First Play placeholder.**

   The theme now appears in the main screen and in the First Play placeholder.

5. **Click the Text button.**

   A list of fonts appears.

6. **Drag a font to the main screen area to create a text object.**

   A text object that simply says "Text" appears on the screen. To edit the text, click it once to select it, wait a moment, then click it again. Start typing your text. If you want to add some buttons to the screen, you can click the Buttons button (sorry!) and drag buttons to the screen just as you did with text. As you can see in Figure 14-13, I've created one button and a text object that says "Play Movie."

   To adjust the color, size, and other characteristics of text, select the text and choose Effects➪Text Properties. Make sure that any text you add contrasts adequately with the background image.

7. **To turn a button or text object into a link, first click the object to select it.**

   A white outline appears around the object to indicate that it is selected.

Drag movie from here

Drop movie here to create link. First Play placeholder Theme menu

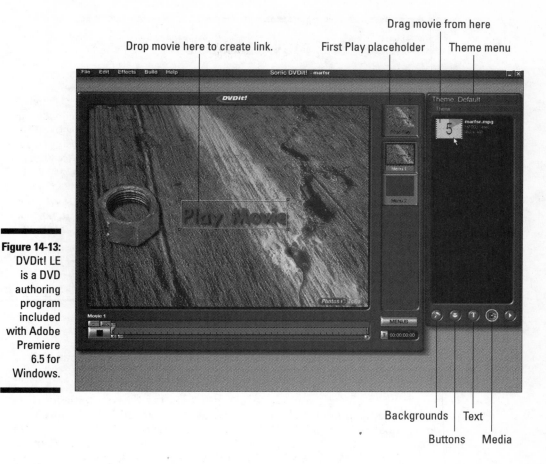

Figure 14-13:
DVDit! LE
is a DVD
authoring
program
included
with Adobe
Premiere
6.5 for
Windows.

Backgrounds | Text

Buttons | Media

8. **Click the Media button to bring the list of media files to the front, and drag the desired movie file onto the button or text that will serve as a link.**

9. **Choose File⇨Project Settings.**

   The Project Settings dialog box appears.

10. **Choose the type of disc that you will be using to record the project in the Output Size menu.**

11. **Review your current project size to ensure that you aren't exceeding the capacity of the disc.**

   The maximum capacity for each Output Size disc type is listed in the dialog box.

12. **Click OK to close the Project Settings dialog box.**

DVD movies on CDs?

In the previous section, I mentioned two other possible destinations for your MPEG-2 movies — VCD (Video Compact Disc) and SVCD (Super VCD). Both use regular CD-R (Compact Disc-Recordable) media for recording. Believe it or not, you can record up to 74 minutes of full-motion MPEG-2 video and audio onto a VCD. An SVCD can only hold about half as much video, but the quality is slightly higher and you can include more audio and subtitle tracks. The video quality of VCD and SVCD video is generally lower than that of DVD video, but it's as good as — or better than — VHS video.

The appeal of VCDs and SVCDs is obvious. Although DVD burners and blank DVD media are getting cheaper, they are still quite expensive compared to CD burners and blank CD-Rs. Blank CD-Rs are also cheaper than blank VHS tapes, and they are cheaper to mail because CD-Rs are smaller and lighter than tapes. VCDs and SVCDs provide an economical way to share high-quality video, although you should keep in mind that some DVD players cannot play VCDs and SVCDs. For player-compatibility information, I recommend that you check out a Web site such as that maintained by VCDHelp.com (www.vcdhelp.com), featured in **Chapter 15** of this book.

13. **Burn the disc or create a disc image.**

Use options in the Build menu to either make a DVD using your DVD or CD burner, or create an image by choosing Make DVD Folder.

If you create an image, you have a folder on your hard drive (in the location you specified) containing all the files needed to create a DVD. Of course, you'll probably spend a lot more time playing around in DVDit! LE, but this is the basic procedure. You should also check the documentation for your DVD burner; it may have come with additional software to help you author DVDs. And of course, test your DVDs carefully to ensure functionality — *before* you send them out into the world.

If you are creating a master disc image that will be mass produced by someone else, ask the manufacturing facility that you are working with about special formatting requirements and submission procedures before creating a disc image.

Exporting for Analog Playback

Although analog video may seem old-fashioned, it is still the most common method for sharing video. It's also pretty reliable. When you share movies on CD-ROM or the Internet, you have to worry about your possible users' mishmash of bandwidth capabilities — and whether they have the right playback software. And even with DVDs, some players simply refuse to play some discs.

But in the case of VHS videotapes, you know that your tapes play reliably in almost any VHS tape deck. You also know that virtually every human being in your target audience already owns at least one VHS tape deck and a TV.

Of course, you still need to be wary of broadcast standards. A PAL-format VHS tape doesn't play in an NTSC-format VHS deck.

Exporting video to an analog source is also a far less complicated process than exporting for a digital source. The main difference is that you don't have to worry about codecs and player software. Your only real concern is that you have the right hardware for export, and that your computer runs well enough to export without dropping frames or causing other problems.

Videotape

Though DVDs are quickly becoming the standard for video exchange, VHS videotapes are still the most common video medium. If your ultimate plan is to put your video on a VHS tape, you can use one of three methods:

- ✔ **Export directly to a VHS deck connected to your computer.** This generally requires special hardware such as a high-quality video card. If you were able to capture video from a VHS deck, then you should be able to export to it as well. Device control is only available on higher-quality, professional-grade tape decks.

- ✔ **Export video through the analog outputs on your digital camcorder.** With your camcorder connected to your FireWire port, the camcorder can serve as a digital-to-analog converter to the VHS deck. Some camcorders do not allow analog output and FireWire input at the same time. Also, when using this method, Premiere's device control can only control the camcorder, not the analog deck.

- ✔ **Export video to your digital camcorder, and then dub it to the analog deck later.** This approach should work even with the cheapest consumer-grade hardware. If your camcorder doesn't allow simultaneous digital input and analog output, simply export the video to a tape in the camcorder and then later dub it to a VHS tape using the camcorder's analog outputs.

The following sections describe exporting video to an analog source, both with and without device control.

Getting ready for export

Remember back when you were getting ready to capture video into your computer? You probably spent some time preparing your system to ensure that you didn't drop any frames during capture. As with capturing, exporting video is also resource intensive, and you must carefully prep your computer to ensure there aren't any dropped frames as you lay the movie down on tape. Before you export a movie to tape, double-check the following:

- Make sure that all unnecessary programs are closed, including your e-mail program and Web browser. Every open program uses up memory and processor resources that should be devoted to video export.

- Disable memory-resident programs — for example, antivirus programs, programs that have icons in the Windows system tray, and unneeded Macintosh extensions.

- Disable screen savers and power-management settings to ensure they don't kick on in the middle of a long export operation. (You weren't *really* going to create a movie using battery power, right? I thought not.)

- Defragment your hard drive. A recently defragmented hard drive is important with any operating system, but doubly so if you are using Windows 98 or Windows ME.

Before exporting to tape, you should also check your project settings in Premiere. Open the project, and choose Project➪Project Settings➪General. In the General settings dialog box, click the Playback Settings button. The Playback options dialog box appears, as shown in Figure 14-14. The exact settings available vary according to the type of project you are working with.

I recommend that you disable the Playback on Desktop option before exporting your project. This frees up additional resources on your computer and hopefully make dropped frames even less likely.

Figure 14-14:
Review your playback options to ensure that the Timeline plays correctly to your external device.

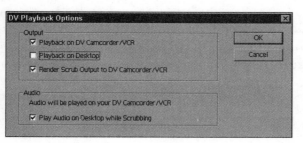

Exporting to tape with device control

Years ago, when Apple and Microsoft introduced Plug and Play hardware, many old-timers scoffed. "Plug-and-*pray*," it was often called, especially when it didn't work. Thankfully, years of development have made Plug and Play — combined with device control — a crucial asset of IEEE-1394 (FireWire) technology. Connect a digital camcorder to your FireWire port, turn it on, and

---

Blacking and coding a tape

As you'll see in the next section, some export-to-tape operations assume that there is already timecode on the videotape to which you are about to export video. But if you are using a brand-new tape that you just peeled out of its plastic shrink-wrap, the tape has no timecode yet. You can rectify this situation by doing what video pros call *blacking and coding* the tape — recording black video and timecode onto the tape before you record anything else.

The easiest way to black and code a tape is to simply create a project in Premiere that contains nothing but black video (with *no* audio), and then export that project to the tape. You might be tempted to just black and code the first minute or two of a tape, but I have found that with some devices this can cause a recording glitch when the end of the original timecode is reached during export.

---

within seconds you should be controlling camcorder functions using your computer. I've been using digital video equipment for a couple of years now, and it still amazes me every time I click Play in Premiere and the tape in my camcorder starts to roll. In fact, thanks to device control, I have *more* control over the camcorder in Premiere than I do when trying to manipulate the buttons on the camcorder itself.

Device control also makes exporting video to tape really easy. If you are exporting to a device that has device control (such as a digital camcorder) follow these steps:

1. **Connect your recording device (your camcorder or tape deck) to your computer and turn it on.**

2. **In Premiere, choose File⇨Export Timeline⇨Export to Tape.**

   The Export to Tape Settings dialog box appears as shown in Figure 14-15.

3. **Select the Activate Recording Deck option.**

4. **If the tape already has timecode on it, select the Assemble at Time Code option and specify a timecode where you want recording to begin.**

   As you can see in Figure 14-15, I am starting my movie at the one-minute mark on my tape.

5. **Enter the number of quarter frames, if any, that you want to delay before the movie starts playing.**

   Some devices need a delay between receiving the record command and the actual movie.

6. **Enter the number of frames that you want to preroll the tape in the Preroll (Macintosh) or Timecode Offset (Windows) field.**

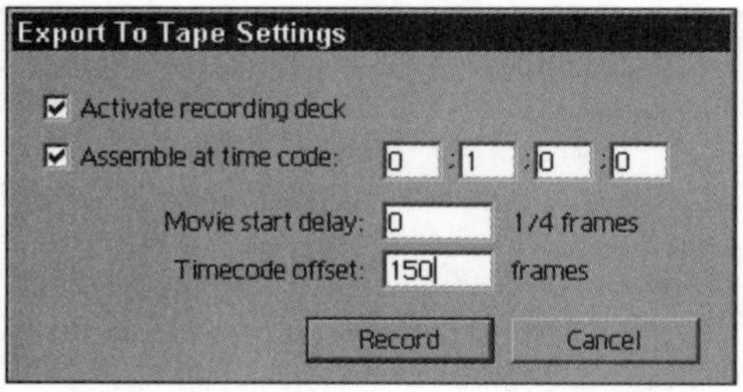

Figure 14-15:
Adjust
settings
here before
exporting
your movie
to tape.

Export To Tape Settings

☑ Activate recording deck

☑ Assemble at time code: [0] : [1] : [0] : [0]

Movie start delay: [0]   1/4 frames

Timecode offset: [150]   frames

[Record]   [Cancel]

Preroll allows the reels in the tape deck to spin up to the correct speed before recording begins. I recommend at least five seconds (150 frames for NTSC video) of preroll.

7. Click Record.

Your movie is recorded on the tape.

Steps 4 through 6 above require that there is already timecode on the tape to which you are exporting. Although you can often get away with skipping those three options — especially if you already placed a section of black video at the beginning of your Timeline — I recommend that you black and code your tapes before exporting to them.

Exporting to tape without device control

Exporting to tape without device control is a tad clumsy, but it is possible. You basically just use magic flying fingers to press Record on the tape deck as you click Play in Premiere. Here's how:

1. Connect your hardware and cue the tape to the point at which you want to start recording.

2. Play the Timeline by clicking Play in the Monitor.

Make sure that the movie plays on your external monitor or camcorder display. Once you are sure that your movie is playing on your external monitor, stop the Timeline.

3. Place the Edit line at the beginning of the Timeline.

4. Press Record on the tape deck or camcorder you are using to record.

5. Click Play in the Program view of the Monitor to play the Timeline.

Step 2 in this list is basically a test to make sure that your hardware setup is going to work. This test is crucial because if you don't see the video from the Timeline playing out on the external hardware, you can bet that nothing is recorded onto your tape either.

Exporting for Further Editing

If you're relatively new to video editing and you recently spent $500 or so for Adobe Premiere, you may be surprised to find out that there are even more-sophisticated and expensive video-editing systems out there. Personally, I find that Premiere satisfies almost all my editing needs, but you may find that once you are done editing in Premiere you need to do a bit more work somewhere else. You may need to do advanced animation editing in a specialty program like Adobe After Effects. Or you may want to take your project to a professional postproduction video-editing facility.

Creating edit decision lists

In Chapter 8 I described the Timeline as Adobe Premiere's kitchen. If the Timeline is like a kitchen, an edit decision list (EDL) can be thought of as a recipe for a specific movie that you can create in the kitchen. An EDL contains the names of all the clips in your project, the in and out points for all your edits, and information about the transitions and effects that you apply. The idea is that you can take the tapes (a.k.a. reels) with all your source material and the EDL to a postproduction facility, and all your edits are automatically reproduced using the EDL.

You may find that the theory of EDLs does not match the reality of them. Before you start exporting EDLs for use at a postproduction facility, work with the people at the facility and find out what exactly they need in the EDL. They'll probably tell you to generate an EDL for a specific edit controller. Premiere includes built-in support for CMX, Grass Valley, and Sony controllers, and you can add support for others.

To generate an EDL, follow these steps:

1. **Complete your edits in Premiere and save your project.**
2. **Choose File⇨Export Timeline⇨EDL.**
3. **Select a format from the submenu that appears.**

    The EDL Output dialog box appears, unless you choose Generic EDL, in which case a standard Save As dialog box will appear. If the EDL Output dialog box appears, set options as needed. Again, consult with the postproduction facility for specific settings to use when you export the EDL. When you click OK to close the EDL Output dialog box, the standard Save As dialog box will appear.

4. **Name and save the EDL.**

5. Copy the EDL to a floppy disk.

Double-check with the folks at the postproduction facility to find out what kind of disk they want. EDLs are simply text files and are small, so fitting one onto a floppy disk shouldn't be a problem, even for a large and complex project.

You can open an EDL in a text editor such as Notepad or SimpleText, but don't edit it unless you really know what you're doing. If you need to make changes in your Timeline after generating an EDL, the best solution is to simply export a new EDL.

Exporting for Adobe After Effects

As I've said throughout this book, Adobe Premiere is a truly amazing program. However, you may find that there are times when you want or need to do some work in another program. For example, if you want to create graphics or animation for your movie, Adobe's After Effects is one of the best tools available anywhere. To export your Timeline (or a portion of the Timeline) for use in After Effects, simply export it as a QuickTime movie. Export the movie at full frame size, frame rate, and quality, and do not use a compressor. You can then import the QuickTime movie into After Effects for further editing.

Exporting Audio

We usually think of Adobe Premiere as a video-editing program, but it can also edit and export audio. You can export audio in several different formats, including Apple Sound (SND), QuickTime, MP3, RealAudio, Windows waveform (WAV), and Windows Media (WMA). The SND format can only be generated with the Macintosh version of Premiere, and WAV and WMA are limited to Windows users. The simplest way to export audio from Premiere is to choose File⇨Export Timeline (or Export Clip)⇨Audio. The Export Audio dialog box appears. The default audio export format for Macintosh is QuickTime, and the default format for Windows is AVI. If you don't like the default, click Settings and choose a different format.

Of the various formats available, I like MP3 the best because it can be played on almost any computer — as well as on countless MP3 player devices. To export an audio clip directly from Premiere as MP3, you need to use Cleaner 5 EZ, an audio and video compression program that helps you prepare media for use on the Internet and elsewhere. Cleaner 5 EZ came with both Macintosh and Windows versions of Premiere 6.0, but it only comes with the Macintosh version of Premiere 6.5. Cleaner 5 EZ only works with OS 9; if you are using OS X you will not be able to use Cleaner 5 EZ. If you have Premiere 6.5 for Windows or OS X, export your audio as a Windows waveform or QuickTime file and then use a third-party MP3 encoding program to convert the file. You can find a comprehensive list of freeware and shareware audio encoding programs online at TUCOWS (`www.tucows.com`). If you have a version of Premiere that includes Cleaner 5 EZ, follow these steps:

1. **Select the clip in the Project window or Timeline that you want to export.**

2. **Choose File⇨Export Clip⇨Save for Web.**

   The Cleaner 5 EZ dialog box appears. (Refer to Figure 14-9.)

3. **In the Settings menu, choose MP3, and then choose a quality option.**

   I recommend the High Quality, Stereo option.

4. **Click Start.**

   Cleaner 5 EZ launches.

5. **Choose a name and location to save the file.**

   The MP3 file is exported by Cleaner 5 EZ.

As I mentioned above, you can export audio in various other formats as well. For RealAudio, choose the Advanced RealMedia Export option from the Export Clip or Export Timeline submenus in the Premiere File menu. For Windows Media, use the Advanced Windows Media option in the Export menus.

Exporting Still Images

Premiere enables you to export still graphics from your movies, which can be handy for a variety of reasons. For example, you may want to display some stills from the movie on a Web page that promotes it. Just keep in mind that stills extracted from video are of much lower quality than stills shot with a conventional still camera (film or digital).

If you want poster-quality promotional shots of your movie, bring a high-quality still camera along with you during a video shoot and use it to take some pictures of the scenes or subjects in the movie.

It is possible to save stills directly to JPEG format using the Export⇨Save for Web option, but I don't recommend it. Instead, I suggest that you export the frame as a bitmap or TIFF image and then touch it up in Adobe Photoshop. After all, Photoshop comes free with Premiere, so you might as well use it. To export a still image, follow these steps:

1. **Move the Edit line in the Timeline to the exact frame that you want to export.**

2. **Choose File⇨Export Timeline⇨Frame.**

   The Export Still Frame dialog box appears.

3. **If you want to change the export format or any other attributes of the frame, click Settings and adjust the attributes there.**

4. **Choose a location and name the file, and then click Save.**

    The still image is saved.

It is crucial that you edit any still images exported from video, especially if the image comes from interlaced video. Fast-moving objects in the image may have interlacing *jaggies*, which are horizontal distortions of the image caused by interlacing, and if the video came from a rectangular-pixel video image, it appears distorted on computer screens. Check out Chapter 16, where I show you how to correct these problems using Adobe Photoshop.

Part V
The Part of Tens

The 5th Wave — By Rich Tennant

"Well, shoot — I know the animation's moving a mite too fast, but <u>dang</u> if I can find a 'mosey' function anywhere in the toolbox!"

In this part . . .

If you have ever used a *For Dummies* book before, you know what this part is all about. The chapters in this part provide top-ten lists to help you find useful stuff by tens — ten great online resources, ten great plug-ins for Adobe Premiere, and ten cool tools (well, okay, some are enough fun that you *could* call 'em toys) for your movie production studio.

Chapter 15

Ten Online Resources

In This Chapter

▶ Adobe user-to-user forums

▶ AppleErrorCodes

▶ C|NET

▶ Digital Producer

▶ DV.com

▶ eBay

▶ Tiffen

▶ VCDHelp.com

▶ VersionTracker.com

▶ videoguys.com

I probably don't have to tell you what a valuable resource the Internet can be. This is especially true if you're looking for information on a high-tech issue such as digital video. DV is a hot topic these days, so you'll find no shortage of Web sites and other resources ready to help you answer questions and spend your money.

This chapter features ten resources that I think you might find useful. Rather than just list a bunch of commercial Web sites, I have tried to list sites that are learning resources for anyone who wants to continue growing as a movie producer. Whether you are just starting out making home movies, or you make a living producing wedding videos and other movie projects, I think you'll find some useful Web sites listed here.

Adobe User-to-User Forums

www.adobe.com/support/forums/main.html

Adobe's support site includes a section of User-to-User forums for the various programs that they publish. There are forums for Acrobat, GoLive, Illustrator, Photoshop, and, of course, Premiere. Many of the Web sites featured throughout this chapter feature forums where moviemakers and editors (such as yourself) can get together and solve problems and share advice. So why feature an Adobe-hosted forum? Frankly, the Premiere User-to-User forms at Adobe are the best Premiere-specific forums that I have found. One problem with forums at other sites is that if you ask a question about Premiere you'll get some useful answers and some less helpful responses. For example, if you ask a Premiere-specific question in a general NLE (nonlinear editor) forum, someone is bound to respond, "I like (Final Cut Pro/Avid XPress) better." That opinion may be interesting, but it doesn't really help you use Premiere, which you already own and have paid for.

The Premiere User-to-User forum is subdivided into four sections:

- ✔ **Macintosh:** For questions about Premiere for Macintosh, go here.
- ✔ **Windows:** For questions about Premiere for Windows, go here.
- ✔ **Video editing techniques:** For questions about editing techniques while using Premiere, go here. This is a subforum and is where you should go if, say, you want to know how to create a tunnel-vision effect for a video clip.
- ✔ **RealMedia export:** Have questions about or trouble with Advanced RealMedia Export? Visit this subforum.

Although the Adobe User-to-User forums can be extremely helpful, you should spend some time reading the FAQs (frequently asked questions) as well as recent posts. There is also a search feature that enables you to search posts for keywords. My observations show that some forum regulars get a bit sensitive when forum newbies ask the same question that has already been asked and answered 40 times this year. Save yourself some embarrassment (and flames) and do a bit of research before you ask.

Amazingly, Adobe doesn't seem to censor the User-to-User forums for content; if someone is critical of Adobe or identifies a bug or flaw in the software, some bureaucrat from the company PR department won't rush in to delete the post. If you want to discuss almost any aspect of Adobe Premiere, the Premiere User-to-User forum is a great free resource.

AppleErrorCodes

www.appleerrorcodes.com/

Although I try to avoid the "religious" Mac-versus-Windows debates, one of the things I have always liked about Apple Macintosh computers is their general dependability. If an error occurs on a Mac, there is usually a good reason, and it is thus usually easier to troubleshoot. I've certainly seen my share of Macintosh error messages, but they were always the result of either a hardware failure or a basic configuration problem.

Countless online resources can help you troubleshoot errors on your Mac, and one of the best is the AppleErrorCodes Web site. Macintosh Error messages almost always have error codes in them, and this code can tell you a lot about what caused the problem. (Don't get me wrong, I love my Windows PCs too, but the generic "Illegal Operation Errors" and the ubiquitous BSOD — Blue Screen of Death — are usually not helpful.) The AppleErrorCodes Web site describes the various Macintosh error codes and offers useful troubleshooting information to help you identify and resolve the problem. When you use Premiere to capture video or perform other editing operations, the most common errors you're likely to encounter seem to be caused by

✔ Insufficient memory allocated to Premiere.

✔ Too many other memory-intensive programs running in the background.

✔ Extension conflicts.

If you experience an error while using Premiere (or any program) on your Mac, write down the error code and visit AppleErrorCodes. The site also contains links to specific troubleshooting articles residing at the Apple Web site and elsewhere.

CINET

    www.cnet.com/

When it comes time to buy computer hardware, software, or other electronics, C|NET offers one of the most comprehensive online shopping resources available. C|NET offers all the resources of a traditional magazine — product reviews, comparison tests, editorial ratings, glossy advertisements — without filling up your recycling bin every month.

The product and gear reviews at C|NET are really cool, because they are accompanied by links to various online stores that currently offer that product for sale. Current prices (as well as shipping charges, don't forget about those) for each store are listed right there on C|NET's site, so you can quickly compare prices before you buy. Stores are also rated based upon their customer service performance using the "C|NET Certified Store" star ratings. C|NET has made its store listing criteria more stringent in recent years, which is good for you if you're concerned about getting ripped off. C|NET even guarantees you against unauthorized charges (click the "CNET Certified Store" link for details and limitations).

Digital Producer

`www.digitalproducer.com/`

Digital Producer is an excellent online magazine catering to digital video producers. Like many of the sites featured in this chapter, *Digital Producer* is aimed more towards the professional and semiprofessional user, but I believe this is where you can learn the most as you get deeper into the world of DV production.

The *Digital Producer* Web site delivers much of the same types of content that you would expect to find in a paper magazine. In particular, you'll find comprehensive product reviews and news on the latest technologies to affect digital video production. You'll also find some useful tutorials to help you choose equipment and edit video more effectively. In addition, as with many other Web sites these days, a forum gives you the chance to discuss problems and ask questions of others (perhaps one of the most valuable things about the Internet).

Another feature of *Digital Producer* that I like is the Classifieds section. If you're looking for pro-quality gear but you don't have a pro-quality budget, you may be able to save some money by purchasing preowned stuff.

DV.com

`www.dv.com/`

If this chapter had an award for "Easiest-to-Remember Web URL," `www.dv.com` would have to be it. DV.com is an offshoot of *DV Magazine,* a publication aimed at digital video professionals. Like the magazine, the content of the Web site is aimed towards the professional audience as well. DV.com offers some indispensable features:

- **Forums:** Ask questions and discuss various issues relating to video production.

- **Feature articles:** The site offers insightful articles by people working in the business of moviemaking. I've found a lot of practical advice on editing and production techniques in the articles here. Even if you aren't a "pro" yet, you can learn a lot from their experiences.

- **Product reviews:** As with virtually all DV-oriented Web sites, product reviews are a key feature of DV.com. The reviews here are a good place to see what's new for video professionals.

To use the resources on DV.com you must register (registration is free). Although DV.com is oriented towards professional users, articles and topics are easy to follow even if you are a video newbie. Technical issues are spelled out in language that anyone can understand.

eBay

www.ebay.com/

Is a description even necessary here? eBay has quickly become one of the favorite Web sites for almost anyone who is shopping for almost anything. It is an online auction site where anyone can offer items for sale, new or used. Many regular retail stores now sell items on eBay, often at deeply discounted prices.

I include eBay here because despite the difficulty of finding some specific video gear, eBay is so large and comprehensive that you can find almost anything for sale here. No matter how obscure your item may seem — a SECAM MiniDV video deck, or a light that fits on the accessory shoe of your-three year-old Hitachi camcorder — a quick keyword search at eBay should turn up some results. There is even a category for professional video equipment. On the main eBay page, click the link for Consumer Electronics, and then click the link for the "Pro Video Equipment" category. If you're looking for a good deal on new or used gear, eBay is a great place to start.

Buyers and sellers at eBay can rate each other on promptness and reliability in payment and delivery. If you're shopping for more-expensive items such as camcorders, you may find that many sellers are unwilling to accept your bid if you are a new eBay user. For high-ticket items, they prefer bidders who have a lot of positive feedback. To build a base of positive feedback for yourself, start by buying small items, such as blank tapes and other cheaper gear. Once you have at least ten positive feedbacks on your eBay record, most sellers will be more than happy to do business with you.

Tiffen

www.tiffen.com/

I have tried not to include specific manufacturer Web sites in this chapter, but Tiffen's Web site truly is a valuable source for digital video equipment. Tiffen is primarily a manufacturer of filters for camera lenses. However, the Tiffen site is also a good place to purchase other gear, such as

- ✔ Tripods

- ✔ Mobile-camera stabilization devices (for example, Steadicam)

- ✔ Camera cases

One of the reasons I like the Tiffen Web site is that it (ahem) focuses on photographic gear. Tripods, filters, and other such gear can be difficult to find on other Web sites that primarily sell computers and digital camcorders. The Tiffen site also features Steadicam camera stabilization equipment — perhaps not too surprising, considering that Tiffen acquired Steadicam a couple of years ago.

Of course, Tiffen is all about lens filters, and the Tiffen Web site is one of the best resources on the Web for information about filters. When you click the "Filters" link near the top of the page, you will be taken to a list of the various filters that Tiffen offers. Most filters feature photographic comparisons of scenes shot with and without a filter. This helps you identify the exact effect of each filter.

VCDHelp.com

```
www.vcdhelp.com/
```

Since you're using Adobe Premiere to digitally edit movies, doesn't it make sense to distribute your movies in a digital format? I think so, and so do a lot of other people, which is why DVD (Digital Versatile Disc), VCD (Video Compact Disc), and SVCD (Super Video Compact Disc) are becoming popular distribution mediums for Premiere users. These are new technologies, however, and as with any new technology you may find that you have questions or problems that require expert help. For this help, I recommend VCDHelp.com.

I could not list all the great reasons to frequent VCDHelp.com, but some of the great things you'll find at this site include these:

- ✔ **How-Tos:** Need step-by-step instructions on how to do something that isn't described in this book? VCDHelp.com has countless "How Tos" for performing various actions, such as creating DVDs, converting media, and playing video on a computer.

- ✔ **News:** Keep up-to-date on the latest news in digital-video technologies and standards.

- ✔ **Product Reviews:** Read reviews on all kinds of hardware, including capture hardware, DVD players, CD and DVD burners, and more. VCDHelp.com also provides a "pricewatch" section to help you find the current lowest prices on various items.

✔ **Compatibility Lists:** Alas, not all DVD players were created equal. Some play VCDs and SVCDs, and some don't. VCDHelp.com includes complete compatibility cross-reference lists for numerous DVD players and other hardware, broken down by make and model. Users are encouraged to contribute feedback, so if you see a listing for a device you own, consider sharing your own experiences, be they positive or negative.

✔ **DVD Hacks:** The DVD player in your home entertainment system probably has a menu with a few basic options. However, some crafty users have discovered that some players have more features and adjustments than are noted in the manufacturers' documentation. Find out about secret features and adjustments in the DVD Hacks section.

✔ **Forum:** Like many other Web sites today, VCDHelp.com provides a forum where users can discuss various DVD and VCD technology issues with each other.

VersionTracker.com

`www.versiontracker.com/`

Checking to make sure you have the latest version of Adobe Premiere is easy enough. Just click Help➪Updates and go online to see if Adobe has any downloadable updates and patches available. But what about all your other software? A surprising number of computer problems can be traced to having out-of-date software and drivers. Drivers — the software elements that control hardware inside and connected to your computer — should continuously be kept up-to-date to ensure optimal performance of your system. Rather than visiting half a million different sites trying to figure out if updated versions of your software and drivers are available, I recommend using VersionTracker.com as your central place for checking and updating software.

VersionTracker.com is renowned throughout the Internet as an outstanding resource for both Windows and Macintosh users. From this site, you can link directly to downloadable updates for your software and drivers. You can also visit VersionTracker.com to download

✔ Beta software
✔ Shareware
✔ Freeware
✔ Commercial software

videoguys.com

www.videoguys.com/

The first impression one gets when visiting videoguys.com is that the site is merely another online store for video editing stuff. Yes, videoguys.com is an online store that sells a lot of really cool hardware and software for video editors, and those items are advertised all over the main page for the site. But there is so much more information here that it has become one of my favorite Web sites. Although many video-related Web sites are Mac-oriented, videoguys.com stands out as one of the more Windows-centric video sites you'll find. Key features of the site include these three:

- **The Desk Top Video Handbook On Line.** This section includes product reviews and articles to help you decide what's hot and what's not in the world of digital video. One might argue that a store is not going to write truly objective reviews of the products it sells, but articles at videoguys.com also cover items that the store does not sell. For example, one article I read recently compared new computers from various resellers and pointed out features that video editors should look for.

- **OS Tweaks.** The videoguys.com Web site provides pages with specific, detailed instructions to help you tweak your operating system's settings for optimal video-editing performance. You may think that your computer's performance is good enough, but after applying some of the videoguys.com tweaks your system will run better.

- **Desktop Video Q & As and tips.** You can find some pretty good Q & A sections at videoguys.com that cover a variety of video-related technologies, including FireWire, DVD, and more. There are also sections of tips, including a page of Adobe Premiere tips.

Many online stores are ready to take your money when it's time to purchase video-editing hardware and software. But videoguys.com also gives back, in the form of outstanding online technical resources.

Chapter 16

Ten Plug-ins for Adobe Premiere

· ·

In This Chapter

▶ AccessFX

▶ Adobe After Effects

▶ Adobe Photoshop

▶ BorisFX

▶ Media players

▶ PanHandler

▶ Panopticum effects

▶ Pixelan Effects

▶ SmartSounds QuickTracks

▶ Ultimatte compositing plug-ins

· ·

Many years ago, software companies worked hard to make single software programs that could serve a variety of needs. If you used office productivity software ten or more years ago, you may remember massive software packages like Enable or Symphony. You may also remember that although those packages did many things, they didn't do any of those things *well*.

In recent years, the trend in software development has been to create individual programs that do a few things very well. Not only does this provide us users with more powerful applications, it is also more profitable for the software companies because they can sell many smaller (but still expensive) programs rather than one big, discounted software suite that not everybody uses in the same way. This approach does seem to ensure that the well-crafted special tools will find their way to the users who can appreciate them best.

Adobe Premiere is a good example of this modern style of software development. It does video editing extraordinarily well, but other tasks — such as illustration, image editing, word processing, e-mail, card games — are left out. To really make effective use of Premiere, you're probably going to need some additional programs to use alongside it. This chapter identifies some programs that I think you may find useful as you edit video projects with Premiere.

AccessFX

Adobe Premiere 6.5 comes with a lot of built-in transitions, but if you want some even wilder and more sophisticated transitions, you may want to check out some of the transitions from AccessFX (www.accessfx.com/). AccessFX currently offers two Windows-only plug-ins for Premiere:

- ✔ **TransLux** — Pixel-based wipe transitions
- ✔ **Lord of the Wipe** — Gradient wipes and highly-customizable transitions

Adobe After Effects

Adobe has long been a leader in multimedia and graphic arts software. You already know that Premiere is well regarded as a pro-caliber, nonlinear video-editing program, but Adobe makes many other programs that are also favored by multimedia professionals. One of Adobe's most beloved programs is After Effects, a special-effects and animation program used by video specialists all over the world. Even among editors who prefer to edit video in Apple Final Cut Pro or Avid Xpress, Adobe After Effects is a favorite tool.

As the name implies, After Effects is all about creating special effects for your otherwise-complete video projects. In fact, the Adobe Premiere 6 (and higher) Effects palette includes many effects that were formerly available *only* in After Effects, including the capability to represent on-screen objects in both two- and three-dimensional environments. If you want to create radical effects that seemed impossible (even for Hollywood megastudios) just a few years ago, this is the tool for you.

As a standalone product, After Effects retails for $649, although as a registered Premiere owner you can save $150 off that amount.

Using After Effects with your Premiere projects is easy. Simply export a QuickTime movie from Premiere and import it into After Effects. Once you are done editing in After Effects, simply re-import your QuickTime footage back into Premiere.

Adobe Photoshop

In the previous section, I mentioned that Adobe After Effects is a wildly popular effects and animation program, even among video editors who don't use Premiere. When it comes to still-image editing, Adobe's Photoshop is widely recognized as the industry standard. A basic version of Photoshop comes free with Premiere — meaning that if you have Premiere, you already have the world's best still-image editor.

For information on preparing still images for import into a video project in Premiere, see "Preparing Stills for Your Movie" in Chapter 6.

You'll probably find that Photoshop is an invaluable tool as you work. Photoshop includes a variety of filters that allow you to apply special effects to images or fix various problems. Of special interest are the Video filters. Consider the image shown in Figure 16-1 — a frame I exported from a DV-format project in Premiere (File⇨Export Timeline⇨Frame). Look carefully at the image and you'll notice that it has two main problems:

✔ If you look closely at Figure 16-1 (or any still-image that you export from a DV-based movie project), it appears elongated and the subjects seem slightly distorted. This is because the DV footage from which the frame was exported has rectangular pixels, but Photoshop works with square pixels.

✔ The image has what I call "interlacing jaggies." Because the original footage was interlaced, fast-moving portions of the image have an ugly pattern of horizontal distortions.

Both these problems are easily fixed in Photoshop. First, we can fix the elongation problem by simply adjusting the size of the picture:

1. **In Photoshop, choose Image⇨Image Size.**

   The Image Size dialog box appears.

2. **In the Image Size dialog, remove the check mark next to "Constrain Proportions."**

   If the frame was exported from DV footage with a 4:3 aspect ratio, the image size will be 720 x 480 pixels. All you need do is change the image size so it conforms to a 4:3 aspect ratio.

3. **Change the Width value from 720 pixels to 640 pixels. Make sure that the Height is still 480 pixels.**

4. **Click OK.**

   The image shape should now be more natural, but there are still those interlacing jaggies to get rid of.

5. Choose Filter➪Video➪De-Interlace.

A small dialog box appears. Here you can choose to eliminate odd or even fields, and whether to generate the replacement fields by duplication or interpolation. I generally recommend that you choose Interpolation, but the Odd or Even choices may need some experimentation on your part.

Interlacing jaggies

Figure 16-1: Still graphics exported from interlaced DV footage will appear distorted in Photoshop and other still-graphics programs.

When Photoshop de-interlaces an image, it actually deletes every other horizontal line of the image and replaces each one with new lines. It can generate these replacement lines in one of two ways: *duplication* or *interpolation*. If the lines are generated through duplication, the line above (if you deleted the even lines) or below (if you deleted the odd lines) is copied to create the new replacement line. If the lines are generated through interpolation, Photoshop compares the lines above and below the missing line and generates a new line that is halfway between in terms of appearance. This usually gives a smoother appearance to the image, which is why I normally recommend using the Interpolation option when de-interlacing a video image.

6. **Click OK and view the results.**

   If you're not satisfied, choose Edit⇨Undo, and then open the De-Interlace filter again and choose different options.

My finished result looks like Figure 16-2.

Figure 16-2: The picture looks much better after Photoshop is used to adjust the size and de-interlace the image.

The version of Photoshop that comes with Premiere is not the latest and most powerful version. As you might expect, the more expensive version of Photoshop offers more filters, more editing tools, and scripting ability. (Although scripting may not sound important right now, if you are using Photoshop to adjust video footage, you might appreciate being able to automate a lot of repetitive actions.) Check Adobe's Web site (www.adobe.com) for pricing information, and be on the lookout for special upgrade pricing.

BorisFX

Premiere comes with a lot of built-in effects, but even so you may find that none of the included effects are exactly what you were hoping for. Fear not; plenty of third-party software developers such as Boris (www.borisfx.com/) produce plug-ins for Premiere that give you bigger and better special effects to use in your projects.

Boris produces a variety of visual effects plug-ins for programs such as After Effects, Final Cut Pro, and Premiere. BorisFX — available for Mac and Windows systems — helps you create animations, image distortions, unlimited layers of composition, rain and other weather effects, and more. If you want, you can even wrap a video image around a 3-D sphere and then shatter the image into a hundred pieces.

Another software tool available from Boris is Graffiti. Graffiti is an advanced titling tool that provides you with a huge array of options for animation and text creation — the results of which can then be imported into your Premiere project.

Media Players

Rather than list a specific program here, I'm going to talk about a category of programs. If you'll be producing movies for computer playback, either over the Internet or on CD-ROM, you must carefully consider what format you'll use to export the movie as well as what player the audience will use. To ensure that you can accurately test the viewing experience that various people in your audience will have, you must have the latest versions of any media-player programs they are likely to use.

For more on selecting media players for your output projects, see "Selecting a Player" in Chapter 14.

Even if you have a specific format and/or player that you favor, you owe it to yourself to keep current on the latest technologies. You may find that as you experiment with various formats and players, some formats offer a more favorable quality-versus-file-size balance than what you've been using. Whether you are using a Macintosh or Windows, I strongly recommend that you download and install the following four players:

- **Apple QuickTime:** www.apple.com/quicktime/
- **DivX Player:** www.divx.com/
- **RealNetworks RealPlayer:** www.real.com/
- **Microsoft Windows Media Player:** www.microsoft.com/windows/windowsmedia/

PanHandler

Starting in the 1970s, there was a long period during which not much changed in the realm of home-audio technology. Home stereos sprouted remote controls, and CD players replaced LP turntables, but the state of the art for speakers and amplifiers remained largely unchanged. Beginning in the 1990s, however, home theater systems became common, where a system of at least five speakers provided a true surround-sound experience in suburban living rooms.

Today it seems almost everyone has a home theater system, and you can produce movies that take advantage of surround sound. If you try that, however, you may find out in a hurry that you can't really take advantage of surround sound if the only audio tools you use are those that come with Premiere. Instead, you need a more powerful audio plug-in such as PanHandler from Kelly Industries (www.kellyindustries.com/). Pan-Handler, available for both Mac and Windows versions of Premiere, enables you to encode your sound for surround-sound systems and control audio panning throughout the audio track.

Panopticum Effects

Panopticum (www.panopticum.com/) is another developer of numerous plug-ins for Adobe programs, including After Effects, Illustrator, Photoshop, and of course, Premiere. Premiere plug-ins are available from Panopticum for both Mac and Windows platforms. Interesting plug-ins include:

- ✔ **Engraver:** Adds the appearance of an engraving to images. The plug-in does this by adding thin engraving lines like you might see on paper currency.

- ✔ **Fire:** Fire and explosions are always fun in movies, but they aren't always safe or cost effective to shoot. Panopticum's Fire effect helps you create realistic burning effects without worrying that you might singe your eyebrows off.

- ✔ **Lens Pro:** Create lens and glass distortion effects with this plug-in.

Panopticum effects act as plug-ins in Premiere; once they're installed, you can access them directly from the Premiere Effects palette.

Pixelan Effects

One of the things I love about Adobe software is that third parties can expand the original program's capabilities by developing plug-ins. I've featured a number of third-party plug-in developers for Premiere throughout this chapter, and another developer to consider is Pixelan (www.pixelan.com/). Pixelan produces truly advanced transition and effects plug-ins for Premiere and various other editing applications. Pixelan's plug-ins are available for both Mac and Windows versions of Premiere.

Pixelan's SpiceMaster is an effects plug-in that provides over 500 custom effects and wipes. SpiceMaster effects can be controlled with fine precision, allowing you to get just the right look, be it mild or wild.

SmartSounds QuickTracks

I probably don't have to tell you how important good music is for your movie projects. And if you've spent time trying to locate and get permission for good music, I probably also don't have to tell you how expensive good music can be. Thankfully, Adobe has come to your rescue with a program called Smart-Sounds QuickTracks. SmartSounds QuickTracks comes free with Adobe Premiere and includes a wide variety of music that you can use in your projects. Best of all, the music that comes with SmartSounds QuickTracks is royalty-free!

The SmartSounds QuickTracks CD is located in the jewel case that contained your Adobe Premiere program disc. If you open the jewel case, you'll notice that the black plastic panel holding the Premiere disc flips up to reveal the SmartSounds QuickTracks disc underneath. (That's even better than getting a free plastic pterodactyl in your cereal box.)

SmartSounds QuickTracks acts as a plug-in for Adobe Premiere. Once you have installed the software, you create a new sound by choosing File⇨New⇨SmartSound. In the SmartSound window, click Start Maestro to select some music for your project. A wizard like the one shown in Figure 16-3 takes you through the process of selecting music that best fits your needs.

Click to preview.

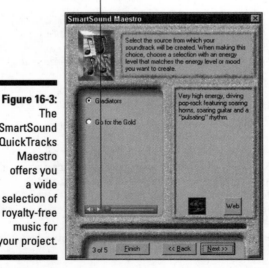

Figure 16-3:
The SmartSound QuickTracks Maestro offers you a wide selection of royalty-free music for your project.

Additional royalty-free music is always being added to the SmartSounds library. You can download new sounds by clicking the Web links in the SmartSounds QuickTracks program, or by visiting www.smartsounds.com.

Ultimatte Compositing Plug-ins

Many of the most advanced special effects involve compositing multiple images, layering them upon one another. Premiere does have some pretty good compositing tools built in, but if you want even more control, you may want to use a plug-in from Ultimatte (www.ultimatte.com/), a maker of professional video-compositing hardware and software. Ultimatte (it's a pun, not a typo) offers plug-ins for Premiere that include

- **Ultimatte software for Macintosh and Windows:** Exercise precise control over bluescreen and greenscreen removal with the Ultimatte software.

- **Screen Correction:** Use this plug-in to correct for unevenly lit blue- or greenscreens. Unevenly lit screens usually cause problems for Premiere's own bluescreen and greenscreen transparency keys.

- **Grain Killer:** Use this plug-in to filter out blue- or greenscreen noise in an image.

Chapter 17

Ten Tools (And Toys) for Your Production Studio

- -

In This Chapter

▶ Audio recorders

▶ Dream camcorders

▶ DVD burners

▶ Filters

▶ Microphones

▶ Monitors

▶ Multimedia controllers

▶ Tripods and other stabilization devices

▶ Video converters

▶ Video decks

- -

The bare essentials of what you need to make great movies are a digital camcorder, a good computer equipped with a FireWire port, and Adobe Premiere. Those are the three basics that can get you started. But so many other tools (some would say "toys") can make your editing life easier and your movies that much better. This chapter features ten items you may find invaluable as you work with Premiere. (Well, okay, maybe some items aren't indispensable, but at least they're a whole lot of fun!)

Before you buy any video gear, make sure it matches the video-broadcast standard (NTSC, PAL, or SECAM) that you are using before placing your order. This is especially important when purchasing camcorders, monitors, and video decks. For more on broadcast standards, see Chapter 4.

Audio Recorders

I know, I know, your camcorder records audio along with video, and it's already perfectly synchronized. So what is the point of a dedicated audio recorder? Well, you may need the capabilities of an audio recorder in many situations. Take, for example, these three:

- ✔ You may want to record a subject who is across the room, in which case, have the subject hold a recorder (or conceal it so it's off-camera), and attach an inconspicuous lavalier microphone.

- ✔ You may want to record only a special sound, on location, and add it to the soundtrack later. For example, you might show crashing waves in the distant background, but use the close-up sound of those waves for dramatic effect.

- ✔ You can record narration for a video project, tweak it till it suits you, and then add it to the soundtrack of your movie.

Countless other uses for audio recorders exist. You may simply find that an external, dedicated recorder records better-quality audio than the built-in mic in your camcorder.

Recording decent audio used to mean spending hundreds of dollars for a DAT (digital audio tape) recorder. However, these days I think the best compromise for an amateur moviemaker is to use a MiniDisc recorder. MiniDisc player/recorders can record CD-quality audio onto MiniDiscs as computer files in .WAV format — which can be easily imported into a Premiere project. Countless MiniDisc recorders are available for less than $200 from companies that include Aiwa, Sharp, and Sony.

Don't forget a slate!

If you use a secondary audio recorder, one of the biggest challenges you may face is synchronizing the audio it records with video. Professionals ensure synchronization of audio and video using a *slate* — that black-and-white board that you often see production people snapping shut on camera just before the director yells "Action!"

The slate is not just a kitschy movie thing. The snapping of the slate makes a noise that can be picked up by all audio recorders on scene. When you are editing audio tracks later, this noise will show up as a visible spike on the audio waveform. Because the slate is snapped in front of the camera, you can later match the waveform spike on the audio track with the visual picture of the slate snapping closed on the video track. If you're recording audio with external recorders, consider making your own slate. This will make audio-video synchronization a lot easier during the postproduction process.

Dream Camcorders

If you recently purchased your first digital camcorder, you're probably impressed by the image quality it produces, especially in comparison to older consumer technologies like 8mm, Hi8, and S-VHS. Most digital camcorders are also packed with features that were considered wildly advanced just a few years ago.

But you know how the old saying goes: The grass is always greener, and all that. As impressive and wonderful as your camcorder may seem, you'll soon find even better products out there. If you get really serious about moviemaking, one of the first things you should do is upgrade to a really serious camera. High-end DV camcorders are becoming so advanced now that even the pros are using them. Several pro-grade features now claim to have been shot exclusively using the Canon XL1, a MiniDV camcorder that costs less than $5,000.

If $5,000 sounds like a lot, keep in mind that until recently, broadcast-quality video cameras started at $20,000, and often cost $100,000 or more!

When you're ready to step up to the next level of DV camcorder, look for the following features that make some digital camcorders better than others:

- ✔ **CCD:** The *charged coupled device* is the unit in a camcorder that captures a video image from light. Most consumer-grade camcorders have one CCD, but higher-quality units have three, one for each of the standard video colors (red, green, and blue). Three-CCD cameras — also called *three-chip* cameras — capture much sharper, more saturated images.

- ✔ **Progressive scan:** Many cheaper camcorders only capture interlaced video. This can create a variety of problems — such as the interlacing "jaggies" that I've shown in Chapter 16 and elsewhere in this book — especially if you are editing a project for distribution on the Web. Higher-quality camcorders offer a progressive scan mode.

- ✔ **Resolution:** Okay, this one can get confusing; resolution is defined and listed in many different ways. Some spec sheets tell you how many thousands of pixels, but this isn't always a good indication of ultimate video quality. I recommend that you look (instead) at horizontal resolution lines. A high-quality digital camcorder should capture at least 500 lines of resolution.

- ✔ **Audio:** Many high-end DV camcorders have big, condenser-style microphones built onto them — a definite improvement in audio quality compared to the built-in mics on cheaper camcorders, but also look for external audio connectors so you can use a remote microphone if you need to. For external audio, I recommend XLR-style microphone connectors.

✔ **Lens:** Any digital camcorder still needs a good old-fashioned "analog" glass lens to collect and focus light. A bigger, higher-quality lens produces better video images. Make sure that any camcorder you get accepts filters on the lens. Many more-expensive cameras offer interchangeable lenses.

✔ **Zebra pattern:** Many professional-grade camcorders display a zebra-stripe pattern in the viewfinder on overexposed areas of a shot. This can be extremely helpful, especially when you are manually adjusting exposure.

✔ **Manual focus ring:** A lot of cheaper digital camcorders have manual focus controls on a small dial or slider switch — often difficult to use (provided you can *find* the thing). Try to get a camera with a large, easy-to-use focal ring around the lens.

If you're willing to spend at least $1,500 for a camcorder, there are lots of good units to choose from. The camcorder market is always changing, but Table 17-1 lists some longtime-favorite, high-quality "prosumer" digital camcorders. Just imagine the great movies you'll make with one of these cameras!

Somebody must have worked overtime to coin the term *prosumer* to mean high-end consumer products that give you pro-level output. (Will the word itself catch on? I wouldn't "prosume" to say.)

Table 17-1	Dream Camcorders	
Manufacturer	*Model*	*Street Price*
Canon	GL1	$1,800-$2,400
Canon	XL1S	$3,200-$4,500
JVC	GY-DV500U	$4,000-$4,500
Panasonic	PV-DV952	$1,500-$2,000
Sony	DCR-VX2000	$2,200-$3,000
Sony	DCR-VX9000	$4,000-$5,000

The "street prices" listed in Table 17-1 are estimates I made by surveying various Web sites and retail outlets. The actual price you pay may be quite different, but the table gives you a ballpark figure so you can make a general price comparison for these various cameras.

DVD Burners

When Apple first released its G4 Macintosh with SuperDrive in 2001, it seemed remarkable that a complete DVD (Digital Versatile Disc) authoring system could be had for *just* $5,000. But prices dropped fast, and in less than a year Apple was already selling iMacs capable of recording DVDs for less than $2,000. Many new Macintosh computers can now be purchased with the SuperDrive (Apple's DVD burner), and third-party DVD burners are now widely available for both Macintosh and PC systems. As of this writing, DVD-R (DVD-Recordable) drives can be found for less than $300, and I don't even want to speculate what they'll cost next week (or a few months from now, when you read this).

DVD burners — *burner* is the not-so-technical term used interchangeably with *recorder* — are useful for a variety of reasons. First, they can record up to 4.7GB (gigabytes) of data onto a single disc. Second, with software like Adobe's MPEG Encoder and Sonic's DVDit! LE (which comes free with Adobe Premiere 6.5 for Windows) you can record your Premiere projects directly onto movie DVDs so they can be watched in virtually any DVD player.

It's only a matter of time before DVD becomes the most preferred and affordable method of movie distribution. With a DVD burner, you can be ahead of the game and start recording your own DVDs now. If you have a Macintosh, I recommend that you stick with Apple's SuperDrive for now. If you have a Windows PC, check with your local computer-hardware expert to find out about upgrading your computer with an add-on DVD burner. Most current offerings use the EIDE interface, which involves some complexity and PC hardware experience to install and configure. LaCie also offers an external DVD burner that plugs into a FireWire port — which makes it far easier to set up on your computer.

Filters

Adobe Premiere 6.5 contains many effects and tools that you can use to improve the quality — or change the appearance — of your video images. But sometimes it's quicker to tweak the light coming into the camera than to fuss with the digital image later — and some image issues are better dealt with using lens filters. Filters usually attach to the front of your camcorder's lens using a threaded fitting. Check your camcorder housing to determine whether it has a threaded filter fitting. Also check the documentation that came with your camcorder to find out what size and type of filter(s) can be used with your camcorder.

Many consumer-grade camcorders accept 37mm filters; prosumer camcorders usually accept 58mm or larger filters.

Filters can serve many important purposes, including

- **Protecting the lens:** A UV filter is often used primarily to protect the camcorder's lens. If the filter gets scratched or damaged, it will be a lot cheaper to replace than the camcorder's lens.

- **Improving lighting:** Countless filters are available to help you improve lighting problems on your shots. A neutral-density filter, for example improves color in bright sunlight; color-conversion and color-compensation filters can increase or decrease the saturation of a specific color in a shot.

- **Reducing glare and reflections:** If a window or other shiny surface appears in your shot, an undesired glare or reflection may appear. Use a polarizing filter to eliminate or control the glare.

- **Creating special effects:** Certain filters can be used to create star patterns around light points, soften the video image, simulate fog, and more.

Filters can usually be purchased at photographic supply stores, although some consumer electronics stores may have them in their camcorder accessories sections. If nothing else, I recommend that you use a UV filter at all times to prevent damage to your camcorder's lens. But filters can greatly improve or enhance your video images, so you may find it worthwhile to look seriously at a wide range of them.

For more on filters, check out the Tiffen Web site (www.tiffen.com). The Tiffen Web site is also featured in Chapter 15.

Microphones

Virtually all camcorders have built-in microphones. Most digital camcorders boast 48-bit stereo sound-recording capabilities, but you'll soon find that the quality of the audio you record is still limited primarily by the quality of the microphone you use. Therefore, if you care even a little about making great movies, you *need* better microphones than the one built into your camcorder.

Your camcorder should have connectors for external microphones, and your camcorder's manufacturer may offer accessory microphones for your specific camera.

One type of special microphone you may want to use is a *lavalier* microphone — a tiny unit that usually clips to a subject's clothing to pick up his or her voice. You often see lavalier mics clipped to the lapels of TV newscasters. Some lavalier units are designed to fit inside clothing or costumes, though some practice and special shielding may be required to eliminate rubbing noises.

You might also use a condenser microphone to record audio. Some prosumer camcorders come with large, boom-style condenser mics built in. Although these are nice, if you want to record the voice of a subject speaking on camera they may still be inferior to a hand-held or lavalier mic.

Microphones are generally defined by the directional pattern in which they pick up sound. The three basic categories are cardioid (which has a heart-shaped pattern), omnidirectional (which picks up sound from all directions), and bidirectional (which picks up sound from the sides). Figure 17-1 illustrates these patterns.

A good place to look for high-quality microphones is a musician supply store. Just make sure that the connectors and frequency range are compatible with your camcorder or other recording device (check the documentation). You may also want to check with your camcorder's manufacturer; it may offer accessory microphones specially designed to work with your camcorder. Finally, the Internet is always a good resource as well. One especially good resource is www.shure.com, the Web site of Shure Incorporated. Shure sells microphones and other audio products, and the Web site is an excellent resource for general information about choosing and using microphones.

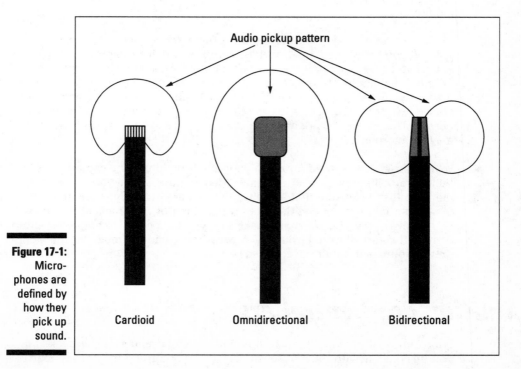

Figure 17-1: Microphones are defined by how they pick up sound.

Audio pickup pattern

Cardioid   Omnidirectional   Bidirectional

Monitors

Although the computer on which you use Adobe Premiere already has a monitor (at least, I *hope* it does), computer monitors are not the ideal place to preview video as you edit. This is especially true if you ultimately plan to output your movie back to tape or DVD where it will be played on regular TVs. If you want to ensure the highest quality for your video image, you need to use an external video monitor.

An external monitor must be a broadcast-style monitor. This is because broadcast TV monitors display colors differently than computer monitors. Colors that look fine on the computer screen may be distorted or washed out on an NTSC or PAL monitor.

Okay, from a strictly technical standpoint, your monitor can be any old TV, although if your budget allows, I recommend buying a high-quality monitor intended for video production use. With an external monitor connected, you can configure Premiere to play the video out to the monitor at full quality, while playing video on your computer screen at partial quality or not at all. This saves processing power on your computer for other tasks, such as rendering previews. To adjust these settings in Premiere, choose Project➪Project Settings➪General. In the General options, click Playback Settings. Remove the check mark next to "Playback on Desktop" to stop playback on the computer monitor.

The only trick now is to actually connect the external monitor to your computer. If you have a high-quality video capture card, it probably already has analog video outputs, or it has a breakout box with analog video outputs. Connect the monitor to the correct output as instructed in your card's documentation. Alternatively, you might be able to connect your DV camcorder to your FireWire port, and then connect the monitor to the camcorder's analog output. This may not work on some camcorders, so some experimentation may be in order.

 Is your desk too crowded for a video monitor? Build up! You can purchase or build a rack that stacks your external video monitor above your computer monitor. Just make sure that all your monitors are properly ventilated, use monitors that don't exceed the rated weight limit of your rack, and make sure you secure everything for earthquake safety (which can also help your equipment withstand vibration from severe weather outside, rampaging small children indoors, and other miscellaneous chaos).

Multimedia Controllers

I don't know about you, but manipulating some of Premiere's playback and editing controls with the mouse isn't always easy. Sure, there are keyboard shortcuts for most actions, and you may find yourself using those keyboard shortcuts quite a bit. In particular, I find that controlling playback with the J and L keys is a lot easier than using the mouse, and using the arrow keys to frame forward or back is vastly superior to dragging the jog control back and forth.

Useful though the keyboard may be, there is an even better way. You can also control Premiere with an external multimedia controller, such as the ShuttlePro from ContourDesign. The ShuttlePro, shown in Figure 17-2, features 13 buttons and a two-part dial control in an ergonomically designed housing. The overall design of the ShuttlePro is based on professional video-editing controllers. The unit plugs into a USB port, which can be found on virtually any modern computer. You can find out more about the ShuttlePro online at:

`www.contourdesign.com`

Figure 17-2:
Contour-
Design
ShuttlePro
makes
editing in
Premiere
fun and
easy!

At the risk of sounding like an advertisement, I have to say that I'd be lost without my ShuttlePro. Well, maybe not lost, perhaps, but I certainly do enjoy editing a lot more because of ShuttlePro (and if you enjoy what you're doing, the result is often better). ContourDesign provides control sets for the ShuttlePro for a variety of video editing programs (such as Premiere), as well as other multimedia programs like Macromedia Director.

The array of buttons may look intimidating at first, but I found that I learned the function of each one very quickly. The ShuttlePro was certainly easier to master than the Premiere keyboard shortcuts. In Premiere, ShuttlePro buttons can be used to play forward, play backward, pause, move to edit points, or quickly set (or clear) in points and out points. But most useful are the dials. The spring-loaded outer ring acts as a shuttle control, and the inner dial rolls video forward or back a frame at a time (like Premiere's Jog control, only a *lot* easier). It even works with device control to control external camcorders and tape decks during capture. The buttons are customizable, too, meaning you can apply new functions to them if you wish.

ContourDesign offers downloadable drivers and control sets for a variety of operating systems, including Mac OS 8.6 through OS X, and Windows 98, ME, 2000, and XP.

Tripods and Other Stabilization Devices

The need for image stabilization will probably become apparent the first time you watch your footage on a large TV screen. No matter how carefully you try to hold the camera still, some movement is going to show up on the image. Of course, there are plenty of times when hand-held is the way to shoot, but there are plenty of other times when a totally stable image is best. For this, you need a tripod.

Tripods are generally available (starting as low as $20) at your local department store. Alas, as with so many other things in life, when you buy a tripod you get what you pay for. High-quality video tripods incorporate several important features:

- **Dual-stanchion legs and bracing:** This gives the tripod greater stability, especially during panning shots. Braces at the base or middle of the tripod's legs also aid stability.

- **High-tech materials:** You'll soon get tired of lugging a 15- to 20-pound tripod around with your camera gear. Higher-quality tripods usually use high-tech materials (including titanium, aircraft-quality aluminum, and carbon fiber) both strong and lightweight, making the gear less cumbersome to transport and use.

- **Bubble levels:** This helps you ensure that your camera is level, even if the ground underneath the tripod isn't.

- **Fluid heads:** This ensures that pans will be smooth and jerk-free.

- **Counterweights:** The best tripods have adjustable counterweights so the head can be balanced for your camera and lens (telephoto lenses, for example, can make the camera a bit front-heavy). Counterweights allow smooth use of the fluid head while still giving you the option of letting go of the camera without having it tilt out of position.

For a tripod with all these features, you can expect to spend at least $300, if not much, much more. If that kind of money isn't in your tripod budget right now, try to get a tripod that incorporates as many of these features as possible.

Monopods

Tripods aren't the only stabilization devices available. You may also want to keep a monopod handy for certain occasions. As the name suggests, a monopod has only one leg (just as tripods have three legs, octopods have eight, and . . . never mind). Although this means that some camera movement is inevitable — you have to keep the camera balanced on the monopod — resting the monopod on the ground can give you more stability than you'd have if you simply hand-held the camera. I used a monopod recently when I was shooting some video at a local Taekwondo tournament. The tournament floor was crowded with parents and competitors, so the wide footprint of a regular tripod would not have been practical. As a bonus, I could also use the monopod as a makeshift boom for overhead shots.

Mobile stabilizers

If you've watched a sporting event on TV recently, you may have seen footage of a player running along where the camera appears to stay with the player as he or she runs. And although the camera operator was obviously moving to get the shot, the image appears to be as stable as any tripod shot. How can this be? There are two possibilities:

- ✔ The camera operator is a superhero with the special ability to hold heavy objects absolutely still, even while riding a Radio Flyer wagon down a rocky, rutted slope.
- ✔ The camera operator was using a Steadicam device.

Steadicam (www.steadicam.com) is a brand of camera stabilizer that allows both superstable images and hand-held mobility. A Steadicam device attaches to the camera operator with an elaborate harness and includes an LCD monitor which allows the operator to see the video image without taking her eyes off her path of travel. Steadicams are incredibly effective, but they are also incredibly expensive. The "affordable" Steadicam JR, which is aimed at semi-professionals and prosumers, retails for $899! (You don't even want to know what the professional-grade units cost.)

Other, more-affordable devices are available. Check your local camera shop to see what is available for mobile stabilization. If you're handy with a needle and thread, you can even make a sling to help stabilize your arm while shooting. Fashion a sling that enables you to support your forearm with your neck and shoulders. This will reduce fatigue and thus result in smoother images.

Video Converters

You have a computer with a FireWire port, and you want to capture some analog video. What are you going to do? You have many, many solutions, of course. You could install a video capture card, but a good one is expensive and installing it means tearing apart your computer. If you're lucky, you might be able to connect an analog video source to the analog inputs on your digital camcorder and then connect the camcorder to the FireWire port. This method is clumsy, however, and it simply won't work with some camcorders.

A simpler solution may be to use an external *video converter* — usually a box that connects to your computer's FireWire port. The box includes analog inputs, so you can connect an analog VCR or camcorder to the box. The unit itself converts signals from analog media into DV-format video, which is then captured into your computer — where you can easily edit it using Premiere.

If you have worked with analog video a lot, you're probably aware that each time you make a copy of the video some quality is lost. This is called *generational loss*. Video converters like the ones described here don't present any more of a generational-loss problem than a standard video capture card, because once the signal is converted to digital, generational loss is no longer a problem until you output the video back to an analog tape again.

Most converter boxes can also be useful for exporting video to an analog source. You simply export the DV-format video from Premiere, and the converter box converts it into an analog signal that you can record on your analog tape deck. Among other advantages, this method of export saves a lot of wear and tear on the tape-drive mechanisms in your expensive digital camcorder. Features to look for in a video converter include

- Analog output
- Broadcast standard support (NTSC or PAL)
- Color-bar output
- Multiple FireWire and analog inputs/outputs

Video converters typically range in price from $250 to $700 or more. Table 17-2 lists a few popular units.

Table 17-2		Video Converters	
Manufacturer	*Model*	*Street Price*	*Web Site*
Canopus	ADVC-100	$250-$300	www.canopuscorp.com/
Data Video	DAC-2	$600-$750	www.datavideo-tek.com/
Dazzle	Hollywood DV Bridge	$225-$275	www.dazzle.com/

Video Decks

Because it's so easy to simply connect a FireWire cable to your camcorder and capture video right into your computer, you may be tempted to use your digital camcorder as your sole MiniDV tape deck. If you're on a really tight budget, you may not have much of a choice, but otherwise I strongly recommend a high0quality video deck. A video deck not only saves wear and tear on the tape drive mechanisms in your expensive camcorder, but it can also give you greater control over video capture and export back to tape. Professional video decks are expensive, but if you do a lot of video editing, they quickly pay for themselves — both in terms of the greater satisfaction and quality you're likely to get from your finished movie and in less money spent on camcorder maintenance. Table 17-3 lists some decks to consider.

Table 17-3		DV Video Decks	
Manufacturer	*Model*	*Formats*	*Street Price*
JVC	DVS2U	MiniDV, S-VHS	$1,000
Panasonic	AG-DV1000	MiniDV	$950
Sony	GVD-1000 VCR Walkman with 4-inch LCD screen	MiniDV	$1,200

When shopping for a professional-grade MiniDV deck, you can also look for decks that support the DVCAM or DVCPRO tape formats. These are more-robust professional-grade DV-tape formats, and decks that support these formats generally also support MiniDV.

Part VI
Appendixes

In this part . . .

The appendixes of many books are where authors stick information that seems somehow important yet doesn't seem to fit anywhere else. *Adobe Premiere For Dummies* is no exception. The first appendix provides a glossary of terms relating to video editing and Adobe Premiere. I throw the odd technical term into the discussion in this book now and then — and if you see something you don't understand, check the glossary. The next appendix serves as a guide to using Premiere's Help resources — and you find out where else you can look for help if you need it.

Appendix A

Glossary

• •

alpha channel — Some digital images have transparent areas; the transparency is defined using an alpha channel.

analog — Data that is recorded as a wave with infinitely varying values is analog data. Analog recordings often suffer from generational loss. *See also: digital, generational loss.*

aspect ratio — The shape of a video image (its width compared to height) is the *aspect ratio*. Traditional television screens have an aspect ratio of 4:3, meaning the screen is four units wide and three units high. Image pixels can also have various aspect ratios. *See also: pixel.*

bars and tone — A video image that serves the function of the "test pattern" used in TV broadcasting: Standardized color bars and a 1-kHz tone are usually placed at the beginning of video programs. This helps broadcast engineers calibrate video equipment to the color and audio levels of a video program. The format for color bars is standardized by the SMPTE. *See also: SMPTE.*

bit depth — The amount of data that a single piece of information can hold depends upon how many bits are available. Bit depth usually refers to color or sound quality. A larger bit depth means a greater range of color or sound.

CCD (charged coupled device) — This is the unit in camcorders that interprets light particles (photons) and converts the information into an electronic video signal. This signal can then be recorded on tape. Digital still cameras also use CCDs.

clip — Segments making up the scenes of a video program. Individual clips are edited into Premiere's Timeline to form complete scenes and a complete storyline.

codec — A scheme used to compress — and later decompress — video and audio information so it can pass more efficiently over computer busses, hard drives, Internet connections, and other components.

color gamut — The total number of colors a given system can create (by combining several basic colors) to display a video image. The total number of individual colors that are available is finite. If a color cannot be displayed correctly, it is considered out of gamut.

data rate — The volume of data per second contained in a signal is the data rate. The data rate of DV-format video is 3.6MB (megabytes) per second.

digital — A method of recording sound and light by converting it into data that uses discrete, binary values (expressed as ones and zeros). *See also: analog.*

drop-frame timecode — A type of timecode specified by the NTSC video standard, usually with a frame rate of 29.97 fps. To maintain continuity, two frames are dropped at the beginning of each minute, except for every tenth minute. *See also: timecode.*

DV (Digital Video) — A standard format and codec for digital video. Digital camcorders that include a FireWire interface usually record DV-format video. *See also: codec, FireWire.*

EDL (Edit Decision List) — A file or list that contains information about all edits performed in a program. This list can then be used to reproduce the same edits on another system, such as at a professional video-editing facility. An editing program such as Premiere can generate an EDL automatically.

field — Interlaced video frames consist of two separate fields. Each field contains every other horizontal resolution line and is drawn in a separate pass. *See also: frame.*

FireWire — Also known by its official designation IEEE-1394, or by other names such as i.Link, FireWire is a high-speed computer interface standard developed by Apple Computer. The speed of FireWire has contributed greatly to the affordability of modern video editing.

frame — Still image, one in a sequence of many; taken together, they make up a complete moving picture. *See also: frame rate.*

frame rate — The speed at which the frames in a moving picture change. Video images usually display 25 to 30 frames per second, providing the illusion of movement to the human eye. Slower frame rates save storage space but can produce jerky motion; faster frame rates produce smoother motion but have to use more of the recording medium to store and present.

gamut — *See: color gamut.*

generational loss — A worsening of the signal-to-noise ratio (less signal, more noise) that occurs every time an analog recording is copied; some values are lost in the copying process. Each copy (especially a copy of a copy) represents a later, lower-quality *generation* of the original. *See also: analog.*

HDTV (High-Definition Television) — A new set of broadcast video standards that incorporates resolutions and frame rates higher than those used for traditional analog video. *See also: NTSC, PAL, SECAM.*

IEEE-1394 — *See: FireWire.*

interlacing — Most video images are actually composed of two separate fields, drawn on consecutive passes of the electron gun in the video tube. Each field contains every other horizontal resolution line of a video image; while the completed field is fluorescing, the second field is drawn, resulting in a complete video image. Such displays are called interlaced. *See also: field, progressive scan.*

jog — *See: scrub.*

NLE (nonlinear editor) — Computer programs that can edit video, audio, or other multimedia in a nonlinear manner (meaning you can edit the work in any order you choose, as opposed to working from the first frame to the last) are called nonlinear editors. Adobe Premiere is an NLE.

NTSC (National Television Standards Committee) — The broadcast-video standard used in North America, Japan, the Philippines, and elsewhere. *See also: PAL, SECAM.*

online/offline editing — When you edit using full-quality footage, you are performing online editing. If you perform edits using lower-quality captures and intend to apply those edits to the full-quality footage later, you are performing offline editing.

PAL (Phase Alternating Line) — The broadcast-video standard used in Western Europe, Australia, Southeast Asia, South America, and elsewhere. *See also: NTSC, SECAM.*

pixel — The smallest element of a video image, also called a picture element. Bitmapped still images are made up of grids containing thousands, even millions of pixels. A screen or image size that has a resolution of 640 x 480 is 640 pixels wide by 480 pixels high.

progressive scan — A scan display that draws all the horizontal resolution lines in a single pass. Most computer monitors use progressive scan. *See also: interlacing.*

RAM (Random Access Memory) — The electronic working space for your computer's processor and software. To use Premiere effectively, your computer needs lots of RAM.

render — If an effect, speed change, or transition is applied to a video image, Premiere must figure out how each frame of the image should look after the change. The process of applying these changes is called rendering. Usually, the rendering process generates a preview file that is stored on the hard drive. *See also: transition.*

sampling rate — When audio is recorded digitally, the sound is sampled thousands of times per second. The number of samples per second is the sampling rate. 48 kHz audio has 48,000 samples per second.

scrub — To move back and forth through a video program, one frame at a time. In Premiere, the slotted line just under the video image is the scrub bar (also called Jog control). *See also: shuttle.*

SECAM (Sequential Couleur Avec Memoire) — The broadcast video standard used in France, Russia, Eastern Europe, Central Asia, and elsewhere. *See also: NTSC, PAL.*

shuttle — To roll a video image slowly forward or back, often to check a detail of motion. Professional video decks and cameras often have shuttle controls. Premiere's Capture dialog box also has a Shuttle control. *See also: scrub.*

SMPTE (Society for Motion Picture and Television Engineers) — This organization develops standards for professional broadcasting equipment and formats. Among other things, the SMPTE defines standards for bars and tone, counting leaders, and timecode.

timecode — The standard system for identifying individual frames in a movie or video program. Timecode is expressed in `hours:minutes:seconds:frames` (as in `01:20:31:02`). This format has been standardized by the SMPTE. Non-drop-frame timecode uses colons between the numbers, and drop-frame timecode uses semicolons. *See also: SMPTE.*

title — Words that appear on screen to give the name of the movie, or to give credit to the people who made the movie, are called titles. Subtitles are often used during a video program to show translations of dialogue spoken in foreign languages.

transition — The method by which one clip ends and another begins in a video program is with transitions. A common type of transition is when one clip gradually fades out as the next clip fades in. *See also: clip, render.*

waveform — A visual representation of an audio signal. Viewing a waveform on a computer screen allows precise synchronization of sound and video.

Appendix B

Finding Help!

● ●

*P*lease believe that I endeavored to answer as many questions as possible throughout *Adobe Premiere For Dummies*. Still, I realize that at times you will have questions or need information that you cannot find here. This appendix introduces you to some resources that can help answer even your toughest questions regarding Adobe Premiere.

Using Premiere's Built-in Help

As with virtually all modern computer programs, Adobe Premiere includes a built-in help system. By now, you're probably familiar with how to use such a system. You can access Premiere's help using all the typical methods:

✔ Press F1.

✔ Click the Help button that appears in some dialog boxes.

✔ Choose an option from the Help menu.

When you open the Help menu, you'll notice some options that are typical of most programs — and some options that are not as common. Some basic tips for using the system include the following:

✔ **Premiere's Help system is HTML-based.** The system includes a table of contents, an alphabetical index, and a search engine. Use the Help system by clicking links, just as you would a Web page.

✔ **For a list of keyboard shortcuts, click the help system's table of contents.** Both Macintosh and Windows shortcuts are available.

✔ **Periodically click Help⇨Updates.** Premiere will check Adobe's Web site for updates, and if updates are available, you will be given the opportunity to download them.

Using Online Resources

This newfangled thing called the *Internet* — perhaps you've heard of it? — just happens to be a fantastic communication medium. It's a virtual place where people can get together and exchange information and ideas on nearly any topic. Premiere users are among those who get together online and share knowledge and wisdom. There is almost no aspect of using Premiere that doesn't get discussed regularly online. The next two sections help you find some of those discussions.

Adobe's online support

I have been using Adobe software for a long time, and I love it. One thing I do not love, however, is Adobe's free technical support. "But," you interject, "Adobe doesn't offer free technical support." That is my point exactly.

Actually, I am not being entirely fair to Adobe Systems. Although they do not provide free *live* technical support, they do offer a vast library of online resources that can answer many of your questions. To access Adobe's support resources, visit the main Adobe site (www.adobe.com) and click the Support link at the top of the page. Online support resources include the following:

- ✔ **Support by Product:** This page includes online tutorials, knowledgebase articles, and other product-specific information. Of particular interest is the DV hardware compatibility database. Here you can check specific brand names and model numbers of DV cameras to see whether Adobe Premiere supports them.

- ✔ **User-to-User Forums:** I have the URL for the forums (www.adobe.com/support/forums/main.html) in my Web browser's favorites list, and I use them all the time. Here you can find forums on most Adobe products, including Premiere. The forums allow you to post questions or answer questions asked by others. Adobe does not seem to censor the forums for content, which means you can even voice criticisms in the forums. Just keep in mind that the forums are *User-to-User,* not User-to-Adobe. You can usually get help from other Premiere experts, but don't expect responses from Adobe personnel.

Before you post a question in a User-to-User Forum, spend some time perusing older posts — try the search link — to see if your question has already been asked and answered. You should also read the Frequently Asked Questions (FAQ) for the forum for answers to some of the most common questions. An FAQ link can be found at the top of the topic list in each User-to-User Forum. The forums get a lot of the same questions over and over, and some participants get really nasty if you ask them again.

- ✔ **Training:** Adobe offers some online tutorials and stuff here. You will also find information about offline training that Adobe provides, including a number of seminars. Some seminars are free, and some aren't. I've attended a couple of the free ones and they seem designed primarily to sell more Adobe products. However, there is usually at least some useful information to be gleaned.

- ✔ **Adobe Support Marketplace:** Now we're back into the support that you have to pay for. Prices and services are listed here. Prices are based on per-incident charges. The service isn't free, but if you have a really stubborn problem, you may find that it is money well spent.

Getting third-party help

Adobe's Web site isn't the only place to find Premiere wisdom online. A simple Web search will reveal countless Web sites with information about Adobe Premiere, but my favorite resources tend to be the places where people get together and discuss Premiere issues with each other. Some good resources include these:

- ✔ **Creative Cow** (www.creativecow.net): Here you'll find a pretty-active forum devoted to Adobe Premiere. Creative Cow specializes in forums for creative communities (or "*cow*munities" as they would call them).

- ✔ **Macworld** (www.macworld.com): Macworld is a good place to start if you have any Mac-related questions, and they also offer forums. You won't find a Premiere-specific forum, but there is a forum devoted to digital music, video, and photography.

- ✔ **Postforum** (www.postforum.com): This is a forum where you can post questions about digital postproduction (get it?) subjects, including Adobe Premiere.

- ✔ **tutorialfind** (www.tutorialfind.com): This site offers a searchable database of tutorials on how to perform various tasks in Adobe Premiere (among other programs).

You'll find some additional online resources in Chapter 15.

Index

• Numerics •

256MB, 25
3D motion transition, 161
512MB, 25
5400-rpm drives, 25
7200-rpm drives, 25
8mm analog video format, 69
80GB disk storage, 25
800MHz, system requirements, 25

• A •

AccessFX Web site, 284
accessing. See also opening
  Adobe Premiere, 19–20
  EDL (Edit Decision List), 90
  palettes, 17
Active Recording Deck option (Export to
    Tape Settings dialog box), 267
active track (Timeline window), 135
Add Command command (Commands
    palette menu), 53
Add Default Transition button (Monitor
    window), 164
Add/Delete Keyframe button (Keyframe
    and Rendering dialog box), 178–179
Add Keyframes at Edits option (Keyframe
    and Rendering dialog box), 87
Add Keyframes at Markers option
    (Keyframe and Rendering dialog
    box), 87
Add Tracks dialog box, 152
adding
  audio to clips, 203
  bars and tones to projects, 234
  graphics to titles, 219–220
  items to bin, 14
  keys to clips, 170–171
  markers to Timeline, 153
  shadows to text, 213–214
  styles to titles, 214

titles to Timeline, 221
tracks to Timeline, 152
transitions to projects, 159–160
adjust effect, 176
Adobe After Effects feature, 270, 284
Adobe MPEG Settings window, 261
Adobe Photoshop, 285–287
Adobe Premiere
  launching, 19–20
  overview, 9–10
Adobe Title Designer window.
    See Title Designer window
Adobe Web site, 314
Advanced RealMedia dialog box, 254
Advanced RealMedia Export
  exporting movies using, 253–256
  quality settings, list of, 256
After Effects feature (Adobe), 55, 270, 284
All frames option (Timeline Window
    Options dialog box), 47
alpha channel, 169, 309
AMD K6-2-400 processors, 25
analog hardware, configuring for video
    capture, 97–99
analog playback, exporting, 264–268
analog video
  capture devices, 34
  digital video versus, 60–61
  formats, types of, 69
animating
  clips, 183–186
  text, 218–219
Apple Final Cut Pro, 9
Apple menu
  overview, 19
  Recent Documents command, 83
AppleErrorCodes Web site, 276–277
Arrange command (Title menu), 220
aspect ratios
  defined, 64, 309
  for images, 65
  for pixels, 65–66

ATI All-In-One Wonder adapter cards, 34
audio. *See also* media; video
  adding to clips, 203
  background noise, removing, 203
  for camcorders, purchasing
      considerations, 30
  cross-fading, 200–201
  effects, list of, 202–203
  exporting, 270–271
  fades, 86
  licensing issues, 195
  linking to video, 201–202
  muting, 196
  popping noises, 86
  production of, 193
  quality of, selecting, 11
  recorders, capability considerations, 294
  recorders, purchasing considerations, 32
  recording guidelines, 194–195
  rubber bands, 86
  sampling rate and, 194
  sound reflection, minimizing, 195
  synchronization, 232
  visually editing, 204
audio capture, 103–106
Audio Capture command (File menu), 105
Audio Gain dialog box, 200
Audio Mixer (Audio Workspace)
  balance in, adjusting, 198–199
  customizing, 50–51
  illustration of, 39
  Mute button, 197
  overview, 40, 196
  Solo button, 197
  Volume Sliders, 197–198
Audio Mixer Window Options dialog
      box, 50–51
Audio Previews drop-down menu
      (Preferences dialog box), 41
Audio Settings dialog box, 85–86
Audio Workspace, 39–40
authoring tools (QuickTime Pro), 239
Auto Pan audio effect, 202
Auto Save and Undo command
      (Edit menu), 42–43, 131
Automate to Timeline command
      (Project menu), 165

Automatically Save Projects option
      (Preferences dialog box), 42
Automation Write options
      (Audio Mixer Option dialog box), 50
Avid Xpress DV, 9

● *B* ●

background lighting, 76
Backgrounds button
      (Look In dialog box), 262
backlight situations, 182
balance, audio balance, adjusting, 198–199
bandwidth
  dial-up connections and, 249
  video requirements, 70
bars and tones
  adding, 234
  defined, 309
batch captures, 108–110
batteries
  for camcorders, purchasing
      considerations, 30
  extra, 73
Betacom SP camcorders, 68–69
Bin command (File menu), 13
bins
  adding items to, 14
  creating for titles, 221
  creating new, 13–14
  naming, 14
  organizing media using, 116
  viewing contents within, 14
bit depth, 194, 309
black alpha matte key type, 169
Black & White filters, 189
black video, 235–236
Block Select tool (Timeline), 146–147
blue screen key type, 170
bluescreening, 168
blur effects
  Camera Blur, 188
  overview, 176
Boost audio effect, 202
borders, thickness of, adjusting, 163
BorisFX Web site, 287–288
bright lighting in video footage, 76

Broadcast color effects, 177
broadcast standards
  frame rates for, 64
  resolution values for, 64
  selecting, 11
  types of, 63
Building a PC For Dummies
    (Mark Chambers), 29
Building Preview dialog box, 227
building versus purchasing PCs, 29
burning discs, 260, 297
buttons
  Add Default Transition
    (Monitor window), 164
  Add/Delete Keyframe, 178–179
  Backgrounds (Look In dialog box), 262
  Close, 17, 19
  Collapse, 19
  Collapse/Expand Track, 151
  Create Item (Project window), 120
  Custom, 81
  Device Info, 95
  Display Opacity Rubberbands, 168
  Dual View (Monitor window), 144
  Edit Line, 209
  Frame Back, 100, 122
  Frame Forward, 100, 122
  Go Online, 95
  Insert (Monitor window), 135
  Lock/Unlock Track, 151
  Log In/Out, 109
  Mark In, 125
  Mark Out, 125
  Minimize, 17, 19
  Mute (Audio Mixer), 197
  New Bin, 116
  New Percentage
    (Clip Speed dialog box), 129
  Palette Menu, 52
  Pause, for clips, 121
  Play, 14
  Play, for clips, 121
  Remove Effect, 181
  Select A/B Editing (Initial Workspace
    dialog box), 10–11, 36
  Select Single-Track Editing (Initial
    Workspace dialog box), 10–11
  Set In, 100

Set Poster Frame, 121
Solo (Audio Mixer), 197
Sort By In Point, 110
Stop, for clips, 121
Templates (Title Designer window), 210
Text (Look In dialog box), 262
Toggle Edge Viewing
    (Timeline window), 136
Toggle Shift Tracks Options
    (Timeline window), 137
Toggle Snap to Edges (Timeline window),
    136, 138
Toggle Sync Mode
    (Timeline window), 137
Track Output/Shy State, 150
Zoom, 19

• C •

`C:WINDOWS` folder, 105
`C:WINDOWSApplication Data Adobe
    Premiere` file, 44
calibrating color, 232
camcorders
  audio recorders, purchasing
    considerations, 32
  Betacom SP, 68
  CCDs (charged coupled devices), 30
  Digital8, 67–68
  DVCAM, 68
  DVCPro, 68
  iris, 77
  manual exposure control, 77
  manuals for, reviewing, 76–77
  MiniDV format, 67
  prices of, 295
  purchasing consideration, 30–31
  Sony DCR-TRV103, 67
Camera Blur effect, 188
Camera View effect, 187
Cancel option (Fit Clip dialog box), 145
Canon GL1 camcorders, 30
Canopus ADVC-100, 34
capture cards, 34
capture hardware
  analog video devices, 34
  FireWire (IEEE-1394) devices, 33
  overview, 32–33

Capture In/Out option (Logging tab), 101
Capture Movies menu
    (Preferences dialog box), 41
Capture Project Settings dialog box, 94, 99
Capture settings, changing, 87–88
capturing audio. *See* audio capture
capturing stop-motion video.
    See stop-motion video capture
capturing video. *See* video capture
cathode ray tube (CRT) monitors, 25
CCDs (charged coupled devices),
    62, 295, 309
CD-ROM
  cross platforms, creating, 248
  recording video onto, 244–247
CD-RW (Compact Disc-
    Recordable/reWritable), 68
central processing unit (CPU), system
    requirements and, 25
Chambers, Mark (*Building a PC For
    Dummies*), 29
Change Speed option
    (Fit Clip dialog box), 145
channel effects, 176
Channel Map, 161
characters. *See* text
charged couple devices (CCDs),
    62, 295, 309
Check for Updates drop-down menu
    (Online Preferences dialog box), 44
children, shooting video of, 73–75
Chorus audio effect, 203
chroma key type, 169
Cleaner 5EZ
  exporting audio using, 270–271
  exporting movies using, 251–253
clean-up video problems, 182
Clear command (Marker menu), 126
Clear History option (History palette), 132
Clear Timeline Marker command
    (Timeline menu), 153
Clip Capture Parameters dialog box, 110
Clip Duration dialog box, 128, 163, 235–236
Clip Duration field (Monitor window), 125
Clip menu commands
  Audio Gain, 200
  Duration, 149
  Frame Hold, 149

Mute Left or Mute Right, 199
Properties, 120
Speed, 129
Swap Channels, 199
Unlink Audio and Video, 201
Clip Speed dialog box, 129–130, 149, 190
clips
  adding audio to, 203
  adding keys to, 170–171
  animating, 183–186
  appearance of, smoothing, 163
  black video, generating, 235–236
  copying, 127
  Cross Dissolve transition option, 124
  defined, 309
  dragging from Project window to
      Monitor window, 38
  dragging from Project window to
      Timeline, 36
  duration of, adjusting, 128, 149
  generating, 120
  logging, 108–109
  moving between, 121
  moving into Timeline window, 134–136
  naming, 127
  opacity of, adjusting, 167
  overlaying, 137–138
  playing, 116, 121–122
  poster frame, setting, 121
  properties of, viewing, 120
  rotating, 184
  selecting for capture, 110
  selecting multiple, 145–146
  slicing, 151
  sorting, 46
  speed of, adjusting, 128–130, 148–149
  summary of, viewing, 120
  synchronized, 137
  transitions, adding to beginning, 124
  types of, 119
  virtual, creating, 147
Close button, 17, 19
closing palettes, 17
C | NET Web site, 277
codecs (compressor/decompressor)
  defined, 67, 70, 309
  keyframes as reference points, 87
  selection considerations, 70–71

Collapse button, 19
Collapse/Expand Track button, 151
color
  calibrating, 232
  of text, setting, 212
  of transitions, selecting, 164
Color Balance effects, 182
color gamut, 309
Color Matte command (File menu), 172
Command Options dialog box, 52–53
commands
  Add Command
      (Commands palette menu), 53
  Arrange (Title menu), 220
  Audio Capture (File menu), 105
  Audio Gain (Clip menu), 200
  Audio Mixer Window Options (Window
      menu), 50
  Auto Save and Undo (Edit menu), 42, 131
  Automate to Timeline (Project menu), 165
  Bars and Tone (File menu), 234
  Bin (File menu), 13
  Black Video (File menu), 235–236
  Clear (Marker menu), 126
  Clear Timeline Marker
      (Timeline menu), 153
  Color Matte (File menu), 172
  Command Options (Palette menu), 52
  Desktop (Start menu), 19
  Documents (Start menu), 83
  Duplicate Clip (Edit menu), 127
  Duration (Clip menu), 128, 149
  EDL (File menu), 90
  Export Timeline (File menu), 246
  File List (File menu), 90
  Frame (File menu), 271
  Frame Hold, Video Options command
      (Clip menu), 148
  General (Project), 89
  General and Still Image (Edit menu), 42
  Go To (Marker menu), 125
  Go To Timeline Marker
      (Timeline menu), 154
  Image Size (Image menu), 112
  Import (File menu), 113
  keyboard, 52–53
  Marker, Set Clip command
      (Clip menu), 148

Monitor Window Options
    (Window menu), 49
Movie Capture (File menu), 94, 99
Mute Left or Mute Right (Clip menu), 199
New Project (File menu), 79
Online Settings (Edit menu), 44
Open (File menu), 43, 83, 106
Open Recent Project (File menu), 82
Print (File menu), 110
Print to Video, Export Timeline command
    (File menu), 234
Project Window Options
    (Window menu), 45
Properties (Clip menu), 120
Recent Documents (Apple menu), 83
Recent Projects (File menu), 228
Redo command (Edit menu), 131
Render Work Area (Timeline menu),
    168, 171
Replace command (Edit menu), 144
Ripple Delete (Timeline menu), 143, 233
Save (File menu), 81, 155
Save As (File menu), 81
Save for Web (Export menu), 271
Save for Web (File menu), 252
Save Workspace (Window menu), 36
Scratch Disks and Device Control
    (Edit menu), 40
Send To (Start menu), 19
Set Timeline Marker (Timeline menu), 153
Settings (Project menu), 84
Settings Viewer (Project menu), 83
Show Commands (Windows menu), 17
Show Effect Controls button (Window
    menu), 178, 181
Show History (Window menu), 132
Show Transitions (Windows menu),
    17, 158
Show Video Effects (Windows menu),
    17, 175
Sound Input (Audio Capture menu), 105
Speed (Clip menu), 129, 190
Stop Motion (File menu), 106
Storyboard, New command
    (File menu), 154
Swap Channels (Clip menu), 199
Text Properties (Effects menu), 262

commands *(continued)*
  Timeline Window Options
    (Window menu), 47
  Title command (File menu), 208
  Undo (Edit menu), 131, 287
  Universal Counting Leader
    (File menu), 231
  Unlink Audio and Video, 201
  View command (Title menu), 208
  Workspace (Window menu), 36
Commands palette, 52–53
Compact Disc-Recordable/reWritable
  (CD-RW), 68
compositing, 137
composition techniques, 73–75
compressing video, 245
Compressor option (Settings Viewer), 83
compressor/decompressors (codecs)
  defined, 67, 70
  keyframes as reference points, 87
  selection considerations, 70–71
computer selection
  minimum system requirements, 24–25
  overview, 23–24
  real system requirements, 25–26
configuring
  analog hardware for video capture, 97–99
  DV hardware for video capture, 94–97
connections, Internet dial-up, 242
Constrain Proportions option (Image Size
    dialog box), 112
Contour Design ShuttlePRO, 123
copying clips, 127
Count menu (Timeline Window Options
    dialog box), 49
counting leaders, 230–233
CPU (central processing unit), system
    requirements and, 25
Create audio preview files option (Audio
    Settings dialog box), 86
Create Bin dialog box, 13–14
Create Item button (Project window), 120
creating
  bins, new, 13–14
  bins for titles, 221
  cross-platform CD-ROMs, 248
  EDLs (Edit Decision Lists), 269–270
  folders for transitions, 158
  keyframes, 184

  leaders, 230–233
  lines, 219
  mattes, 171–172
  presets, 89
  split-screen effects, 172–173
  storyboards, 154–155
  titles, 208
  virtual clips, 147
  Web links, 191–192
Creative Cow Web site, 315
Cross Dissolve transition option, 124, 161
Cross-Fade tool (Timeline), 201
cross-fading audio, 200–201
cross-platform CD-ROMs, creating, 248
CRT (cathode ray tube) monitors, 25
Custom button, 81
customizing
  Audio Mixer, 50–51
  Monitor window, 49–50
  Project window, 45–46
  Timeline window, 47–49
  views, 116

• *D* •

DAT (digital audio tape), 294
data rate, 310
Dazzle Hollywood DV-Bridge, 34
DDR (double data rate), 25
default, duration default, setting, 130
Default Effect dialog box, 165
defragmenting, 92
deleting
  effects, 180–181
  in points, 126
  items from batch capture, 110
  keyframes, 178
  out points, 126
  video files from scratch disks, 82
Desktop command (Start menu), 19
deterioration, in analog data, 61
device control
  for cameras, 32
  exporting analog playback to tape using,
    266–268
  overview, 98
Device Control section
    (Capture settings), 88
Device Info button, 95

dialog boxes
  Add Tracks, 152
  Advanced RealMedia, 254
  Audio Gain, 200
  Audio Mixer Window Options, 50–51
  Audio Settings, 85–86
  Building Preview, 227
  Capture Project Settings, 94, 99
  Cleaner 5EZ, 271
  Clip Capture Parameters, 110
  Clip Duration, 128, 163, 235–236
  Clip Speed, 129–130, 149, 190
  Command Options, 52–53
  Create Bin, 13–14
  Default Effect, 165
  Distortion box, 185
  Duplicate, 127
  DV Capture Options, 94
  DV Device Control Options, 95–96
  EDL Output, 269
  Export Audio, 270
  Export Movie, 246
  Export Movie Settings, 246–247
  Export Still Frame, 271
  Export to Tape Settings, 267
  File Name, 109
  Fit Clip, 145
  Frame Hold Options, 148
  General and Still Image Preferences, 42
  Image Size, 112–113
  Initial Workspace, Select A/B Editing
      button, 10–11
  Initial Workspace, Select Single-Track
      Editing button, 10–11
  Keyframe and Rendering, 86–87
  Load Project Settings, 10–11, 42, 80–81
  Look In, 262
  Marker Properties, 192
  Monitor Window Options, 49–50
  Motion Settings, 183–184
  Name Track, 152
  New Project Settings, 42
  Online Preferences, 44
  Open File, 83
  Open Project, 42
  Pinch Settings, 186
  Playback Options, 229
  Preferences, 41
  Print to Tape, 231
  Project Settings, 84, 87–89
  Project Settings, Optimize Stills
      option, 228
  Project Window, 45–46
  Properties, 120
  Roll/Crawl Options, 218–219
  Save Project Settings, 89
  Scratch Disks and Device Control
      Preferences, 94–95, 114
  Stop Motion Options, 106–107
  Timeline Window Options, 47–48
  Track Options, 136, 152
  Transparency Settings, 170–171
  Universal Counting Leader Setup, 232
  Video Settings, 85
  Windows Media Export Plug-in, 257
dial-up connections, 242, 249
difference matte key type, 170
digital audio tape (DAT), 294
digital camcorders. *See* camcorders
digital playback, exporting
  overview, 237
  using Advanced RealMedia Export,
      253–256
  using Cleaner 5EZ, 251–253
  using DivX player, 242–243
  using QuickTime File Exporter, 250–251
  using QuickTime Player, 240–241
  using RealPlayer, 240–241
  using Windows Media Player, 241–242
  using WMV (Windows Media Video)
      format, 256–260
Digital Producer Web site, 278
Digital Versatile Disc (DVD)
  burning, 260, 297
  Macintosh support for, 260
  recorder drives, cost of, 28
  recorder drives, placing movies on, 238
  recorder drives, widescreen format, 65
  Windows support for, 260
digital video (DV). *See also* video
  analog data versus, 60–61
  configuring for video capture, 94–97
  defined, 310
  overview, 23, 60
  technological advances in, 61
Digital8 camcorders, 67–68

disabling
  effects, 177
  Playback on Desktop, 229
  Snap to Edges feature, 138
disk storage, system requirements for, 25
Display Opacity Rubberbands button, 168
dissolve transitions, 161
distortion effects, 176, 185–187
DivX player, 242–243
documenting projects, 89–90
Documents command (Start menu), 83
double data rate (DDR), 25
dragging. *See also* moving
  clips from Project window to Monitor
    window, 38
  clips from Project window to Timeline, 36
  files from Project window into Source
    view, 15
  palettes, 17
drawing tools, 219
drives
  external, warning against, 26
  hard drives, selection of, 25
drop-frame timecode, 66, 310
dropped frames
  gaps between, 103
  video capture and, 99, 102
Dual View button (Monitor window), 144
Duplicate Clip dialog box, 127
duration
  of black video clips, adjusting, 236
  of clips, adjusting, 128, 149
  of clips, default for, setting, 130
  of titles, adjusting, 221
  of transitions, adjusting, 162–163
Duration command (Clip menu), 128
DV (digital video). *See also* video
  analog data versus, 60–61
  configuring for video capture, 94–97
  defined, 310
  overview, 23, 60
  technological advances in, 61
DV Capture Options dialog box, 94
DV Device Control Options dialog box,
    95–96
DV Magazine, 278
DVCAM camcorder, 68

DV.com Web site, 278–279
DVCPro camcorders, 68
DVD (Digital Versatile Disc)
  burning, 260, 297
  Macintosh support for, 260
  recorder drives, costs of, 28
  recorder drives, placing movies on, 238
  recorder drives, widescreen format, 65
  Windows support for, 260
DVDit! LE feature, 262–264
DV-NTSC command, Standard 48kHz, 11
DV-NTSC preset (Load Project Settings
    dialog box), 80
DV-PAL preset (Load Project Settings
    dialog box), 80

• E •

eBay Web site, 279
echo effects, 203
Edit Decision List (EDL)
  creating, 269–270
  defined, 90, 310
  generating, 90
Edit line (Timeline window), 17
Edit menu commands
  Auto Save and Undo, 42, 131
  Duplicate Clip, 127
  General and Still Image, 42, 130
  Online Settings, 44
  Redo, 131
  Replace, 144
  Scratch Disks and Device Control, 40
  Undo, 131, 287
Edit tool (Timeline toolbar), 139
edit types
  four-point edits, 144–145
  list of, 139
  ripple edits, performing, 140–142
  roll edits, performing, 140
  selecting, 139
  slide edits, performing, 142
  slip edits, performing, 142
  three-point edits, 144–145
editing. *See also* editing video
  clips, duration of, 128
  clips, speed of, 128–130, 148–149

opacity, 167
text, size of, 216
titles, duration of, 221
transitions, duration of, 162–163
transitions, sequence of, 163
transitions, start and end points, 163
editing video
  linear editing method, 71–72
  nonlinear editing method, 71–72
  offline editing method, 72
  online editing method, 73
EDL (Edit Decision List)
  creating, 269–270
  defined, 72, 90, 310
  generating, 90
EDL Output dialog box, 269
effects. *See also* special effects
  applying, 177
  audio, list of, 202–203
  Camera Blur effect, 188
  Camera View effect, 187
  categories, list of, 176–177
  Color Balance, 182
  deleting, 180–181
  disabling, 177
  distortion, 185
  Ghosting effect, 188
  Pinch effect, 186
  rendering, 177
  rotation effects, 184
  split-screen, creating, 172–173
  transparency, 166–167
  view of, expanding, 177
  viewing, 176
Effects Controls palette, 38
Effects menu, Text Properties
    command, 262
800MHz, system requirements, 25
8mm analog video format, 69
80GB disk storage, 25
Enable Automation Of option
    (Audio Mixer Options dialog box), 51
energy management settings, adjusting
    for video capture, 93
Enhanced Rate Conversion option
    (Audio Settings dialog bog), 86
Equalize audio effect, 203
Export Audio dialog box, 270

Export menu, Save for Web command, 271
Export Movie dialog box, 246
Export Movie Settings dialog box, 246–247
Export Still Frame dialog box, 271
Export Timeline command (File menu), 246
Export to Tape Settings dialog box, 267
exporting. *See also* exporting movies
  analog playback, 264–268
  audio, 270–271
  still images, 271–272
exporting movies
  overview, 237
  using Advanced RealMedia Export,
      253–256
  using Cleaner 5EZ, 251–253
  using QuickTime File Exporter, 250–251
  using QuickTime Player, 240–241
  using RealPlayer, 240–241
  using Windows Media Player, 241–242
  using WMV (Windows Media Video)
      format, 256–260

• F •

fades, audio fades, 86
Field Interpolate effect, 177
fields, 64, 310
Fields option (Keyframe and Rendering
    dialog box), 87
File List command (File menu), 90
File list option (Project window), 14
File menu commands
  Audio Capture, 105
  Bars and Tone, 234
  Bin, 13
  Black Video, 235–236
  Color Matte, 172
  EDL, 90
  Export Timeline, 234, 246
  File List, 90
  Frame, 271
  Import, 113
  Movie Capture, 94, 99
  New Project, 79
  Open, 43, 83, 106
  Open Recent Project, 82
  Print, 110
  Print to Video, 234

File menu commands *(continued)*
Recent Projects, 228
Save, 81, 155
Save As, 81
Save for Web, 252
Stop Motion, 106
Storyboard, 154
Title, 208
Universal Counting Leader, 231
File Name dialog box, 109
File name option (Timeline Window
  Options dialog box), 48
files
  previewing, in Project window, 14
  video files, loading into Source view, 15
Fill Color box (Motion Settings
  dialog box), 184
Fill Left/Right video effect, 202
filters
  Black & White, 189
  threaded filter fitting, 297
  uses of, 298
Final Cut Pro, 9
Finder menu (Macintosh), 54
firehosing, 74
Firewire
  camcorder purchasing considerations, 30
  defined, 310
  ports, system requirements, 25
Firewire (IEEE-1394) devices
  expansion cards, installation
    requirements, 33
  MiniDV formats and, 67
Fit Clip dialog box, 145
512MB, 25
5400-rpm drives, 25
fixing video problems, 182
flat-panel monitors, 27
flicker problems, 177
flipping video, 190
floating palettes, 17–18
folders
  creating for transitions, 158
  opening, 17
formats, media import formats, 111
four-point edits, 144–145
fps (frames per second), 63–64
Frame Back button, 100, 122

Frame command (File menu), 271
Frame Forward button, 100, 122
Frame Hold Options dialog box, 148
Frame Jog control, 122
frame rate
  defined, 310
  selecting, 11
  for video standards, 63–64
Frame Rate option (Settings Viewer), 83
Frame Size option (Settings Viewer), 83
frames
  defined, 310
  freezing, 148
  size of, selecting, 11
  size of, viewing, 14
  viewing, 49
Frames Only at Marker option (Keyframe
  and Rendering dialog box), 87
frames per second (fps), 63–64
freezing frames, 148
frequency, 193

• *G* •

gamma correction, 182
gamut, 309
General and Still Image command
  (Edit menu), 42, 130
General and Still Image Preferences dialog
  box, 42
General menu command
  (Project menu), 89
General page (Project Settings
  dialog box), 229
General Settings dialog box, 84–85
generational loss, 61, 310
Ghosting effect, 188
Go Online button, 95
Go To command (Marker menu), 125
Go to Timeline Marker command
  (Timeline menu), 154
graphical user interface. *See* GUI
graphics
  adding to titles, 219–220
  opacity, reducing, 220
grayscale, 189
green line (Work Area bar), 225
green screen key type, 170

GUI (graphical user interface)
  for Macintosh, 19
  overview, 51
  for Windows, 19–20

• *H* •

hard drives, selection of, 25
HDTV (High Definition Television)
  defined, 310
  interlaced formats and, 64
  resolution in, 64
Height field (Pixel Dimensions option), 112
help resources, 313–315
HFS (Hierarchical File System), 248
Hi-8 videotapes, 67–69
hiding
  palettes, 132
  tracks, 150
High Definition Television (HDTV)
  defined, 310
  interlaced formats and, 64
  resolution in, 64
Highpass audio effect, 202
History palette, 132
Horizontal flip option, 190
Horizontal text tool (Title Designer
  window), 209, 215

• *I* •

Icon view (Project Windows Options
  dialog box), 46
IEEE-1394. *See* Firewire (IEEE-1394) devices
i.Link, 33
The iMac For Dummies, 93
image control effects, 176
image matte key type, 169
Image menu, Image Size command, 112
Image Size dialog box, 112–113
images
  aspect ratios for, 65
  size of, adjusting, 112–113
  still images, exporting, 271–272
Import command (File menu), 113
import/export option (QuickTime Pro), 239

importing
  media, 111–113
  stills into video, 112–113
  titles, 222
In point, file name and out point option
  (Timeline Window Options
  dialog box), 47
in points. *See also* markers; out points
  deleting, 126
  moving in Timeline window, 136
  overview, 15, 123
  setting, 124–125
Include Device Control Settings check box
  (Save Project Settings dialog box), 89
Initial Workspace dialog box, 10–11
Insert button (Monitor window), 135
installations
  Firewire expansion card requirements, 33
  plug-ins, 54–55
interlaced video standards, 64
Interleave option (Audio Settings
  dialog box), 86
Internet
  dial-up connections, 242, 249
  packet delivery and, 249
interpolation, 286
iris
  defined, 77
  iris transitions, 161

• *J* •

jog. *See* scrubbing
JPEG format file, saving still images
  using, 271

• *K* •

Kelly Industries Web site, 289
keyboard shortcuts
  Commands palette, 52
  creating, 53
  naming, 52
  overview, 51
Keyframe and Rendering dialog box, 86–87
Keyframe options (Keyframe and
  Rendering dialog box), 87

keyframes
  creating, 184
  defined, 86, 177
  deleting, 178
  as reference points, 87
  setting, 178–180
  uses of, 86
keys
  applying to clips, 170–171
  types of, 169–170

• L •

Latch option (Audio Mixer Options
    dialog box), 51
launching. *See* accessing; opening
lavalier microphones, 298
LCD (liquid crystal display) monitors, 27
leaders, creating, 230–233
leading, 220
lens, telephoto, 75
Lens Pro plug-in, 289
licensing agreements
  QuickTime, 239
  RealPlayer, 240–241
lighting tips, for video footage, 75–76
linear editing, 71–72
lines, creating, 219
List View mode (Project Window Options
    dialog box), 46
Load Project Settings dialog box,
    10–11, 42, 80–81
loading video files into source view, 15
Lock/Unlock Track button, 151
Log In/Out button, 109
logging clips, 108–109
Logging tab, 101, 108–109
Look In dialog box, 262
Lowpass audio effect, 202
luminance key type, 169
Luminance Map, 161

• M •

Mac OS 9 For Dummies, 18, 93
Mac OS X For Dummies, 18, 93
Macintosh
  DVD (Digital Versatile Disc) support, 260
  Finder menu, 54

GUI (graphical user interface) for, 19
  minimum system requirements, 24
  purchasing considerations, 26–27
Macs For Dummies, 18
Macworld Web site, 315
margins
  changing from default settings, 49
  title margins, setting, 208
  in video images, 54
Mark In button, 125
Mark Out button, 125
Marker menu commands
  Clear, 126
  Go To, 125
Marker Properties dialog box, 192
markers. *See also* in points; out points
  adding to Timeline, 153
  clearing from Timeline, 126, 153
  moving between, 126
  navigating within Timeline using, 154
  numbered, 126
  unnumbered, 126
mattes
  creating, 171–172
  uses for, 172
media. *See also* audio; video
  importing, 111–113
  organizing, using Project window, 115–116
  organizing, using source clips, 114–115
Media Player, 241–242
megabytes, 70
microphones
  purchasing considerations, 32
  recording audio and, 194
  types of, 298–299
Microsoft Windows Me For Dummies, 18, 93
Microsoft Windows Movie Maker, 9
*Microsoft Windows Movie Maker For
    Dummies* (Underdahl, Keith), 260
MiniDisc recorders, 294
MiniDV standard format, 67
Minimize button, 17, 19
minimizing palettes, 17
minimum system requirements, 24
mistakes, fixing, 131
mobile stabilizers, 303
modifying. *See* editing

Monitor window
  Add Default Transition button, 164
  Clip Duration field, 125
  customizing, 49–50
  Dual View button, 144
  Insert button, 135
  Marker menu, 125
  moving clips into, 38
  playing clips in, 121–122
  Program view, 15–16
  Single and Dual Pane modes, switching
    between, 50
  Source view, loading video files into, 15
  Trim Mode view, 16
  views, switching between, 16
Monitor Window Options dialog box, 49–50
monitors
  flat-panel, 27
  LCD (liquid crystal display), 27
  purchasing considerations, 300
  system requirements, 25
monopods, purchasing considerations, 303
Motion Settings dialog box, 183–185
Move tool (Title Designer window), 209
Movie Capture command (File menu),
    94, 99
Movie Maker, 9
movie projects. *See* projects; video
moving. *See also* dragging
  clips into Timeline Window, 134–136
  between markers, 125
  out points in Timeline window, 136
  palettes, 17
  in points in Timeline window, 136
  text, 216
MP3 option (Cleaner 5EZ dialog box), 271
MPEG Export feature, 260–262
Multimedia preset (Load Project Settings
    dialog box), 80
multiply key type, 170
Multitrack Selection tool (Timeline),
    146, 232
music. *See* audio
Mute button (Audio Mixer), 197
Mute Left or Mute Right command (Clip
    menu), 199
muting sound, 196
My Documents, 41

• *N* •

Name Track dialog box, 152
naming
  bins, 14
  clips, 127
  keyboard commands, 52
  presets, 89
  titles, 221
  tracks, 152
  workspaces, 36
National Television Standards Committee
    (NTSC), 63, 311
network drives, as scratch disks, warning
    against, 41
New Bin button, 116
New command (File menu), 154
New Percentage button (Clip Speed dialog
    box), 129
New Project command (File menu), 79
New Project Settings dialog box, 42
New Rate percentage option (Clip Speed
    dialog box), 190
NLE (nonlinear editing), 71–72, 311
noninterlaced video standards, 64
non-red key type, 170
NTSC (National Television Standards
    Committee), 63, 311
numbered markers, 125

• *O* •

offline editing, 72, 311
old video, simulating, 188–190
online editing, 73, 311
Online Preferences dialog box, 44
online resources
  AppleErrorCodes, 276–277
  C∣NET, 277
  Digital Producer, 278
  DV.com, 278–279
  eBay, 279
  Tiffen, 279–280
  User-to-User forums, 275–276
  VDCHelp.com, 280–281
  VersionTracker.com, 281
  videoguys.com, 282
Online Settings command (Edit menu), 44

opacity
  of clips, adjusting, 167
  of graphics, reducing, 220
Open command (File menu), 43, 83, 106
Open File dialog box, 83
Open Project dialog box, 42
Open Recent Project command (File menu), 82
opening. *See also* accessing
  folders, 17
  History palette, 132
  projects, existing, 82–83
Optimize Stills option (Keyframe and Rendering dialog box), 87
orienting text, 214–216
out points. *See also* in points; markers
  deleting, 126
  moving in Timeline window, 136
  overview, 15, 123
  settings, 124–125
overlaying clips, 137–138
overscan, 43, 209

• P •

Page Peel transitions, 161
PAL (Phase Alternating Line), 63, 311
PAL QuickTime or Video for Windows preset (Load Project Settings dialog box), 81
Palette Menu button, 52
palettes
  accessing, 17
  closing, 17
  Commands, 52–53
  Effects Controls, overview, 38
  floating, 17–18
  folders for, opening, 17
  hiding, 132
  History, 132
  minimizing, 17
  moving, 17
  showing, 132
  Transitions, 55, 158
PanHandler program, 288–289
panning techniques, 74

Panopticum Effects program, 289
Path Text tool (Title Designer window), 215
Pause button, for clips, 121
perspective effects, 176
Phase Alternating Line (PAL), 63, 311
Photoshop, 285–287
Pinch effect, 186
Pinch Settings dialog box, 186
Pinnacle DV500+ analog capture card, 34
Pixel Aspect Ratio (Settings Viewer), 84
Pixel Dimensions options (Image Size dialog box), 112
Pixelan Web site, 289–290
pixelate effects, 176
pixels
  aspect ratios for, 65–66
  defined, 311
  HDTV (High Definition Television) resolution and, 64
Play button, 14, 121
playback, analog, exporting, 264–268
playback, digital, exporting
  overview, 237
  using Advanced RealMedia Export, 253–256
  using Cleaner 5EZ, 251–253
  using QuickTime File Exporter, 250–251
  using QuickTime Player, 240–241
  using RealPlayer, 240–241
  using Windows Media Player, 241–242
  using WMV (Windows Media Video) format, 256–260
Playback on Desktop feature, 229
Playback Options dialog box, 229
playing clips, 116, 121–122
plug-ins
  After Effects plug-ins, 55
  Boris, 287–288
  installing, 53–55
  overview, 53
  Panopticum, 289
  Pixelan, 289–290
  selecting type of, 53
  SmartSounds QuickTracks, 290–291
  Ultimatte, 291
popping noises in audio, ridding, 86
poster frame, 121

Postforum Web site, 315
Preferences dialog box, 41
Premiere. *See* Adobe Premiere
presets
  creating, 89
  QuickTime Capture, 99
  saving, 89
  selecting, 10–11
previewing. *See also* viewing
  files in Project window, 14
  projects, 226–227
  Real-time Preview, 226–227
  titles, 223
  transitions, 160, 166
Print command (File menu), 110
Print to Tape dialog box, 231
Print to Video command (File menu), 234
problems, video problems, fixing, 182
production studio, setting up
  audio recorder selections, 32
  camera selections, 30–31
  computer selections, 23–26
  hardware selections, 32–34
  Macintosh selection, 26–27
  video deck selections, 31–32
  Windows PC selection, 28–29
professional-grade video formats,
    advantages of, 68
Program view (Monitor window), 15–16
progressive download video, 241
progressive scanning, 295
Project menu commands
  Automate to Timeline, 165
  General, 89
  Settings, 84
  Settings Viewer, 83
Project Settings dialog box, 84, 87–89,
    238–239
Project window
  activating, 13
  Bin list, 14
  Create Item button, 120
  creating bins in, 13–14
  customizing, 45–46
  expanding, 14, 115
  File list, 14
  moving clips from, 36, 38

organizing media using, 115–116
  previewing files in, 14
Project Window Options command
    (Window menu), 45
Project Window Options dialog box,
    45–46
projects
  adding bars and tones to, 234
  audio settings, changing, 85–86
  capture settings, changing, 87–89
  compressor options, setting, 83
  documenting, 89–90
  frame rate options, setting, 83
  frame size options, setting, 83
  general settings, changing, 84–85
  keyframe and rendering settings,
    changing, 86–87
  opening existing, 82–83
  pixel aspect ratio, setting, 84
  previewing, 226–227
  saving, 81–82
  starting new, 79–81
  transitions, adding, 159–160
  video settings, changing, 85
Properties command (Clip menu), 120
Properties dialog box, 120
purchasing considerations
  for audio recorders, 32
  versus building PCs, 29
  for camcorders, 30–31
  capture hardware, 32–34
  for Macintosh computers, 26–27
  for microphones, 32, 298–299
  for monitors, 300
  for monopods, 303
  for tripods, 302
  for video converters, 304–305
  for video decks, 305
  for Windows PC, 26–27

• *Q* •

QuickTime, licensing agreement for, 239
QuickTime Capture preset, 99
QuickTime File Exporter, 239, 250–251
QuickTime Pro, 238–239
QuickTime Transition, 161

• R •

RAM (random-access memory)
  defined, 311
  system requirements and, 25
Range Select tool (Timeline), 146
Rate Stretch tool (Timeline toolbar), 140
Razor tool (Timeline), 151
real system requirements, 25–26
RealPlayer, 240–241
Real-time Preview, 226
Recent Documents command (Apple menu), 83
Recent Projects command (File menu), 228
recording audio, guidelines for, 194–195
recording video
  on CD-ROM, considerations for, 244–245
  on CD-ROM, step-by-step instructions, 246–247
red line (Work Area bar), 225
Redo command (Edit menu), 131
Reduce Interlace Flicker effect, 177
reference points, keyframes as, 87
reflective lighting, in video footage, 75
Remove Effect button, 181
Render Work Area command (Timeline menu), 168, 171
rendering. *See also* transitions
  defined, 40, 311
  effects, 177
  frames marked in Timeline, 87
  for projects, setting, 86–87
  rendering time, reducing, 87
  rendering time, speeding up, 227–228
  transitions, 166
Replace command (Edit menu), 144
resolution
  in HDTV (High Definition Television) formats, 64
  system requirements, 25
  for video standards, 64
resources, online
  Digital Producer, 278
  DV.com, 278–279
  User-to-User forums, 275–276
  VCDHelp.com, 280–281
  VersionTracker.com, 281
  videoguys.com, 282

reverb effects, 203
RGB difference key type, 169
Ripple Delete command (Timeline menu), 143, 233
Ripple Edit tool (Timeline toolbar), 141
ripple edits
  description of, 139
  performing, 140–142
Roll Edit tool (Timeline toolbar), 140
roll edits, 139–140
Roll/Crawl Options dialog box, 218–219
rotation effects, 184
Roxio Toast Web site, 248
rubberbands, audio, 86
ruler (Timeline), 17

• S •

Safe Action Margin option (Adobe Title Designer window), 208–209
safe margin, 43
Safe Title Margin option (Adobe Title Designer window), 208–209
sampling rates, 194, 312
Save As command (File menu), 81
Save command (File menu), 81, 155
Save for Web command (Export menu), 271
Save for Web command (File menu), 252
Save Project Settings dialog box, 89
saving
  presets, 89
  projects, 81–82
  storyboards, 155
  titles, 221
  workspaces, 36
scratch disks
  defined, 40
  deleting video files from, warning against, 82
  memory space for, 40
  network drives as, warning against, 41
  setting up, 40–41
Scratch Disks and Device Control command (Edit menu), 40
Scratch Disks and Device Control Preferences dialog box, 94–95, 114
screen key type, 170
screen resolution, system requirements, 25

screen savers, disabling for video capture, 92

scrubbing, 230, 312

SDI (Serial Digital Interface) outputs, 68

SECAM (Sequential Couleur Avec Memoire), 63, 312

Select A/B Editing button (Initial Workspace dialog box), 10–11, 36

Select Single-Track Editing button (Initial Workspace dialog box), 10–11

selection tools, list of, 146

Send To command (Start menu), 19

sequence of transitions, adjusting, 163

Sequential Couleur Avec Memoire (SECAM), 63, 312

Serial Digital Interface (SDI) outputs, 68

Set In button, 100

Set Poster Frame button, 121

Set Timeline Marker command (Timeline menu), 153

Settings command (Project menu), 84

Settings Viewer, 83

7200-rpm drives, 25

shadows, adding to text, 213–214

sharpening effects, 176

Shift Track Option (Timeline Window Options dialog box), 49

shifting tracks, 137

shooting video
  camcorder manuals, reviewing, 76–77
  composition techniques, 73–75
  firehosing, 74
  lighting tips, 75–76
  panning techniques, 74
  planning tips, 73
  zooming techniques, 75

Show All box (Motion Settings dialog box), 184

Show Commands command (Windows menu), 17

Show Effect Controls button (Window menu), 178, 181

Show History command (Window menu), 132

Show Safe Action Margins (Titler option), 43

Show Safe Title Margins check box (Titler option), 43

Show Transitions command (Window menu), 17, 158

Show Video Effects command (Windows menu), 17, 175

Shure Incorporated Web site, 299

ShuttlePro (ContourDesign), 301

Single View Monitor element (Workspace menu), 36

Single-track Timeline (Audio Workspace), 39–40

sites. *See* Web sites

size
  of images, adjusting, 112–113
  of text, adjusting, 216

slate, 294

slicing clips, 151

Slide Edit tool (Timeline toolbar), 142

slide edits
  description of, 139
  performing, 142

slide transitions, 161

Slip Edit tool (Timeline toolbar), 142

slip edits
  description of, 139
  performing, 142

SmartSounds QuickTracks, 290–291

SMPTE (Society of Motion Picture and Television Engineers), 231

Snap to Edges feature
  disabling, 138
  overview, 136

SND (Sound), 270

SNDREC32.EXE file, 105

Society of Motion Picture and Television Engineers (SMPTE), 231

software distribution agreements, 238

Sony DCR-TRV103 camcorder, 67

Sony DCR-VX2000 camcorder, 30

Sony Digital8 camcorder, 67–68

Sort By In Point button, 110

Sort By menu (Project Windows Options dialog box), 46

sorting clips, 46

Sound (SND), 270

Sound Input command (Audio Capture), 105

sound reflection, minimizing, 195

Source Options (Monitor Window Options dialog box), 49

Source view (Monitor window), loading video files into, 15

spaces between text, adjusting, 212

special effects. *See also* effects
bluescreening, 168
key types, list of, 169–170
transitions, 161

speed
of clips, adjusting, 128–130, 148–149
of renders, speeding up, 227–228

Speed command (Clip menu), 129, 190

SpiceMaster feature, 290

split-screen effects, 172–173

Standard 48kHz command (DV-NTSC), 11

Start menu
Desktop command, 19
Documents command, 83
function of, 19
Send To command, 19

starting projects, 79–81

Steadicam Web site, 303

still images
exporting, 271–272
importing into video, 112–113

Stop button, for clips, 121

Stop Motion Options dialog box, 106–107

stop-motion video capture, 106–108

storage, disk storage, system requirements for, 25

storyboards
creating, 154–155
saving, 155
uses for, 156

stretch transitions, 161

styles, adding to titles, 214

stylize effects, 176

sunlight, in video footage, 76

Super Drive feature, 260

superimposing tracks, 138

Surestream option (Advanced RealMedia Export dialog box), 254

SVCD (Super Video Compact Disc), 264

S-VHS analog video format, 69

S-Video inputs, 34

Swap Channels command (Clip menu), 199

Swap Left & Right audio effect, 202

synchronized clips, 137

system requirements for computers
minimum system requirements, 24
real system requirements, 25–26

• T •

tapes. *See* videotapes

Target Audience Settings option (Advanced RealMedia Export dialog box), 255

telephoto lens, 75

templates, adding to titles, 210–211

Templates button (Title Designer window), 210

Terran Interactive, Cleaner 5EZ feature, 251–252

text
animating, 218–219
color of, setting, 212
ending point, 216
moving, 216
orienting, 214–216
properties, setting, 13, 211–212
selecting, 212
shadowing, 213–214
sizing, 216
solid-colored box behind, 219
spacing between, adjusting, 212
underlining, 219
Word Wrap option, 209

Text button (Look In dialog box), 262

Text Properties command (Effects menu), 262

third-party help resources, 315

This movie appears to have DROPPED FRAMES message, 103

3D motion transition, 161

three-point edits, 144–145

Thumbnail view (Project Windows Options dialog box), 46

TIFF format file, exporting still images as, 271

Tiffen Web site, 279–280

timecode
defined, 66, 312
drop-frame, 66
format, adjusting, 49

Timeline toolbar. *See also* Timeline window
  Block Selection tool, 146–147
  Cross-Fade tool, 201
  Edit tool, 139
  Multitrack Select tool, 146, 232
  Range Selection tool, 146
  Rate Stretch tool, 140
  Razor tool, 151
  Ripple Delete command, 143, 233
  Roll Edit tool, 140
  Slide Edit tool, 142
  Track Select tool, 146
Timeline window. *See also* Timeline toolbar
  active track in, 135
  adding markers to, 153
  adding titles to, 221
  adding tracks to, 152
  customizing, 47–49
  Edit line, 17
  moving clips into, 36, 134–136
  moving in points within, 136
  moving items within, 17
  moving out points within, 136
  navigating within, using markers, 154
  overview, 16
  removing markers from, 153
  rendering frames marked in, 87
  ruler, function of, 17
  Toggle Edge Viewing button, 136
  Toggle Shift Tracks Options button, 137
  Toggle Snap to Edges button, 136, 138
  Toggle Sync Mode button, 137
  Zoom Level menu, 136
  Zoom menu, 17
Timeline Window Options dialog box,
  47–48
timing effects, 176
Title Designer window
  Horizontal text tool, 209, 215
  Move tool, 209
  Path Text tool, 215
  Safe Action Margin option, 209
  Safe Title Margin option, 209
  Style menu, 214
  Templates button, 210
  text objects, selecting, 212
  Vertical text tool, 209, 215
  Word Wrap option, 209

Title menu commands
  Arrange, 220
  View, 208
Titler options (Preferences dialog box), 43
titles
  adding to Timeline, 221
  creating bins for, 221
  creating new, 208
  defined, 312
  duration of, adjusting, 221
  fading, 221
  graphics, adding, 219–220
  importing, 222
  naming, 221
  previewing, 223
  Safe Action Margin option, 208
  Safe Title margin option, 208
  saving, 221
  styles, adding, 214
  templates for, 210
  text properties, setting, 13, 211–212
titling images, 188
Toggle Edge Viewing button
  (Timeline window), 136
Toggle Shift Tracks Options button
  (Timeline window), 137
Toggle Snap to Edges button
  (Timeline window), 136, 138
Toggle Sync Mode button
  (Timeline window), 137
tools
  Block Select (Timeline), 146
  Cross-Fade (Timeline), 201
  drawing, 219
  Edit tool (Timeline toolbar), 139
  Horizontal text tool (Title Designer
    window), 209, 215
  Multitrack Select (Timeline), 146, 232
  Path Text tool
    (Title Designer window), 215
  Range Select tool (Timeline), 146
  Razor (Timeline), 151
  Ripple Edit tool (Timeline toolbar), 141
  Slide Edit (Timeline toolbar), 142
  Slip Edit (Timeline toolbar), 142
  Track Select (Timeline), 146
  Vertical text tool (Title Designer window),
    209, 215

Touch option (Audio Mixer Option dialog box), 50
track matte key type, 170
Track Options dialog box, 136, 152
Track Output/Shy State button, 150
Track Select tool (Timeline), 146
tracks
  adding to Timeline, 152
  expanding view of, 17, 151
  hiding, 150
  locking, 151
  naming, 152
  shifting, 137
  superimposing, 138
  unlocking, 151
  views, adjusting, 150–151
transformation effects, 177
transitions. *See also* rendering
  adding to projects, 159–160
  categories, list of, 161
  color of, selecting, 164
  default, uses of, 164–165
  defined, 312
  direction of, adjusting, 163
  duration of, adjusting, 162–163
  folders for, creating, 158
  previewing, 166
  rendering, 166
  selecting, 160
  sequence of, adjusting, 163
  start and end points for, adjusting, 163
  viewing, 158
Transitions palette, 55
Transparency Settings dialog box, 170–171
Trim Mode options (Monitor Window Options dialog box), 16, 49
Trim Source option (Fit Clip dialog box), 145
tripods, purchasing considerations, 302
Tucows Web site, 105, 271
tutorialfind Web site, 315
256MB, 25

• *U* •

Ultimatte Web site, 291
Underdahl, Keith (*Microsoft Windows Movie Maker For Dummies*), 260

underlining text, 219
Undo command (Edit menu), 131, 287
Universal Counting Leader Setup dialog box, 232
Unlink Audio and Video command (Clip menu), 201
unnumbered markers, 125
updates, online settings, 44
Use Logarithmic Audio Fades option (Audio Settings dialog box), 86
User-to-User forums, 275–276

• *V* •

VCD (Video Compact Disc), 264
VCDHelp.com Web site, 280–281
VCR units, purchasing considerations, 30–31
VersionTracker.com Web site, 281
Vertical flip option, 190
vertical hold problems, 177
Vertical text tool (Title Designer window), 209, 215
VHS analog video format, 69
VHS-C analog video format, 69
video. *See also* audio; digital video; media
  analog formats, types of, 69
  aspect ratios, defined, 64
  bandwidth requirements for, 70
  black video, 235–236
  broadcast standards, selecting, 11
  broadcast standards, types of, 63–64
  compressing, using DivX, 245
  Digital8 format, 67
  distorting, 186–187
  dropped frames and, 99
  files, loading into Source view, 15
  flipping, 190
  image aspect ratios, 65
  importing stills into, 112–113
  linking to audio, 201–202
  MiniDV formats, 67
  pixel aspect ratios, 65–66
  problems within, fixing, 182
  process of, 62
  professional-grade formats, advantages of, 68
  progressive download video, 241

shooting good, 73–77
simulating old, 188–190
timecode and, 66
what is not, 62
Video 1A/B track element
(Workspace menu), 36
video capture
batch captures, 108–110
configuring analog hardware for, 97–99
configuring DV hardware for, 94–97
dropped frames and, 99, 102
guidelines for, 92–93
stop-motion video capture, 106–108
video identification, 99–103
video cards, 28
video clips. *See* clips
Video Codec option (Advanced RealMedia
Export dialog box), 255
Video Compact Disc (VCD), 264
video converters, purchasing
considerations, 304–305
video decks, purchasing
considerations, 305
video display adapter cards, 34
Video Filter option (Advanced RealMedia
Export dialog box), 255
video gear, selecting
audio recorders, 32
camcorders, 30–31
capture hardware, 32–34
video deck, 31–32
Video Previews drop-down menu
(Preferences dialog box), 41
Video Settings dialog box, 85
videoguys.com Web site, 282
videotapes
exporting analog playback to, 266–268
Hi-8, 67, 69
View command (Title menu), 208
viewing. *See also* previewing
effects, 176
transitions, 158
views
customizing, 116
in Monitor window, switching between, 16
Program (Monitor view), 15–16
Source (Monitor window), loading video
files into, 15

switching between, 116
track views, adjusting, 150–151
Trim Mode, overview, 16
virtual clips, creating, 147
virtual memory, disabling for video
capture, 93
Volume Sliders (Audio Mixer), 197–198

• *W* •

warnings
for clip speed, adjustments to, 129
against external drives, 26
network drives, as scratch disks, 41
video capture, dropped frames and, 99
video files, deleting from scratch disks, 82
waveform, 312
Web links, creating, 191–192
Web sites
AccessFX, 284
Adobe, 314
AppleErrorCodes, 276–277
BorisFX, 287–288
C|NET, 277
Creative Cow, 315
Digital Producer, 278
DV.com, 278–279
eBay, 279
Kelly Industries, 289
Macworld, 315
Panopticum, 289
Pixelan, 289–290
Postforum, 315
Roxio Toast, 248
Shure Incorporated, 299
SmartSounds, 291
Steadicam, 303
Tiffen, 279–280
Tucows, 105, 271
tutorialfind, 315
Ultimatte, 291
VCDHelp.com, 280–281
VersionTracker.com, 281
videoguys.com, 282
white alpha matte key type, 169
wideangle lens, 75
widescreen format (DVD), 65
Width field (Pixel Dimensions option), 112

Window at Startup drop down menu, 42
Window menu commands
  Audio Mixer Window Options, 50
  Monitor Window Options, 49
  Project Window Options, 45
  Save Workspace, 36
  Show Commands, 17
  Show Effect Controls, 178, 181
  Show History, 132
  Show Transitions, 17, 158
  Show Video Effects, 17, 175
  Timeline Window Options, 47
  Workspace, 36
Windows
  DVD (Digital Versatile Disc) support, 260
  GUI (graphical user interface) for, 19–20
  minimum system requirements, 24
*Windows 2000 Professional
    For Dummies*, 93
Windows Media Export Plug-in
    dialog box, 257
Windows Media Player, 241–242
Windows PC, purchasing considerations,
    28–29
Windows Taskbar, 19
Windows XP For Dummies, 18, 93

wipe transitions, 161
WMV (Windows Media Video format)
  exporting movies using, 256–260
  quality settings, list of, 258–259
Word Wrap option (Title Designer
    window), 209
workspaces
  Audio workspace, overview, 39–40
  naming, 36
  reloading, 36
  saving, 36
  switching between, 36
Write option (Audio Mixer Options dialog
    box), 51
Write/Touch option (Audio Mixer Options
    dialog box), 51

• *Z* •

Zero Point field (Timeline Window Options
    dialog box), 49
Zoom button, 19
Zoom Level menu option
    (Timeline window), 136
zoom transitions, 161
zooming, in video footage, 75

FOR DUMMIES®

The easy way to get more done and have more fun

PERSONAL FINANCE & BUSINESS

Investing
0-7645-2431-3

Home Buying
0-7645-5331-3

Grant Writing
0-7645-5307-0

Also available:

Accounting For Dummies
(0-7645-5314-3)

Business Plans Kit For Dummies
(0-7645-5365-8)

Managing For Dummies
(1-5688-4858-7)

Mutual Funds For Dummies
(0-7645-5329-1)

QuickBooks All-in-One Desk Reference For Dummies
(0-7645-1963-8)

Resumes For Dummies
(0-7645-5471-9)

Small Business Kit For Dummies
(0-7645-5093-4)

Starting an eBay Business For Dummies
(0-7645-1547-0)

Taxes For Dummies 2003
(0-7645-5475-1)

HOME, GARDEN, FOOD & WINE

Feng Shui
0-7645-5295-3

Gardening
0-7645-5130-2

Cooking
0-7645-5250-3

Also available:

Bartending For Dummies
(0-7645-5051-9)

Christmas Cooking For Dummies
(0-7645-5407-7)

Cookies For Dummies
(0-7645-5390-9)

Diabetes Cookbook For Dummies
(0-7645-5230-9)

Grilling For Dummies
(0-7645-5076-4)

Home Maintenance For Dummies
(0-7645-5215-5)

Slow Cookers For Dummies
(0-7645-5240-6)

Wine For Dummies
(0-7645-5114-0)

FITNESS, SPORTS, HOBBIES & PETS

Fitness
0-7645-5167-1

Golf
0-7645-5146-9

Guitar
0-7645-5106-X

Also available:

Cats For Dummies
(0-7645-5275-9)

Chess For Dummies
(0-7645-5003-9)

Dog Training For Dummies
(0-7645-5286-4)

Labrador Retrievers For Dummies
(0-7645-5281-3)

Martial Arts For Dummies
(0-7645-5358-5)

Piano For Dummies
(0-7645-5105-1)

Pilates For Dummies
(0-7645-5397-6)

Power Yoga For Dummies
(0-7645-5342-9)

Puppies For Dummies
(0-7645-5255-4)

Quilting For Dummies
(0-7645-5118-3)

Rock Guitar For Dummies
(0-7645-5356-9)

Weight Training For Dummies
(0-7645-5168-X)

Available wherever books are sold.

Go to www.dummies.com or call 1-877-762-2974 to order direct

FOR DUMMIES®

A world of resources to help you grow

TRAVEL

Italy
FOR DUMMIES
A Travel Guide for the Rest of Us!
0-7645-5453-0

Hawaii
FOR DUMMIES
A Travel Guide for the Rest of Us!
0-7645-5438-7

Walt Disney World & Orlando
FOR DUMMIES
A Travel Guide for the Rest of Us!
0-7645-5444-1

Also available:

America's National Parks For Dummies
(0-7645-6204-5)

Caribbean For Dummies
(0-7645-5445-X)

Cruise Vacations For Dummies 2003
(0-7645-5459-X)

Europe For Dummies
(0-7645-5456-5)

Ireland For Dummies
(0-7645-6199-5)

France For Dummies
(0-7645-6292-4)

Las Vegas For Dummies
(0-7645-5448-4)

London For Dummies
(0-7645-5416-6)

Mexico's Beach Resorts For Dummies
(0-7645-6262-2)

Paris For Dummies
(0-7645-5494-8)

RV Vacations For Dummies
(0-7645-5443-3)

EDUCATION & TEST PREPARATION

Spanish
FOR DUMMIES
A Reference for the Rest of Us!
0-7645-5194-9

Algebra
FOR DUMMIES
A Reference for the Rest of Us!
0-7645-5325-9

U.S. History
FOR DUMMIES
A Reference for the Rest of Us!
0-7645-5249-X

Also available:

The ACT For Dummies
(0-7645-5210-4)

Chemistry For Dummies
(0-7645-5430-1)

English Grammar For Dummies
(0-7645-5322-4)

French For Dummies
(0-7645-5193-0)

GMAT For Dummies
(0-7645-5251-1)

Inglés Para Dummies
(0-7645-5427-1)

Italian For Dummies
(0-7645-5196-5)

Research Papers For Dummies
(0-7645-5426-3)

SAT I For Dummies
(0-7645-5472-7)

U.S. History For Dummies
(0-7645-5249-X)

World History For Dummies
(0-7645-5242-2)

HEALTH, SELF-HELP & SPIRITUALITY

Diabetes
FOR DUMMIES
A Reference for the Rest of Us!
Alan L. Rubin, M.D.
0-7645-5154-X

Sex
FOR DUMMIES
Dr. Ruth K. Westheimer
A Reference for the Rest of Us!
0-7645-5302-X

Parenting
FOR DUMMIES
A Reference for the Rest of Us!
0-7645-5418-2

Also available:

The Bible For Dummies
(0-7645-5296-1)

Controlling Cholesterol For Dummies
(0-7645-5440-9)

Dating For Dummies
(0-7645-5072-1)

Dieting For Dummies
(0-7645-5126-4)

High Blood Pressure For Dummies
(0-7645-5424-7)

Judaism For Dummies
(0-7645-5299-6)

Menopause For Dummies
(0-7645-5458-1)

Nutrition For Dummies
(0-7645-5180-9)

Potty Training For Dummies
(0-7645-5417-4)

Pregnancy For Dummies
(0-7645-5074-8)

Rekindling Romance For Dummies
(0-7645-5303-8)

Religion For Dummies
(0-7645-5264-3)

Available wherever books are sold. Go to www.dummies.com or call 1-877-762-2974 to order direct